Pearson New International Edition

Classroom Assessment
What Teachers Need to Know
W. James Popham
Seventh Edition

PEARSON®

Pearson Education Limited
Edinburgh Gate
Harlow
Essex CM20 2JE
England and Associated Companies throughout the world

Visit us on the World Wide Web at: www.pearsoned.co.uk

© Pearson Education Limited 2014

ISBN 10: 1-292-04135-8
ISBN 13: 978-1-292-04135-3

British Library Cataloguing-in-Publication Data
A catalogue record for this book is available from the British Library

ARP impression 98

Printed in Great Britain by Ashford Colour Press Ltd.

Table of Contents

Why Do Teachers Need to Know about Assessment?

T eachers teach students. That hardly constitutes a breakthrough insight. Just as preachers preach and flyers fly—teachers teach. That's why they're called teachers.

But what is a bit less obvious is that most teachers teach because they *like* to teach. Primary teachers like to teach little people. High school teachers like to teach bigger people. Most high school teachers also like to teach about a particular subject matter. (Have you ever seen how mathematics teachers' eyes get misty when they introduce their students to the raptures of the Pythagorean theorem?) Yes, most teachers love to teach. It is because they enjoy what they do that they waded through a medley of preservice teacher education courses, conquered the challenges of student teaching, and hopped the myriad hurdles of the certification process. Teachers overcame these obstacles in order to earn annual salaries that, particularly during the first few years, are laughably low. Yes, there's little doubt that teachers enjoy teaching.

Although teachers like to *teach,* they rarely like to *test.* Yet, here you are—beginning a text about testing. How can I, the author, ever entice you, the reader, to become interested in testing when your heart has already been given to teaching? The answer is really quite straightforward. Teachers who can test well will be better teachers. Effective testing will enhance a teacher's instructional effectiveness. Really!

If you're willing to suspend any preconceptions about testing while you're reading this text, particularly any negative ones, I'll make a pledge to you. If you tackle this text with even half the enthusiasm you might bring to a teaching assignment, I promise you'll discover how *testing will make you a much better teacher.* And, because I've been a teacher for over 50 years, it's a promise I'll keep. Teachers definitely should not break promises to teachers. Teachers' promises to administrators, on the other hand, should be regarded as eminently renegotiable.

But before I attempt to convince you, ever so subtly, that testing can be a boon to teaching, I want you to get a fix on your own *current* views about educational testing. And, because this is a text about testing, what better way to have you learn about those attitudes than to have you take a self-test I devised just for readers of this chapter?

So, on the adjacent page (it's on the *right* from where you're currently reading!) you'll find a brief self-test similar to the ones you've surely encountered in many widely read magazines. I saw one such self-test in a health magazine recently. It was entitled "How Long Will You Live? A Self-Test." Frankly, I was afraid to try it. As one gets older, one becomes more cautious.

But you have nothing to fear by taking the self-test I've whipped up for you. To emphasize its brevity, I have entitled it "A Terse Self-Test about Testing." It is an example of an attitudinal inventory. Later, you'll learn more about attitudinal inventories. But for now, please take a crack at the teensy self-test. The way to interpret your responses is given as a footnote .

■ Federal Laws Rule

Anyone who has completed even an introductory course in U.S. Government knows that while state laws can overturn the laws enacted by local communities, federal laws can overturn state laws. When it comes to the art of overturning, federal folks hold all the trump cards.

Any consideration of educational testing these days cannot be sensibly undertaken without understanding the nature of whatever assessment-related federal laws are on the books. No Child Left Behind Act (NCLB) exercised considerable influence on the way U.S. teachers tested and taught in their classrooms, the law elicited intense criticism from many quarters. Moreover, NCLB was supposed to be revised sometime during 2009 or, at the latest, 2010. Yet, by late 2012, genuinely serious movement to revise NCLB had not yet surfaced.

Instead, very briefly, I want to describe the background of the most pivotal federal legislation that, in one form or another, will surely have an impact on the way teachers are obliged to think about educational testing. Hopefully, based on that familiarity, you will then be more easily able to learn about the particulars of any federal law bearing directly on how students' achievements are supposed to be assessed. All educators will definitely need to attend to those assessment-related particulars.

A Terse Self-Test about Testing

Directions: For each of the statements below, use the following answer key to indicate how you react to the statement:

SA =	A =	U =	D =	SD =
Strongly	*Agree*	*Uncertain*	*Disagree*	*Strongly*
Agree				*Disagree*

There are no right or wrong answers, so please answer frankly by circling the appropriate response for each statement.

1. The chief reason that teachers should give classroom tests is to determine students' grades   SA   A   U   D   SD

2. Teachers should typically plan instruction that focuses on the skills or knowledge represented by a test.   SA   A   U   D   SD

3. In their classroom tests, teachers should only use items that can be scored objectively.   SA   A   U   D   SD

4. There are other legitimate indicators of a teacher's instructional effectiveness besides students' test scores.   SA   A   U   D   SD

5. A teacher has no business measuring students' confidence in their ability to do schoolwork.   SA   A   U   D   SD

6. Today's nationally standardized achievement tests should never be used to supply evidence about how well teachers are instructing children.   SA   A   U   D   SD

7. Teachers really don't need to determine the reliability of their own classroom tests.   SA   A   U   D   SD

8. It is impossible to judge the quality of students' written compositions with any meaningful accuracy.   SA   A   U   D   SD

9. The enormous pressure to boost students' scores on important tests permits teachers to employ almost any sort of score-improvement preparation activities.   SA   A   U   D   SD

10. Significant classroom tests should typically be built before a teacher plans instruction.   SA   A   U   D   SD

Why Do Teachers Need to Know about Assessment?

By all odds, the most significant federal statute influencing U.S. educational testing was the Elementary and Secondary Education Act (ESEA) of 1965. Enacted as a key component of President Lyndon B. Johnson's "great society," ESEA set out to provide a more appropriate education for historically underserved student groups such as students who were economically disadvantaged. Over the years (actually, every two to eight years), ESEA was periodically reauthorized with, sometimes, serious shifts in its assessment provisions. No Child Left Behind, for instance, the eighth reauthorization of 1965's ESEA, contained some significant alterations to that law's testing requirements. In the earliest incarnations of ESEA, educational assessments were focused on evaluating the progress made by those statutorily designated underserved groups—for example, minority students. However, in the reauthorization immediately preceding NCLB, the reauthorization enacted in 1994, the assessment of *all* students rather than statute-designated underserved groups was required. Clearly, this was a change of considerable importance.

Because the responsibility for education is not identified as a federal responsibility in the United States Constitution, U.S. education has historically been seen as a state rather than federal responsibility. Thus, prior to the 1994 incarnation of ESEA, known as the Improving America's Schools Act (IASA), states were relatively free to carry out whatever sorts of educational assessments they thought appropriate, with the chief exception being the assessment of those students being educated, at least in part, via federal dollars dispensed by the then-operative version of ESEA. But in 1994's IASA, that game changed. When a state took IASA dollars, that state agreed to assess the achievement of all its students in several IASA-designated grade ranges. And when NCLB was signed into law by President George W. Bush on January 8, 2002, the assessment of *all* students became more emphatic by far. Students in twice as many grade levels (grade *levels,* not grade ranges) were to be assessed—even though many of those students were not on the receiving end of federal dollars.

Moreover, whereas in the IASA statute, federal oversight of state-level testing of students in certain grade ranges was fairly light, NCLB's controls over the testing of more than twice as many students assessed under that law was not light but, instead, quite tight indeed. In short, the most recent two versions of ESEA (IASA and NCLB) embodied increasingly stringent requirements regarding which students were to be tested and how this testing was to be done. While the dominant

---

Self-Test Interpretation Guide: For statements 2, 4, 6, 7, and 10, use the following scoring key: SA = 5, A = 4, U = 3, D = 2, and SD = 1. For statements 1, 3, 5, 8, and 9, use the following scoring key: SA = 1, A = 2, U = 3, D = 4, and SD = 5. The highest possible total score is 50; the lowest possible total score is 10. The higher your total score, the more sensible is your view of educational testing. After finishing this text, you might wish to retake this terse self-test (without looking at your earlier answers, of course). If you come up with a postbook score that's substantially *lower* than your prebook score, you and I should *both* be worried.

function of IASA and NCLB was to be accountability—that is, the identification of which schools and districts were doing a satisfactory instructional job—certain specifics of those laws make a real difference in how teachers need to think about educational assessment.

I entreat you to become knowledgeable about the assessment-related aspects of a reauthorized ESEA. Although there may be numerous features of such a law that can have an impact on the way teachers teach, it is almost certain that the assessment-related provisions of such a law will have great impact, if not the greatest impact, on how a teacher needs to think about *instruction*. In the realm of educational assessment, federal laws tend to rule. That's because federal legislators craft their statutes so that unless a state's officials comply with a federal statute's ground rules, that state must forego receipt of substantial federal dollars. The history of American public education is, as you might guess, not replete with instances wherein state authorities turned down federal dollars.

Interestingly, as the NCLB statute neared its decade-old anniversary, the federal government's stance regarding how best to foster state and local accountability initiatives had shifted considerably. The early years of NCLB's existence had been marked by the threat of penalties for low-performing schools. However, after President Barack Obama's administration had taken office, federal officials soon set out meaningful financial incentives for states who subscribed to the U.S. Department of Education's accountability preferences. As usual, state education officials responded predictably to the lure of federal largesse. In essence, then, federal implementation of ESEA had shifted—in just a few years—from the stick to the carrot.

Arrival of the Common Core State Standards

One of the most salient of these carrot-induced shifts in state education policies was associated with the adoption, by all but a few states, of a set of identical curricular aims: the *Common Core State Standards (CCSS)* in English language arts (ELA) and mathematics. Because states that adopted these identical curricular aims became eligible for receipt of substantial federal subsidies, and because a markedly slowing national economy found most states facing serious fiscal shortfalls, we soon saw almost all states accepting—as their state's official curricular aims—the CCSS in ELA and math. This event, almost unthinkable just a few years earlier, will unquestionably have a substantial impact on the instructional and assessment practices of the nation's public school teachers in the coming years.

Let's be clear about what the CCSS are. They represent the curricular outcomes sought for the nation's students—that is, the knowledge and cognitive skills students are supposed to acquire in school. Because NCLB had allowed each state to select its own curricular aims (that is, content standards), its own tests to assess students' mastery of those aims, and its own cut-scores (that is, achievement standards) to signify students' mastery of those curricular aims, making sense out of the NCLB-spawned accountability picture in U.S. public schools was almost impossible. In an effort to rectify this chaotic situation, the Council of Chief State School Officers (CCSSO) and the National Governors Association (NGA) Center for Best Practices set out in late 2009 to provide a more suitable set of curricular targets for the nation's schools. CCSSO is the organization of the state officials, elected or appointed, who head each state's public schools. NGA performs a comparable function for the nation's governors.

On June 2, 2010, CCSSO and NGA released the *Common Core State Standards for English Language Arts and Mathematics* (National Governors Association, 2010). As noted earlier, all but a few states have accepted these standards—these "expectations for student knowledge and skills that high school graduates need to master to succeed in college and careers." Given the long-standing reluctance of U.S. state education officials to abandon "local control" over important educational decisions such as curricular outcomes for students, the widespread adoption of the CCSS was genuinely astonishing. In essentially a single year, CCSSO and NGA crafted sets of national mathematics and ELS curricular aims that seem sufficiently defensible so that all but a few states soon hopped aboard the CCSS Express. Truly astonishing!

But the curricular aims embodied in the CCSS were destined to serve as much more than lofty statements of curricular intent that, like so many previously crafted sets of curricular aims, languished in rarely read reports. This is because, soon after the release of the CCSS in mid-2010, the federal government announced its intention to fund one or more consortia of states whose mission it would be to create assessments suitable for measuring students' mastery of the skills and knowledge embodied in the CCSS. Two such assessment consortia have been selected by federal authorities (from competing bidders) and have been funded at approximately $175 million each to create assessments that, by the 2014–15 school year, can be used to determine students' mastery of the CCSS. One consortium is the *Partnership for the Assessment of Readiness for College and Careers (PARCC)*. The other consortium is the *Smarter Balanced Assessment Consortium (SBAC)*. Each of the consortia was initially composed of about 25 to 30 states, all of which agreed to promote students' mastery of the curricular goals represented by the CCSS.

The work of these two consortia will be well under way by the time you read this text, and I will attempt to describe the very latest developments in the work of the two consortia. It should be clear that the nature of the assessments devised by PARCC and SBAC will have a considerable impact on America's public schools. Because the curricular aims being pursued by so many states will be identical, and the assessments used in those states will also be identical, comparisons among states' student performances will now be possible in ways that heretofore were impossible. The evaluative impact of such evidence, of course, is apt to be substantial.

I am going to assume that, under whatever federal revision of ESEA ultimately is enacted by Congress, there will continue to be state accountability tests. The nature and number of those tests may be modified in any ESEA reauthorization, of course, but it seems likely that in one form or another, we will continue to see federal laws calling for state-operated accountability tests. Perhaps those state tests will have been chosen from the CCSS tests provided by one of the two federally funded assessment consortia. Perhaps a state's accountability tests will be state-grown rather than consortium-built. But, one way or the other, state-level accountability tests are apt to be with us for a long while to come. That's the premise I will be operating on in the coming pages.

■ Assessment versus Testing

So far, I've been contrasting teaching to testing and if you're alert, you've already started to wonder—What's this author trying to pull off? Am I going to learn about *testing* or am I going to learn about *assessment*? Is *assessment* simply a more fashionable word for *testing*? In short, what's he up to? These are reasonable questions, and I'll now try to supply you with a set of compelling, confidence-engendering answers.

Almost everyone knows about the kinds of tests typically encountered in school. Most of today's adults, indeed, were on the receiving end of a hoard of teacher-dispensed tests during their own days in school. There were final exams, midterm exams, end-of-unit tests, pop quizzes, and (in the interest of gender equity) mom quizzes. All of those tests had one thing in common. They represented the teacher's attempt to get a fix on how much the teacher's students had learned. More accurately, such tests were employed to determine a student's status with respect to the knowledge or skills the teacher was attempting to promote. This is an altogether praiseworthy endeavor for teachers—to find out how much students know. If teachers are reasonably sure about what their students currently know, then teachers can more accurately tailor instructional activities to promote what their students need to learn.

The sorts of tests referred to in the preceding paragraph, such as the quizzes and examinations most of us took in school, have historically been paper-and-pencil instruments. When I was a student, many years ago, the three most common forms of tests I encountered were essay tests, multiple-choice tests, and true-false tests. Until the past decade or so, those three kinds of tests were, by far, the most prevalent sorts of tests found in classrooms.

In recent years, however, educators have been urged to broaden their conception of testing so students' status is determined via a wider variety of measuring

Not
measured—

devices—a variety extending well beyond traditional paper-and-pencil tests. The reason teachers have been challenged to expand their repertoire of testing techniques is not merely for the sake of variety. Rather, thoughtful educators have recognized there are a number of important kinds of student learning not measured most appropriately by paper-and-pencil tests. If, for example, a teacher wants to determine how well students can function orally in a job-interview situation, it's pretty clear that a written true-false test doesn't cut it.

Thus, because there are many worthwhile learning outcomes not best measured by paper-and-pencil tests, and because when most people use the word *test* they automatically think of traditional paper-and-pencil tests, the term *assessment* has been increasingly adopted by many educators and measurement specialists. Assessment is a broader descriptor of the kinds of educational measuring teachers do—a descriptor that, while certainly including traditional paper-and-pencil tests, covers many more kinds of measurement procedures. Here is a working definition of ***assessment*** as it is used in an educational context:

> Educational assessment is a formal attempt to determine students' status with respect to educational variables of interest.

Lest you be put off by this fairly foreboding definition, let's briefly consider its chief elements. Note that the kind of assessment we're talking about is aimed at determining the status of students regarding "educational variables of interest." *Variables* are merely things that vary. (I suspect you could have figured this out all on your own!) In education, for example, we find that students vary in how much they know about a subject, how skilled they are in performing such operations as long division, and how positive their attitudes are toward school. Those are the sorts of variables with which a teacher is typically concerned; thus they are the "variables of interest" teachers typically measure. If the teacher's instructional focus is on the industrial revolution, then the teacher may wish to assess how much students know about the industrial revolution. In that case, the variable of interest would be the degree of students' knowledge regarding the industrial revolution. If the teacher is interested in how confident students are regarding their own written composition skills, then students' composition confidence would be a variable of interest. Educational assessment deals with such variables.

Our working definition also indicates that educational assessment constitutes a "formal" attempt to get a fix on students' status. As human beings, we make all sorts of informal determinations regarding people's status. For example, we may conclude that the woman who cut into the supermarket line ahead of us is rude, or that the man who keeps stumbling as he climbs a set of stairs is clumsy. But these are informal status determinations. Teachers, too, make informal judgments about their students. For instance, a teacher might conclude that a student, based on the student's glum demeanor during the first few moments of class, is definitely grumpy. Such informal appraisals, although they may be useful to teachers, should not be regarded as educational assessment.

When I was a high school teacher, for example, I employed informal judgment to conclude that Raymond Gonty, one of the seniors in my U.S. Government class, was not really interested in what I was teaching. I reached this conclusion chiefly because Raymond usually slept during class. I became more firmly convinced, however, when he began arriving at class carrying a pillow!

The kind of educational assessment you'll be reading about in this text is formal—that is, it's a deliberate effort to determine a student's status regarding such variables as the student's knowledge, skills, or attitudes. The kind of educational assessment you'll be considering is more than a teacher's "impressions." Rather, you'll be learning about systematic ways to get a fix on a student's status.

Assessment, therefore, is a broad and relatively nonrestrictive label for the kinds of testing and measuring teachers must do. It is a label to help remind educators that the measurement of students' status should include far more than paper-and-pencil instruments. Assessment is a word that embraces diverse kinds of tests and measurements. In the remaining pages, you'll find that although I'll use the term *assessment,* I'll often use the words **test** and **measurement**. I'll not be trying to make any subtle distinctions at those times. Instead, I'm probably just tired of using the A-word.

9

Why Should Teachers Know about Assessment? Yesteryear's Answers

Let's play a bit of time travel. Suppose you were magically transported back to the 1950s or 1960s. And, as long as we're in a let's-pretend mode, imagine you're a new teacher taking part in a fall orientation for first-year teachers in a large school district. The thematic topic of the particular session you're attending is Why Should Teachers Know about Testing? The session's lecturer, Professor Tess Tumm, is supplying the audience with a set of traditional answers to this thematic question based on how teachers actually can use classroom tests. Because you are a docile new teacher (remember, this is imaginary), you are compliantly taking notes to help guide you during the coming school year.

What I'm suggesting, as you've probably guessed, is that there are a number of fairly traditional answers to the question of why teachers should learn about assessment. Those answers have been around for several decades. There is also a set of more current answers to the question of why teachers should know about assessment. Let's give tradition its due and, initially, consider four time-honored answers to the question of why teachers should know about testing. Although these reasons for knowing about classroom assessment may have been around for a while, they're still compelling because they are rooted in the realities of what skilled teachers can do with classroom assessment. These four reasons may well have been the major points treated by Professor Tumm during our imaginary orientation session of yesteryear.

Diagnosing Students' Strengths and Weaknesses

One important reason that teachers assess students is to determine an individual student's weaknesses and strengths. If you're an elementary teacher, you need to know how well Giselle is comprehending what she reads so, if she's having certain difficulties, you can address those problems instructionally. Student weaknesses, once identified via assessment, can be the focus of future instruction.

On the flip side of the issue, teachers need to know what their students' prior accomplishments are. If Jaime is already truly proficient in solving simultaneous equations, it's a waste of Jaime's time to make him plow through practice piles of such equations. When I was growing up, the expression "That's like carrying coal to Newcastle" was used to disparage any scheme that reeked of redundancy. (I always assumed that coal mining was a big deal in Newcastle.) Well, teachers who relentlessly keep instructing students regarding knowledge or skills that the students have already mastered are definitely lugging coal lumps to Newcastle. Assessment can allow teachers to identify students' current strengths and, as a consequence, can help teachers avoid superfluous and wasteful instruction.

Thus, by measuring students' current status, teachers can discern (1) where to put their instructional energies to ameliorate a student's weaknesses and (2) what already mastered skills or knowledge can be instructionally avoided. Such diagnostic assessment is particularly useful for a teacher's planning if the assessment is carried out at the beginning of an instructional sequence. This kind of early diagnosis is often referred to as *preassessment* because it is assessment that takes place prior to the teacher's initiation of instruction.

Monitoring Students' Progress

A second, related answer to the question, Why should teachers assess? is that such assessments help teachers determine whether their students are making satisfactory progress. Sometimes, of course, it's easy for teachers to tell whether their students are or are not progressing satisfactorily. I can still recall, with suitable embarrassment, the absolutely scintillating lesson I provided as a high school English teacher on the topic of Modifying Gerunds with Possessives. It was a lesson designed for a full-class period, and I was confident that at its conclusion my students would not only understand the topic but also be able to explain to others why one of the following sentences contains an appropriate pronoun and one does not:

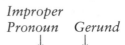

Improper
Pronoun   Gerund
   ↓   ↓
☹ **Sentence 1:** I really appreciate you sending the brownies.

Proper
Pronoun   Gerund
   ↓   ↓
☺ **Sentence 2:** I really appreciate your sending the brownies.

At the end of a bravura 40-minute lesson, replete with all sorts of real-life examples and a host of on-target practice activities, I was certain I had effectively taught students that because a gerund was a noun-form of a verb, any modifiers of such gerunds, including pronouns, must be possessive. And yet, at the end of the lesson, when I looked into my students' baffled faces, I realized that my optimism was unwarranted. After asking several students to explain to me the essence of what I'd been talking about, I quickly discerned that my lesson about gerund modification was not an award-winning effort. Most of my students couldn't distinguish between a gerund and a geranium.

Although teachers can occasionally discern informally, as I did, that their students aren't making satisfactory progress, more often than not we find teachers' believing their students are progressing quite well. (Note in the previous sentence that the modifier of the gerund *believing* is the possessive form of *teachers*. Yes, I'm still trying.) It's only human nature for teachers to believe they're teaching well and their students are learning well. But unless teachers systematically monitor students' progress via some type of assessment, there's too much chance teachers will improperly conclude progress is taking place when, in fact, such progress is not.

Why Do Teachers Need to Know about Assessment?

A useful function of classroom assessment, therefore, is to determine whether students are moving satisfactorily toward the instructional outcomes the teacher is seeking to promote. If progress for all students is satisfactory, of course, then the teacher need make no instructional adjustments. If progress for most students is satisfactory, but a few students are falling behind, then some separate doses of remedial assistance would seem to be in order. If progress for most students is inadequate, then the teacher should substantially modify whatever instructional approach is being used because, it is all too clear, this approach is not working. Progress monitoring is a time-honored and altogether sensible use of classroom assessment.

I've run into a number of teachers in recent years who refer to this use of assessment as "dip-sticking." When I think back to the days that I occasionally used a dip-stick to determine if my second-hand automobile was running low on oil (as it typically was), that label definitely rings true.

A teacher ought to monitor students' progress via classroom assessment because, more often than you'd think, the teacher can stop instructing on a certain topic well in advance of what the teacher had anticipated. Suppose, for instance, you're attempting to get your students to acquire a certain skill, and you've set aside two weeks to promote their mastery of the skill. If you monitor students' progress with an assessment after only a week, however, and discover your students have already mastered the skill, you should simply scrap your week-two plans and smilingly move on to the next topic.

Another way of thinking about the monitoring of student progress is that it positions teachers to use the results of classroom tests as part of *formative assessment*—that is, the use of assessment-elicited evidence intended to improve unsuccessful yet still modifiable instruction. *Summative assessment,* in contrast, refers to the use of tests whose purpose is to make a final success/failure decision about a relatively unmodifiable set of instructional activities. In a review of research studies focused on the instructional payoffs of formatively oriented classroom assessment, two British investigators (Black and Wiliam, 1998) concluded that the use of progress-monitoring classroom assessments can promote striking gains in student learning on *external* exams.

The range of typical improvements in student learning reported by these investigators was such that at the *least* positive level, an average student whose classes featured formative assessments displayed the same achievement as a student in the top 35 percent of students in classes without such formative assessments. And at the *most* positive end of the effect-size range, there were learning gains in classes using formative assessments that, had they been seen in all of a nation's classes, would have raised the score of that nation from the middle of a pack of 40 or so nations to one of the top 5 nations in the world. The British researchers concluded their review of empirical studies about classroom assessments with the assertion that "there is a body of firm evidence that formative assessment is an essential component of classroom work and that its development can raise standards of achievement" (Black & Wiliam, 1998, p. 148).

Based on their conclusions regarding the major instructional dividends of formatively oriented classroom assessment, members of Britain's Assessment Reform Group introduced the idea of classroom assessment *for* learning—in contrast to assessment *of* learning. They describe this approach as follows:

> *Assessment for learning is any assessment for which the first priority in its design and practice is to serve the purpose of promoting pupils' learning. It thus differs from assessment designed primarily to serve the purpose of accountability, or of ranking, or of certifying competence. (Black et al., 2002)*

More recently, Stiggins and Chappuis (2012) have pushed assessment for learning as the cornerstone of effective classroom measurement.

Assigning Grades

If I were somehow able to carry out an instant nationwide survey of beginning teachers and asked them, "What is the most important function of classroom assessment?" I know what answer I'd get from most of the surveyed teachers. They'd immediately respond: *to give grades.*

That's certainly what I thought testing was all about when I taught in public schools. To be honest (confession, I am told, is good for the soul), the *only* reason I tested my students was to give them grades. I've talked to hundreds of teachers during the past few years, and I've been dismayed at how many of them continue to regard testing's *exclusive* function to be grade giving. A third reason, therefore, that teachers assess students is to assemble the evidence necessary to give their students grades. Most school systems are structured so the end-of-course or end-of-year grades a student earns constitute the beginnings of a record of the student's personal accomplishments—a record destined to follow the student throughout life. Thus, it is imperative teachers not assign grades capriciously. Whether we like it or not, students' grades are important.

The best way to assign grades properly is to collect evidence of a student's accomplishments so the teacher will have access to ample information before deciding whether to dish out an A, B, C, D, or F to a student. Some school systems employ less traditional student grading systems—for example, the use of descriptive verbal reports that are relayed to parents. Yet, whatever the reporting system used, it is clear the teacher's assessment activities can provide the evidence necessary to make sensible student-by-student appraisals. The more frequent and varied the evidence of student accomplishments, the more judiciously the teacher can assign to students the grades they deserve.

A corollary principle linked to "tests as grade determiners" is that some teachers also employ the prospect of upcoming tests to motivate their students. Because a student's grade is often dependent on the student's test performances, teachers will frequently employ admonitions such as, "Be sure to study this chapter carefully, because you have an important end-of-chapter exam coming up on Thursday!" Some teachers surely employ impending tests as a motivational device.

Determining One's Own Instructional Effectiveness

A fourth and final reason teachers have traditionally been told they should test students is that students' test performances can help teachers infer how effective their teaching has been. Suppose a teacher sets out to have students master a set of worthwhile skills and knowledge regarding Topic X during a three-week instructional unit. Prior to instruction, a brief test indicated students knew almost nothing about Topic X but, after the unit was concluded, a more lengthy test revealed students had mastered most of the skills and knowledge addressed during the Topic X unit.

Because the comparison of students' pretest and posttest results indicated the teacher's students had acquired ample knowledge and skills regarding Topic X, the teacher has a charming chunk of evidence that the instructional approach being used appears to be working. If the teacher's instruction seems to be promoting the desired outcomes, then it probably shouldn't be altered much.

On the other hand, let's say a teacher's Topic X pretest-to-posttest results for students suggest students' progress has been piffling. After comparing results on the end-of-instruction posttest to students' performance on the preinstruction test, it appears students barely knew more than they knew before the instruction commenced. Such trivial student growth should suggest to the teacher that adjustments in the instructional activities seem warranted when teaching Topic X again next term or next year.

I'm not suggesting students' pretest-to-posttest results are the only way for teachers to tell whether they're flying or flopping, but students' end-of-instruction performances on assessment devices constitute a particularly compelling indication of whether teachers should retain, alter, or jettison their current instructional procedures.

In review, then, we've considered four fairly traditional answers to the question of why teachers should assess students. Here they are again:

Traditional Reasons That Teachers Assess Students
- To diagnose students' strengths and weaknesses
- To monitor students' progress
- To assign grades to students
- To determine instructional effectiveness

You will notice that each of these four uses of educational assessment is directly related to *helping the teacher make a decision*. When a teacher assesses students' strengths and weaknesses, the teacher uses test results to *decide* what instructional objectives to pursue. When a teacher assesses students' progress, the teacher uses test results to *decide* whether certain parts of the ongoing instructional program need to be altered. When a teacher assesses students to help assign grades, the teacher uses students' performances to *decide* which students get which grades. And, finally, when a teacher uses pretest-to-posttest assessment results to indicate how effective an instructional sequence has been, the teacher is trying to *decide* whether the instructional sequence needs to be overhauled. Teachers should never assess students without a clear understanding of what the decision is that will be informed by results of the assessment. The chief function of educational assessment, you see, is to improve the quality of educational decision-making.

Taken in concert, the four traditional reasons just described should incline teachers to assess up a storm in their classrooms. But these days even more reasons can be given regarding why teachers need to know about assessment.

■ Why Should Teachers Know about Assessment? Today's Answers

In addition to the four traditional reasons teachers need to know about assessment, there are three new reasons that should incline teachers to dive joyfully into the assessment pool. Having emerged during the past decade or so, these are compelling reasons why today's teachers dare not be ignorant regarding educational assessment. Let's consider three new roles for educational assessment and see why these new functions of educational testing should incline you to pump up your assessment knowledge.

Influencing Public Perceptions of Educational Effectiveness

When I was a high school teacher a long while ago, teachers were required to give nationally standardized achievement tests. But, to be honest, no one really paid much attention to the test results. My fellow teachers perused the test-score reports, but were rarely influenced by them. The public was essentially oblivious of the testing process and altogether disinterested in the results unless, of course, parents received a report that their child was performing below expectations. Testing took place in the fifties and sixties, but it was definitely no big deal.

During the seventies and eighties, however, a modest journalistic wrinkle changed all that. Newspaper editors began to publish statewide educational test results on a district-by-district and even school-by-school basis. Citizens could see how their school or district stacked up in comparison to other schools or districts in the state. Districts and schools were *ranked* from top to bottom.

From a news perspective, the publishing of test results was a genuine coup. The test scores were inexpensive to obtain, and readers were really interested in the scores. Residents of low-ranked districts could complain; residents of high-ranked districts could crow. More importantly, because there are no other handy indices of educational effectiveness around, test results became the measuring-stick by which citizens reached conclusions about how well their schools were doing. There are many reports of realtors trying to peddle homes to prospective buyers on the basis that a house was located "in a school district with excellent test scores."

Let me be as clear as I can possibly be about this issue, because I think it is a terrifically important one. As matters stand, students' performances on a state's accountability tests are certain to influence the way that *all* teachers are evaluated—even if a particular teacher's own students never come near an accountability test. Here's how that will happen.

Suppose you teach ninth-grade social studies, and your ninth-graders aren't required to take federally required accountability tests. Suppose you're a second-grade teacher, and your students aren't required to take any kind of accountability test. Suppose you're a high school teacher who teaches subjects and grade levels where no federally imposed accountability tests are required. In all these "suppose" situations, *your* students won't be taking accountability exams. However, the public's perception of *your* personal effectiveness will most certainly be influenced by the scores of *your* school's students on any accountability tests that are required for such schools. Let's be honest—Do you want to be a teacher in a "failing" school? Do you want your students' parents to regard *you* as ineffective because you do your teaching in what's thought to be a sub-par school? I doubt it.

The reality is that the performance of any school's students on federally stipulated accountability tests will splash over on every teacher in that school. If you teach in a school that's regarded as successful, then you will be seen as a member of an effective educational team. The opposite is also true. Unless federal accountability requirements are substantially softened, no public school teacher will be able to remain isolated from the impact of externally imposed accountability tests.

And, as I'll try to point out later in the text, the nature of a school's success on high-stakes external assessments, such as federally required accountability tests, will (and, indeed, *should*) have an impact on the sorts of classroom assessments you personally choose to employ. We live in an era when public perceptions of schooling are more important than some educators might prefer. Yet, like it or not, that's the reality today's teachers must face.

Helping Evaluate Teachers

Teaching skill is coming under increasing scrutiny these days. With the push for more rigorous evaluation of a classroom teacher's performance, we now see many teacher appraisal systems in which students' test performances constitute one key category of evidence being used to evaluate teachers. Sometimes, teachers are directed to assemble pretest and posttest data that can be used to infer how much learning by students was promoted by the teacher. And, of course, teachers whose students are *required* to take a state's annual accountability tests understand all too well that their students' scores on those tests will play a prominent role in teacher evaluation—that is, in the evaluation of *their* teaching.

Decision Time

Pressure from "Higher Ups"

Laura Lund has been teaching second-graders at Horace Mann Elementary School for the past three years. During that period, Laura has become increasingly convinced that "developmentally appropriate instruction" is what she wants in her classroom. Developmentally appropriate instruction takes place when the instructional activities for children are not only matched with the typical developmental level of children in that grade but also matched with the particular developmental level of each child. Because of her growing commitment to developmental appropriateness, and its clear implications for individualized instruction, Laura's students now no longer receive, in unison, the same kinds of massed practice drills in reading and mathematics Laura provided earlier in her career.

Having discovered what kinds of changes are taking place in Laura's second grade, however, the third-grade and fourth-grade teachers in her school have registered great concern over what they regard as less attention to academics, at least less attention of the traditional sort. Because state accountability tests are given to all third- and fourth-grade students each spring, Laura's colleagues are afraid their students will not perform well on those tests because they will not be skilled at the end of the second grade.

A year or so earlier, when Laura was teaching her second grade in a fairly traditional manner, it was widely recognized that most of her students went on to the third grade with a solid mastery of reading and mathematics. Now, however, the school's third- and fourth-grade teachers fear that "Horace Mann's accountability scores may plummet."

As Laura sees it, she has to decide whether to (1) revert to her former instructional practices or (2) maintain her stress on developmentally appropriate instruction. In either case, she realizes that she has to try to justify her action to her colleagues.

 If you were Laura Lund, what would your decision be?

Several state legislatures have now enacted laws stipulating that a specified proportion of a teacher's annual evaluations be derived from the test scores of that teacher's students. In Arizona, for example, any local teacher evaluation procedure must base between one-third and one-half of the evaluation on students' tests performances. This is an altogether understandable response by legislators to some taxpayers' expressed dissatisfactions with the performances of their public schools. That is, legislators want to "hold teachers accountable" by requiring a state's teacher to produce satisfactory improvements in students' achievement—as reflected in students' test scores.

However, only certain kinds of educational assessments can properly carry out this sort of test-rooted task. Most of the tests proposed for this purpose are altogether inappropriate for such an evaluative assignment. Nonetheless, if judgments about teachers' quality are—because of well-intentioned legislative actions—to be based in part on students' assessment performances, then it is apparent that teachers need to learn about the kinds of tests that will support or, possibly, distort this sort of evaluative endeavor.

Experienced teachers will be quick to tell you that the caliber of students' test performances is dramatically influenced by the caliber of the students being tested. It should be apparent that a teacher who is blessed with a flock of bright students will almost always get better test results than a teacher who must work with a less able group of students. And let's not forget about the quality of students' previous teachers. Wouldn't you rather be receiving a new group of students who had been well taught by Mrs. X than a group of students who had been badly taught by Mrs. Y? Nonetheless, increasing numbers of statewide and districtwide teacher evaluation systems now call for teachers to assemble tangible evidence of student accomplishments based on external exams or teacher-made classroom assessments. It is clear, therefore, that today's teachers need to know enough about educational assessment so they can corral compelling evidence regarding their own students' growth.

Clarifying Teachers' Instructional Intentions

For many years, educational tests were regarded as instructional afterthoughts. Once an instructional unit was over, the teacher got busy cranking out a test. Tests were rarely created before instruction was initiated. Instead, tests were devised *after* instruction to fulfill some of the traditional functions of educational assessment described earlier in the chapter—for example, the assignment of grades.

Today, however, many educational measuring instruments have become high-stakes tests. A **high-stakes test** is an assessment for which important consequences ride on the test's results. One example of an educational high-stakes test would be a statewide basic skills test that must be mastered before a student graduates. (Note that the important consequences are for the test taker.) Another example would be a districtwide achievement test whose results are publicized so local taxpayers' judgments about educational effectiveness are influenced by the test results. (Note that in this second case the important consequences apply to the educators who prepared the students, not the test takers themselves.)

A federally required accountability test will fall into this second category of high-stakes tests. Because students' performances on these tests will so powerfully influence the way people regard a school staff's quality, such accountability tests will be genuinely high stakes in nature. You should know, however, there was nothing in NCLB that required diploma denial or that obliged students to be held back at grade level if they fail to perform well enough on a test. A *state's* decision can transform a federal test into one that has an adverse impact on a particular student. Many people continue to be confused by this, for they assume that any federally mandated accountability test automatically requires diploma-denial or promotion-denial testing. It's just not so.

Insofar as important consequences are directly linked to assessment results, the content of such high-stakes tests tends to be emphasized instructionally by teachers. Because teachers want their students to perform well on high-stakes tests (for the students' own good and/or for the teacher's benefit), high-stakes tests tend to serve as the kind of curricular magnet seen in Figure 1.

On some educational grounds, teachers might prefer that tests did not influence instruction so directly, but the reality is that high-stakes assessment will definitely have an impact on classroom instructional practices. Because this curricular influence is certain to be present, it will be in teachers' and students' best interests if the nature of the upcoming assessment is sufficiently well understood so the teacher can organize the most effective, on-target instruction possible. In a sense, however, the more that teachers understand what the innards of a test are, the more effectively they can use this understanding to clarify what's to be sought instructionally.

Even the low-stakes classroom tests routinely employed by teachers can be used to help teachers clarify their instructional targets. Tests should obviously not, then, be instructional afterthoughts. Rather, classroom assessment instruments should always be prepared *prior* to any instructional planning in order for the

figure 1 ■ The Curricular Impact of High-Stakes Tests

teacher to better understand what is being sought of students and, therefore, what to incorporate in instructional activities for students. Assessment instruments prepared prior to instruction concretely exemplify a teacher's instructional intentions and, as a consequence, clarify those intentions. Clarified instructional intentions characteristically lead to more effective instructional decisions by the teacher. The better you understand where you're going, the more efficiently you can get there.

To reiterate, we've now looked at three reasons today's teachers, unlike their counterparts of a few decades ago, need to know about assessment. These reasons are supplemental to, not in place of, the previously considered traditional reasons teachers assess students. Here are the three new reasons for teachers' familiarization with educational assessment:

Today's Reasons for Teachers to Know about Assessment

- Test results determine public perceptions of educational effectiveness.
- Students' assessment performances are increasingly being included as part of the teacher evaluation process.
- As clarifiers of instructional intentions, assessment devices can improve instructional quality.

These reasons are also linked to decisions. For instance, when citizens use test results to reach judgments about a school district's effectiveness, those judgments can play a major role in determining what level of taxpayer support will be provided in that district. There are also decisions on the line when students' test scores are used as evidence to evaluate teachers. Such decisions as whether the teacher should be granted tenure or receive merit-pay awards are illustrative of the kinds of decisions that can ride, at least in part, on the results of educational assessments. Finally, from the teacher's perspective, when tests serve as clarifiers of the teacher's instructional intentions, the teacher can make better decisions about how to put together instructional activities likely to help students attain the instructional intentions represented by the assessment. With these three current roles of educational assessment, as was true with the four more traditional roles of educational assessment, test results should contribute to educational *decisions*.

What Do Classroom Teachers Really Need to Know about Assessment?

Whether you are already a teacher or are preparing to become a teacher, you really do need to know about educational assessment. But the field of educational assessment contains huge chunks of information. In fact, some educators devote their entire careers to assessment. Clearly, there's more to educational assessment than you probably care to know. The question is, What should *classroom teachers* know about assessment?

There are oodles of fascinating things about assessment you might learn. You'd even find a few of them interesting (not all that many, I suspect). But to help your students learn, you really don't *need* to know a host of assessment esoterica. This text about educational assessment is deliberately focused on only those things that you really *must know* in order to promote your students' learning most effectively. I am altogether reluctant to clutter your skull with a galaxy of nice-to-know but nonessential knowledge about educational assessment. Such nice-to-know content often crowds out the need-to-know content. There is, after all, only so much skull space available.

It may be easier for you to get a handle on what you'll be reading if you realize you'll be covering topics dealing chiefly with:

1. Constructing your own assessment instruments
2. Using assessment instruments constructed by others
3. Planning instruction based on instructionally illuminating assessments

Creating Classroom Assessment Devices

Let's start with the kinds of classroom assessment devices you will personally need to create. The chief thing you will learn in this text is how to construct a wide variety of assessment instruments you can use as part of your day-to-day classroom instruction. You really do need to know how to determine what your students have learned—for example, whether they comprehend what they have read. You also really do need to know how to get a fix on your students' educationally relevant attitudes—such as how positively disposed your students are toward the subject(s) you're teaching. Thus, you are going to be learning about how to create classroom assessment approaches to measure students' *achievement* (that is, the knowledge and/or skills students acquire) as well as students' *affect* (that is, the educationally pertinent attitudes, interests, and values influenced by school).

As suggested earlier, the kinds of classroom assessment procedures you'll be learning about will extend well beyond traditional paper-and-pencil testing instruments. You may even learn about several assessment approaches with which you are currently unfamiliar.

In a related vein, you will also learn how to judge the quality of the assessment devices *you* create. And, at the same time, you will learn how to judge the quality of assessment devices created by others. Those "others" might be your own colleagues or, perhaps, the folks who devise large-scale assessment instruments such as districtwide or statewide tests. It may seem presumptuous for me

Assessment Literacy: Only for Grown-Ups?

Students' performances on tests can have an enormous impact not only on the students who actually take educational tests but also on the test-taker's family. Teachers, too, are often affected by their students' test scores. To illustrate, today's teachers seem to be frequently buffeted by educational accountability tests on which students' test scores can have an impact on teachers' tenure, assignment, and salaries. Clearly, educators at all levels, whether teachers or administrators, need to learn enough about educational tests to carry out their responsibilities successfully.

What those educators need, therefore, is a reasonable dose of *assessment literacy*. And here's a definition of it: *Assessment literacy consists of an individual's understandings of the fundamental assessment concepts and procedures deemed likely to influence educational decisions.*

Notice that this definition is focused on someone's understandings of educational measurement's *basic* concepts and procedures of educational assessment. The stuff an assessment-literate person needs to understand is not esoteric and incomprehensible. Rather, most of what an assessment-literate person should know is just common sense applied to educational measurement. Describing assessment literacy a bit differently, it represents the main-line measurement procedures and concepts thought to make a difference in the decisions made about the students who take educational tests.

Well, if that's what assessment literacy is, who needs to have it? There's considerable pressure these days on teachers to become more assessment literate. You are currently reading a book that, unless the book's author has really mucked up, ought to help you personally become more assessment literate. But what about educational policymakers? And what about parents of school-age children? And, finally, *what about students themselves?* Don't all three of these groups need to beef up their understandings about the key assessment-related principles and processes that can influence students' lives?

I certainly think so. I hope, as you read this text, you'll occasionally pause to think how you might relay to policymakers (such as school board members), parents (such as the ones you had yourself), and students (such as the ones you're teaching) the most essential things about the assessment-related concepts and procedures you're encountering in these pages. Remember, because test results these days can increasingly enhance or impair the decisions made about students, don't *at least* those students have the right to know what's going on behind the assessment curtain? A reasonable lump of assessment literacy is good for almost everyone!

to suggest that you, a classroom teacher (in practice or in preparation), could be judging the efforts of folks who create large-scale standardized educational tests. But you'll discover from this text that you will, indeed, possess the knowledge and skills necessary to distinguish between tawdry and terrific practices by those who create such large-scale educational tests. In particular, you can use your new knowledge to judge the quality of any accountability tests that may be used in your state. Those tests are going to be so important that, if you are teaching in a state whose accountability tests are educationally unsound, you definitely need to know it.

Fundamentally, educational assessment rests on a foundation of common sense. Once you learn the technical vocabulary of assessment, you'll be able to identify departures from commonsensical assessment practices, whether those departures are seen in your own tests, in the tests of a teacher down the hall, or in the tests created by district, state, or national assessment specialists. In short, after you finish this text, you really need not be deferent to any "measurement experts." You'll know enough to spot serious shortcomings in their work.

You will learn about three criteria you can use to evaluate all educational tests. Those criteria apply with equal force to tests you might develop as well as to tests that are commercially developed. Once you get the hang of how to evaluate tests, you can apply this evaluative skill in many settings.

Interpreting Standardized Test Results

Because your students will often be assessed with nationally standardized or state-developed tests, you will need to know how to interpret the results of such tests. In general, commercially developed educational tests focus either on students' *achievement,* which, as noted earlier, deals with the knowledge and skills that students have acquired, or commercial tests focus on *aptitude,* which is a term used to describe a student's learning *potential.* You should know, however, that the term *aptitude* is definitely falling from grace these days. In the old days, when I was a tyke, people talked about intelligence. As a prospective teacher, I learned all about the intelligence quotient (IQ), which was a numerical way of indicating the degree to which a particular individual's intellectual abilities exceeded or fell short of conventional expectations for such individuals.

But "intelligence" has fallen decisively out of favor with educators during the past few decades. The term *intelligence* conveys the notion that students possess an inborn potential about which schools can do little to influence. Yet, the so-called intelligence tests, widely used until recently, often measured what students had learned at school or, more importantly, what students had learned at home. Thus, the term *aptitude* has been increasingly used rather than *intelligence* in order to convey a notion of a student's academic potential. But even the term *aptitude* tends to create the perception there is some sort of innate cap on one's potential. Because of this perception, we now find that the commercial test makers who formerly created so-called intelligence tests, and then renamed them aptitude tests, are looking for a less negatively loaded descriptor. Interestingly, the tests themselves, although they've been relabeled, haven't really changed all that much.

At any rate, you'll learn how to make sense out of the kinds of reports regarding student performance released by those who conduct large-scale assessments. You will need this knowledge not only to inform your own decisions about classroom instruction but also to interpret students' test performances to

but what does this have to do with
Teaching?

This chapter contains over a half-dozen reasons teachers need to learn about assessment. Actually, there are seven reasons in the chapter, and that's one more reason than a half-dozen. (Notice how low-level the arithmetic in this text is going to be!)

But let me single out the *two* reasons I think, *from an instructional perspective,* all teachers need to know about testing. The first of these reasons is the last of the seven reasons cited in the chapter—namely, the *instructional-planning payoffs* teachers can get from a more clear understanding of what they're trying to have their students accomplish. Because a properly constructed classroom test can truly exemplify what a teacher is trying to achieve, the resulting *clarity of intention* helps teachers make more astute decisions when they plan their instruction.

When I recall my own early years as a high school teacher, I remember how often I simply whipped together lesson plans that *seemed* somewhat instructional. Yet, my planning was almost never guided by a truly clearheaded notion of what knowledge, skills, or attitudes I wanted my students to possess when the instruction was over. If I had relied on my classroom tests to clarify what I wanted my students to become, I'm certain my lessons would have been far better focused on my intended instructional outcomes.

The second reason I think all teachers should become more astute regarding assessment is also instructionally rooted. It's the second of the four traditional reasons considered in the chapter—namely, so teachers can *monitor students' progress.* If teachers use students' assessed levels of achievement to determine whether the current instructional plan is stellar or sickly, then teachers' adjustments in lessons can, if warranted, be made. Without the evidence yielded by classroom formative assessments, a teacher will often fail to spot instructional inadequacies. As Black and Wiliam, the British investigators, made quite clear, the instructional dividends from monitoring students' progress can be striking. And their views were based on solid research investigations, not wishful yearnings. My grandparents came to the United States from Great Britain, so I typically groove on anything that's asserted with a British accent. But, then, doesn't everyone?

parents who may demand answers to questions such as, "What does my son's standardized test performance at 40th percentile really mean?" or "If my fifth-grade daughter earned a grade-equivalent score at the eighth-grade level on this year's standardized achievement test, why shouldn't she be promoted?" In short, you'll learn how to interpret students' performances on both *achievement tests* and *aptitude tests*.

Instructionally Illuminating Assessment

Earlier, it was suggested that because assessment devices exemplify a teacher's instructional intentions, those assessment instruments can clarify the teacher's instructional decision-making. You'll learn more about how the link between testing and teaching can prove beneficial to your students because you can provide more on-target and effective instruction.

On the other hand, you'll also learn how some teachers inappropriately prepare their students for tests, particularly for high-stakes tests. You will learn about ways of judging whether a given test-preparation practice is (1) in students' best interests from an educational perspective and (2) in educators' best interests from an ethical perspective. In short, you'll learn about the increasingly important relationship between instruction and assessment.

You'll learn about a way to build classroom assessments so that they'll have a decisively positive impact on how well you teach. *Tests,* if deliberately created with instruction in mind, *can boost your personal success as a teacher.*

There's one other issue that I'd like to bring to your attention—namely, the possibility of your helping *parents* learn more about educational assessment. And why, you might ask, should a teacher be messing around trying to promote parental measurement moxie? It's a good question. And the answer is this: Parents who are *assessment literate* will be better able to *help you help their children learn* more successfully.

You see, most parents know little more about testing than what they can recall, often vaguely, from their own classroom days as students. But the nature of classroom testing has changed dramatically since that time. Not only are there new approaches to assessment being used in classrooms, but students' test scores are also being used to judge the success of teachers' instructional efforts. If you and your students' parents truly understand the fundamentals of educational assessment, you can work together in many ways that will benefit your students. Assessment-literate parents can be a potent force to counter the serious misuses of educational tests we see so often today. And, if you are teaching in a state whose officials have opted to use instructionally insensitive accountability tests, you'll find that assessment-literate parents can be a potent political force who might, if you're lucky, help get more appropriate accountability tests installed in your state.

There's another audience for assessment literacy that you'll hopefully give some thought to as you wend your way through this text. Please recognize that the lives of today's students are increasingly influenced by their performances on various kinds of educational tests. Why not, therefore, provide at least a dose of assessment literacy to students themselves? As you will see, most of the assessment concepts treated in the text are not particularly complicated. Indeed, the truly essential assessment understandings needed by students are well within the grasp of those students. Why not splash a bit of assessment literacy on those students? They really need it!

Parent Talk

Mr. and Mrs. Smothers are attending a back-to-school night at a middle school where their daughter, Cathy, is a fifth-grader. After briefly leafing through Cathy's math port-folio and language arts portfolio, they get around to the real reason they've come to school. Mrs. Smothers, looking more than a little belligerent, says, "Cathy tells us she gets several teacher-made tests in class every week. All that testing can't be necessary. It obviously takes away the time you spend teaching her! Why is there so darn much testing in your class?"

 If I were you, here's how I'd respond to Mrs. Smothers:

"I suppose that it might seem to you there's too much testing going on in my class, and I can understand your concern about testing-time taking away from teaching-time. But let me explain how the time my students spend doing classroom assessments really leads to much *better* use of instructional time.

"You see, the way I use classroom assessment is to make sure my instruction is on target and, most importantly, that I don't waste the children's time. Last month, for in-stance, we started a new unit in social studies and I gave students a short pretest to find out what they already knew. To my delight, I discovered that almost all of the students—including Cathy—knew well over half of what I had been planning to teach.

"Based on the pretest's results, I was able to shorten the social studies unit substan-tially, and spend the extra time giving students more practice on their map-interpretation skills. You probably saw some of the maps Cathy was interpreting as part of her home-work assignments.

"Mr. and Mrs. Smothers, I want Cathy's time in class to be as well spent as possible. And to make sure of that, I use formal and informal classroom tests to be certain that I'm teaching her, and her classmates, what they really need to learn."

 Now, how would you respond to Mrs. Smothers?

■ Chapter Summary

In this chapter, the emphasis was on why teachers really need to know about as-sessment. Early in the chapter, the assessment-related features of various reauthor-izations of the Elementary and Secondary Education Act of 1965 were briefly described because this oft-revised federal law's impact on most teachers' instruc-tional and assessment decisions is becoming profound. *Educational assessment* was defined as a formal attempt to determine students' status with respect to edu-cational variables of interest. Much of the chapter was devoted to a consideration of why teachers must become knowledgeable regarding educational assessment. Based on teachers' classroom activities, four traditional reasons were given for why teachers assess—namely, to (1) diagnose students' strengths and weaknesses, (2) monitor students' progress, (3) assign grades, and (4) determine a teacher's own instructional effectiveness. Based on recent uses of educational assessment results, three more current reasons teachers need to know about instruction were identified. Those more recent functions of educational tests are to (1) influence public perceptions of educational effectiveness, (2) help evaluate teachers, and (3) clarify teachers' instructional intentions. Regardless of the specific application of test results, however, it was emphasized that teachers should use the results of assessments *to make better decisions*. That's really the only excuse for taking up students' time with assessment.

The chapter identified three major outcomes to be attained by those reading the text—namely, becoming more knowledgeable about how to (1) construct and evaluate their own classroom tests, (2) interpret results of standardized tests, and (3) teach students to master what's assessed in classroom and high-stakes tests. It was also suggested that an assessment-literate teacher should attempt to promote parents' and students' assessment literacy.

 # Self-Check

This chapter was decisively heavier on pep talk and previewing than on solid assessment-related content. I've included a brief self-check exercise section so you can become familiar with what will be coming up at the end of this chapter. An answer key for self-check exercises is provided immediately after the discussion questions (entitled Pondertime to encourage you to devote meaningful time to pondering) and immediately before the references section (entitled Additional Stuff because it is, in fact, additional stuff). The answer key will be presented in slightly smaller type to make you pay careful attention and to make your eyes hurt.

1. Without referring to the text, and using your own words (although, if you're stuck, you can borrow some of mine), how would you define *educational assessment*?

   _____

   _____

   _____

2. An educational *test* is a term that's been around for a long time. Why was it suggested in the chapter that educational *assessment* is the preferred descriptor these days?

_____

_____

_____

3. Review the following list of six fictitious quotes from classroom teachers and decide which four quotations represent the *traditional* reasons that teachers are likely to give in response to the question, Why should you, as a teacher, test your students?
   a. "Because I need to base my students' grades on something other than smiling faces."
   b. "Because I can figure out, before I begin to teach, what my students already know and don't know."
   c. "Because testing takes up classroom time, and I have so many classroom hours to fill and so little content to cover."
   d. "Because I can tell whether my pupils have learned, hence whether I've taught well."
   e. "Because I can see what kinds of progress my students are making, and can give more instruction to those who need it."
   f. "Because I want to learn more about what kinds of pronouns to use when modifying gerunds."

4. Which of the following four statements does *not* represent one of the *current* reasons cited in the chapter that today's teacher should either learn about educational assessment or be considered a consummate cluck?
   a. Educational measuring devices, as clarifications for instructional intentions, can improve instructional quality.
   b. Student performances on high-stakes tests substantially influence public perceptions of educational effectiveness.
   c. Today's teacher evaluation systems increasingly incorporate students' performances on educational assessment devices.
   d. Educational assessment devices are now being used to advertise young people's fashionwear.

(Self-Check Key is provided following the Pondertime questions.)

Pondertime

Here are a few assessment-related questions for you to ponder. Such pondering can be done in public, as in a class discussion, or in private, as in by yourself. A recent survey of pondering practices in Pennsylvania indicated that public pondering was preferred over private pondering, even by consenting adults, almost two to one. (There was a sampling error for this survey of ±100%.)

1. Why do you think we have witnessed such an increased interest in educational assessment during the past decade or so?

2. In many states, prospective teachers are not required to take any courses dealing with educational assessment. Why do you think this is so?

3. What kinds of rights, if any, does the public have regarding educational assessment?

4. Recalling your personal days in school, what level of expertise do you think your own teachers possessed regarding educational assessment?

5. Do you think the movement to discourage the use of the terms *intelligence* and *aptitude* is appropriate? Why?

6. Do you believe that classroom teachers will derive any advantages from promoting parental assessment literacy? If so, what might those advantages be?

Self-Check Key

1. Any reasonable paraphrase of the following definition will be acceptable: "Educational assessment is a formal attempt to determine students' status with respect to educational variables of interest."

2. Two related reasons were given—namely, that (1) the phrase *educational test* conjures up notions of only paper-and-pencil instruments and (2) many worthwhile educational outcomes are not best assessed by paper-and-pencil tests.

3. Choices a, b, d, and e are winners. Choices c and f, therefore, are losers.

4. If you did not choose d for this warm-up, giveaway item, you are hereby sentenced to a rereading of the entire chapter.

■ Additional Stuff

Andrade, H. (Ed.). (Winter 2009). "A special issue on classroom assessment," *Theory Into Practice, 48,* no. 1.

Black, P., and Wiliam, D. (1998). "Inside the black box: Raising standards through class-room assessment," *Phi Delta Kappan, 80,* no. 2 (October): 139–148.

Della-Piana, G. M. (2008). "Enduring issues in educational measurement," *Phi Delta Kappan, 89,* no. 8 (April): 590–592.

Gordon, W. E. (2008). The transformation of key beliefs that have guided a century of assessment. In C. A. Dwyer (Ed.), *The future of assessment: Shaping teaching and learning* (pp. 3–6). New York: Lawrence Erlbaum.

Hess, F. M. (2008/2009). "The new stupid," *Educational Leadership, 66,* no. 4 (December/January): 12–17.

National Governors Association Center for Best Practices and Council of Chief State School Officers. (2010). *Common Core State Standards for English Language Arts and Mathematics.* Washington, D.C.: Author.

Nichols, S. L., and Berliner, D. C. (2008). "Testing the joy out of learning," *Educational Leadership, 65,* no. 6 (March): 14–18.

Popham, W. J. (2009). *Unlearned lessons: Six stumbling blocks to our schools' success.* Cambridge, MA: Harvard Education Press.

Stiggins, R. J., and Chappuis, J. (2012). *An introduction to student-involved assessment FOR learning* (6th ed.). Boston: Pearson.

Stobard, G. (2008). *Testing times: The uses and abuses of assessment.* New York: Routledge.

■ Cyber Stuff

- ■ *The Council of Chief State School Officers (CCSSO)* is a nationwide, nonprofit organization of public officials who lead K–12 education in the 50 states. This website is a rich resource for those who wish to monitor state-level assessment activities throughout the United States. The website also contains a host of practical guidelines regarding how states can satisfy federal accountability requirements. **www.ccsso.org**

- ■ *The National Governors Association* was founded in 1908. Its bipartisan membership included the governors of the 50 states, three territories, and two commonwealths. The Center for Best Practices of the National Governors Association (NGA) played a prominent collaborative role in the generation of the Common Core State Standards. Use of this website's search engine under "educational assessment" yields more than 60 results on the topic. **www.nga.org**

- ■ *U.S. Department of Education* provides a full-ranging website offering detailed information about federal accountability/assessment statutes currently in force. For example, for the currently approved version of the Elementary and Secondary Education Act, this website supplies guidelines not only to state and local officials regarding the law's implementations, but also to parents of school-age children about the law's influence on local schools. An excellent search engine accompanies the site. **www.ed.gov**

Extended Applications

It is a truism that the more a person uses something, the more familiar with this something the person becomes. This self-evident notion surely applies to the assessment-related knowledge, skills, and concepts you have been reading about in the foregoing pages. Thus, to provide readers of *Classroom Assessment* with additional opportunities to apply the content contained in this text, this final section contains a variety of exercises intended to give readers an opportunity to use what they've been reading about.

In a sense, of course, the Self-Check exercises found at the close of each chapter provided an opportunity for readers to apply a chapter's content. Nonetheless, the more times you use a concept, skill, or a body of knowledge, the more likely it is that you will master this content so you can employ it in varied situations.

For each of the text, you will find an extended-application exercise calling for you to do some thinking about that chapter's content as it applies to a real-world situation. Each exercise is preceded by a brief introduction setting forth the reason that the upcoming extended-application exercise has been selected.

Because many of these exercises call on you to generate an original response rather than select a response from a set of options, it is difficult to supply an "answer key" for readers' unpredictable responses. So, what you'll find following all the exercises is One Possible Response—an indication of how I would have personally responded to the exercise if I had been asked to do so. Please don't regard my response as the only way to respond to an exercise. After all, by definition, this is only "one possible" response. Instead, please think of my response as a fairly flimsy form of feedback. You can certainly disagree with me, even emphatically, yet still profit from doing the exercise.

Remember, what is being provided in this section. The exercises deliberately intended to extend how you apply the content treated in *Classroom Assessment*. I hope you find these exercises useful in enhancing your understanding of what teachers need to know about classroom assessment.

Electronically Induced Thinking

Introduction

During the past half-dozen years or so, whenever I've had an article published in an educational journal (typically these days I write about some aspect of educational assessment), the article is concluded by saying that I'm a UCLA emeritus professor and my e-mail address is wpopham@ucla.edu. In a fair number of instances, readers of these articles send me an e-mail—typically seeking clarification, expressing agreement, or registering thoroughgoing disdain for my views. Because those folks took the time to e-mail me, I always respond. And that's what I want you to do in this very first exercise—that is, I'm asking you to read three e-mails and respond to each one. Please assume *you* have written an article about assessment and you've just had it published. (Congratulations!)

Why Do Teachers Need to Know about Assessment?

For the purposes of this exercise, please pretend the article was published in a state-level education journal, and is entitled "Assessment Makes a Difference." Assume the three e-mails in this exercise have been sent to you by folks who've read your article. Your task is to compose an appropriate response to each of the three e-mails you'll find in the exercise.

In this chapter of *Classroom Assessment,* the focus is on "*why* teachers need to know about assessment." Near the chapter's conclusion, however, three "*what* teachers need to know about assessment" topics were given. The three e-mails in this exercise deal with each of these three *whats*. The purpose of this exercise, as its title implies, is to get you to do some electronically induced thinking about those three *whats*. You'll have to do so in order to compose sensible responses to issues raised by three educators who (we are assuming) have recently read your article. If you do this thinking well, it should solidify your understanding of why it is that teachers need to know (1) *how to build their own tests,* (2) *how to interpret standardized test results,* and (3) *how a well-designed test can contribute to better instructional decisions.*

I suggest that you come up with a response to one e-mail at a time rather than tackling them en masse. Please think through the reasons for your response carefully before composing your reply. Finally, please try to devise your own reply to each e-mail *before* reading what I've written as my One Possible Response.

 Exercise Directions: This exercise presents you with three fictional e-mails. Your task is to compose an e-mail reply to each.

E-Mail Number 1

To: Author of "Assessment Makes a Difference"
From: Jane Carruthers
Subject: 24 Hours in a Day

Hello:

I teach third-graders in Laidlaw, a small community in the southern part of our state. I've been teaching for six years now, and I have come to appreciate the importance of classroom testing.

However, in your article you recommend that classroom teachers become skilled in developing their own assessment instruments. I really think this is a case of wishful thinking. I simply don't have the time to construct first-rate assessment instruments.

And why, indeed, should classroom teachers have to do this sort of test-building in the first place? Are surgeons required to make their own scalpels? Are plumbers obliged to make their own pipe wrenches?

Isn't the creation of classroom tests something a district or state should be doing? If teachers were presented with a collection of properly constructed assessment devices, then we could *choose* the ones that were most appropriate for our own instructional situations.

Wouldn't this be better than having teachers churn out their own tests—some of which will surely be terrible? I'd appreciate your reactions.

Sincerely,

Overworked Jane

 One Possible Response (to E-Mail Number 1)

To: Overworked Jane
From: Author of "Assessment Makes a Difference"
Subject: Re: 24 Hours in a Day

Hi Jane:

I really do understand what you're saying. My years as a public school teacher taught me all too well just how physically and mentally draining a teacher's job can be. I taught high school kids, and they were tough enough. I doubt if I could have stayed in teaching had I been surrounded by third-grade squirmers.

Okay, getting down to your idea of having states or districts create a flock of first-rate tests from which teachers could select—it's a great idea! The trouble is that in our state there seems to be absolutely no interest on the part of our State Department of Education's staff in creating such a resource. Moreover, I haven't heard about any districts in the state whose administrators intend to do what you're asking for. It is a wonderful approach but, until it actually happens, it's merely a well-conceived wish.

Realistically, then, you're going to need to come up with appropriate assessments for your third-graders on your own time. And here's the point at which I think there's some hope. If you are willing to learn more about classroom assessment, then I think your mission should be the following: "How can I learn about *efficient* ways to assess my students so that, while retaining a smattering of sanity, I can use classroom tests effectively?"

Clearly, you appreciate the importance of good classroom testing. Thus, in the absence of a set of "choose-from" tests supplied by your district or by the state, you'll need to construct good tests yourself. The more you learn about classroom assessment, the greater the likelihood will be that you can adopt a "less is more" assessment strategy so you can get by with fewer tests, but tests that measure the most important things you want to teach. You'll find that a handful of really first-rate tests can have a dramatic and beneficial impact on your teaching.

Why Do Teachers Need to Know about Assessment?

If you don't employ as many classroom assessments as your time and energy permit, you are apt to be instructionally short-changing your students. I know you don't want that.

Good luck.

■ ■ ■

E-Mail Number 2

To: "Assessment Makes a Difference" Author
From: Guy Phelps
Subject: A Task for Specialists?

Hi:

In your recent article, "Assessment Makes a Difference," you claimed that all teachers should know quite a bit about standardized achievement tests and standardized aptitude tests. I really think that you are expecting too much—way too much—of regular class-room teachers. Aren't such tests the proper domain of school counselors and school psychologists, not teachers? After all, that's why school psychologists and school counselors completed so much additional training focused on standardized testing!

I think that you are especially unrealistic in expecting busy classroom teachers to become knowledgeable regarding *aptitude* tests. Surely the interpretation of such tests is a job for specialists. I've been a language arts teacher in a middle school for about two years, and I am far too busy to acquire a ton of truths about educational testing!

However, I thought that the rest of your article was very good. Thanks for writing about these issues.

Guy Phelps

Hunter Middle School

 One Possible Response (to E-Mail Number 2)

To: Guy Phelps
From: "Assessment Makes a Difference" Author
Subject: Re: A Task for Specialists?

Hello Guy:

I'm glad that you liked the bulk of my recent article. I feel strongly that today's educators just don't know enough about assessment—especially its potential contribution to instruction. However, let me address the concerns you raised in your e-mail.

Why Do Teachers Need to Know about Assessment?

Classroom teachers would certainly be better off if specialists, such as counselors and school psychologists, were constantly on hand to deal with issues related to standardized tests. Unfortunately, in the education world that I know, such specialists are few in number and, sadly, seem to be becoming an endangered species in many parts of the country. So if you have convenient access to a school counselor and/or school psychologist at Hunter Middle School, count yourself lucky. These days you are definitely an exception!

Even in specialist-blessed Hunter Middle School, I think that *you* need to know what makes the ticking sound inside standardized achievement tests *and* standardized aptitude tests. I guess I didn't defend my views very well in the article, so let me clarify why I hold that position.

Today, more than ever, students' test scores are playing major roles in the decisions made about those students. Because most standardized achievement and aptitude tests are intended to yield results from which *comparative* score-interpretations can be made (for instance, when a student's score is contrasted—often in the form of a percentile—with the scores of students in a norm group), the focus of almost all standardized tests is on *an individual student*. In most instances, teachers can pick up at least some limited information from those tests that might help them in understanding a student's overall achievement or aptitude. In many cases, however, students' parents will be calling on *you* to tell them the precise meaning of such scores.

Parents of your students will want, and those parents will deserve, information about the meaning of their children's standardized test scores. If parents ask you what it means when their child earns a score "at the 78th percentile," or "a scale-score of 320," you need to be able to answer those parents with something other than a lame response such as, "That's the interpretive job of a counselor."

Besides, many of your students will soon be taking preliminary versions of either the SAT or ACT, our nation's most widely used college entrance exams. Your students, and their parents, will have many questions about those exams. You should have some answers on hand.

I really don't think teachers can be true professionals if they are unfamiliar with an important form of evidence bearing on the status of their students. You don't need to become an assessment expert, Guy, but you can't farm out sense-making about standardized tests to a set of increasingly scarce specialists.

It is said that "ignorance is bliss." In the case of teachers' familiarity with standardized tests, however, this sort of "bliss" is harmful to students.

■ ■ ■

Why Do Teachers Need to Know about Assessment?

E-Mail Number 3

To: The Writer of "Assessment Makes a Difference"
From: George Marshall
Subject: A Decade Done Wrong?

Dear Writer:

I enjoyed your recent article, "Assessment Makes a Difference," because it certainly clarified why it is that teachers need to become more conversant with measurement— particularly these days when accountability tests seem to be smothering us.

I've been an elementary teacher for almost a decade, and I've certainly built my share of classroom tests—ten years' worth of such tests to be accurate. Yet, you said one thing in your article that runs directly counter to the way I have been creating tests for my students. You recommend that teachers build their important classroom tests *before* actually planning their instructional activities. I do precisely the opposite!

I almost always wait until my instruction is finished before I generate my tests. Naturally, I am guided by our state's and our district's curricular objectives, but I don't think it is fair to my students to test them on content that I may not have had time in class to get to. (As I'm sure you know, all sorts of unforeseen events take place in a classroom—some of them providing serendipitous opportunities for learning.) Some-times such learning opportunities prevent me from getting to certain content that I had planned to cover. Anyway, it seems more fair to devise tests only a day or two before I want to use them instead of building those tests many weeks in advance.

I have 10 years' worth of experience in doing it this way, and I think it works well. What's wrong with my approach?

Respectfully,

George Marshall

Elk Grove Elementary School

 One Possible Response (to E-Mail Number 3)

To: George Marshall
From: The Writer of "Assessment Makes a Difference"
Subject: Re: A Decade Done Wrong?

Howdy George:

I understand your concern, for one rarely likes to learn about one's mistakes, and the possibility of discovering that you've made 10 years' worth of assessment errors is certain to be unnerving. Clearly, you've been trying to do the best, most fair assessment job you can for your students. That's commendable, and I can't imagine anyone who would not applaud your efforts.

Nonetheless, *in the interest of your students,* I'm still going to urge you to do your test-building differently. I'll try to explain here why you will almost certainly provide better instruction for your students if you construct their important exams *prior* to devising your instructional plans. I guess I didn't do a very good job of explaining this in the article. Sorry.

The reason for creating key exams prior to designing your instructional activities boils down to one word: *clarity*. The more clearheaded you are about the skills and knowledge you want your students to achieve as a consequence of your instruction, the better you will design your instructional activities for those students. I realize that, as you say, you try to build your instructional activities in an attempt to promote students' mastery of state and district curricular goals. But, in my experience, those sorts of goals are often stated in a remarkably ambiguous manner. Thus, many teachers have only a general idea of where they are headed instructionally when they attempt to develop their unit plans and lesson plans on the basis of official curricular goals. By using your tests themselves to *exemplify* what those curricular goals really mean, you'll find you become far more clearheaded about where you want to go instructionally. The students you teach, therefore, will be the beneficiaries of clarity-induced improvements in what will almost certainly turn out to be more on-target instruction.

You fear that if you fail to treat a topic on the test, your students will be unfairly penalized. That concern tells me a good deal about the caring sort of teacher you are. Well, suppose in a given school year you experience loads of serendipitous events in your classroom. (I always liked serendipity in bunches when I was teaching.) If these fortuitous events have prevented you from addressing a topic on your test—the one you made up well in advance of your instructional planning—all you have to do is write a note on the board saying, "Please skip Items 7, 8, and 13 on today's test." Be assured that your students will not feel ill-used because of your test-shortening decision.

Thanks so much for writing. I am, as I hope you can sense from my response, thoroughly committed to *clarity of instructional intent* as the single, most important precursor of good teaching. Teachers who truly understand where they want their students to be at the end of instruction are usually successful. Teachers who possess only murky notions about their end-of-instruction aims will, all too often, provide off-target teaching destined to fall short of high-quality instruction.

■ Glossary

achievement tests   A measurement of the knowledge and/or skills a student possesses. Although often thought to assess what a student has *achieved* in school, some commercially published achievement tests contain many items measuring a student's out-of-school learning or the students' inherited academic aptitudes.

Common Core State Standards (CCSS)   These are curricular goals developed as targets for the nation's instructional programs. The reading and mathematics curricular aims created for the Common Core State Standards have been accepted as official curricular aspirations by all but a few of the 50 U.S. states.

high-stakes test   An assessment whose consequences have important implications either for students (such as grade-to-grade promotion) and/or for educators (such as when schools are qualitatively ranked on the basis of students' test scores).

Partnership for the Assessment of Readiness for College and Careers (PARCC)   One of the two state assessment consortia established with substantial federal funding to create "next generation" tests to assess students' mastery of the Common Core State Standards.

preassessment   A pretest given prior to instruction, typically to (1) determine a student's entry skills and knowledge or (2) employ as part of a pretest-posttest collection of evidence regarding instructional quality.

Smarter Balanced Assessment Consortium (SBAC)   One of the two state assessment consortia formed to generate assessments suitable for measuring students' mastery of the Common Core State Standards.

test   A formal attempt to determine a student's status with respect to an educational variable of interest. Synonyms: *assessment, measurement.*

Deciding What to Assess and How to Assess It

If classroom assessment does not help teachers do a better job of educating their students, then classroom assessment has no reason to exist. Well-conceived classroom assessment will almost invariably lead to better educated students. So, before getting into some of the measurement concepts typically linked to educational testing, this chapter addresses two overridingly important *educational* questions that each teacher must answer about classroom assessment. Those two whopper questions, suitably highlighted in uppercase type, are presented below:

1. WHAT SORTS OF THINGS SHOULD A CLASSROOM TEACHER TRY TO ASSESS?
2. HAVING DECIDED ON WHAT TO ASSESS, HOW SHOULD A CLASSROOM TEACHER GO ABOUT ASSESSING IT?

Let's tackle the first of these two questions—that is, the what-to-assess question. Having given you some ways to answer it, we'll then figure out how to respond to the second, how-to-assess-it question.

What to Assess

Far too many teachers simply stumble into an assessment pattern without giving serious consideration to why they're assessing what they're assessing. Typically, teachers test students in order to dispense grades in a manner that somehow

From Chapter 2 of *Classroom Assessment: What Teachers Need to Know*, Seventh Edition.
W. James Popham. Copyright © 2014 by Pearson Education, Inc. All rights reserved.

resembles the levels of academic performances students have displayed. Students who score well on the teacher's tests are given good grades; low-scoring students get the other kind. Traditionally, the need to dole out grades to students has been the chief factor spurring teachers to assess their students. Many teachers, of course, also employ classroom tests as motivational tools—that is, to encourage students to "study harder."

Yet, there are a number of other significant reasons these days that teachers construct and use assessment instruments. For example, results of classroom assessments may be employed to identify certain students' areas of deficiency so the teacher can more effectively target additional instruction at those content or skill areas where there's the greatest need. Another important function of classroom assessment is to help teachers, *prior* to the design of an instructional sequence, understand more clearly what their end-of-instruction targets really are. This clarification occurs because properly constructed assessment procedures can exemplify and, thereby, illuminate the nature of instructional targets for teachers.

Decision-Driven Assessment

Teachers use tests to get information about their students. Teachers typically make score-based interpretations about their students' status with respect to whatever curricular aims are being represented by the tests. Based on these interpretations, teachers then make decisions. Sometimes the decisions are as straightforward as whether to give Steve Smith an A or a B. Sometimes the decisions are more difficult, such as how to adjust an ongoing instructional unit based on students' performances on a mid-unit exam. But, whatever the decisions are, classroom assessment should be unequivocally focused on the *action options* teachers have at their disposal. The information garnered from assessing students is then used to help a teacher make the specific decision that's at issue. Because the nature of the decision to be serviced by the test results will usually influence the kind of assessment approach the teacher selects, it is important to clarify, *prior to the creation of a test*, just what decision or decisions will be influenced by students' test performances.

I realize it may seem silly to you, or at least somewhat unnecessary, to identify *in advance* what decisions are linked to your classroom assessments, but it really does make a difference in determining what you should assess. For instance, suppose the key decision riding on a set of test results is how to structure a series of remedial instructional activities for those students who performed poorly during a teaching unit about a higher-order thinking skill. In this sort of situation, the teacher would definitely need some fine-grained diagnostic information about the "building block" subskills or enabling knowledge each student did or didn't possess. Thus, instead of designing a test so it merely assessed students' mastery of the overall thinking skill being taught, there would also need to be a sufficient number of items assessing students' mastery of each building-block subskill or enabling knowledge. Based on the diagnostic data derived from the test, a sensible set of remedial instructional activities could then be designed for the low performers.

If, on the other hand, the key decision linked to test results is a simple determination of whether the teacher's instruction was sufficiently effective, a pretest-posttest assessment of more global (and less diagnostic) outcomes would suffice. It's also appropriate, by the way, when judging the effectiveness of a teacher's instruction, that separate assessments should be used containing items intended to assess students' *attitudes* about what was being taught, not merely the knowledge and/or skills being addressed.

In short, the decisions to be benefitted by assessment results should always influence the nature of classroom assessment. Teachers should, therefore, routinely consider the decision(s) at issue prior to creating a classroom assessment device.

A fairly easy way to decide if a test's results will really influence a classroom teacher's decision is to imagine the test results turn out in two opposite ways—for example, a set of excellent student test performances versus a set of inferior student test performances. If the teacher would be apt to make a *different* decision based on those disparate sets of performances, then the teacher truly has a test that can help inform decisions. If the teacher's decision would be pretty much the same no matter what the test results were, there's a strong likelihood the assessment procedure is more ritual than genuine help for the teacher.

The Role of Curricular Aims

Much classroom assessment takes place after an instructional sequence has been completed. There are exceptions, of course, such as the during-instruction monitoring of students' progress as part of the formative-assessment process . There's also the pretesting a teacher might use as part of a pretest-posttest evaluation of the teacher's instructional effectiveness. Yet, many classroom tests are used at the close of instruction. And, because much classroom instruction is intended to help students achieve specified outcomes, it is quite reasonable to think that if teachers consider the content of the outcomes they want their students to achieve, those teachers can more readily answer the what-to-assess question. What teachers should assess will, in most instances, stem directly from the intended consequences of instruction because it will be those hoped-for consequences that influence what the teacher will be teaching and, in all probability, what the students will be learning.

Let's pause for just a moment to consider how best to label a teacher's instructional intentions. This might seem unnecessary to you because, after all, why should the way teachers label their instructional aspirations make any real difference? Aren't a teacher's instructional aspirations simply what a teacher hopes, as a consequence of the teacher's instruction, will happen to kids?

Regrettably, there is considerable confusion among educators regarding how to describe the outcomes we hope students will achieve. If you become aware of this potential confusion, you can adroitly dodge it and move on to more important concerns. If you don't understand the nature of curriculum-label confusion, however, it is likely you will end up either being confused or, worse, adding to the confusion.

Getting down to basics, **curriculum** refers to the sought-for *ends* of instruction—for example, changes in students' knowledge or skills that a teacher hopes students will experience as a result of what was taught. In contrast, **instruction** describes the *means* teachers employ in an attempt to promote students' achievement of the curricular ends being sought. Instruction, therefore, refers to the set of activities a teacher has students carry out in an attempt to accomplish one or more intended curricular outcomes. Simply put, *curriculum equals ends* and *instruction equals means*. Where confusion careens onto the scene is when educators try to plaster diverse sorts of labels on the curricular ends they hope their students will accomplish.

No widespread consensus among educators exists regarding what to call the intended outcomes of instruction. During my own 50-plus years in the classroom, I've been in settings where curricular outcomes are referred to as goals, objectives, outcomes, expectations, benchmarks, and standards. In most of those locales, certain labels were supposed to apply to broader, more general curricular outcomes while other labels were given to more specific, less general outcomes. What's important when carving out what you want your classroom assessments to measure is that you understand precisely the meaning of whatever curricular labels are being used by colleagues in your school, district, or state. In most instances, whatever the curricular labels are, they are presented (often with examples) in some sort of official curricular document. Be sure you have a handle on what sorts of curricular descriptors are being used in your own part of the world. You'll dodge much potential curricular chaos if you do.

More often than not, I will be employing the label **curricular aim** to characterize the desired outcomes of instruction. That phrase, *curricular aim*, has not been around for all that long and, therefore, has not had all of its meaning leeched from it. I'll sometimes use such phrases as "educational objectives" or "instructional objectives" to describe curricular aims—just for a descriptive change-of-pace. But, as indicated above, you need to find out what sorts of curricular labels are being used where you teach. Odds are that those labels will be different from the descriptors I'm using here. That's okay, as long as you know what's going on.

Consideration of your own curricular aims, therefore, is one action you can take to help get a fix on what you should assess. The more clearly you state those aims, the more useful they will be to you in answering the what-to-assess question. In the 1960s and 1970s, there was widespread advocacy of *behavioral objectives*—that is, educational objectives stated in terms of the postinstruction behavior of learners. The push for behavioral objectives was fueled, at least in part, by dissatisfaction with the traditional form of general and ambiguous instructional objectives historically used by educators. An example of such general objectives would be the following: "At the end of the course, students will understand the true function of our federal government." My favorite gunky instructional objective of that era was one I ran across in a state-level language arts syllabus: "The student will learn to relish literature." After that time, I kept on the lookout for an objective such as "The student will mayonnaise mathematics." I haven't encountered one—yet.

Decision Time

On-Demand Assessment

Dolly Davis is a fourth-grade teacher who has set up her social studies activities on a mastery learning basis. Students are allowed to work through most of their social studies assignments at their own speed. Much of the social studies program in Dolly's class is based on reading assignments, so students can move at their own pace. When students believe they are ready to demonstrate mastery of the social studies skills and knowledge Dolly has described in written documents she distributes early in the school year, students set up an oral assessment. Dolly then spends 10 to 15 minutes presenting a series of short-answer items students must answer orally. So students do not discover from previously assessed students what the items on the assessment are, Dolly selects items at random from a pool of nearly 50 items for each of the four major social studies assessments during the year.

Although most students seem to appreciate Dolly's willingness to let them be assessed when they're ready, several students have complained that they "got a harder test" than some of their classmates. The dissatisfied students have encouraged Dolly to retain her mastery learning model, but to assess all students at the same time.

Dolly is deciding whether to maintain her on-call oral assessments or to revert to her former practice of written examinations administered to the entire class at the same time.

 If you were Dolly, what would your decision be?

Still, in their attempt to move from unclear general objectives toward super-clear behavioral objectives, the proponents of behavioral objectives (and I was right in there proponing up a storm) made a serious mistake. We failed to realize if we encouraged teachers to use instructional objectives that were *too* specific, the result would be an abundance of small-scope behavioral objectives. The resulting piles of hyperspecific instructional objectives would so overwhelm teachers that those overwhelmed teachers would end up paying attention to no objectives at all.

If you are currently a classroom teacher, you know you can't realistically keep track of whether your students are achieving hundreds of curricular aims. If you are preparing to be a classroom teacher, you'll soon discover that dozens and dozens of curricular aims will overwhelm you. The trick in conceptualizing curricular aims that help rather than hinder is to frame those aims broadly enough so you can sensibly organize instruction around them while making sure that the aims are still measurable. The degree of *measurability* is clearly a key in the way you should state your curricular aims. The broader the objective is, while still measurable, the more useful the objective will be because you can be guided by an intellectually manageable set of curricular intentions. If you can conceptualize your curricular aims so that one broad, measurable aim subsumes a bevy of lesser, smaller-scope objectives, you'll have a curricular aim that will guide your instruction more effectively and, at the same time, will be a big help in deciding what to assess.

In language arts instruction, for example, when teachers set out to have their students become good writers, a curricular aim focused on the students' ability to generate an original composition is an aim that, although still measurable (by simply having students churn out an original essay), encompasses a number of smaller-scope aims such as the students' ability to employ appropriate syntax, word choice, and proper spelling.

The concept of *measurability* is trickier than it first appears to be. Let's see why. Although two paragraphs ago you were urged to frame your curricular aims broadly—so they subsumed more specific curricular intentions, be sure your students' mastery of a curricular aim can be measured by a single, conceptually *unitary* assessment approach—not a fragmented flock of separate assessment tactics.

To illustrate, when we measure a student's ability to compose an original persuasive essay by asking the student to whip up such an essay (a writing sample) from scratch, we can use the writing sample to get a fix on the student's punctuation skills, content mastery, spelling, and word usage—all at one time. A unitary assessment strategy has been employed that, in one fell swoop, captures students' mastery of lesser, contributory subskills and bodies of knowledge. The way we use students' writing samples to arrive at an inference about the student's composition prowess—and the separate subcomponents of that prowess—represents an example of *unitary* measurability.

On the other hand, if the only way we can measure a student's mastery of a curricular aim is by relying on a collection of substantively *different* assessment tactics, then unitary measurability is not present. To illustrate, suppose a teacher had formulated a curricular aim labeled "Geometry" that embraced (1) congruence, (2) similarity, (3) circles, (4) equations, and (5) geometric measurement. However, in order to determine students' mastery of the "Geometry" goal, five separate sets of items were constructed, each focused on one of the five separate subcomponents of the "Geometry" curricular aim. This conceptualization, as you can see, does not constitute unitary measurement of students' curricular-aim mastery. The five distinct subcomponents of the curricular aim have not been truly coalesced in such a way that a single assessment strategy can accurately reflect students' attainment of an amalgam of the five subcomponents. What we would have here is what might be characterized as "counterfeit coalescence." What teachers should try to identify is a modest number of high-import curricular aims that can be measured via a unitary assessment approach. A flock of different, noncoalesced subtests clearly does not constitute unitary measurability.

Many educators these days use the concept of **grain-size** to represent the breadth of a curricular aim. More specific curricular aims are considered "small grain-size" instructional objectives, whereas more general curricular aims are regarded as "large grain-size" instructional objectives. One useful way of distinguishing among curricular aims according to their grain-sizes is to estim[ ] amount of instructional time it will take for students to accomplish what's embodied in a particular curricular aim. If the curricular aim can be achieved by students in a short while, perhaps in a few days or even in one class session, then the aim is usually thought of as a small grain-size outcome. If, on the other hand, a curricular aim seems likely to take days, weeks, or months to accomplish, such an aim is regarded as a large grain-size outcome.

Here's an example of two small-scope (small grain-size) curricular aims in language arts:

- When presented with reading passages containing unfamiliar words, students can employ context clues to infer the unfamiliar words' meanings.
- The student will be able to write sentences in which verbs agree in number with relevant nouns and pronouns.

Now let's look at a broad-scope (large grain-size) language arts curricular aim that subsumes these small-scope objectives plus a load of similar small-scope objectives:

- After reading an age-appropriate nonfiction essay, the student will be able to compose two paragraphs, the first of which summarizes the essay's central message and the second of which provides the student's personal reaction to the essay's message.

Strive to come up with a half dozen or so truly salient, broad, yet measurable, curricular aims for your own classroom. Too many small-scope, hyperspecific objectives will be of scant value to you because, if you're at all normal, you'll soon disregard an overwhelming array of super-specific curricular targets. On the other hand, a small number of intellectually manageable, broad, yet measurable, curricular aims will not only prove helpful to you instructionally but will also help you answer the what-to-assess question. Simply put, you need to create assessments to help you determine whether your students have, as you hoped, achieved your curricular aims.

Cognitive, Affective, and Psychomotor Assessment

In thinking about what to assess, classroom teachers can often be helped by considering potential assessment targets according to whether they are chiefly focused on cognitive, affective, or psychomotor targets. *Cognitive assessment* targets are those that deal with a student's intellectual operations—for instance, when the student displays acquired knowledge or demonstrates a thinking skill such as decision-making or problem solving. *Affective assessment* targets are those that deal with a student's attitudes, interests, and values, such as the student's self-esteem, risk-taking tendencies, or attitudes toward learning. *Psychomotor assessment* targets are those focused on a student's large-muscle or small-muscle skills. Examples of psycho-motor assessments that take place in schools would include tests of the student's keyboarding skills in a computer class or the student's prowess in shooting a basket-ball in gym class.

The distinction among cognitive, affective, and psychomotor educational outcomes was first introduced in 1956 when Benjamin Bloom and his colleagues (Bloom et al., 1956) proposed a classification system for educational objectives organized around those three categories. While recognizing there are usually ad-mixtures of all three domains of behavior in most things that teachers ask students to do on tests, the 1956 *Taxonomy of Educational Objectives* made it clear there is typically a dominant kind of student behavior sought when teachers devise edu-cational objectives for their students. For example, if a student is completing an essay examination in a social studies class, the student may be using a pencil to write *(psychomotor)* the essay and may be feeling remarkably confident *(affective)* about the emerging quality of the essay, but the chief domain of performance in-volved is *cognitive* because it is the student's intellectual analysis of the test's items and the student's intellectual organization of a response that mostly account for what the student's essay contains. Bloom's cognitive taxonomy included six levels of students' intellectual activity—ranging from the lowest level, *knowledge*, all the way up to the highest level, *evaluation*.

Standards-Based Classroom Assessment

Whether you are an elementary teacher who has instructional responsibility for a number of subject areas, or a secondary teacher who has instructional responsibil-ity for one or two subject areas, you should be concerned that your instruction and your assessments address appropriate content. Fortunately, in the last decade or so, various national organizations have attempted to isolate the most important content to teach in their respective subject areas. These content-delineation efforts can prove quite helpful to teachers who are trying to "teach the right things." These national content-delineation efforts were a pivotal part of the 1990s *educational standards movement*.

First off, let's define what an educational *standard* actually is. Unfortunately, you'll find that different educators use the term all too loosely and often incorrectly. Actually, there are two types of educational standards you need to know about:

- A *content standard* describes the knowledge or skills that educators want students to learn. Such curricular aims are also referred to as "academic con-tent standards."
- A *performance standard* identifies the desired level of proficiency at which educators want a content standard mastered. Such sought-for performance levels are also referred to as "academic achievement standards."

It should be apparent that although we might refer to both of the above as "standards," they are very different creatures. Just as cowboys in a western movie might loosely refer to "cattle," those cowpokes know that boy-cattle and girl-cattle perform decisively different functions. It's the same story today when educators utter the many-meaning word *standards*. An academic content standard (a curricular aim) is patently different from an academic achievement standard (a performance level). To refer to them both as "standards" can cause a cattle-car full of confusion!

From a classroom teacher's perspective, the most useful kinds of standards, without question, will be *content* standards because those standards set forth the things that whoever chose the standards regarded as the most important content for children to learn. Years ago, when I was a high school teacher, we had a district "curriculum guide" and a state "scope and sequence" manual, both of which attempted to identify the most important knowledge and skills that students should learn in each subject area. To be honest, those documents weren't all that wonderful. My fellow teachers and I found those curriculum materials to be vague, ambiguous, and altogether unhelpful.

During the 1990s, however, standards were recommended by many organizations, led by the National Council of Teachers of Mathematics (NCTM) 1989 publication of *Curriculum and Evaluation Standards for School Mathematics*. In that publication, NCTM made a major effort to reconceptualize how mathematics should be taught by identifying a set of important new content standards. Those content standards defined the chief curricular aim of mathematics education as the promotion of students' mathematical power—that is, students' ability to use mathematical thinking and understanding to solve problems and communicate the results of those solutions mathematically.

Soon thereafter, other national subject-matter associations began to bring forth their own sets of content standards and, in some instances, performance standards as well. I have had a chance to review many of these standards documents. Most of them are very impressive. All of the standards documents represent the efforts of top-flight subject-area specialists who devoted enormous time to circumscribing the knowledge and skills that students should learn.

I think it would be great if *you* spent some time reviewing these standards documents to identify what you might be teaching (and, therefore, testing). But I do *not* believe you should meekly succumb to the curricular preferences expressed in those standards collections. The reason for such a warning is straightforward. These standards documents were produced by subject-matter *specialists*. And subject-matter specialists really adore their subject matters. Subject-matter specialists would like to see students master almost *everything* in their field.

Subject specialists often approach their standards-identification tasks not from the perspective of a busy classroom teacher, but from the perch of a content devoteé. Content devoteés and classroom teachers, just like steers and cows, are different members of the cattle crowd. If teachers tried to teach students to do *all* the things set forth in most standards documents, there'd be no time left for food, sleep, or movies! So, what I recommend you do is *consult* the most recent national standards document(s) relevant to your own teaching responsibilities, and then see which of the content standards you have time to address. Without question, you'll get some wonderful ideas from the standards documents. But select your own content standards judiciously; don't try to stuff the whole wad of standards into your students' skulls. That wad won't fit.

■ A State's Official Curricular Aims

A state's designated educational policymakers typically decide on the curriculum aims—that is, the content standards—to be promoted for the state's public-school students. This is because education, not having been identified in the U.S. Constitution as a federal responsibility, has historically been regarded as a state obligation. Until recently, the usual way for a state to identify the curricular targets for its schools was to assemble groups of content-capable educators who, after substantial deliberation, identified the content standards to be promoted in the state's public schools. While, as might be expected, considerable agreement was seen between the official curricular aims of different states, meaningful differences in curricular preferences were also seen among states. But with the arrival of the Common Core State Standards (CCSS) in 2010, all this changed—dramatically. All but a few states have now accepted the mathematics and English language arts (ELA) curricular aims represented by the CCSS. As was true in earlier years when state-specific curricular aims were identified by each state, the adoption of the CCSS was usually accomplished by a state board of education or, in some instances, a state legislature.

The CCSS seem certain to play a prominent role not only in the nature of U.S. classroom instruction and assessment but also in the sorts of assessment instruments that will be available so that educators can measure students' achievement of the CCSS. If only from an assessment perspective, then, we need to take a look at the CCSS.

The Common Core State Standards

As noted earlier, on June 2, 2010, the CCSS were released by the Council of Chief State School Officers (CCSSO) and the National Governors Association (NGA) Center for Best Practices. In the next section of this chapter an attempt will be made to provide a brief introductory picture of the CCSS in ELA and mathematics. Yet, because these curricular aims have now been accepted by almost all of the 50 states, it should be apparent that any teacher in a state where the CCSS curricular aims have been adopted should possess much more than a nodding acquaintance with these curricular targets. Accordingly, educators are encouraged to consult either the CCSSO or the NGA websites , for each of those websites supplies a far more detailed depiction of what makes up the CCSS. Moreover, if you are a teacher in a state where the CCSS have been adopted, it is likely that your state or district will have information available regarding the nature of these curricular aims.

Before presenting what I hope will be an accurate but terse introduction to the CCSS, however, I feel compelled to offer one or two stage-setting remarks regarding these important curricular aims. First off, remembering that the CCSS, at least their official publication, did not take place until June 2010—at least in the early months thereafter—it was clear that many U.S. educators were not familiar with the nature of the CCSS. As many educators began to dig into the substance of the CCSS, they anticipated that these newly spawned curricular targets would be similar to the sets of state-specific content standards seen throughout the U.S. during recent decades. Those state-identified curricular aims had typically consisted of a list of content standards (that is, sets of the knowledge and skills students were supposed to master)—typically grouped under subject-area headings such as reading, writing, mathematics, and so on. Beneath those subject headings, the content standards themselves usually were grouped under a set of general labels (often called "strands") such as in math, geometry, numeration, algebra, and so on. Beneath those content standards, we usually found further particularization such as the specific bodies of knowledge or skills a student should achieve in order to attain mastery of any content standard. Although these collections of state curricular aims were often too numerous, as least in the view of the educators who had to promote students' mastery of those aims, these state-specific aims—as typically formulated—were relatively easy to understand.

I regret to report that such is not the case with the CCSS. Several categorization strata have been employed to describe the curricular targets in the CCSS and, unfortunately, the labeling schemes employed for the ELA curricular targets is not the same as the labeling approach employed in mathematics. Thus, elementary teachers who are instructionally responsible for both English language arts and math will be obliged to engage in gobs of mental gear-shifting when seeking guidance from CCSS documents regarding appropriate curricular targets for those two content fields.

In the next few paragraphs, then, a particularly brief introduction to the organizational structure of the CCSS ELA and mathematics content standards will be provided. This "handshake" with the CCSS should, hopefully, be followed up with a much more meaningful "hug" that can only be obtained by your spending time—more than might be initially thought—with the actual content of the CCSS (NGA and CCSSO, 2010). Let's begin with ELA.

English Language Arts Common Core Standards In an effort to identify K–12 standards to help ensure that all American students would be college and career ready in *literacy* no later than the close of high school, those crafting the CCSS identified a set of curricular targets in both English language arts as well as Literacy in History/Social Studies, Science, and Technical Subjects. When reviewing the complete array of these standards, your comprehension of them will usually be enhanced if you are aware of the several ways the ELA and literacy standards have been categorized in the CCSS. Let's consider those categorizations.

For openers, there's a fairly straightforward distinction between grades K–8 and grades 9–12. For grades K–8, the standards are set out on a grade-by-grade basis. At the secondary level, however, we find grade bands being used to describe the standards for grades 9–10 and 11–12.

Then, at each K–8 grade level you will find sets of standards for *reading, writing, speaking and listening*, and *language*. For the reading outcomes, there's an important distinction drawn between standards based on students' reading of *literature* versus *informational text*. Architects of the CCSS reading standards definitely wanted U.S. students to have greater exposure to informational text than has often been the case in years past. In grades K–5, in fact, the standards are broken out separately for literature and for informational texts. Ten "College and Career Readiness Anchor Standards" are presented under the following four general categories: (1) Key Ideas and Details, (2) Craft and Structure, (3) Integration of Knowledge and Ideas, and (4) Range of Reading and Level of Text Complexity. In addition to a more equitable split between students' exposure to informational texts and literature, framers of the CCSS reading standards want students to be able to read increasingly complex texts through the grades. After grades K–5, the reading standards are identified separately for literature and informational text at grades, 6, 7, and 8 as well as for grade ranges 9–10 and 11–12.

Here, then, is an example of a CCSS grade 5 standard in *reading*—in this instance for students' reading of informational text (rather than literature):

> *Explain how an author uses reasons and evidence to support particular points in a text, identifying which reasons and evidence support which point(s).*

In addition to the ELA reading standards, the CCSS also spell out anchor standards for writing, for speaking and listening skills, and for language. As was the case with reading, these curricular aims are broken out by separate grades in K–8, and then use two grade ranges in grades 9–10 and 11–12. Here's an example of a CCSS *writing* standard for grade 3 students:

> *Write informative/explanatory texts to examine a topic and convey ideas and information clearly. (This standard is accompanied by four attributes sought of these early writers—for example, "Provide a concluding statement or section.")*

Beyond the identification of ELA standards as described above, separate standards are also provided in the CCSS for literacy in grades 6–12 dealing with history/social studies, science, and technical subjects. Both reading and writing standards are given for students in three grade ranges, that is, 6–8, 9–10, and 11–12. Authors of these grade 6–12 literacy standards in reading intend for instructional attention to those standards to be integrated along with instruction focused on the K–5 reading standards described earlier. It was hoped by the shapers of the CCSS that attention to the K–5 reading standards would provide broad curricular targets, while the literacy standards in 6–12 reading would supply additional specificity (NGA and CCSSO ELA Standards, 2010, p. 61).

The original June 2, 2010, publication by CCSSO and NGA (2010) not only contains substantial introductory material related to the CCSS but, in the case of the ELA standards, also presents a number of components intended to assist in the implementation of the standards. To illustrate, the CCSS authors strongly advocate that students become ever more able to engage in "close analysis" of increasingly complex textual materials. Accordingly, helpful illustrations of increasingly complex materials—both literary and informational text—are supplied (NGA and CCSSO ELA Standards, 2010, p. 32). Suggestions are also proffered regarding how to stay on topic within a grade and across grades (NGA and CCSSO ELA Standards, 2010, p. 33).

Given the several ways in which the designers of the CCSS attempt to organize the curricular aims embodied in their conceptualization of what students should learn, educators who wish to take full advantage of the CCSS, not only in ELA but also in mathematics, should become flat-out familiar with any CCSS segments in which they are interested. Thus, rather than being overwhelmed and/or confused by a set of seemingly off-putting curricular aims, educators can become truly knowledgeable about these significant collections of curriculum goals.

Mathematics Common Core Standards Let's look now at the CCSS for *mathematics*. The working group that identified the math standards divided those standards into two groups, the mathematical *practice* standards and the mathematical *content* standards. The content standards are identified for each grade level, kindergarten through grade 8, and also at high school. These mathematics curricular aims are categorized in three ways as seen below:

> *Standards* define what students should understand and be able to do. An example of a standard would be: "Use place value understanding to round whole numbers to the nearest 10 or 100."
>
> *Clusters* represent groups of related standards. An example of a cluster that includes the illustrated standard (above) would be: "Use place value understanding and properties of operations to perform multi-digit arithmetic."
>
> *Domains* are larger groups of related standards, for example, "Number and Operations in Base Ten."

To illustrate how this sort of categorization system works, let's take a look at one grade level and the numbers of domains, clusters, and standards identified for that particular grade. In the fourth grade, for instance, we find five domains, each of which contains one, two, or three clusters of standards. And each of these grade 4 clusters contains one to three standards. (Several of the standards have been broken down further into subdivisions reflecting two, three, or four different aspects of a student's understanding of a given standard.) In all, then, there are 28 grade 4 CCSS standards with, if one also considers the three "subdivided" standards, a grand total of 37 curricular targets in the CCSS mathematics standards.

A given grade's domains, then, constitute the broadest descriptors of the curricular aims designated at that grade level. In some instances, we encounter slight differences between the mathematical domains at two different grade levels, but frequently these domains are identical at different grades. To Illustrate, the CCSS grade 6 overview in mathematics presents the following five domains: (1) Ratios and Proportional Relationships, (2) The Number System, (3) Expressions and Equations, (4) Geometry, and (5) Statistics and Probability. In the seventh grade, precisely the same five domains are seen. However, beneath these domain labels, there are often differences in the set of standards that a given cluster represents.

Clearly, then, although there is surely substantial coherence and consistency in mathematical emphases as one moves through the grades, there are also meaningful differences in the math skills and knowledge sought of students. Teachers whose state authorities have adopted the CCSS should certainly become conversant with relevant grade-level variations in the knowledge and skills sought of students not only for the particular grade at which a teacher teaches but also at nearby grade levels. The creators of the CCSS mathematics curricular targets have attempted to fashion a series of multigrade curricular emphases that, from an instructional perspective, build sensibly on one another.

Turning from the math *content* standards, let's look at the mathematical *practice* standards. The practice standards remain the same across the grades because they describe varieties of expertise that mathematics educators at all levels should seek to foster in their students. These practice standards are drawn from processes and proficiencies that have traditionally occupied important places in mathematics education. They are presented in Figure 1.

figure 1 ■ CCSS Standards for Mathematical Practice

1. Make sense of problems and persevere in solving them.
2. Reason abstractly and quantitatively.
3. Construct viable arguments and critique the reasoning of others.
4. Model with mathematics.
5. Use appropriate tools strategically.
6. Attend to precision.
7. Look for and make use of structure.
8. Look for and express regularity in repeated reasoning.

As the designers of the CCSS see it, the Mathematical Practice standards describe ways in which those who engage in the discipline of mathematics should increasingly engage with the subject matter as they grow in mathematical expertise and maturity. It is the hope of those who crafted the CCSS mathematical standards that educators will make a serious effort to connect the Standards for Mathematical Practice to the Standards for Mathematical Content. Candidly, given the relatively short time that the CCSS math standards have been with us, there is much work to be done in discerning the most sensible ways to interrelate these two meaningfully different sets of standards.

Turning to high school, the CCSS mathematics standards are listed as conceptual categories: (1) Number and Quantity, (2) Algebra, (3), Functions, (4) Modeling, (5) Geometry, and (6) Statistics and Probability. These six categories are believed to represent a coherent view of high school mathematics. To illustrate, a student's work with functions can cross a number of traditional course boundaries up through and including calculus.

Each of these conceptual categories is broken out at the high school level by the CCSS architects. For example, the geometry category is subdivided into (1) Congruence, (2) Similarity, Right Triangles, and Trigonometry, (3) Circles, (4) Expressing Geometric Properties with Equations, (5) Geometric Measurement and Dimension, and (6) Modeling with Geometry. And each of these subdivisions typically represents several further subdivisions. Slight differences also exist for high school in the mathematical *practices* for the conceptual categories that, in elementary grades, had remained the same.

It should be apparent that the manner in which the CCSS mathematics standards are organized and presented to the nation's educators could easily become confusing. There are so many curricular targets—in different categories and at different levels—embraced by the math standards, that educators really do need to arrive at a "mentally manageable" way of representing the diverse mathematical outcomes being sought of students.

When one spends much time with the CCSS mathematics standards, it is apparent that those who built these mathematical curricular aims desperately wish the nation's educators to stress "greater focus and coherence." Indeed, in the initial paragraphs of the materials describing the math standards, we are given frequent reminders that not only should mathematical *focus* be achieved, but *coherence* among those standards should also be attained. "The mathematics curriculum in the United States must become substantially more focused and coherent in order to improve mathematics achievement in this country" (NGA and CCSSO Mathematics Standards, 2010, p. 3).

In their quest for "focus," the architects of the CCSS in mathematics are not merely advocating a smaller number of curricular targets—as might be achieved merely by stuffing numerous narrow but clearly stated standards into a smaller collection of broader curricular statements that mask much, if not all, of the original standards' clarity. Jason Zimba, one of three CCSS mathematics team coordinators, provides a powerful argument supporting the need for focus in the

CCSS mathematics standards. As he suggests, "Not everything in the Standards *should* have equal priority," (Zimba, 2011, p. 2). He continues:

> *Moreover, at every level in mathematics, there are intricate, challenging, and necessary things that serve as prerequisites for the next level's intricate, challenging, and necessary things. In order to keep as many students as possible on the path to readiness for college and careers, we need to give students enough time to succeed in these areas. (Zimba, 2011, pp. 2–3)*

To illustrate, the CCSS mathematics team coordinators believe there should be a definite focus on numbers and operations in the elementary school, but that this focus should be diminished in later grades. In short, the developers of the CCSS mathematics standards clearly recommend that more time be spent on fewer things at each grade level. Because both focus *and* coherence are emphasized throughout the CCSS mathematics standards, the designers of these standards want teachers to recognize how the curricular aims focus on progress from one grade to the next. According to *Webster's*, when something *coheres*, it "sticks together, that is, holds together as parts of the same mass." Well, such *coherence* among the *focused* CCSS mathematics curricular aims is what the originators of these mathematics standards apparently had in mind.

Mathematics curricular aspirations that are both coherent *and* focused will surely constitute a collection of curricular targets capable of influencing what takes place in our nation's classrooms. Teachers who set out to have their students master the CCSS goals in math (or ELA) need to become sufficiently familiar with what (to some educators) is the initially off-putting CCSS structure to arrive at their own judgments regarding the coherence and focus of the CCSS curricular aims.

"Many a Slip . . ."

The older I get, there are fewer and fewer folks who know the maxims that I've relied on most of my life. One of those sayings is: "There's many a slip twixt the cup and the lip!" Besides giving me an opportunity to use the word "twixt" (an option that doesn't come along all that often), the maxim reminds us that, as we raise our cups of hot cocoa toward our mouths, numerous things can go wrong. Through the years, loads of laps have definitely been doused by errant, about-to-be-consumed drinks of one sort or another. Yet, this little-used adage still alerts us to the possibility, perhaps the *probability*, that well-conceived hopes often take a tumble en route to the finish line. And so it is with curricular aims such as those embodied in the CCSS.

I have concluded that the CCSS English language arts and mathematics curricular targets are really quite commendable. For the most part, I believe the CCSS curricular aims are equal to or better than the state curricular goals they are replacing—that is, the ones we have seen adopted by individual states during the last several decades. Some months after I had reached this conclusion, a report was issued in late 2011 by the respected nonpartisan Center on Education Policy in Washington, DC, which seemed to confirm such an estimate of CCSS quality. After surveying school districts in 44 states where the CCSS had been officially adopted, this report concluded that almost 60 percent of officials in those districts agreed "that the new standards in math and English language arts are more rigorous than the ones they are replacing" (Center on Educational Policy Press Release, September 14, 2011, p. 1).

So it appears that the curricular aims embodied in the CCSS may, indeed, be worthwhile. Moreover, many district-level officials recognize the merits of those curricular aims. Where, then, does "slip twixting" slither into this happy picture? Here's my answer to that question: *Curricular aims—whether local, state, or national—until decisions have been made about how students' mastery of those aims will be assessed, are just words—sometimes fairly meaningless words.* That's right, no matter how laudable the curricular aspirations embodied in the CCSS are, if they are poorly assessed, then the positive impact of the CCSS will most certainly be minimal.

You see, curricular aims set an outer limit of how a sensible assessment might take place. For instance, if a curricular aim calls for students to be able to comprehend the main idea of a written passage, then we know that measuring such an aim by asking students to perform long division is obviously off target. Long division is *outside* the limits set by a main-idea curricular aim. However, *within* that main-idea curricular aim, there are various ways to get at a student's main-idea mastery. And it is the way students perform on the tests chosen to measure attainment of a curricular aim that really lets us know the degree to which we've been successful in promoting students' curricular-aim mastery.

To determine how well a teacher, school, or district has succeeded in getting students to master any of the CCSS curricular aims, we must consider students' postinstruction performances. Those postinstruction performances will most often be displayed as *scores on tests*. And that's where two assessment consortia will come rumbling onto our education's center-stage.

If one or both consortia do a nifty job in generating instructionally useful assessments—assessments that can provide accurate evidence regarding students' attainment of the CCSS targets—then all will be well. But, as has been pointed out, "twixt-slips" often happen between aspiration and culmination. Accordingly, it becomes particularly important for U.S. educators to carefully scrutinize the caliber of the assessments that will emerge from the SBAC and PARCC consortia. Wonderful curricular hopes can be hobbled by less than wonderful assessments. Wonderful curricula can be made even more marvelous by truly wonderful assessments. Because the two assessment consortia need not deliver their assessments until the 2014–15 school year, substantial watching while waiting is definitely warranted from all of us.

I carried out a check on the progress of the two assessment consortia. Although those consortia are not obligated to have tests available for use until the

2014–15 school year, at that time both consortia were well on their way, and in the next few paragraphs I will describe what seemed to me to be the chief emphases of their test-development efforts.

It is invariably expected that a state's accountability tests should be *aligned* with the state's official curricular aims. Let's look briefly at the term *alignment*. In the field of education, *alignment* is the only 9-letter word that seems to function as a 4-letter word. This is because many people play fairly fast and loose with a term that, by its nature, seems to evoke fast-and-loose play. **Alignment** refers to the degree to which there is a meaningful agreement between two or more of the following: curriculum, instruction, and assessment. What is generally called for, of course, is the agreement of a state's accountability tests with a state's content standards. To the extent that such a *curriculum-assessment* alignment has been achieved, a teacher would have to be a ninny not to recognize that it is sensible to also align the teacher's classroom curricula and assessments with whatever state content standards are to be assessed by the accountability tests in that teacher's state.

A major difficulty with the concept of alignment, unfortunately, is that it is decidedly *squishy*. What constitutes alignment in one educator's eyes may be seen as nonalignment by another educator. And there is often much self-interested "seeing alignment where none exists." So, whenever you hear someone touting the alignment between instruction and curriculum and assessment, try to dig a bit deeper so you can see whether the alignment being described is based on rigorous or relaxed ways of determining agreement levels.

But what do teachers do to align their classroom tests with important exams such as a state's annual accountability tests? This constitutes a nontrivial quandary for most teachers, and it turns out to depend—almost totally—on the quality of the accountability exams. If your state's accountability exams are capable of accurately detecting instructional quality, then you should make sure your classroom assessments mesh with what's assessed on those accountability tests. If your state's accountability tests, on the other hand, are *not* capable of accurately detecting instructional quality, then you need to pay less heed to what's assessed by those statewide tests. You'll learn how to distinguish between state-level accountability tests that are grubby versus those that glisten.

Of Standards and Emperors

Then a small voice called out from the crowd, "But the emperor's not wearing new standards at all; he's wearing old objectives!" According to a classic but uncorroborated fairy tale, a ruler can be persuaded to parade around in the buff if he's made to believe he's wearing wonderful but invisible garments. The moral of "The Emperor's New Clothes" fable, of course, is that a ruler is not apt to redress his state of undress unless someone informs him that he's naked as a jaybird.

Standards, of course, is a warmth-inducing word. Although perhaps not in the same league with *motherhood, democracy*, and *babies*, I suspect that *standards* ranks right up there with *oatmeal, honor*, and *excellence*. It's really tough not to groove on *standards*, especially if those standards are *high*. Everyone wants students to reach high standards. And, because high standards are so intrinsically praiseworthy, if teachers pursue such standards, then teachers can sleep tranquilly at night. Teachers are clearly questing after that which, like the Holy Grail, warrants such questing.

If by the expression *content standards* we refer to the knowledge and skills we want our students to achieve as a consequence of education, how is a content standard different from an instructional objective? The answer (all emperors and emperors-in-training take heed) is that there really is *no* difference between instructional objectives and content standards. Both phrases describe the educational intentions—that is, the curricular aims—we have for our students.

One reason that content standards are much more appealing to almost everyone than instructional objectives, as noted earlier, is that *content standards* is a warmth-inducing phrase; *instructional objectives* is not. What right-minded politician or educational policymaker would not leap with enthusiasm to be "in solid support of high content standards"? It's far less exciting for someone to applaud even meritorious instructional objectives.

So, for both of these reasons, I foresee continued widespread support for the identification and promotion of defensible content standards. As I listen, however, to today's enthusiastic endorsements of "challenging" or "world-class" content standards and their pivotal role in educational improvement, I find myself doing a bit of mental transformation, so I'm covertly thinking about curricular aims or instructional objectives. (I don't tell anyone, of course. One needs to be regarded as up-to-date.)

NAEP Frameworks

The National Assessment of Educational Progress (NAEP) is a congressionally mandated project of the U.S. Department of Education. It assesses U.S. students' knowledge and skills in geography, reading, writing, mathematics, science, U.S. history, the arts, civics, and other academic subjects. Since 1969, NAEP has periodically surveyed the achievement of students at *ages* 9, 13, as well as 17 and, since the 1980s, in *grades* 4, 8, and 12. As originally conceptualized, NAEP was intended to measure U.S. students' levels of academic achievement over time.

The National Assessment Governing Board (NAGB) was created by Congress in 1988 to formulate policy for NAEP. Among its responsibilities is the development of assessment objectives for NAEP through a national consensus approach. Although NAGB strives to avoid the perception that its objectives for various academic subjects at grades 4, 8, and 12 constitute a national curriculum, the assessment frameworks produced under NAGB's aegis are typically first-rate curricular documents, hence represent another source teachers might wish to consult as they attempt to decide what to assess.

The NAEP frameworks can be downloaded from the NAGB website listed at the chapter's close. Although never intended to serve as a one-size-fits-all set of assessable objectives for an entire nation, the NAEP assessment/curricular frameworks typically reflect thoughtful analyses regarding what ought to be assessed (taught) at three key grade levels.

No Child Left Behind required all states to participate in the biennial administration of NAEP reading and mathematics tests to representative samples of students in grades 4 and 8. The NAEP results are reported as the numbers of students who score in each of the following three categories: *advanced*, *proficient*, and *basic*. Scores that fail to be classified in one of these three categories are regarded as *below basic*. Most states currently report the percentages of students who score in those categories *on the state's own accountability tests*. Accordingly, how do you think it will look to the public if on the state's accountability test, 60 percent of the students score at proficient-or-above but, on NAEP, only 20 percent of the state's students earned proficient-or-above scores? That's right, it will look fiercely fishy!

Assessment Blueprints

A number of teachers find it helpful, especially when constructing major examinations, to develop what's called an *assessment blueprint* or a *test blueprint*. These blueprints are essentially two-way tables in which one dimension represents the curricular aims the teacher wants to assess, while the other dimension represents the levels of cognitive functioning being sought. For instance, the following example from a teacher's assessment blueprint will illustrate how these sorts of organizational schemes work by dividing each curricular aim's items into (1) knowledge (low-level recall of information) and (2) cognitive levels higher than mere recall.

	Number of Items	
	Cognitive Level	
Curricular Aim	*Knowledge*	*Above Knowledge*
1	3	1
2	1	4
3	2	2
etc.	etc.	

Assessment blueprints can help teachers identify curricular aims not being measured with sufficient items or with sufficient items at an appropriate level of **cognitive demand**.

Collar a Colleague

Too many classroom teachers carry out their professional chores in isolation. If you're trying to figure out what to assess in your own classroom, one straightforward scheme for tackling the task is to seek the counsel of a colleague, particularly one who teaches the same sort of class and/or grade level you teach.

Always keeping in mind that what you assess should be governed by the decisions to be influenced by your students' assessment results, simply solicit the advice of a respected colleague regarding what sorts of things you should be assessing in your class. If you're uncomfortable about making such a request, simply read (with feeling) the following scripted question: "If you were I, what would you assess?" I admit the phrasing of the question isn't all that exotic, but it will get the job done. What you're looking for is some sensible advice from a nonpartisan co-worker.

If you've already devoted a significant chunk of thought to the what-to-assess question, you might simply ask your colleague to review your ideas so you can discern whether your planned assessment targets seem reasonable to another teacher. A second pair of eyes can frequently prove useful in deciding whether you've really staked out a defensible set of emphases for your planned classroom assessments.

What-to-Assess Considerations

In review, then, we've looked at several factors that can help classroom teachers in deciding what they should measure in their classroom assessment procedures. From the discussion of those points, seven possible ways of addressing the what-to-assess question can be derived:

1. Focus all class assessment procedures on clearly explicated decision options.
2. A small number of significant curricular aims can provide a useful framework for deciding what to assess.
3. An analysis of whether assessments should focus on cognitive, affective, or psychomotor behavior (and, if cognitive, at what cognitive-demand level) can prove helpful.
4. A review of relevant collections of content standards prepared by national subject-matter organizations (such as NCTM in mathematics) can help a teacher identify key knowledge and skills to be pursued.
5. A consideration of the NAEP assessment frameworks can present a useful view of what curricular aims to assess in a number of curriculum fields.
6. Advice from a colleague about what to assess can prove beneficial.
7. A serious analysis of the way your state's official content standards are assessed by its accountability exams can help you plan your classroom assessments after being influenced by that analysis.

Tests as Instructional Influencers

Historically, teachers have used classroom tests at or near the close of an instructional sequence. And, of course, teachers would like their students to perform well on any end-of-instruction tests. If students are successful on end-of-instruction classroom tests, it usually means that students have learned well and, accordingly, teachers have taught well. More often than not, teachers' classroom tests have been constructed only *after* instruction is over or when instruction is nearing its conclusion (for instance, near the end of a semester, a school year, or a short-duration teaching unit). Obviously, classroom assessments devised *after* instruction is over will have scant impact on what the teacher teaches. The teacher's instruction, or at least the majority of it, is a "done deal" by the time the test is constructed.

Classroom assessments, therefore, have typically had little impact on instructional planning. At least this was true until the era of *educational accountability* arrived in the 1970s and 1980s. During that period, legislators in most states enacted a string of laws requiring students to pass basic skills tests in order to receive high school diplomas or, in some cases, to be advanced to higher grade levels. Thus was born what educators have come to call "high-stakes" tests because there were important consequences for the students who were required to take those tests.

There was another sense in which statewide tests became high schools where all, or almost all, students passed the tests, a school's te[...] and administrators were applauded. But in schools where many students failed the tests, a school's teachers and administrators were blamed. The stakes associated with statewide testing were elevated even more when newspapers began, in the 1980s, to publish annual statewide test scores of all districts and all schools in the state. Each school and district was *ranked* in relation to the state's other schools and districts. There were, of course, numerous winners as well as an equal number of losers.

What was being measured by the tests began to influence the nature of what was taught in classrooms. The phrase **measurement-driven instruction** became widely used during the eighties to depict an educational reform strategy in which it was hoped the content of high-stakes tests would have a substantial and positive influence on the content of classroom instruction.

Because of this heightened attention to student performance on important statewide and districtwide tests, we also saw increased attention being given to the evidence of student success on teacher-made *classroom* tests. Many educational administrators and policymakers concluded that if students' performances on statewide tests reflected a school's educational effectiveness, then even at the classroom level, test results could indicate whether good teaching was taking place. Greater and greater emphasis was given to "evidence of effectiveness" in the form of improved student performance on whatever types of classroom tests were being employed. Increasingly, *evidence* of student learning—evidence in the form of student performance on classroom tests—is being used in personnel appraisals of teachers. In many settings, a teacher's competence is currently being determined, at least in part, by how well a teacher's students perform on the teacher's classroom tests. During the past several years, considerable pressure has been brought on educational leaders to make students' test scores a prominent factor when evaluating individual teachers.

Given this ever-increasing administrative reliance on student test results as one indicator of a teacher's instructional effectiveness, it was only natural that many teachers tried to address instructionally whatever was to be tested. Tests had clearly begun to influence teaching. And it was increasingly recognized by teachers not only that the content of their tests *could* influence their teaching but also that, perhaps, the content of those tests *should* influence their teaching.

If testing should influence teaching, why not construct classroom assessments *prior* to instructional planning? In this way, any planned instructional sequence could mesh more effectively with the content of the test involved. Moreover, why not build classroom assessments with the instructional implications of those assessments deliberately in mind? In other words, why not build a classroom assessment not only before any instructional planning, but in such a way that the assessment would beneficially inform the teacher's instructional planning? A contrast between a more traditional educational approach in which instruction influences assessment and the kind of assessment-influenced instruction being described here can be seen in Figure 2.

figure 2 ■ Traditional Instruction-Influenced Assessment versus Assessment-Influenced Instruction, Both of Which Are Governed by Curricular Aims

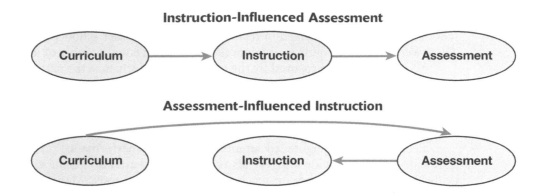

In a traditional approach to instructional design, an approach in which instruction influences assessment, the teacher (1) is guided by the curriculum that's been adopted by the state and/or district, (2) plans instructional activities to promote the educational objectives set forth in that curriculum, and (3) assesses students. In an assessment-influenced approach to instructional design, also indicated in Figure 2, the teacher still (1) starts with curricular aims, (2) then moves to create assessments based on those goals, and (3) only thereafter plans instructional activities intended to promote students' mastery of the knowledge, skills, and/or attitudes to be assessed. In both approaches, curriculum is the starting point. Curricular aims still govern the entire process. But in the two contrasting approaches, the sequence of instructional planning and assessment development is reversed.

A Cautious Convert

(Text ssuch as this one are not regarded as suitable places for authors to toss out opinion essays. Let's face it: If an author has a hankering to share an opinion piece with the world, all sorts of newspapers and Internet outlets exist to which such essays can be sent. Nonetheless, I need to break this unwritten rule. I do so because of the importance of the issue I'll be addressing—namely, a set of curricular goals that are almost certain to alter how we teach this nation's children—and how educators might react to those goals.)

The Common Core State Standards (CCSS) were released in mid-2010 by the Council of Chief State School Officers (CCSSO) and the National Governors Association (NGA). These curricular aims, in mathematics and English language arts, identify the knowledge and skills that students ought to be learning in school. The CCSS curricular aims have now been officially adopted by all but a few of our 50 states. Accordingly, because the curricular goals embodied in the CCSS are almost certain to influence classroom instruction in any state where they've been adopted, these CCSS curricular aspirations will, unarguably, have a huge impact on what goes on in U.S. public schools. I'd like to briefly describe my own reactions to what most folks now regard as these "national" curricular aims, and then ask you to do the same.

Perhaps you've never devoted much thought to how you personally regard the Comon Core State Standards. I certainly have. Maybe you didn't observe the frequently furtive manner in which the CCSS goals were born. I definitely did. Indeed, it's because I've expended a good deal of energy not only in discovering the nature of the CCSS, but also in thinking about my response to these important curricular aims, that I decided to whomp up this short essay. You see, given the potential impact of the CCSS on our schools, and hence on our society itself, I think all educators need to be clearheaded about how they personally regard this set of remarkably important curricular targets.

In 2009, when I first heard some rumblings about the emergence of a generic set of curricular targets for our schools, I was an immediate fan. For more than a half-century, I had seen firsthand the negative consequences of state-spawned curricular anarchy wherein some states shot for the stars and other states scurried to the cellar. I was convinced that our nation's schools, and the children they serve, would benefit from a set of in-common, well-conceived curricular goals.

I soon discovered that CCSSO and NGA were officially in charge of this curricular conclave, and they were making good noises. To illustrate, an early and oft-mouthed mantra of the CCSS initiative was that the curricular goals to be carved out would be "fewer, clearer, and higher." I resonated to this message, for some states' curricular goals were too numerous, often ambiguous, and patently puerile. Whoever the leaders of this CCSS project were, they appeared to be headed in a defensible direction.

So, time and energy permitting, I tried to find out more about these emerging curricular goals. Who were the people who were creating this collection of curricular goals that, if widely adopted, would most certainly change the nature of U.S. public schooling? And that's when I started getting concerned about the project. Despite my being on the alert for information describing the early and en route accomplishments of the CCSS curricular crew, I rarely encountered such information. When it came to getting details regarding the innards of the CCSS-development process, the project seemed to be slathered with secrecy.

Granted, I did not go to the trouble of hiring a private investigator to discover what was taking place behind CCSS closed doors. Nor did I choose

(*Continued*)

to devote most of my waking hours to figuring out what was up with this curriculum-determination activity. I just wanted, without Herculean effort, to find out more about this quest for curricular goals destined to be fewer, clearer, and higher. I had the feeling that important curricular work was afoot, but those doing it had chosen to maintain an almost invisible profile.

Dismayed by my unsuccessful efforts to learn more about this project, I soon began to get frustrated. And, not surprisingly, frustration fostered suspicion. If these emerging curricular goals were going to be so blinking important to our schools, thought I, why aren't educators—at least the educators who are interested (including me)—being given an opportunity to learn what's under way with the project? And, perhaps more importantly, who are the individuals who are actually doing this curriculum building? Are they first-rate folks or mediocre mutton-heads?

Given the potential importance of the CCSS, I wanted to know not only who was holding the steering wheel, but would there be sufficient opportunities for concerned constituencies to review the emerging curricular standards? Absent such information, and I assure you this information was not *readily* available, I became suspicious of those building the CCSS. Nor were my worries allayed when I learned that some sort of "validation" group had met to review a not-yet-final version of the CCSS curricular aims, but had not been allowed to offer improvement suggestions. Only an on/off approbation of the "as is" CCSS had been sought. The CCSS project seemed to be an effort to swiftly push forward, but without any meaningful pauses for scrutiny by nonpartisans. Again, my apprehensions soared.

Yet, as the initial release of the CCSS in June 2010 approached, and the federal government began laying out formidable financial incentives for states who adopted these standards, more and more states chucked aside their own state's official curricular aims and, instead, embraced the new CCSS aims. In fact, Kentucky was the first state to choose the CCSS over its own state's curricular aims, and Kentucky officials did so while the CCSS were *still in draft form*!

So, despite my misgivings, within months following the release of the CCSS, all but a few states had signified their intention to clamber aboard the Good Ship CCSS. I had to concede that, despite the speed, secrecy, and insufficient vetting of these new math and ELA curricular aims, those devising and advocating adoption of these new common curricular aims had pulled it off. Just as someone can admire the skill of a baseball pitcher who throws a no-hit ball game even if he or she is a member of the hitless team, I needed to take my hat off to the CCSSO and NGA designers of the CCSS game plan. It was a hands-down winner.

But I was still suspicious about the specific math and ELA goals embodied in the CCSS. As I familiarized myself with the new standards, I conceded that the CCSS crew seemed to have done well in cleaving to their "clearer" and "higher" promises, but I thought there still were too many curricular targets for teachers to pursue. For example, in fourth-grade mathematics, a teacher is given 37 specific curricular targets to promote. In view of a fourth-grade teacher's other curricular responsibilities, almost 40 curricular targets in math are simply too many. So, the architects of the CCSS appeared to have stumbled in their quest for "fewer" curricular targets.

In the months following the release of the CCSS, however, the individuals who were the designers of those curricular targets began to hit the road—that is, they began to speak at various conferences where they described the thrust of their curricular vision. They also began to elaborate, in writing, about the viscera of the CCSS. They even supplied some videos capturing the "main idea" of the ELA and mathematics standards. As soon as I soaked up those dissemination efforts, I came away with one solid inference—the folks who were in charge of carving up the mathematics and ELA curricular aims were, obviously and gratifyingly, *smart*. Moreover, *they knew their content fields*. This curricular caper had not been headed by a carload of lummoxes. Good people had been at the helm of the CCSS gestation game—good people who brought first-rate intellects and content moxie to their tasks.

Another reassuring theme could be seen in the messages provided by the CCSS architects—namely, the need for *focus* when using the identified content standards. In other words, those who fashioned the CCSS recognized the necessity to engage in meaningful prioritizing so that certain curricular aims would be emphasized at different grade levels. The CCSS experts had staked out a substantial set of curricular targets for the nation's schools, but they realized that any sensible instructional or assessment implementation of those targets would require some serious choices about which aims to emphasize—and when.

Summing up, then, I've definitely had a roller-coaster response to the Common Core State Standards. I initially regarded them as a terrific idea, but cooled toward them when it seemed their birthing process was insufficiently transparent. Yet, after applauding the game plan by which the CCSS leaders had gotten their curricular aims accepted nationally, I found the caliber of the curricular aims—and the individuals who crafted them—to be encouragingly excellent. And, finally, when the developers of the CCSS kept stressing the need for *focus* as a way of dealing with what I regarded as too many curricular aims, I had been won over.

Perhaps, just as the making of sausage should rarely be seen, the creation of national curricular aims should remain quasi-secret. If the *assessments* intended to measure students' mastery of these curricular targets can be fashioned with the same skill, the promise of the CCSS will be realized.

Well, this describes my own interaction with the curricular aims constituting the CCSS. If you have not personally undertaken such a safari, perhaps it is time for you to do so. These curricular aims, given their potential to significantly shape our schools, really are that important.

Dividends of Assessment Illumination

Assessment-illuminated instruction rests on the assumption that, in many instances, what is to be assessed *will* influence the teacher's instructional decisions. Consequently, if the assessment can be created prior to the teacher's instructional planning, the resultant clarity provided to the teacher will help the teacher make more appropriate instructional choices.

When teachers develop their classroom assessments *before* instructional plans are made, teachers are meaningfully *clarifying* the curricular aims being pursued. In other words, the assessment serves as the operational definition of whether a curricular aim has been achieved. Such clarity provides far more insight for teachers when, subsequently, they make their instructional plans.

It is important to remember that classroom assessments *represent* the knowledge and/or skills being promoted. Teachers should *never* teach toward the classroom test itself. Instead, teachers should teach toward the knowledge, skills, and/or attitudes sampled by the classroom test. But, when teachers construct classroom assessments prior to instructional decision-making, those teachers will have a markedly better understanding of what the instructional objectives really are. And, of course, the more clearheaded teachers are about curricular *ends*, the more skillfully such teachers can select suitable instructional *means* to accomplish those ends.

With increased clarity regarding the nature of the curricular aims being promoted, there are all sorts of derivative instructional-planning benefits. Here are a few of the most salient dividends you, as a teacher or a teacher-in-preparation, will receive:

- *More accurate learning progressions.* Because you'll know more clearly what the terminal results of an instructional sequence are supposed to be, you can better pinpoint the enabling knowledge or the subskills your students must acquire before mastering what's being taught.
- *More on-target practice activities.* Because you'll know better what kinds of end-of-instruction outcomes are being sought for your students, you can make sure to select guided-practice and independent-practice activities more accurately aligned with the target outcomes.
- *More lucid expositions.* Because you'll understand more clearly what's to be assessed at instruction's conclusion, during instruction you can provide clearer explanations to your students about the content involved and where the instructional activities are heading.

Instructional planning will benefit from early development of classroom assessments most fundamentally because you will, as a consequence of prior assessment development, better understand what it is hoped that your students will be able to do when instruction has been concluded.

■ How to Assess It

Let's assume you've decided what you're going to measure in your classroom assessments. Now the task turns to how you're going to assess it. In the remainder of the chapter, we'll look at several choices to consider when deciding how to answer the how-to-assess-it question. More specifically, we'll be dealing with the following choices:

1. Whether to adopt a norm-referenced or a criterion-referenced assessment approach
2. Whether to emphasize selected-response or constructed-response assessment schemes
3. What kind of item type(s) to select from such alternatives as multiple-choice, short-answer, or performance tests

Norm-Referenced versus Criterion-Referenced Interpretations

There are two rather distinctive, yet widely used, assessment strategies available to educators these days: *norm-referenced measurement* and *criterion-referenced measurement*. The most fundamental difference between these two approaches to educational assessment is the nature of the interpretation that's used to make sense out of students' test performances.

With *norm-referenced* measurement, educators interpret a student's performance in relation to the performances of students who have previously taken the same examination. This previous group of test takers is referred to as the *norm group*. Thus, when educators try to make sense out of a student's tests score by "referencing" the score back to the norm group's performances, it is apparent why these sorts of interpretations are characterized as norm referenced.

To illustrate, when a teacher asserts a student "scored at the 90th percentile on a scholastic aptitude test," the teacher means the student's test performance has exceeded the performance of 90 percent of students in the test's norm group. In education, norm-referenced interpretations are most frequently encountered when reporting students' results on academic aptitude tests, such as the SAT, or on widely used standardized achievement tests, such as the Iowa Tests of Basic Skills or the California Achievement Tests. In short, norm-referenced interpretations are *relative* interpretations of students' performances because such interpretations focus on how a given student's performance stacks up in relation to the previous performances of other students.

In contrast, a *criterion-referenced* interpretation is an *absolute* interpretation because it hinges on the extent to which the criterion (that is, curricular aim) represented by the test is actually mastered by the student. Once the nature of an assessed curricular aim is properly described, the student's test performance can be interpreted according to the degree to which the curricular aim has been mastered. For instance, instead of a norm-referenced interpretation such as the student "scored better than 85 percent of the students in the norm group," a criterion-referenced interpretation might be that the student "mastered 85 percent of the test's content and can be inferred, therefore, to have mastered 85 percent of the curricular aim's skills and/or knowledge represented by the test." Note that a criterion-referenced interpretation doesn't depend at all on how other students performed on the test. The focus is on the curricular aim represented by the test.

As you can see, the meaningfulness of criterion-referenced interpretations is directly linked to the clarity with which the assessed curricular aim is delineated. Accurately described curricular aims can yield crisp, understandable criterion-referenced interpretations. Ambiguously defined curricular aims are certain to yield fuzzy criterion-referenced interpretations of little utility.

Although loads of educators refer to "criterion-referenced tests" and "norm-referenced tests," there are, technically, no such creatures. Rather, there are criterion- and norm-referenced *interpretations* of students' test performances. For example, educators in a school district might have built a test to yield criterion-referenced interpretations, used the test for several years and, in the process, gathered substantial data regarding the performances of district students. As a consequence, the district's educators could build normative tables permitting norm-referenced interpretations of the test which, although born to provide criterion-referenced inferences, can still provide meaningful norm-referenced interpretations.

Because most of the assessment-influenced decisions faced by classroom teachers are benefited by those teachers' understanding of what it is students can and cannot do, not merely their relative standing in relationship to one another, classroom teachers will generally want to arrive at criterion-referenced rather than norm-referenced interpretations. A teacher's instructional choices, for example, are better serviced by evidence about particular students' skills and knowledge than by evidence about how those students compare with one another.

About the only instance in which classroom teachers will need to employ norm-referenced interpretations occurs when there are fixed-quota settings—that is, when there are insufficient slots for all of a teacher's students to be assigned to a given educational experience. For example, suppose there were five students to be chosen for a special outside-of-class enrichment program in mathematics, and the teacher had been directed by the school principal to choose the "best" mathematics students for the program. In such a situation, because *best* is, by definition, a relative descriptor, norm-referenced interpretations would be warranted. A teacher might build a test to spread students out according to their mathematics skills so the top students could be identified. Barring those rare situations, however, most classroom teachers would be better off using tests yielding criterion-referenced interpretations. Criterion-referenced interpretations provide a far more lucid idea of what it is students can and can't do. Teachers need such clarity if they're going to make solid instructional decisions.

Later, you'll be considering standardized achievement tests, assessment devices usually built to provide norm-referenced interpretations. At that time, the appropriate and inappropriate uses of test results from such commercially distributed assessment instruments will be identified. For most *classroom assessment*, however, the measurement strategy should almost always be criterion referenced rather than norm referenced.

Before saying farewell to the distinction between criterion-referenced and norm-referenced assessment strategies, I need to highlight a confusion that I first encountered about 40 years ago, but am running into again in recent years.

When Robert Glaser first introduced the notion of criterion-referenced measurement more than four decades ago (Glaser, 1963), there were actually two different meanings he provided for the term *criterion*. On the one hand, Glaser used it in a fairly traditional manner to represent a *level of performance*, such as one might employ when saying, "Let's get the quality of all trainees' performance up to a suitable criterion." In the sixties, most people I knew tended to use the word *criterion* in precisely that way—as a desired level of performance. On the other hand, in Glaser's article he also used "criterion" to represent a clearly defined criterion behavior such as a well-explicated cognitive skill or a tightly delineated body of knowledge. Well, in those early days, many educators who were beginning to learn about criterion-referenced testing were not sure which of those two very different notions to employ.

Yet it soon became apparent that only the "criterion as defined behavior" notion really made much sense because, if the "criterion as level of performance" interpretation were adopted, then all of the existing education tests could become instantly criterion-referenced simply by designating a desired performance level for those tests. Such an approach to assessment would be fundamentally no different from the traditional approaches to educational testing so widely used at the time. Glaser was looking for a new way of thinking about educational testing, not more of the same. Thus, in the '70s and '80s, criterion-referenced testing was seen as a way of ascertaining a test taker's status with regard to one or more well-defined criterion behaviors. This interpretation was sensible.

Just during the last few years, however, I have encountered measurement specialists who are once more touting the "criterion as level of performance" notion. This is a clear instance of regression. It is not a suitable way to think about criterion-referenced assessment. I just want you to be on guard so you can spot such flawed thinking when it crosses your path. Criterion-referenced measurement is built on an assessment strategy intended to determine a test taker's status with respect to a clearly defined set of criterion behaviors, typically well-defined skills or knowledge.

Selected Responses and Constructed Responses

Assuming a classroom teacher has come up with a reasonable answer to the what-to-assess question, an important point in determining how to assess it arises when the teacher must choose between assessment strategies that elicit *selected responses* or *constructed responses* from students. If you think for a moment about the way educators assess students' educational status, you'll realize there are really only two kinds of responses students can make. Students *select* their responses from alternatives we present to them—for example, when we give students multiple-choice tests and students' responses must be selected from each item's available options. Other examples of selected-response assessment procedures are binary-choice items such as those found in true-false tests where, for each item, students must select either a true or a false answer.

In contrast to selected-response sorts of tests, students *construct* all kinds of responses. In an English class, for instance, students construct original essays. In a woodshop class, students construct end tables. In a speech class, students construct five-minute oral speeches. In a drama class, students construct their responses while they present a one-act play. In a homemaking class, students construct souf-flés and upside-down cakes. Constructed-response tests lead either to student *products*, such as the end tables and soufflés, or to *behaviors*, such as the speeches and the one-act plays. When the students' constructed responses take the form of a tangible product, classroom teachers have the luxury of judging the quality of the product at their leisure. For instance, once students create an original essay, the teacher can take this product home on the weekend and, while relaxing in the jacuzzi, either grade or immerse each essay.

When students' constructed responses are in the form of behaviors, however, such as when students are asked in a physical education class to run a mile in less than 12 minutes, the teacher must somehow make a record of the behavior or else it disappears. The record might be created by the teacher's use of written records or be captured electronically via an audio or video recording. For example, when students in a speech class give a series of impromptu speeches, the teacher typically fills out some sort of evaluation form for each speech. Similarly, physical education teachers use their stopwatches to note how much time it takes for students to run a mile, and then note the elapsed time in a record book.

It was formerly thought that although selected-response tests were difficult to create, they were easy to score. Similarly, it was once believed constructed-response tests were just the opposite—simple to create but tough to score. These days, however, educators have become more sophisticated about constructed-response tests and are employing many more types of constructed-response assessment procedures than only essay tests or short-answer tests. It is generally conceded that both selected-response and constructed-response tests require considerable care when being created. It is still true, however, that the scoring of selected-response tests is substantially easier than the scoring of constructed-response tests.

If, as a classroom teacher, you're really choosing between these two assessment schemes, you need to focus less on the ease of scoring than on the nature of the score-based inference you wish to make. Some score-based inferences simply shriek out for selected-response assessment schemes. For instance, if you want to make inferences about how many historical facts your students know, a selected-response procedure will not only fill the bill but will also be simple to score. Other score-based inferences you might wish to make really require students to display complex behavior, not merely choose among options. If, for example,

Parent Talk

Suppose that Ms. Collins, a parent of one of your students, has cornered you after school and asked for a few minutes of your time. She wants to know what all the talk about "new, challenging standards" really means. She's read an article about educational standards in the local newspaper, and she wonders whether the "new" standards are really new. Her question to you is, "Why is there all this fuss about educational standards these days when it seems that teachers in this school are still teaching pretty much what they've always taught and testing what they've always tested?"

 If I were you, here's how I'd respond to Ms. Collins:

"I really understand your concern about educational standards, Ms. Collins. They've certainly been receiving plenty of attention from educators during recent years. But, regrettably, there's still a fair amount of confusion about standards, even among educators.

"Actually, there are two kinds of educational standards that you and I need to consider. A *content standard* simply identifies the skills and knowledge we want students to acquire in school. For example, your daughter has recently been improving her composition skills quite dramatically. She can now write narrative and persuasive essays that are quite wonderful. An example of a content standard would be *'Students' mastery of written communication skills.'*

"A *performance standard,* on the other hand, indicates *how well* a content standard should be mastered. We score our students' essays on a four-point scale, and the school's teachers have agreed that a student should achieve at least a three in written communication to be considered satisfactory.

"What we now call *content standards,* we used to describe as goals, objectives, or outcomes. What we now call *performance standards,* we used to describe as passing levels or cut scores. So some of the descriptive labels may be new, but the central idea of trying to teach children important skills and knowledge—this hasn't really changed very much.

"What is new, at least to me, is a much greater concern about the *defensibility* of our content and performance standards. All across the nation, educators are being urged to adopt more challenging standards—standards that demand more of our children. This has been taking place in our school, as well. So if you look more closely at what we're teaching and testing here, I think you'll see important differences in the kinds of skills and knowledge we're pursuing—and the levels of excellence we expect of our students."

 Now, how would you respond to Ms. Collins?

you want to make inferences about how well students can compose sonnets, then selected-response assessment schemes just won't cut it. To see if students can churn out a sonnet, you need to have them construct sonnets. Reliance on a selected-response test in such a situation would be psychometrically silly. It is, as usual, the *test-based inference* the teacher needs to make that should guide the choice between selected-response and constructed-response assessment strategies.

It is always possible, of course, for teachers to rely on both of these two assessment strategies in their classrooms. A given assessment, for instance, might represent a blend of both selected- and constructed-response approaches. As always, the assessment procedure should be employed to help the teacher get a fix on the students' status with respect to an otherwise unobservable variable in which the teacher is interested.

A Profusion of Item Types

Beyond the basic constructed-response versus selected-response distinction just considered, there are numerous types of items available for inclusion in classroom assessment procedures. Certain of these item types have been employed for many, many years. The essay test, for example, has probably been around since Socrates was strutting his instructional stuff. Multiple-choice tests have been with us for more than a century. True-false tests were probably used, at least in oral form, by prehistoric teachers who might have put such true-false toughies to their students as "True or False: Today's dinosaur was a leaf-munching brontosaurus rather than a people-munching tyrannosaurus rex."

During recent years, however, there have been some significant advances in educational measurement procedures so that, for example, some educational measurement specialists now advocate wider use of *portfolio assessment* and *performance assessment*. These significant item types must now be added to the menu of assessment alternatives open to today's classroom teacher. I'll be describing how to create classroom assessments using all of the major item types now available in the classroom teacher's assessment arsenal. And, of course, as each hour goes by, we find advances being made in technology—advances that allow teachers to rely on a number of sophisticated computer programs to provide online or otherwise computer-controlled assessments. States and districts are substantially expanding the range of electronic options available to today's (and tomorrow's) teachers.

We're going to start off with the more traditional sorts of selected- and constructed-response types of items because, quite frankly, you're more likely to be familiar with those item types, and you'll have less difficulty in learning about how to crank out, for instance, a simply splendid short-answer test item. Thereafter, we'll be considering portfolios and how they can be used for classroom assessment, as well as performance tests and how they can be employed. After that, we'll deal with the special kinds of item types to be used when you're trying to get a fix on students' affective status.

but what does this have to do with

Teaching?

As a first-year teacher, I had only a foggy idea of what stuff I should be teaching. Oh, of course, there was a state curriculum syllabus setting forth a seemingly endless array of knowledge and skills that students such as mine might possess. But, as was true with most of my colleagues, I found the syllabus altogether overwhelming.

So, when a new teacher is curricularly overwhelmed, the teacher gravitates toward whatever content is addressed in textbooks. And that's just what I did. Along with courses in high school English, speech, and U.S. government, I also had to teach a course in geography. Having never taken a college course in geography, and knowing barely more than the four major directions on a compass, I thanked heaven each night for the bright red geography text that allowed me to appear geographically suave. Had it not been for that comforting red textbook, I surely would have perished pedagogically before I learned the difference between the equator and a Mercator map projection.

In short, my first year's curricular choices were often made almost unthinkingly. I simply scrambled to fill my lesson plans with something resembling relevant content. But, during my *second* year of teaching, I had a solid basis for my curricular choices—namely, I had taught about those things the previous year!

It should be apparent to you that if teachers carry out a consummately classy instructional act, yet focus on the wrong curricular content, this would be a genuine waste. Yet, many beginning teachers (like me) don't devote sufficient thought to what they need to teach and, therefore, what they need to assess. And even seasoned teachers often can't provide a solid rationale for what they're teaching.

The impact of the federal accountability legislation on most teachers' instruction—and classroom assessment—has been considerable. That's why you really need to find out how *your* state carries out its accountability program. If your state's leaders have installed suitable accountability tests, you'll be in a good position to key off those tests and supply your students with equally sensible classroom tests and on-target instruction. If your state's accountability tests are inappropriate, however, you'll find yourself in the midst of an insoluble testing-teaching puzzle.

This chapter's focus on what to test and how to test it should help you recognize that you should be *assessing* the most important skills, knowledge, and affect you want your students to acquire. And this recognition, of course, should help you realize you should make sure that you're *teaching* your students such stuff.

Unless, of course, you're using a red textbook. If so, forget everything I've just said.

The following types of items can be employed in classroom assessments:

- Binary-choice items
- Multiple binary-choice items
- Multiple-choice items
- Matching items
- Short-answer items
- Essay items
- Observational approaches
- Performance tests
- Portfolios
- Affective assessment procedures

As you can see, there are plenty of options open to classroom teachers when it comes to item types. When I was preparing to be a classroom teacher in the 1950s, my professors familiarized me with several different item types (all as traditional as they could be) and then encouraged me to employ different types of items "for variety's sake." This, to be honest, was dumb advice. Classroom assessment is not akin to a fashion show where you need to change styles in your examinations simply to maintain students' interest.

When you're choosing among item types, select the one that best allows you to make the test-based inference in which you're interested and whatever decision is linked to it. Sometimes it won't make much difference which types of items you choose. I suspect in many instances it really isn't the case that a batch of multiple-choice items is vastly superior to a set of matching items. In other cases, however, there will be substantial differences in the suitability of differing item types. To make your own choice, simply ask yourself the question, Will my students' responses to this type of item allow me to reach a defensible inference contributing to the educational decision facing me?

As we consider various types of items, you'll become more conversant with the particulars of each item type, and thus more skilled in identifying their utility to you in your own classroom assessments.

■ What Do Classroom Teachers Really Need to Know about What to Assess and How to Assess It?

What is the main message of this chapter for classroom teachers who must decide what to assess and how to assess it? The answer is rather straightforward. All you need to do is to think seriously about both questions. Any experienced teacher will, if pressed, confess that *instructional inertia* plays a key role in what usually goes on in the teacher's classroom. Classroom teachers find it far easier to engage in activities this year that they engaged in last year simply because it takes less effort to employ "same-old, same-old" instructional procedures than to install new instructional procedures. There's also *assessment inertia* inclining teachers to rely on whatever assessment schemes they've previously utilized. It's so much simpler to re-use or slightly massage last year's true-false exams than to whip out a brand-new performance test.

In recognition of these all-too-human tendencies to adopt the path of least resistance, it becomes more important to try to "get it right the first time" or, putting it in more pedantic parlance, to "eschew egregiously inferior initial assessment conceptualizations." In other words, the more up-front thought teachers give to answering the what-to-assess and how-to-assess-it questions, the more likely they'll be to avoid the kind of serious assessment errors that, because of practical pressures, may plague them for years.

Because of the impact of federal accountability laws on you and your fellow teachers, you need to understand the nature of the tests your state's leaders have chosen to satisfy the state's accountability needs. For instance, you may end up teaching in a state in which the state's officials have chosen to employ the assessments constructed during recent years to measure students' mastery of the Common Core State Standards described earlier in the chapter. Do not assume, without careful consideration, those tests are going to help you do a better teaching job. Nor should you assume your state's accountability tests will have an adverse impact on what goes on in the state's classrooms. You definitely need to find out whether the state's accountability tests are winners or losers. Those tests will have an enormous impact on what you try to teach, what you try to test, and how you try to test it.

■ Preview

Later in the text, you'll learn all sorts of nifty ways to assess your students. Not only will you learn how to create a variety of traditional paper-and-pencil tests, such as the true-false and multiple-choice instruments, but you'll also discover how to generate many of the alternative forms of educational assessment receiving so much attention these days. To illustrate, you will learn how to create really demanding performance tests, student portfolios, and assessment devices that can gauge your students' attitudes and interests. But when you read about these assessment approaches, it will make it easier for you to determine their worth *to you* if you know how to evaluate the quality of educational assessment approaches.

table 1 ■ Potential Criteria for Brownie Judging

Criterion	Optimal Status
■ Fudginess	Should reek of chocolate flavor—so much, indeed, as to be considered fundamentally fudgelike.
■ Chewiness	Must be so chewy as to approximate munching on a lump of fudge-flavored Silly Putty.
■ Acceptable Additives	Although sliced walnuts and extra chocolate chips are praiseworthy, raw shredded brussels sprouts are not.

If you're evaluating a test—whether it's your own test, a test developed by another teacher, or a test distributed by a commercial test publisher—you will need some criteria to help you decide whether the test should be wildly applauded or, instead, sent swiftly to a paper shredder.

Judging educational tests, in fact, is fundamentally no different from evaluating brownies. If, for example, you are ever called on to serve as a judge in a brownie bake-off, you'll need some evaluative criteria to use when you appraise the merits of the contending brownies. I realize your preferences may differ from mine, but if I were chief justice in a brownie-judging extravaganza, I would employ the three evaluative criteria presented in Table 1. If you are a brownie aficionado and prefer other evaluative criteria, I can overlook such preferences. You may, for example, adore nut-free and high-rise brownies. However, I have no personal interest in establishing a meaningful brownie-bond with you.

When we evaluate just about anything, we employ explicit or implicit evaluative criteria to determine quality. And although there may be substantial disagreements among brownie devoteés regarding the criteria to employ when appraising their favorite baked goods, there are far fewer disputes when it comes to judging the quality of educational assessment devices. There are three widely accepted criteria that are used to evaluate educational assessment procedures. Two of the criteria have been around for a long while. The third is a relative newcomer, having figured in the evaluation of educational tests only during the last couple of decades.

In Table 2 are the three criteria we'll be considering . The capsule description of each criterion presented in the table will let you know what's coming. After considering each of these three criteria I'll level with you regarding what classroom teachers *really* need to know about the three criteria. In other words, I'll toss out my personal opinion regarding whether you should establish an intimate relationship or merely a nodding acquaintance with each criterion.

Of all the things you will learn from reading this text, and there will be lots of them, reliability of assessment, validity, and absence-of-bias are regarded by

table 2 ■ A Preview of the Three Test-Evaluation Criteria to Be Considered

Criterion	Brief Description
■ Reliability	Reliability represents the *consistency* with which an assessment procedure measures whatever it's measuring.
■ Validity	Validity reflects the accuracy of the *score-based inference* made on the basis of an educational assessment procedure.
■ Absence-of-Bias	Absence-of-bias signifies the degree to which assessments are free of elements that would *offend* or *unfairly penalize* students on the basis of students' gender, ethnicity, and so on.

psychometricians as the most important. (*Psychometrician*, by the way, is simply a ritzy descriptor for a measurement specialist.) Related discussions will familiarize you with the pivotal criteria by which assessment specialists tell whether educational assessment procedures are fabulous or feeble. But because this text is focused on classroom assessment, we'll be looking at the content in relation to *educational decisions* that must be made by classroom teachers.

■ Chapter Summary

Two major questions guided the content of this chapter—namely, what should a classroom teacher assess and, having answered this question, how should it be assessed? It was contended that both of these decisions must be primarily influenced by the decisions the teacher hopes to illuminate on the basis of assessment data gathered from students.

In determining what to assess, it was suggested that a teacher's curricular aims play a prominent role in the teacher's choice of assessment emphases. In particular, large grain-size measurable objectives were recommended as helpful vehicles for identifying potential assessment targets. The three domains of student outcomes contained in Bloom's *Taxonomies of Educational Objectives* were also suggested as a helpful framework to decide whether there are instructional or assessment overemphases on certain kinds of outcomes. Because most of the nation's educators will soon be, if not already doing so, promoting their students' mastery of the Common Core State Standards now adopted by almost all states, the background and nature of those standards in mathematics and English language arts were described in the chapter. It was emphasized that those curricular aims, as is true with almost all intended curricular outcomes, will only be clearly understood when assessments to measure students' mastery of the aims have been created. Accordingly, teachers were urged to be particularly attentive to the nature of the tests being developed by two large, federally funded assessment consortia of states whose tests are scheduled to be available by the 2014–15 school year.

When addressing the how-to-assess-it question, the chapter dealt with three topics. First, a distinction was drawn between norm-referenced and criterion-referenced assessment approaches. It was suggested that the bulk of a classroom teacher's assessment needs will be better served by criterion-referenced rather than norm-referenced interpretations because criterion-referenced interpretations tend to provide teachers with a clearer picture of what it is students can or can't do. Second, a discussion of selected-response and constructed-response test options was concluded with a listing of the numerous types of assessment items classroom teachers have at their disposal. Third, it was recommended, because descriptions of how these various types of test items should be constructed are beyond the scope of this chapter, the reader should hold off on deciding which item types for which decisions until you are familiar with the different types of test items.

Self-Check

We'll start off this chapter's self-check exercises with several binary-choice items about *grain-size*. Look over the following five curricular aims and then decide whether each is *small scope (S S)* or *broad scope (B S)*. I assure you that, at least for the moment, you should regard the initials *B S* as *only* indicative of a broad scope curricular aim—nothing else.

1. Students will be able to select, from four options, the correct answer to any double-digit multiplication problem. (S S or B S?)

2. At the end of the Australasia unit, students will write, without prompting, 10 new facts learned about the geography of Australia or New Zealand. (S S or B S?)

3. When presented with descriptions of educational research situations requiring statistical analyses, students will be able to choose the appropriate analytic technique from any of the 40 statistical procedures treated during the statistics course. (S S or B S?)

4. The student will correctly spell aloud any 10 of the words the teacher identifies from the 50-word "spelling terrors" test. (S S or B S?)

5. The student will be able to write an original essay suitably synthesizing any three related but dissimilar newspaper articles on the same general topic. (S S or B S?)

6. What is the key difference between "academic content standards" and "academic achievement standards"?

7. Supply at least two examples of constructed-response test tasks and at least two examples of selected-response test tasks.

_____

_____

_____

_____

_____

_____

8. What is the critical difference between norm-referenced and criterion-referenced approaches to educational measurement?

_____

_____

_____

 # Pondertime

1. It was argued in the chapter that most classroom assessment tasks call for criterion-referenced approaches to measurement. Do you agree? Why or why not?

2. Although widely accepted curricular aims such as the Common Core State Standards should obviously be considered when teachers are deciding what to teach, why do some writers urge teachers to wait until the assessments for the curricular aims are in place before trying to interpret what those aims really mean?

3. If you discovered that your state's educational accountability tests (a) attempt to measure too many content standards, (b) are based on badly defined content standards, and (c) don't supply teachers with per-standard results, how do you think such shortcomings would influence your classroom assessments? How about your classroom instruction?

4. Suppose you were asked to give your best answer to the question, "How should a classroom teacher decide what to assess?" How would you respond?

5. Suppose you were asked to give your best answer to the question, "How should a classroom teacher decide to assess whatever has been determined to be assessed?" How would you respond?

Self-Check Key

The answers for the first five self-check exercises should have been these: 1: S S, 2: S S, 3: B S, 4: S S (although, as the number of words on the list gets longer, the curricular aim becomes broader in its scope), 5: B S.

6. Your answer should have approximated the distinction drawn between the two standards that was discussed earlier.

7. You might have supplied examples such as these:

Constructed-response test tasks: Compose a sonnet; give an impromptu speech; create a watercolor; or produce, direct, and market a major motion picture.

Selected-response test tasks: Choose from multiple-choice options; select true or false for each statement; from three choices select the most (or least) plausible solution for the problem presented; or select from three major motion pictures the film most likely to get universal "thumbs up" from film critics.

8. At bottom, norm-referenced assessment approaches require interpretations of test scores based on the student's performance relative to performances of other students. In contrast, criterion-referenced assessment approaches require interpretations of test scores according to the degree of a clearly described curricular aim the student has mastered.

■ Additional Stuff

Bloom, B. S., et al. (1956). *Taxonomy of educational objectives: Handbook I: Cognitive domain.* New York: David McKay.

Center on Education Policy. (2011). *District officials view common state standards as more rigorous, expect new standards to improve learning.* Press Release, September 14. Washington, DC: Author.

Glaser, R. (1963). "Institutional technology and the measurement of learning outcomes: Some questions," *American Psychology, 18,* 519–521.

Herman, J. L., and Webb, N. M. (Eds.). (2007). "A special issue on alignment methodologies," *Applied Measurement in Education, 20,* no. 1 (October–December).

McMillan, J. H. (2011). *Classroom assessment: Principles and practice for effective standards-based instruction* (5th ed.) Boston: Pearson.

National Council of Teachers of Mathematics. (1989). *Curriculum and evaluation standards for school mathematics.* Reston, VA: The Council.

National Governors Association and the Counsel of Chief State School Officers. (2010). *The Common Core State Standards initiative.* Washington, DC: Author.

Pellegrino, J. W., Chudowsky, N., and Glaser, R. (Eds.). (2001). *Knowing what students know: The science and design of educational assessment.* National Research Council, Division of Behavioral and Social Sciences and Education, Center for Education, Board on Testing and Assessment, Washington, DC: National Academy Press.

Sternberg, R. J. (2007/2008). "Assessing what matters," *Educational Leadership, 65*, no. 4 (December/January): 20–26.

Zimba, J. (2011). *Priorities in the* Common Core State Standards' *standards for mathematical content,* Discussion Draft, March 31, 2011.

■ Cyber Stuff

- *Achieve, Inc.* is an independent, nonprofit organization founded in 1996 by governors and corporate CEOs who were committed to the view that high-level content standards, rigorous tests to assess those standards, and performance-based accountability could promote excellence in the nation's schools. Links to federal agencies, state agencies, educational organizations, and other resources are available. **www .achieve.org**

- *The Council of Chief State School Officers (CCSSO)* is a nationwide, nonprofit organization of public officials who lead K–12 education in the 50 states. This website is a rich resource for those who wish to monitor state-level assessment activities throughout the United States. The website also contains a host of practical guidelines regarding how states can satisfy federal accountability requirements. **www.ccsso.org**

- *The Mid-continent Regional Educational Laboratory (McREL)* is a private, nonprofit organization based in Denver, Colorado. Established in 1966, this regional laboratory has taken a major leadership role in the analysis of how educators can most effectively employ content and performance standards. This website lists a variety of McREL online resources dealing with standards-relevant topics. A searchable database regarding standards and benchmarks is also available. **www .mcrel.org**

- *The National Assessment Governing Board (NAGB)* is an independent, bipartisan group established by the U.S. Congress in 1988 to set policy for, and oversee the activities of, the National Assessment of Educational Progress (NAEP), frequently referred to as "The Nation's Report Card." This website, as would be expected, provides considerable information about current and past NAEP endeavors. The website contains a modest set of links to other sites, mostly governmental, but is dominantly focused on NAGB policies and NAEP activities. A search capacity allows users to easily locate NAEP information of interest. **www.nagb.org**

- *National Association for the Education of Young Children (NAEYC),* founded in 1926, has a membership of nearly 80,000—most of whom are early childhood educators. The association's website contains a rich array of resources dealing with the education of young children, such as NAEYC position statements dealing with guidelines for appropriate curriculum and assessment of children, ages 3 through 8. Using "assessment" in the website's search engine yields several hundred citations. **www.naeyc.org**

- *The National Governors Association was founded in 1908.* Its bipartisan membership included the governors of the 50 states, three territories, and two commonwealths.

The Center for Best Practices of the National Governors Association (NGA) played a prominent collaborative role in the generation of the Common Core State Standards. Use of this website's search engine under "educational assessment" yields more than 60 results on the topic. **www.nga.org**

■ *The OECD Programme for International Student Assessment (PISA)* is a multination student testing project in reading, mathematics, and science conducted under the auspices of the Organization for Economic Co-operation and Development. In 2006, PISA completed its first set of every-three-years surveys of the knowledge and skills of 15-year-olds in OECD member countries and partner countries, covering 90 percent of the world's economy. This website describes the project's activities and also lists the assessment domains measured. **www.pisa .oecd.org**

■ Extended Applications

It is a truism that the more a person uses something, the more familiar with this something the person becomes. This self-evident notion surely applies to the assessment-related knowledge, skills, and concepts you have been reading about in the foregoing pages. Thus, to provide readers of *Classroom Assessment* with additional opportunities to apply the content contained in this text, this final section contains a variety of exercises intended to give readers an opportunity to use what they've been reading about.

In a sense, of course, the Self-Check exercises found at the close of this chapter provided an opportunity for readers to apply a chapter's content. Nonetheless, the more times you use a concept, skill, or a body of knowledge, the more likely it is that you will master this content so you can employ it in varied situations.

For each of the text, you will find an extended-application exercise calling for you to do some thinking about that chapter's content as it applies to a real-world situation. Each exercise is preceded by a brief introduction setting forth the reason that the upcoming extended-application exercise has been selected.

Because many of these exercises call on you to generate an original response rather than select a response from a set of options, it is difficult to supply an "answer key" for readers' unpredictable responses. So, what you'll find following all the exercises is One Possible Response—an indication of how I would have personally responded to the exercise if I had been asked to do so. Please don't regard my response as the only way to respond to an exercise. After all, by definition, this is only "one possible" response. Instead, please think of my response as a fairly flimsy form of feedback. You can certainly disagree with me, even emphatically, yet still profit from doing the exercise.

Remember, what is being provided in this section. The exercises deliberately intended to extend how you apply the content treated in *Classroom Assessment*. I hope you find these exercises useful in enhancing your understanding of what teachers need to know about classroom assessment.

■ Reviewing an Actual Curriculum Document

Introduction

In this chapter centers on a pair of major foci. (Because of the Latin I studied while in high school and college, I try to trot out a Latin plural whenever I can.) Anyway, plurals aside, the two emphases of this chapter are conveniently set forth in the chapter's title—namely, figuring out what should be assessed, then determining how to assess it.

Many teachers will have an opportunity, sometime during their careers, to wrestle with the problem of what to assess in certain subjects. Dealing successfully with such a curriculum-determination task involves far more than simply listing a set of skills or bodies of knowledge for students to learn. This exercise will give you a chance to work with an actual curriculum document—in this case, a framework of considerable importance to those educators who have any responsibility for teaching science.

Clearly, the more significant the use of a test, the more attention should be given to those two issues. In the field of education, one of the most significant tests is surely the National Assessment of Educational Progress (NAEP). This test assesses samples of U.S. students in grades 4, 8, and 12, and its results are reported for the United States and its 50 states according to three achievement levels—basic, proficient, and advanced—as stipulated by the National Assessment Governing Board (NAGB), the group that oversees NAEP.

Since 1969, NAEP has regularly conducted sample-based assessments of students attending public and private schools at the elementary, junior high, and high school levels. The goal of NAEP is to provide reliable information about the academic performance of American students in various subject areas. NAEP comparisons are sure to be made by policymakers; it is obvious that whatever skills and knowledge are to be assessed via NAEP will be given considerable attention by most states' educational leaders.

What this exercise calls on you to do is take a thoughtful look at what's to be assessed in the NAEP 2009 science assessment. In November 2005, NAGB approved the 2009 NAEP Science Framework. More specifically, this exercise asks you to review the highlights of that science framework, then supply your personal reaction to it in the form of written summary remarks for a group of fellow educators. Even in excerpted form, the material from NAGB is *lengthy*. So, you'll need to give yourself a solid chunk of time to read it with care. But these additional exercises are to be based on real-world challenges, so it is often the case that actual curricular materials will be genuinely complicated and require more than two or three pages.

Science is a subject that's laden with ways to go wrong—both from a curricular perspective and from an assessment perspective. There's a huge amount of content in the several fields of science, and a number of key science-related cognitive skills. So, the upcoming exercise is designed to get you to think about how the 2009 NAEP science assessment seems to have turned out. If you are intrigued by this exercise, and wish to learn more about the 2009 science assessment or the many other subject areas measured by NAEP, be sure to scurry electronically to the NAGB website at www.nagb.org.

The purpose of this exercise is to familiarize you with the sorts of actual curricular documents you are apt to encounter if you ever must take part in a significant curricular-determination endeavor. Please think carefully about the conclusions in this curriculum document reached by a number of thoughtful people who worked for a long time on the curricular aims to be assessed by using an especially important assessment. You will be looking at an actual NAEP curricular document, but much of what you will see therein will be found in comparable curricular documents.

 Exercise Directions: For this exercise, you need know very little about science. What you are to do is assume you are a social studies teacher in a middle school who knows almost nothing about science. Your district's deputy superintendent, however, has given you several printed excerpts that were downloaded from www .nagb.org regarding the 2009 NAEP science assessment. The deputy superintendent has asked you, after carefully considering the nature of the way the science framework attempts to conceptualize the content/skills of science, to make a brief written report to the six-member District Curriculum Committee. The deputy superintendent wants your report to (1) evaluate the 2009 NAEP science framework and (2) indicate whether you believe the conceptual approach embodied in the science framework would be suitable for assessing district students' achievement in social studies.

   The district superintendent encourages you to review the following excerpts, but to go for more information, if you wish, to www.nagb.org.

■ ■ ■

Excerpts from the Science Framework for the 2009 National Assessment of Educational Progress (drawn from www.nagb.org)

Content of the Framework

Science Content

The science content for the 2009 NAEP is defined by a series of statements that describes key facts, concepts, principles, theories, and laws in three broad areas:

- Physical Science
- Life Science
- Earth and Space Science

   Physical Science deals with matter, energy, and motion; Life Science with structures and functions of living systems and changes in living systems; and Earth and Space Science with Earth in space and time, Earth structures, and Earth systems. . . .

Science Practices

The second dimension of the *Framework* is defined by four science practices:

- Identifying Science Principles
- Using Science Principles
- Using Scientific Inquiry
- Using Technological Design

These practices can be combined with any science content statement to generate student performance expectations, and assessment items can then be developed based on these performance expectations. The cognitive demands placed on students as they engage in assessment tasks are also described. . . .

Distribution of Items

As measured by student response time, the distribution of items by content area should be as follows: approximately equal across Physical Science, Life Science, and Earth and Space Science at grade 4; more emphasis on Earth and Space Science at grade 8; and a shift to more emphasis on Physical Science and Life Science at grade 12. With respect to science practices, at all grades, the greatest emphasis should be on Identifying and Using Science Principles; and slightly less than a third of the time should be spent on items related to Using Scientific Inquiry. . . .

Types of Items

Item types for the 2009 NAEP Science Assessment fall into two broad categories: selected-response items such as multiple-choice items and constructed-response items such as short-answer items. As measured by student response time, 50 percent of the assessment items at each grade level should be selected-response items and 50 percent should be constructed-response items. In order to further probe students' abilities to combine their understandings with the investigative skills reflective of practices, a sub-sample of students should receive an additional 30 minutes to complete hands-on performance or interactive computer tasks. At each grade, there should be at least a total of four of these tasks. Of these four tasks, there should be at least one hands-on performance *and* one interactive computer task; the number of interactive computer tasks should not exceed the number of hands-on performance tasks. . . .

In hands-on performance tasks, students manipulate selected physical objects and try to solve a scientific problem involving the objects. NAEP hands-on performance tasks should provide students with a concrete task (problem) along with equipment and materials. Students should be given the opportunity to determine scientifically justifiable procedures for arriving at a solution. Students' scores should be based on both the solution and the procedures created for carrying out the investigation. . . .

Interactive computer tasks may be of four types: (1) information search and analysis, (2) empirical investigation, (3) simulation, and (4) concept maps. Information search and analysis items pose a scientific problem and ask students to query an information database and analyze relevant data to address the problem. Empirical investigation items put hands-on performance tasks on the computer and invite students to design and conduct a study to draw conclusions about a problem. Simulation items model systems (e.g., food webs), manipulate variables, and predict and explain resulting changes in the system. Concept map items probe aspects of the structure or organization of students' scientific knowledge by providing concept terms and having students create a logical graphic organizer. . . .

Model of Assessment Development and Methods

NAEP assessment frameworks and specifications documents are themselves used as resources for international, state, and local curriculum and assessment. The broad-based process used in the development of the frameworks and specifications means that current thinking and research is reflected in these descriptions of what students should know and be able to do in a given subject. In addition, NAEP uses a rigorous and carefully designed process in developing the assessment instruments themselves. Pilot tests and internal and external reviews ensure that NAEP assessments are reliable and valid with respect to what they attempt to accomplish. This sophisticated methodology serves as a model for other assessment developers. Given the requirements contained in federal accountability laws to assess students in science, states may wish to use NAEP as one model to guide their own assessment development.

Research and Policy

The data NAEP provides include subject-matter achievement results (reported as both scale scores and achievement levels) for various subgroups; background information about schools, teachers, and students at the subgroup level (e.g., course-taking patterns of Hispanic male 12th graders); state-level results; reports for a set of large urban districts; history of state and district participation; and publicly released assessment questions, student responses, and scoring guides. . . .

Challenges of Developing an NAEP Assessment

There are three major challenges in developing an NAEP framework, and, in particular, this *Framework*. One such challenge arises from measurement constraints and the nature of the items included on the assessment; the next relates to time and resource constraints and how much can be assessed in NAEP; and the last comes from the time horizon for the *Framework* and the difficulty of developing a ten-year framework with the rapid explosion of knowledge in the Information Age. Each of these is discussed in detail below.

Measurement Constraints

NAEP, like any large-scale assessment in education, the workplace, or clinical practice, is constrained in what it can measure. This has implications for the proper interpretation of NAEP Science Assessment results. The *Framework* is an assessment framework, not a curriculum framework. Although the two are clearly interrelated, each has a different purpose and a different set of underlying assumptions. A curriculum framework is designed to inform instruction, to guide what is taught, and often, how it is taught. It represents a very wide universe of learning outcomes from which teachers pick and choose what and how they teach. An assessment framework is a subset of the achievement universe from which assessment developers must choose to develop sets of items that can be assessed within time and resource constraints. Hence, the science content to be assessed by NAEP has been identified as that considered central to the Physical, Life, and Earth and Space Sciences. As a result, some important outcomes of science education that are difficult and time-consuming to measure—such as habits of mind, sustained inquiry, collaborative research—but valued by scientists, science educators, and the business community, will be only partially represented in the *Framework* and on the NAEP Science Assessment. Moreover, the wide range of science standards in the guiding national documents that could be incorporated into the *Framework* had to be reduced in number so as to allow some in-depth probing of fundamental science content. As a result, the *Framework* and the *Specifications* represent a careful distillation that is not a complete representation of the original universe of achievement outcomes desirable for science education.

Time and Resource Constraints

What NAEP can assess is limited by time and resources. Like most standardized assessments, NAEP is an "on demand" assessment; it ascertains what students know and can do in a limited amount of time (50 minutes for paper-and-pencil questions and, for a sub-sample of students, an additional 30 minutes for hands-on performance or interactive computer tasks), with limited access to resources (e.g., reference materials, feedback from peers and teachers, opportunities for reflection and revision). The national and state standards, however, contain goals that require extended time (days, weeks, or months). To assess the achievement of students in the kinds of extended activities that are a central feature of the national and state standards and many science curricula, then, it would be necessary to know, for example, the quality of students':

- reasoning while framing their research questions;
- planning for data collection and the execution of that plan;
- abilities to meet unpredictable challenges that arise during an actual, ongoing scientific investigation;
- lines of argument in deciding how to alter their experimental approach in the light of new evidence;
- engagement with fellow students and/or the teacher in interpreting an observation or result and deciding what to do about it; and
- deliberations and reasoning when settling on the defensible conclusions that might be drawn from their work.

NAEP, like other "on demand" assessments, then, cannot be used to draw conclusions about student achievement with respect to the full range of goals of science education. States, districts, schools, and teachers can supplement NAEP and other standardized assessments to assess the full range of science education standards. In addition to describing the content and format of an examination, assessment frameworks, like this one, signal to the public and to teachers what elements of a subject are important. The absence of extended inquiry in NAEP, however, is not intended to signal its relative importance in the curriculum. Indeed, because of the significance of inquiry in science education, the *Framework* promotes as much consideration of inquiry as can be accomplished within the time and resources available for assessment.

Balancing Current and Future Curricula

The *Framework* attempts to strike a balance between what can reasonably be predicted about future school science and what students are likely to encounter in their curriculum and instruction now and in the near future. It is a significant challenge to write a framework for the future. Cutting-edge science research creates new knowledge at the intersection of disciplinary boundaries. For example, research on human and natural systems has generated new understandings about environmental science that are closely linked to knowledge generated in the Physical, Life, and Earth and Space Sciences. Although the *Framework* is organized into the more traditional Physical, Life, and Earth and Space Sciences, features of current science research are woven throughout.

Another example of burgeoning knowledge relates to technology and technological design and the role of both in the NAEP Science Assessment. Technology and technological design are closely interrelated with science, yet the focus of this assessment is science. Hence, technology and technological design are included in the *Framework* but are limited to that which has a direct bearing on the assessment of students' science achievement. . . .

The *Framework* is intended to be both forward-looking (in terms of what science content will be of central importance in the future) and reflective (in terms of current school science). Because it is impossible to predict with certainty the shape of school science in 2009 and beyond, the choices made for 2009 should be revisited in response to future developments in school science. . . .

Introduction to the Assessment Framework

Science is comprised of both content and practices. The NAEP Science Assessment provides a snapshot view of what the nation's 4th, 8th, and 12th graders know and can do in science. One expects students, as a result of their education and life experiences, to have learned about the principles[1] (along with the facts, concepts, theories, and laws) that have been verified by the community of scientists, as well as how scientists discover regularities in the natural world. NAEP will assess students' abilities to identify and use science principles, as well as use scientific inquiry and technological design. While the *Framework* distinguishes content from practice, the two are closely linked in assessment and in real life. . . .[1] "Science principles" is used throughout this *Framework* to denote not only the principles but also the facts, concepts, theories, and laws of science.

The design of the NAEP Science Assessment is guided by the *Framework's* descriptions of the science content and practices to be assessed. Figure 1 illustrates how content and practices are combined ("crossed") to generate performance expectations. The columns contain the science content (defined by content statements in three broad areas), and the rows contain the four science practices. A double dashed line distinguishes Identifying Science Principles and Using Science Principles from Using Scientific Inquiry and Using Technological Design. The former two practices can be generally considered as "knowing science," and the latter two practices can be considered as the application of that knowledge to "doing science" and "using science to solve real-world problems." The cells at the intersection of content (columns) and practices (rows) contain student performance expectations. Since content and practice categories are not entirely distinct, some overlap in the resultant performance expectations is to be expected, as denoted by dashed lines.

Figure 2 illustrates the fuller process of generating and interpreting assessment items. An item is an individual question or exercise on the NAEP Science Assessment and is used to gather information about students' knowledge and abilities. Figure 2 begins with student performance expectations, which describe in observable terms what students are expected to know and do on the assessment. These performance expectations guide the development of assessment items. The cognitive demands . . . of the items can

[1] "Science principles" is used throughout this Framework to denote not only the principles but also the facts, concepts, theories, and laws of science

then be used to interpret students' responses as evidence of what students know and can do in science. . . . Figure 2 suggests a linear process, but the development of an assessment is iterative (e.g., assessment items are modified based on student responses provided on trials of pilot versions).

■ ■ ■

All right, that's the end of a lengthy, real-world excerpt of a curriculum document drawn from the NAGB website. Your task is to come up with a succinct report to the District Curriculum Committee focusing on (1) the quality of the science framework and (2) whether you think the approach used for the 2009 NAEP science assessment is likely to work in the assessment of students' status with respect to their achievement levels in social studies.

figure 1 ■ Crossing Content and Practices to Generate Performance Expectations

		Science Content		
		Physical Science content statements	**Life Science** content statements	**Earth and Space Science** content statements
Science Practices	**Identifying Science Principles**	*Performance Expectations*	*Performance Expectations*	*Performance Expectations*
	Using Science Principles	*Performance Expectations*	*Performance Expectations*	*Performance Expectations*
	Using Scientific Inquiry	*Performance Expectations*	*Performance Expectations*	*Performance Expectations*
	Using Technological Design	*Performance Expectations*	*Performance Expectations*	*Performance Expectations*

One Possible Response

A Report to the District Curriculum Committee

I was asked to review a set of documents (downloaded from www.nagb.org) supplied to me by the district's deputy superintendent. Using these excerpts, I was asked to provide this report. (I have attached copies of the excerpts I was given to this report so that you may refer to them if you need to.) As a preview, in the report I conclude that the assessment framework (hereafter described as the *Framework*) for the 2009 NAEP science assessment is (1) well conceived and (2) applicable to the assessment of students' levels of learning in the field of social studies. Although unasked to do so by the district superintendent, I register a worry about NAEP-type frameworks.

figure 2 ■ Generating and Interpreting Items

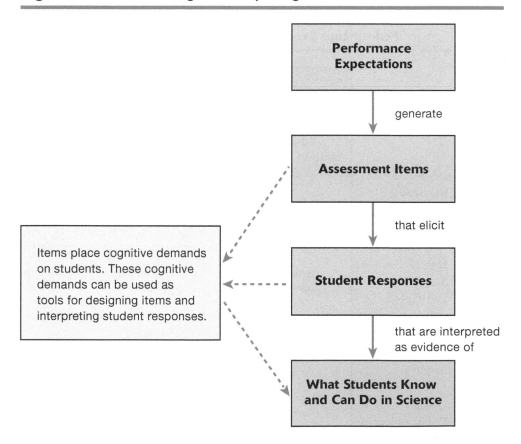

Deciding What to Assess and How to Assess It

The National Assessment of Educational Progress (NAEP) has, since 1969, periodically assessed samples of students at grades 4, 8, and 12 in various subject areas. Federally funded, NAEP is supervised by the National Assessment Governing Board (NAGB). The NAGB has an excellent website (www.nagb.org), and I spent several hours reviewing what kinds of NAEP tests are offered in fields other than science. If any members of the District Curriculum Committee are interested, I recommend this website.

My overall reaction to the *Framework* for science is extremely positive. I know relatively little about science, but I recognize that it consists of three major content areas: Physical Science, Life Science, and Earth/Space Science. Moreover, there seems to be a series of specific cognitive skills that are applied to this content. I think that if you will look at Figure 1 in the attached materials, you will see how the people who created the science *Framework* (I guess I should refer to them as the "framers" of the *Framework*!) attempted to resolve this by "crossing science content with science practices." This seems like an excellent solution to me.

I was also favorably impressed with the realism reflected in the description of how the *Framework* was born—especially how the *Framework* was created against a backdrop of practical constraints and the need to balance current scientific knowledge with future scientific knowledge. In sum, I thought the assessment conceptualization for the 2009 NAEP science assessment was quite wonderful.

Turning to the applicability of the science framework's approach to my own field, social studies, I believe it is altogether suitable. In social studies we have different content areas, such as history, government, economics, geography, and so on. These content areas are comparable to those found in science. In addition, we need to get our students to master certain cognitive skills in all of those content fields. Accordingly, I see that a "crossed" content-by-skills matrix akin to the one seen in the appended Figure 1 would be highly suitable for the assessment of students' social studies achievement levels.

I will wrap up this report by expressing a concern I have as I learned more about the way the architects of NAEP assessment frameworks carry out their work. When subject-matter specialists identify what they want students to learn, those specialists usually end up with assessment targets (and, therefore, instructional targets) that are way too numerous. Because the NAEP 2009 *Framework* in science will surely influence the way states try to build their own state science tests, I am afraid that NAEP's myriad content and skill emphases will simply overwhelm classroom teachers.

There's only so much that can be taught to children in the hours we have available. But, because NAEP tests are given to students on a sampling basis—that is, in such a way that different students get different subsets of items—NAEP tests can measure much more content than would be possible if the same test were to be given to every student. But just because that kind of different-subtest approach means you can measure many more bodies of knowledge and cognitive skills, this doesn't mean that teachers can *teach* all that content in the time they have with their students. Overwhelmed teachers are certain to be ineffective teachers. I worry that the immensity of content coverage replicated in the NAEP assessment frameworks may overwhelm those of us who teach in the district.

I hope members of the District Curriculum Committee can find a way to balance the excellent features of the 2009 NAEP Science Framework with its potential too-much-to-teach drawback.

Glossary

affective assessment A measurement of a student's attitudes, interests, and/or values.

alignment The substantive agreement between two or more of the following: curriculum, instruction, and assessment.

cognitive assessment Measurement of a student's knowledge and/or intellectual skills.

cognitive demand The essence of the intellectual operation(s) a student must carry out in order to respond successfully to a test's items or tasks.

constructed responses A student's answers to assessment tasks, such as essay items, that require a response to be generated by the student "from scratch."

content standards The knowledge and skills that a student is supposed to learn.

criterion-referenced measurement An approach to assessment in which a student's test performance is interpreted according to how much of a defined assessment domain has been mastered by the student.

curricular aim A skill, body of knowledge, or affective outcome that teachers intend their students to acquire.

curriculum The set of educational aims—for instance, goals or objectives—teachers wish their students to achieve.

educational accountability The imposition of required evidence, usually a student's test scores, as a way of holding educators responsible for the quality of schooling.

grain-size The breadth of a curricular aim, ranging from small grain-size to large grain-size aims. Typically, the breadth of a curricular aim—that is, its grain-size—is directly linked to the amount of instructional time it is thought will be required for students to master the curricular aim.

instruction The activities carried out by teachers with their students intended to help students achieve teachers' curricular aims.

measurement-driven instruction An approach to educational reform in which the installation of high-stakes assessments is intended to influence teachers to teach toward the knowledge and skills those assessments purport to measure.

norm-referenced measurement An approach to assessment in which a student's test performance is interpreted relatively—that is, according to how the student's performance compares with that of other test takers.

performance standards The level of proficiency at which content standards should be mastered.

psychomotor assessment Measurement of a student's small-muscle or large-muscle skills.

selected responses A student's answer to test items that present options from which the student must choose—for instance, multiple-choice or binary-choice items.

Selected-Response Tests

I n this text, you will learn how to construct almost a dozen different kinds of test items you might wish to use for your own classroom assessments. You really need to choose item types that mesh properly with the inferences you want to make about students—and to be sure those inferences are directly linked to the educational decisions you need to make. Just as the child who's convinced that vanilla is ice cream's only flavor won't benefit from a 36-flavor ice cream emporium, the more item types you know about, the more appropriate your selection of item types will be. In this chapter you'll be learning about blackberry-ripple exams and mocha-mango assessment devices.

Let me level with you regarding what you can really expect after wading through the exposition about item construction. Unless you're a remarkably quick study, you'll probably finish the text and *not* be instantly transformed into a consummately skilled test constructor. It takes more than reading to turn someone into a capable item developer. But, just as the journey of a thousand miles begins with a single step, you'll have initiated a tentative trot toward the Test Construction Hall of Fame. You'll have learned the essentials of how to construct the most common kinds of classroom assessments.

What you'll need after you complete the five test-construction text is tons of practice in churning out classroom assessment devices. And, if you remain in teaching for a while, such practice opportunities will surely come your way. Ideally, you'll be able to get some feedback about the quality of your classroom assessment procedures from a supervisor or colleague who is clearheaded and/or conversant with educational measurement. If a competent cohort critiques your test-construction efforts, you'll profit by being able to make needed modifications in how you create your classroom assessment instruments.

■ Ten (Divided by Two) Item-Writing Commandments

As you can discern from this chapter's title, it's going to describe how to construct selected-response kinds of test items. You'll learn how to create four different varieties of selected-response test items—namely, binary-choice items, multiple binary-choice items, multiple-choice items, and matching items. All four of these selected-response kinds of items can be used effectively by teachers to derive defensible inferences about students' cognitive status—that is, the knowledge and skills teachers typically try to promote in their students.

But no matter whether you're developing selected-response or constructed-response kinds of test items, there are several general guidelines that, if adhered to, will lead to better assessment procedures. Because the original Ten Commandments were stated in fairly stern "Thou shall not" form, and have proven successful in shaping many folks' behavior, I shall now dish out five general item-writing commandments structured along the same lines. If followed, these commandments won't get you into heaven, but they will make your assessment schemes slightly more divine. All five commandments are presented in the box below. A subsequent discussion of each commandment will help you understand how to adhere to the five item-writing mandates being discussed. It will help if you refer to each of the following item-writing commandments before reading the discussion of that commandment.

Five General Item-Writing Commandments

1. Thou shall not provide opaque directions to students regarding how to respond to your assessment instruments.
2. Thou shall not employ ambiguous statements in your assessment items.
3. Thou shall not provide students with unintentional clues regarding appropriate responses.
4. Thou shall not employ complex syntax in your assessment items.
5. Thou shall not use vocabulary that is more advanced than required.

Opaque Directions

The first item-writing commandment deals with a topic most teachers haven't thought seriously about—the directions for their classroom tests. Teachers who have been laboring to create a collection of test items typically know the innards of those items very well. Thus, because of the teacher's intimate knowledge not only of the items but also how students are supposed to deal with those items, it is often the case that only sketchy directions are provided to students regarding how to respond to a test's items. Yet, of course, unclear test-taking directions can result in confused test takers. And the responses of confused test takers don't lead to very accurate inferences about those test takers.

Flawed test directions are particularly problematic when students are being introduced to forms of assessment with which they're not very familiar, such as the performance tests or the multiple binary-choice tests to be discussed later in this chapter. It is useful to create directions for students early in the game when you're developing an assessment instrument. When generated as a last-minute afterthought, test directions typically turn out to be tawdry.

Ambiguous Statements

The second item-writing commandment deals with ambiguity. In all kinds of classroom assessments, ambiguous writing is to be avoided. If your students aren't really sure about what you mean in the tasks you present to them, the students are apt to misinterpret what you're saying and, as a consequence, come up with incorrect responses even though they might really know how to respond correctly. For example, sentences in which pronouns are used can frequently be unclear about the individual or individuals to whom the pronoun refers. Suppose, in a true-false test item, you asked your students to indicate whether the following statement was true or false: "Leaders of developing nations have tended to distrust leaders of developed nations due to their imperialistic tendencies." Because it is ambiguous regarding whether the pronoun *their* refers to the "leaders of developing nations" or to the "leaders of developed nations," and because the truth or falsity of the statement depends on the pronoun's referent, students are likely to be confused.

Because you will typically be writing your own assessment items, *you* will know what you mean. At least you ought to. However, try to slide yourself, at least figuratively, into the shoes of your students. Reread your assessment items from the perspective of the students, and modify any statements apt to be even a mite ambiguous to those less well-informed students.

Unintended Clues

The third of our item-writing commandments calls for you to *intentionally* avoid something *unintentional*. Well, nobody said that following commandments was going to be easy! What this commandment is trying to sensitize you to is the tendency of test-development novices to inadvertently provide clues to students about appropriate responses. As a consequence, students come up with correct responses even if they don't possess the knowledge or skill being assessed.

For example, inexperienced item writers often tend to make the correct answer to multiple-choice items twice as long as the incorrect answers. Even clucko students will opt for the lengthy response; they get so many more words for their choice. As another example of how inexperienced item writers unintentionally dispense clues, absolute qualifiers such as *never* and *always* are sometimes used for the false items in a true-false test. Because even uninformed students know there are few absolutes in this world, they gleefully (and often unthinkingly) indicate such items are false. One of the most blatant examples of giving unintended clues occurs when writers of multiple-choice test items initiate those items with incomplete statements such as "The bird in the story was an . . ." and then offer answer options in which only the correct answer begins with a vowel. For instance, even though you never read the story referred to in the previous incomplete statement, if you encountered the following four response options, I bet you'd know the correct answer: A. Falcon, B. Hawk, C. Robin, D. Owl. The article *an* gives the game away.

Computer-Adaptive Assessment: Its Seductive Allure

Large-scale assessments, such as statewide accountability tests or nationally standardized achievement tests, are definitely different from the classroom tests teachers might, during a dreary weekend, whip up for their students. Despite those differences, the assessment tactics used in large-scale tests should not be totally unknown to teachers. After all, parents of a teacher's students might occasionally toss out questions at a teacher about such tests, and what teacher wants to be seen, when it comes to educational tests, as a no-knowledge ninny?

One of the two multistate assessment consortia (the Smarter Balanced Assessment Consortium) is committed to have its major tests use ***computer-adaptive assessment*** to measure students' mastery of the Common Core State Standards (CCSS) adopted as curricular aims by so many states during 2010 and 2011. Therefore, given the likelihood that students in many states will be tested by computer-adaptive assessments, a brief description of this assessment approach is in order.

Not all assessments involving computers are computer-adaptive. ***Computer-based assessments*** rely on computers to deliver test items to students. Moreover, students respond to these computer-transmitted items by using a computer. This form of computer-abetted assessment is becoming more and more popular as (1) schools acquire enough computers to make the approach practicable and (2) states and school districts secure sufficient "bandwidth" (whatever that is!) to transmit tests and receive students' responses electronically. Computer-based assessments, as you can see, rely on computers only as delivery and retrieval mechanisms. Computer-adaptive assessment is something quite different.

Here's how computer-adaptive assessment works. Notice, incidentally, the key term *adaptive* in its name. That word is your key to understanding how this approach to educational assessment functions. As a student takes this kind of test, the student is given items of known difficulty levels. Then, based on the student's responses to those initial items, the computer supplies new items whose difficulties mesh with the student's earlier answers. For instance, if a student is answering correctly the early items doled out by the computer, then the next items popping up on the screen will be more difficult ones. Conversely, if the student stumbles on the initially received items, the computer will then provide easier items to the student, and so on. In short, the computer's program constantly *adapts* to the student's responses by providing items matched to the student's assessment-determined level of achievement.

Using this adaptive approach, a student's mastery level regarding whatever the test is measuring can be determined with far fewer items than would typically be the case. This is because, in a typical test, many of the test's items might be too difficult or too easy for a particular student. Accordingly, one of the payoffs of computer-adaptive testing is that it saves testing time—and the stolen instructional minutes that are often snatched away from teachers because of externally imposed assessment obligations.

But there's a limitation of computer-adaptive testing you need to recognize. It stems from the necessity for all the items in such an approach to be measuring a *single variable*, such as students' "mathematical mastery." Because many, many items are needed to make computer-adaptive assessment purr properly, and because the varying difficulties of these items must *all* be linked to what's sometimes referred to as "a unidimensional trait" (such as a child's overall reading prowess), computer-adaptive assessment precludes the possibility of providing student-specific diagnostic data. Too few items dealing with a particular subskill or a body of enabling knowledge can be administered during a student's abbreviated testing time. In other words, whereas computer-adaptive assessment can supply teachers with an efficiently garnered *general fix* on a student's status with respect to what's often a broadly conceptualized curricular aim, it won't reveal a student's specific strengths and weaknesses.

Unintended clues are seen more frequently with selected-response items than constructed-response items, but even in supplying background information to students for complicated constructed-response items, the teacher must be wary of unintentionally pointing truly unknowledgeable students down the correct-response trail.

Complex Syntax

Complex syntax, although it sounds like an exotic surcharge on cigarettes and alcohol, is often encountered in the assessment items of neophyte item writers. Even though some teachers may regard themselves as Steinbecks-in-hiding, an assessment instrument is no setting in which to wax eloquent. This fourth item-writing commandment directs you to avoid complicated sentence constructions and, instead, use very simple sentences. Although esteemed writers such as Thomas Harding and James Joyce are known for their convoluted and clause-laden writing styles, I'll wager they would have been mediocre item writers. Too many clauses, except at Christmas-time, mess up test items. (For readers needing a clue regarding the previous sentence's cryptic meaning, think of a red-garbed guy who brings presents.)

Difficult Vocabulary

Our fifth and final item-writing commandment is fairly straightforward. It indicates that when writing educational assessment items, *you should eschew obfuscative verbiage*. In other words, in almost *any* other words, use vocabulary suitable for the students who'll be taking your tests. Assessment time is not the occasion for you to trot out your best collection of polysyllabic terms or to secure a series of thesaurus-induced thrills. The more advanced the vocabulary level is in your assessment devices, the more likely you'll fail to get a good fix on your students' true status. They will have been laid low by the overblown vocabulary. In the case of the terminology to be used in classroom assessment instruments, simple wins.

In review, you've now seen five item-writing commandments that apply to any kind of classroom assessment device you develop. They certainly apply to tests containing selected-response items. And that's what we'll be looking at in the rest of the chapter. More specifically, you'll be encountering a series of item-writing guidelines to follow when constructing particular kinds of selected-response items. The guidelines are based either on empirical research evidence or on decades of teachers' experience in using such items. If you opt to use any of the item types to be described here in your own classroom tests, try to follow the guidelines for that kind of item. Your tests will typically turn out to be better than if you hadn't.

■ Binary-Choice Items

A *binary-choice item* gives students only two options from which to select. The most common form of binary-choice item is the *true-false item*. Educators have been using true-false tests probably as far back as Socrates. (True or False: Plato was a type of serving-dish used by Greeks for special meals.) Other variations of binary-choice items would be those in which students must choose between yes-no, right-wrong, correct-incorrect, fact-opinion, and so on.

The virtue of binary-choice items is they are typically so terse that students can respond to many items in a short time. Therefore, it is possible to cover a large amount of content in a brief assessment session. The greatest weakness of binary-choice items is that, because there are only two options, students have a 50-50 chance of guessing the correct answer even if they don't have the foggiest idea of what's correct. If a large number of binary-choice items are used, however, this weakness tends to evaporate. After all, although students might guess their way correctly through a few binary-choice items, they would need to be extraordinarily lucky to guess their way correctly through 30 such items.

Here are five item-writing guidelines for binary-choice items. A brief discussion of each guideline is provided in the following paragraphs.

Item-Writing Guidelines for Binary-Choice Items

1. Phrase items so that a superficial analysis by the student suggests a wrong answer.
2. Rarely use negative statements, and never use double negatives.
3. Include only one concept in each statement.
4. Have an approximately equal number of items representing the two categories being tested.
5. Keep item length similar for both categories being tested.

Phrasing Items to Elicit Thoughtfulness

Typically, binary items are quite brief, but brevity need not reflect simplistic choices for students. In order to get the most payoff from binary-choice items, you'll want to phrase items so students who approach the items superficially will answer them incorrectly. Thus, if you were creating the items for a true-false test, you would construct statements for your items that were not blatantly true or blatantly false. Blatancy in items rarely leads to accurate inferences about students. Beyond blatancy avoidance, however, you should phrase at least some of the items so if students approach them unthinkingly, they'll choose false for a true statement and vice versa. What you're trying to do is to get students to *think* about your test items and, thereby, give you a better idea about how much good thinking they can do.

Minimizing Negatives

With binary-choice items, many students have a really difficult time responding to negatively phrased items. For instance, suppose in a true-false test you were asked to decide about the truth or falsity of the following statement: "The League of Nations was not formed immediately after the conclusion of World War II." What the item is looking for as a correct answer to this statement is *true,* because the League of Nations was in existence prior to World War II. Yet, the existence of the *not* in the item really will confuse some students. They'll be apt to answer *false* even if they know the League of Nations was functioning before World War II commenced.

Because I've churned out my share of true-false items over the years, I know all too well how tempting it is to simply insert a *not* into an otherwise true statement. But don't yield to the temptation. Only rarely succumb to the lure of the nagging negative in binary-choice items. Items containing double negatives or triple negatives (if you could contrive one) are obviously to be avoided.

Avoiding Double-Concept Items

The third guideline for binary-choice items directs you to focus on only a single concept in each item. If you are creating a statement for a right-wrong test, and have an item in which half of the statement is clearly right and the other half is clearly wrong, you make it mighty difficult for students to respond correctly. The presence of two concepts in a single item, even if both are right or both are wrong, tends to confuse students and, as a consequence, yields test results apt to produce inaccurate inferences about those students.

Balancing Response Categories

If you're devising a binary-choice test, try to keep an approximately equal number of items representing the two response categories. For example, if it's a true-false test, make sure you have somewhat similar proportions of true and false statements. It's not necessary to have exactly the same number of true and false items. The proportion of true and false items, however, should be roughly the same. This fourth guideline is quite easy to follow if you simply keep it in mind when creating your binary-choice items.

Maintaining Item-Length Similarity

The fifth guideline is similar to the fourth because it encourages you to structure your items so there are no give-away clues associated with item length. If your two response categories are *accurate* and *inaccurate,* make sure the length of the accurate statements is approximately the same as the length of the inaccurate statements. When creating true-false tests, there is a tendency to toss in qualifying clauses for the true statements so those statements, properly qualified, are truly true—but also long! As a result, there's a systematic pattern wherein long statements are true and short statements are false. As soon as students catch on to this pattern, they can answer items correctly without even referring to an item's contents.

In review, we've considered five item-writing guidelines for binary-choice items. If you'll follow those guidelines and keep your wits about you when creating binary-choice items, you'll often find this type of test will prove useful in the classroom. And that's true, not false.

Multiple Binary-Choice Items

A *multiple binary-choice item* is one in which a cluster of items is presented to students, requiring a binary response to each of the items in the cluster. Typically, but not always, the items are related to an initial statement or set of statements. Multiple binary-choice items are formatted so they look like traditional multiple-choice tests. In a multiple-choice test, the student must choose one answer from several options, but in the multiple binary-choice test, the student must make a response for each statement in the cluster. Figure 1 is an example of a multiple binary-choice item.

David Frisbie (1992) reviewed research regarding such items and concluded that multiple binary-choice items are (1) highly efficient for gathering student achievement data, (2) more reliable than other selected-response items,

figure 1 ■ An Illustrative Multiple True-False Item

• • • Suppose that a dozen of your students completed a 10-item multiple-choice test and earned the following number of correct scores:

5, 6, 7, 7, 7, 7, 8, 8, 8, 8, 9, 10

9. The median for your students' scores is 7.5.   (True)

10. The mode for the set of scores is 8.0.   (False)

11. The range of the students' scores is 5.0.   (True)

12. The median is different than the mean.   (False)

(3) able to measure the same skills and abilities as multiple-choice items dealing with comparable content, (4) a bit more difficult for students than multiple-choice tests, and (5) perceived by students to be more difficult but more efficient than multiple-choice items. Frisbie believes that when teachers construct multiple binary-choice items, they must be attentive to all of the usual considerations in writing regular binary-choice items. However, he suggests the following two additional guidelines.

Item-Writing Guidelines for Multiple Binary-Choice Items

1. Separate item clusters vividly from one another.
2. Make certain that each item meshes well with the cluster's stimulus material.

Separating Clusters

Because many students are familiar with traditional multiple-choice items, and because each of those items is numbered, there is some danger students may become confused by the absence of numbers where such numbers are ordinarily found. Thus, be sure to use some kind of formatting system to make it clear a new cluster is commencing. In the illustrative item seen in Figure 1, notice that three dots (• • •) have been used to signify the beginning of a new cluster of items. You can use asterisks, lines, boxes, or some similar way of alerting students to the beginning of a new cluster.

Coordinating Items with Their Stem

In multiple-choice items, the first part of the item—the part preceding the response options—is called the *stem*. For multiple binary-choice items, we refer to the first part of the item cluster as the cluster's stem or stimulus material. The second item-writing guideline for this item type suggests you make sure all items in a cluster are, in fact, linked in a meaningful way to the cluster's stem. If they're not, then you might as well use individual binary-choice items rather than multiple binary-choice items.

There's another compelling reason you should consider adding multiple binary-choice items to your classroom assessment repertoire. Unlike traditional binary-choice items, for which it's likely students will need to rely on *memorized* information, that's rarely the case with multiple binary-choice items. It is rare, that is, *if* the stimulus materials contain content that's not been encountered previously by students. In other words, if the stem for a subset of multiple binary-choice items contains material that's new to the student, and if each binary-choice item depends directly on the previously unencountered content, it's dead certain the student will need to function above the mere recollection of knowledge, the lowest level of Bloom's cognitive taxonomy. So, if you make certain your stimulus material for multiple binary-choice items contains new content, those items will surely be more intellectually demanding than the run-of-the-memory true-false item.

In review, we've considered an item type that's not widely used but has some special virtues. The major advantage of multiple binary-choice items is that students can respond to two or three such items in the time it takes them to respond to a single multiple-choice item. Other things being equal, the more items students respond to, the more reliably we can gauge their abilities.

I must confess to a mild bias toward this often overlooked item type because for over 20 years I used such tests as the final examinations in an introductory educational measurement course I taught in the UCLA Graduate School of Education. I'd give my students 20 one- or two-paragraph descriptions of previously unencountered educational measurement situations and then follow up each description with five binary-choice items. In all, then, I ended up with a 100-item final exam that really seemed to sort out those students who knew their stuff from those who didn't. The five items in each cluster were simply statements to which students were to respond *accurate* or *inaccurate*. I could just as appropriately have asked for *true* or *false* responses, but I tried to add a touch of suave to my exams. After all, I was teaching in a *Graduate* School of Education. (In retrospect, my decision seems somewhat silly.) Nonetheless, I had pretty good luck with my 100-item final exams. I used a 50-item version for my midterm exams, and they worked well too. For certain kinds of purposes, I think you'll find multiple binary-choice items will prove useful.

■ Multiple-Choice Items

For a number of decades, the **multiple-choice test item** has dominated achievement testing in the United States and many other nations. Multiple-choice items can be used to measure a student's possession of knowledge or a student's ability to engage in higher levels of thinking. A strength of multiple-choice items is they can contain several answers differing in their *relative* correctness. Thus, the student can be called on to make subtle distinctions among answer options, several of which may be somewhat correct. A weakness of multiple-choice items, as is the case with all selected-response items, is that students need only *recognize* a correct answer. They need not *generate* a correct answer. Although a fair amount of criticism has been heaped on multiple-choice items, particularly in recent years, properly constructed multiple-choice items can tap a rich variety of student skills and knowledge, and thus can be useful tools for classroom assessment.

The first part of a multiple-choice item, as noted earlier, is referred to as the item's *stem*. The potential answer options are described as **item alternatives**. Incorrect alternatives are typically referred to as the item's **distractors**. Two common

figure 2 ■ Illustrative Multiple-Choice Items

Direct-Question Form (best-answer version)

Which of the following modes of composition would be most effective in explaining to someone how a bill becomes a law in this nation?

      A. Narrative
   * B. Expository
      C. Persuasive
      D. Descriptive

Incomplete-Statement Form (correct-answer version)

Mickey Mouse's nephews are named

      A. Huey, Dewey, and Louie.
      B. Mutt and Jeff.
      C. Larry, Moe, and Curly.
   * D. Morty and Ferdie.

ways of creating multiple-choice items are to use an item stem that is either a direct question or an incomplete statement. With younger students, the direct-question approach is preferable. Using either direct-question stems or incomplete-statement stems, a multiple-choice item can ask students to select either a correct answer or, instead, to select a best answer.

In Figure 2 there are examples of a direct-question item requesting a best-answer response (indicated by an asterisk) and an incomplete-statement item requesting a correct-answer response (also indicated by an asterisk).

Let's turn now to a consideration of item-writing guidelines for multiple-choice items. Because of the widespread use of multiple-choice items over the past half-century, there are quite a few experience-sired suggestions regarding how to create such items. Here, you'll find five of the more frequently cited recommendations for constructing multiple-choice items.

Item-Writing Guidelines for Multiple-Choice Items

1. The stem should consist of a self-contained question or problem.
2. Avoid negatively stated stems.
3. Do not let the length of alternatives supply unintended clues.
4. Randomly assign correct answers to alternative positions.
5. Never use "all-of-the-above" alternatives, but do use "none-of-the-above" alternatives to increase item difficulty.

Stem Stuffing

A properly constructed stem for a multiple-choice item will present a clearly described task to the student so the student can then get to work on figuring out which of the item's options is best (if it's a best-answer item) or correct (if it's a correct-answer item). A poorly constructed stem for a multiple-choice item will force the student to read one or more of the alternatives in order to figure out what the item is getting at. In general, therefore, it's preferable to load as much of the item's content as possible into the stem. Lengthy stems and terse alternatives are, as a rule, much better than skimpy stems and long alternatives. You might try reading the stems of your multiple-choice items without any of the alternatives to see if the stems (either direct questions or incomplete statements) make sense all by themselves.

Knocking Negatively Stated Stems

It has been alleged, particularly by overly cautious individuals, that "one robin does not spring make." Without debating the causal relationship between seasonal shifts and feathered flyers, in multiple-choice item writing we could say with confidence that "one negative in an item stem does not confusion unmake." Negatives are strange commodities. A single *not,* tossed casually into a test item, can make students crazy. Besides, because *not* is such a tiny word, and might be overlooked by students, a number of students (who didn't see the *not*) may be trying to ferret out the best alternative for a positively stated stem that, in reality, is negative.

For example, let's say you wanted to do a bit of probing of your students' knowledge of U.S. geography and phrased the stem of a multiple-choice item such as this: "Which one of the following cities is located in a state west of the Mississippi River?" If your alternatives were: A. San Diego, B. Pittsburgh, C. Boston, and D. Atlanta, students would have little difficulty in knowing how to respond. Let's say, however, that you decided to add a dollop of difficulty by using the same alternatives but tossing in a *not.* Now your item's stem might read something like this: "Which one of the following cities is not located in a state east of the Mississippi River?" For this version of the item, the student who failed to spot the *not* (this, in psychometric circles, is known as not-spotting) would be in big trouble.

By the way, note in both stems, the student was asked to identify which *one* of the following answers was correct. If you leave the *one* out, a student might have interpreted the question to mean there were two or more cities being sought.

If there is a compelling reason for using a negative in the stem of a multiple-choice item, be sure to highlight the negative with italics, boldface type, or underscoring so that students who are not natural not-spotters will have a fair chance to answer the item correctly.

Attending to Alternative Length

Novice item writers often fail to realize the length of a multiple-choice item's alternatives can give away what the correct answer is. Let's say choices A, B, and C say blah, blah, blah, but choice D says blah, blah, blah, blah, blah, and blah. The crafty student will be inclined to opt for choice D not simply because one gets many more blahs for one's selection, but because the student will figure out the teacher has given so much attention to choice D that there must be something special about it.

Thus, when you're whipping up your alternatives for multiple-choice items, try either to keep all the alternatives about the same length or, if this isn't possible, to have at least two alternatives be of approximately equal length. For instance, if you were using four-alternative items, you might have two fairly short alternatives and two fairly long alternatives. What you want to avoid, of course, is having the correct alternative be one length (either short or long) while the distractors are all another length.

Incidentally, the number of alternatives is really up to you. Most frequently, we see multiple-choice items with four or five alternatives. Because students can guess correct answers more readily with fewer alternatives, three alternatives are not seen all that often except with younger students. Having more than five alternatives puts a pretty heavy reading load on the student. I've usually employed four alternatives on my own multiple-choice tests, but in a few instances, the nature of the test's content has led me to use three or five alternatives.

Assigning Correct Answer Positions

A fourth guideline for writing multiple-choice items is to make sure you scatter your correct answers among your alternatives so students don't "guess their way to high scores" simply by figuring out your favorite correct answer spot is, for instance, choice D or perhaps choice C. Many novice item writers are reluctant to put the correct answer in the choice-A position because they believe it gives away the correct answer too early. Yet, the choice-A position deserves its share of correct answers too. Absence-of-bias should also apply to answer-choice options.

As a rule of thumb, if you have four-alternative items, try to assign roughly 25 percent of your correct answers to each of the four positions. It may be necessary to do some last-minute shifting of answer positions in order to achieve what is essentially a random assignment of correct answers to the available positions. But always do a last-minute check on your multiple-choice tests to see you haven't accidentally overbooked your correct answers too heavily in a particular answer-choice position.

Dealing with "of-the-above" Alternatives

Sometimes a beginning item writer who's trying to come up with four (or five) reasonable alternatives will toss in a none-of-the-above or an all-of-the-above alternative simply as a "filler" alternative. But both of these options must be considered more carefully.

The fifth guideline for this item type says quite clearly you should never use the all-of-the-above alternative. Here's the reason why. Let's say you're using a five-option type of multiple-choice item and you want to set up the item so the fifth option (choice E), "all of the above," would be correct. This indicates the first four answers, choices A through D, must all be correct. The problem with such an item is that even a student who only knows two of the first four alternatives are correct will be able to select the all-of-the-above response because if any two responses are correct, choice E is the only possible best answer. Even worse, some students will read only the first alternative, see that it is correct, mark choice A on their response sheet, and move on to the next test item without going over the full array of alternatives for the item. For either of these reasons, you should never use an all-of-the-above alternative in your multiple-choice items.

What about the none-of-the above alternative? The guideline indicates it should be used when you wish to increase an item's difficulty. You should do so only when the presence of the none-of-the-above alternative will help you make the kind of test-based inference you want to make. To illustrate, let's say you want to find out how well your students can perform basic mathematical operations such as multiplying and dividing. Moreover, you want to be confident your students can really perform the computations either "in their heads," by using scratch paper, or by employing a hand-held calculator. Now, if you use only four-alternative multiple-choice items, there's a real likelihood certain students won't be able to perform the actual mathematical operations, but may be able to select by estimation the answer that is most reasonable. After all, *one* of the four options *has* to be correct. Yet, simply by adding the none-of-the-above option (as a fourth or fifth alternative), students can't be sure the correct answer is silently sitting there among the item's alternatives. To determine whether the correct answer is *really* one of the alternatives for the item, students will be obliged to perform the required mathematical operation and come up with the actual answer. In essence, when the none-of-the-above option is added, the task presented to the student more closely approximates the task the teacher is interested in. A student's chance of guessing the correct answer to a multiple-choice item is markedly less likely when a none-of-the-above option shows up in the item.

Here's a little wrinkle on this guideline you might find useful. Be a bit careful about using a none-of-the-above option for a *best-answer* multiple-choice. Care is warranted because there are wily students waiting out there who'll parade a series of answers for you they regard as better than the one option you think is a winner. If you can cope with such carping, there's no problem. If you have a low carping-coping threshold, however, avoid none-of-the-above options for most—if not all—of your best-answer items.

In review, we've taken a cursory look at five guidelines for the creation of multiple-choice items. There are other more subtle suggestions for creating such items, but if you combine these guidelines with the five general item-writing commandments discussed earlier in the chapter, you'll have a good set of ground rules for devising decent multiple-choice items. As with all the item types I've been describing, there's no substitute for oodles of practice in item writing followed by collegial or supervisorial reviews of your item-writing efforts. It is said that Rome wasn't built in a day. Similarly, in order to become a capable constructor of multiple-choice items, you'll probably need to develop more than one such test—or even more than two.

Decision Time

Multiple-Guess Test Items?

For all six years that he has taught, Leroy Larson has worked with fifth-graders. Although Leroy enjoys all content areas, he takes special pride in his reading instruction because he believes his students enter the sixth grade with dramatically improved comprehension capabilities. Leroy spends little time trying to promote his students' isolated reading skills but, instead, places great emphasis on having students "construct their own meanings" from what they have read.

All of Leroy's reading tests consist exclusively of four-option, multiple-choice items. As Leroy puts it, "I can put together a heavy-duty multiple-choice item when I put my mind to it." Because he has put his mind to it many times during the past six years, Leroy is quite satisfied that his reading tests are as good as his reading instruction.

At the most recent open house night at his school, however, a group of five parents registered genuine unhappiness with the exclusive multiple-choice makeup of Leroy's reading tests. The parents had obviously been comparing notes prior to the open house, and Mrs. Davies (the mother of one of Leroy's fifth-graders) acted as their spokesperson. In brief, Mrs. Davies argued that multiple-choice tests permitted even weak students to "guess their way to good scores." "After all," Mrs. Davies pointed out, "do you want to produce good readers or good guessers?"

Surprised and somewhat shaken by this incident, Leroy has been rethinking his approach to reading assessment. He concludes he can (1) stick with his tests as they are, (2) add some short-answer or essay items to his tests, or (3) replace all of his multiple-choice items with open-ended items. As he considers these options, he realizes that he has given himself a multiple-choice decision!

 If you were Leroy, what would your decision be?

■ Matching Items

A *matching item* consists of two parallel lists of words or phrases requiring the student to match entries on one list with appropriate entries on the second list. Entries in the list for which a match is sought are referred to as *premises*. Entries in the list from which selections are made are referred to as *responses*. Usually, students are directed to match entries from the two lists according to a specific kind of association described in the test directions. Figure 3 is an example of a matching item.

Notice in Figure 3's illustrative matching item that both lists are *homogeneous*. All of the entries in the column at the left (the premises) are U.S. military

figure 3 ■ An Illustrative Matching Item

Directions: On the line to the left of each military conflict listed in Column A, write the letter of the U.S. president in Column B who was in office when that military conflict was concluded. Each name in Column B may be used no more than once.

Column A	Column B
____ 1. World War I	A. Bush (the father)
____ 2. World War II	B. Clinton
____ 3. Korea	C. Eisenhower
____ 4. Vietnam	D. Johnson
____ 5. First Persian Gulf	E. Nixon
	F. Roosevelt
	G. Truman
	H. Wilson

conflicts and all of the entries in the column at the right (the responses) are names of U.S. presidents. Homogeneity is an important attribute of properly constructed matching items.

An advantage of matching items is that their compact form takes up little space on a printed page, thus making it easy to tap a good deal of information efficiently. Matching items can also be easily scored by simply holding a correct-answer template next to the list of premises where students are to supply their selections from the list of responses. A disadvantage of matching items is, as with binary-choice items, they sometimes encourage students' memorization of low-level factual information that, in at least some instances, is of debatable utility. The illustrative matching item is a case in point. Although it's relatively easy to create matching items such as this, is it really important to know which U.S. chief executive was in office when a military conflict was concluded? That's the kind of issue you'll be facing when you decide what kinds of items to include in your classroom assessments.

Typically, matching items are used as *part* of a teacher's assessment instruments. It's pretty difficult to imagine a major classroom examination consisting exclusively of matching items. Matching items don't work well when teachers are trying to assess relatively distinctive ideas, because matching items require pools of related entries to insert into the matching format.

Let's consider a half-dozen guidelines you should think about when creating matching items for your classroom assessment instruments. The guidelines are presented here.

Item-Writing Guidelines for Matching Items

1. Employ homogeneous lists.
2. Use relatively brief lists, placing the shorter words or phrases at the right.
3. Employ more responses than premises.
4. Order the responses logically.
5. Describe the basis for matching and the number of times responses may be used.
6. Place all premises and responses for an item on a single page.

Employing Homogeneous Entries

As noted earlier, each list in a matching item should consist of homogeneous entries. If you really can't create a homogeneous set of premises and a homogeneous set of responses, you shouldn't be mucking about with matching items.

Going for Relative Brevity

From the student's perspective, it's much easier to respond to matching items if the entries in both lists are relatively few in number. About 10 or so premises should be the upper limit for most matching items. The problem with longer lists is that students spend so much time trying to isolate the appropriate response for a given premise, they may forget what they're attempting to find. Very lengthy sets of premises or responses are almost certain to cause at least some students difficulty in responding because

Parent Talk

Assume that you've been using a fair number of multiple-choice items in your classroom examinations. Benito's parents, Mr. and Mrs. Olmedo, have set up a 15-minute conference with you during a Back-to-Classroom Night to talk about Benito's progress.

When they arrive, they soon get around to the topic in which they are most interested—namely, your multiple-choice test items. As Mr. Olmedo puts it, "We want our son to learn to use his mind, not his memory. Although my wife and I have little experience with multiple-choice tests because almost all of our school exams were of an essay nature, we believe multiple-choice tests measure only what Benito has memorized. He has a good memory, as you've probably found out, but we want more for him. Why are you using such low-level test items?"

 If I were you, here's how I'd respond to Mr. Olmedo's question:

"I appreciate your coming in to talk about Benito's education and, in particular, the way he is being assessed. And I also realize that recently there has been a good deal of criticism of multiple-choice test items. More often than not, such criticism is altogether appropriate. In far too many cases, because multiple-choice items are easy to score, they're used to assess just about everything. And, all too often, those kinds of items do indeed ask students to do little more than display their memorization skills.

"But this doesn't need to be the case. Multiple-choice items, if they are carefully developed, can assess a wide variety of truly higher-order thinking skills. In our school, all teachers have taken part in a series of staff-development workshop sessions in which every teacher learned how to create *challenging* multiple-choice items that require students to display much more than memory." (At this point, I'd whip out a few examples of demanding multiple-choice items used in my own tests and then go through them, from stem to alternatives, showing Mr. and Mrs. Olmedo what I meant. If I *didn't* have any examples of such items from my tests, I'd think seriously about the legitimacy of Benito's parents' criticism.)

"So, although there's nothing wrong with Benito's acquiring more memorized information, and a small number of my multiple-choice items actually do test for such knowledge, the vast majority of the multiple-choice items that Benito will take in my class call for him to employ that fine mind of his.

"That's what you two want. That's what I want."

 Now, how would you respond to Mr. and Mrs. Olmedo's concerns?

they'll lose track of what's being sought. It would be far better to take a lengthy matching item with 24 premises and split it into three 8-premise matching items.

In addition, to cut down on the reading requirements of matching items, be sure to place the list of shorter words or phrases at the right. In other words, make the briefer entries the responses. In this way, when students are scanning the response lists for a matching entry, they'll not be obliged to read too many lengthy phrases or sentences.

Loading Up on Responses

A third guideline for the construction of matching items is to make sure there are at least a few extra responses. Otherwise, if the numbers of premises and responses are identical, the student who knows, say, 80 percent of the matches to the premises may be able to figure out the remaining matches by a process of elimination. A few extra responses reduce this likelihood substantially. Besides, these sorts of responses are inexpensive.

Ordering Responses

So you'll not provide unintended clues to students regarding which responses go with which premises, it's a good idea in matching items to order the responses in some sort of logical fashion—for example, alphabetical or chronological sequence. Notice that the names of the U.S. presidents are listed alphabetically in the illustrative matching item in Figure 3.

Describing the Task for Students

The fifth guideline for the construction of matching items suggests the directions for an item always make explicit the basis on which the matches are to be made and, at the same time, the number of times a response can be used. The more clearly students understand how they're supposed to respond, the more accurately they'll respond, and the more validly you'll be able to make score-based inferences about your students.

Formatting Items to Avoid Page Flipping

The final guideline for this item type suggests that you make sure all premises and responses for a matching item are on a single page. Not only does this eliminate the necessity for massive, potentially disruptive page turning by students, but it will also decrease the likelihood students will overlook correct answers merely because they were on the "other" page.

In review, matching items, if employed judiciously, can efficiently assess your students' knowledge. The need to employ homogeneous lists of related content tends to diminish the applicability of this type of selected-response item. Nonetheless, if you are dealing with content that can be addressed satisfactorily by such an approach, you'll find matching items a useful member of your repertoire of item types.

What Do Classroom Teachers Really Need to Know about Selected-Response Tests?

If you engage in any meaningful amount of assessment in your own classroom, it's quite likely you'll find that selected-response items will be useful. Selected-response items can typically be used to ascertain students' mastery of larger domains of content than is the case with constructed-response kinds of test items. Although it's often thought selected-response items must, of necessity, measure only lower-order kinds of cognitive capabilities, inventive teachers can create selected-response options to elicit very high levels of cognitive skills from students.

As for the four types of items treated in the chapter, you really need to understand enough about each kind to help you decide whether one or more of those item types would be useful for a classroom assessment task you have in mind. If you do decide to use binary-choice, multiple binary-choice, multiple-choice, or matching items in your own tests, then you'll find the sets of item-writing guidelines for each item type will come in handy.

but what does this have to do with
Teaching?

In this chapter, and the four following it, not only will you become acquainted with varied types of test items but you will learn how to construct them properly. Why, you might ask, does a classroom teacher need to possess such a resplendent repertoire of item types? After all, if a student knows that Abraham Lincoln was assassinated while attending a play, the student could satisfactorily display such knowledge in a variety of ways. A good old true-false item or a nifty multiple-choice item would surely do the necessary assessing.

Well, that's quite true. But what you need to recall, *from a teaching perspective,* is that students ought to master the skills and knowledge they're being taught so thoroughly they can display such mastery in a good many ways, not just one. A cognitive skill that's been learned *well* by a student will be a cognitive skill that can be displayed in all sorts of ways, whether via selected-response items or constructed-response items.

And this is why, when you *teach* children, you really need to be promoting their generalizable mastery of whatever's being taught. Consistent with such a push for generalizable mastery, you will typically want to employ varied assessment approaches. If you gravitate toward only one or two item types (that is, if you become "Multiple-Choice Molly" or "True-False Teddy"), then your students will tend to learn things only in a way that meshes with your favored item type.

Eons ago, when I was preparing to be a teacher, my teacher education professors advised me to employ different kinds of items "for variety's sake." Well, classroom teachers aren't putting on a fashion show. Variety for its own sake is psychometrically stupid. But variety of assessment approaches as a deliberate way of promoting and measuring students' *generalizable mastery* of what's been taught—this is psychometrically suave.

You will learn how to employ selected-response items as part of the formative-assessment process. Rather than complete reliance on paper-and-pencil versions of these items, you will see how to employ such items in a variety of less formal ways.

Yet, in honesty, even if you adhere to the chapter's five general item-writing commandments and the set of guidelines for a particular type of item, you'll still need practice in constructing selected-response items such as those considered here. As was suggested several times in the chapter, it is exceedingly helpful if you can find someone with measurement moxie, or at least an analytic mind, to review your test-development efforts. It's difficult in any realm to improve if you don't get feedback about the adequacy of your efforts. That's surely true with classroom assessment. Try to entice a colleague or supervisor to look over your selected-response items to see what needs to be strengthened. However, even without piles of practice, if you adhere to the item-writing guidelines provided in the chapter, your selected-response tests won't be all that shabby.

The most important thing to learn from this chapter is that there are four useful *selected*-response procedures for drawing valid inferences about your students' status. The more assessment options you have at your disposal, the more appropriately you'll be able to assess those student variables in which you're interested.

■ Chapter Summary

The chapter was initiated with a presentation of five item-writing commandments that pertain to both constructed-response and selected-response items. The five admonitions directed teachers to avoid unclear directions, ambiguous statements, unintentional clues, complex syntax, and hypersophisticated vocabulary.

In turn, then, consideration was given to the four most common kinds of selected-response test items—namely, binary-choice items, multiple binary-choice items, multiple-choice items, and matching items. For each of these four item types, after a brief description of the item type and its strengths and weaknesses, a set of item-writing guidelines was presented. 161, 163, 165. Each guideline was briefly discussed. Readers were encouraged to consider the four item types when deciding on an answer to the how-to-assess-it question.

Self-Check

For this chapter's self-check exercises, you'll be asked to evaluate a series of selected-response items. The items deal with content about assessment. Therefore, you should regard this chapter's self-check as an instructionally reinforcing experience. Specifically, you'll be asked to evaluate a series of selected-response items. In considering each item, think back to the five general item-writing commandments that apply to all the items you'll write. In addition, recall the specific item-writing guidelines associated with the type of item you're being asked to evaluate. To evaluate these *selected*-response items, you'll be asked to supply *constructed* (short-answer) responses. This requirement will either increase your item-writing flexibility or initiate a bit of assessment schizophrenia.

1. Here are two binary-choice items. In the lined spaces below the items, please evaluate the quality of the two items. Be sure to note any particular item-writing deficits you discern.

    Directions: For each of the following statements, indicate whether the statement is right (R) or wrong (W).

R or W ___ (1) The most important attribute of validity evidence is content coverage, whereas the most important attribute of reliability evidence is consistency of results.

R or W ___ (2) Absence-of-bias determinations are not best made only by judgmental procedures.

Your Evaluation: _____

_____

2. Now look over the following two multiple-choice items and make an evaluation of their intrinsic virtues. Evaluate them below.

Directions: Choose the best answer from the alternatives for each of the following items.

(1) Which of the following kinds of validity evidence, when analyzed carefully, is the most comprehensive descriptor for supportive information regarding the validity of test-based inferences?
 a. Content-related evidence of validity
 b. Predictive criterion-related evidence of validity
 c. Concurrent criterion-related evidence of validity
 d. Construct-related evidence of validity

(2) If you were a classroom teacher who wished to improve your students' higher-order thinking skills, in which of the following taxonomic domains should you be most interested?
 a. The cognitive domain
 b. The affective domain
 c. The psychomotor domain
 d. None of the domains given above

Your Evaluation: _____

_____

3. Here's a multiple binary-choice item for you to consider. See what you think of it and then evaluate it in the lined spaces below.

Directions: For *each* statement in the cluster of statements, indicate whether the statement is true (T) or false (F).

In an elaborate effort to ascertain the reliability of a new high-stakes test developed in their district, central-office administrators have calculated the following types of reliability evidence based on a tryout of the test with 2,400 students:

• Internal consistency $r = .82$
• Test-retest $r = .78$
• Standard error of measurement = 4.3

_____ (1) The three types of reliability evidence calculated by the central-office staff are essentially interchangeable.
_____ (2) The minor difference between the stability and internal consistency coefficients constitutes no cause for alarm.
_____ (3) The test-retest r should never be smaller than an internal consistency reliability coefficient.
_____ (4) The standard error of measurement is derived chiefly from the test's reliability indices.

Your Evaluation: _____

_____

4. Let's close out this practice scrutiny of selected-response items with a quick look at the following matching item that grabs its content from this very chapter. Evaluate it in the lined spaces below.

> **Directions:** Choose the best match between the item types in List X and the strengths/weaknesses in List Y.

List X	List Y
_____ (1) matching	a. Can efficiently cover much informational content
_____ (2) binary choice	
_____ (3) multiple binary choice	b. Can measure students' higher-order cognitive skills if properly constructed
_____ (4) multiple choice	c. Often encourages low-level recall of information
	d. Assesses what students can recognize rather than create

Your Evaluation: _____

_____

 # Pondertime

1. If you were asked to take part in a mini-debate about the respective virtues of selected-response items versus constructed-response items, what do you think would be your major points if you were supporting the use of selected-response test items?

2. During your lifetime you've probably completed all, or most, of the item types described in the chapter. Which type was your most favorite and which type was your least favorite? Why?

3. Why do you think that multiple-choice tests have been so widely used in nationally standardized norm-referenced achievement tests during the past half-century?

4. Do you think classroom teachers can become truly effective writers of selected-response test items? If so, how?

5. If you had to build your classroom assessments exclusively using selected-response test items, which item types would you prefer to use? Why?

Self-Check Key

1. The first of the two items violated the third item-writing guideline for binary-choice items: Don't include two concepts in one statement. A student may not be able to keep separate the part of the item dealing with validity evidence from the part that deals with reliability evidence. Incidentally, although the segment of the item dealing with reliability is accurate, the segment about validity is off the mark because not all validity evidence is content related.

   The second of the two items violates Guideline 2: Avoid negative statements. Because the descriptive phrase being used is *absence-of-bias*, the item already has a negative notion built into it. By the time the student reads the *not* and the *only*, full-bodied confusion is apt to have flowered.

2. The first multiple-choice item isn't all that bad. There don't seem to be any major deficits in the item (the correct answer to which is choice d).

   The second multiple-choice item isn't all that bad either, except choice d (a version of "none of the above") is pretty much of a throw-away choice. It would be better to have only three alternatives or to split the cognitive domain based on whether the cognitive behavior deals with the lowest level of cognition (knowledge) or higher than the lowest level of cognition (all other kinds of cognitive behavior). The correct answer, of course, is choice a.

3. Although it's surely possible to improve the phrasing of items such as these, in general, this multiple binary-choice item looks fairly acceptable in that it has violated neither the guidelines for multiple binary-choice items nor the guidelines for more conventional binary-choice items. The correct answers, by the way, are (1) F, (2) T, (3) F, and (4) T.

4. This is a genuinely cruddy item. There are almost more mistakes in the item than the words used to create it. First off, the directions are too sloppy and violate Guideline 5 for matching items by giving neither the basis for matching nor the number of times responses can be used. In addition, there are identical numbers of premises and responses, a violation of Guideline 3. The response list isn't homogeneous (Guideline 1) because it contains advantages *and* disadvantages. Guideline 2 also is violated because the shorter phrases are at the left rather than the right. About the only good thing you can say about the item is that it all fits on a single page. Regarding the correct answers—who knows?

◼ Additional Stuff

Downing, S. M., and Haladyna, T. M. (Eds.). (2006). *Handbook of test development.* Mahwah, NJ: Lawrence Erlbaum.

Frisbie, D. A. (1992). "The multiple true-false format: A status review," *Educational Measurement: Issues and Practice, 11,* no. 4 (Winter): 21–26.

Holler, E. W., Gareis, C. R., Martin, J., Clouser, A., and Miller, S. (2008). "Teacher-made assessments: Getting them right," *Principal Leadership, 9,* no. 1 (September): 60–64.

Nitko, A. J., and Brookhart, S. M. (2011). *Educational assessment of students* (6th ed.). Boston, MA: Pearson.

Waugh, C. K., and Gronlund, N. (2013). *Measurement and assessment in teaching* (10th ed.). Columbus, OH: Pearson.

◼ Cyber Stuff

- *WestEd* was established in 1995 by the consolidation of two western regional educational laboratories. WestEd is a nonprofit agency specializing in educational research, development, and service. One of this agency's chief activities deals with assessment, standards, and accountability. The website contains a substantial number of assessment-related resources and services (for example, professional development workshops and test-alignment analyses). A nicely produced, visually engaging flash video describes to website viewers what WestEd's chief functions are. www.wested.org

◼ Extended Applications

It is a truism that the more a person uses something, the more familiar with this something the person becomes. This self-evident notion surely applies to the assessment-related knowledge, skills, and concepts you have been reading about in the foregoing pages. Thus, to provide readers of *Classroom Assessment* with additional opportunities to apply the content contained in this text, this final section contains a variety of exercises intended to give readers an opportunity to use what they've been reading about.

In a sense, of course, the Self-Check exercises found at the close of this chapter provided an opportunity for readers to apply a chapter's content. Nonetheless, the more times you use a concept, skill, or a body of knowledge, the more likely it is that you will master this content so you can employ it in varied situations.

For each of the text, you will find an extended-application exercise calling for you to do some thinking about that chapter's content as it applies to a real-world situation. Each exercise is preceded by a brief introduction setting forth the reason that the upcoming extended-application exercise has been selected.

Because many of these exercises call on you to generate an original response rather than select a response from a set of options, it is difficult to supply an "answer key" for readers' unpredictable responses. So, what you'll find following all the exercises is One Possible Response—an indication of how I would have personally responded to the exercise if I had been asked to do so. Please don't regard my response as the only way to respond to an exercise. After all, by definition, this is only "one possible" response. Instead, please think of my response as a fairly flimsy form of feedback. You can certainly disagree with me, even emphatically, yet still profit from doing the exercise.

Remember, what is being provided in this section. The exercises deliberately intended to extend how you apply the content treated in *Classroom Assessment*. I hope you find these exercises useful in enhancing your understanding of what teachers need to know about classroom assessment.

■ Biggest-Bopper Badness

Introduction

In this chapter deals with birthing better selected-response test items—specifically, binary-choice items, multiple-choice items, multiple binary-choice items, and matching items. The chapter begins with a presentation of five item-writing commandments applicable to both selected-response and constructed-response items. Thereafter, item-writing guidelines are presented for the chapter's four item types. Clearly, the chapter's chief aim was to get you to be more skilled in whipping up winning selected-response items for your own tests.

One of the best ways to sharpen a teacher's item-writing skills is to give that teacher gobs of practice in ginning up items, then getting a seasoned item-writer to critique those items. But this sort of "you-build, someone-critiques" exercise is tough to pull off. So, this Extended Applications exercise is a sort of surrogate. Ideally, you would be given a set of selected-response test items, then asked to determine if there is anything wrong with each item—anything at all. But, candidly, that's a bit tricky because if someone looks long enough—and hard enough—flaws can be discerned in darn near anything or anyone.

But it seems reasonable to assume that the more familiar you are with violations of the five general item-writing commandments or the item-specific guidelines for selected-response items, the more able you'll be to spot such shortcomings in any items you personally construct. Thus, this exercise will present a set of 10 flawed selected-response items. It will be your job to identify that item's most salient flaw—that is, its *Biggest-Bopper Badness*.

Be sure to arrive at your own determination of an item's most serious deficit *before* you look at the per-item One Possible Response.

 Exercise Directions: Each of the 10 selected-response items in this exercise has one or more deficits. An item's most significant flaw will be based on either the five general item-writing commandments or the item-writing guidelines associated with particular types of items. Following each item (all items are boxed) is a space where you are to come up with the item's most serious weakness—that is, the item's biggest-bopper badness.

1. An "instructionally supportive" test need *not*:
   a. measure only a modest number of extraordinarily important curricular aims such as a student's ability to compose original narrative, persuasive, descriptive, or expository essays.
   b. be accompanied by succinct, clear, teacher-palatable descriptions of each skill or body of knowledge being assessed.
   c. provide reports of students' performances at levels of generality suitable for teachers to use in making day-to-day classroom instructional decisions.
   d. include a ratio of at least one constructed-response test item for every three selected-response items employed in the test.

This item's biggest-bopper badness? _____

_____

_____

One Possible Response: This multiple-choice item's chief problem is that its stem is too short and its alternatives are too wordy, especially in view of the stem's negative phrasing. Whenever possible, as stated in the first item-writing guideline for this kind of stem, the stem should consist of a self-contained question or problem.

2. True or False? When district administrators provide professional-development activities for teachers, it is necessary that they understand all relevant accountability-tested curricular aims.

This item's biggest-bopper badness? _____

_____

_____

One Possible Response: This item's most grievous shortcoming is that it violates the second item-writing commandment about the use of ambiguous statements. Because we can't tell whether the "they" refers to the teachers or to the district administrators, this will make a difference in whether the item's statement is true or false.

---

3. Correct or Incorrect? A plethora of empirical investigations demonstrate that classroom teachers' pedagogical predilections are manifestations of idiosyncratic proclivities rather than reliance on evidence-derivative postulates.

This item's biggest-bopper badness? _____

_____

_____

➤ **One Possible Response:** This item appears to have been created while the item-writer was using two thesauri and sitting on another one. Obviously, because the vocabulary employed is egregiously complex, the item is egregiously rotten.

---

4. On the line to the left of each measurement concept listed in Column A, please write the letter of the most relevant measurement procedure in Column B.

   Column A

   _____ 1. Bias Detection

   _____ 2. Item Difficulty

   _____ 3. Reliability

   _____ 4. Score Interpretation

   _____ 5. Validity

   Column B

   a. Determining DIF indices

   b. Evaluating curricular alignment

   c. Computing K-R formulae

   d. Deriving percentiles

   e. Calculating p values

This item's biggest-bopper badness? _____

_____

_____

➤ **One Possible Response:** This matching item has a pair of problems with it. For one thing, the entries in Column B are not alphabetized as they should have been.

To me, however, a more serious shortcoming is the item's failure to include more responses than premises. That's a violation of the third item-writing guideline for matching items, and I regard it as more serious than the absence of alphabetization in the response entries.

---

5. According to the terminology used in our state's recently enacted "Teacher Appraisal Law," a state-approved skill or body of knowledge that the state's students should learn is described as an:
   a. Academic Content Standard
   b. Curricular Aim
   c. Content Standard
   d. Goal

This item's biggest-bopper badness? _____

_____

_____

 One Possible Response: This multiple-choice item violates the general item-writing commandment that students shouldn't be given unintended clues that would help them stumble onto a correct answer. Because of the *an* that closes out the item's stem, only choice a, the one beginning with a vowel-commencing word, fits grammatically. This is the item's rather obvious deficit.

---

6. True or False? Although assessment of students' attitudes has recently become much more common, it is almost impossible to arrive at an accurate measurement-based inference about an *individual* student's attitudinal status.

This item's biggest-bopper badness? _____

_____

_____

One Possible Response: This item runs afoul of the third item-writing guideline for binary-choice items—the need to include only one concept in each item's statement. Here we see that only one of the two concepts is false. Attitudinal assessment of students is *not* becoming more prevalent, but it is essentially impossible to get an accurate fix on an individual student's attitudinal status. With half of this two-concept item true, and the other half false, what's a student's appropriate response? There isn't one!

---

7. When teachers attempt to arrive at a valid inference regarding a student's skill mastery, which of the following assessment approaches can usually contribute useful evidence to undergird that inference?

   a. A student's performance on selected-response test items

   b. A student's performance on constructed-response test items

   c. Systematic observations of a student's behavior in settings requiring skill usage

   d. All of the above

This item's biggest-bopper badness? _____

_____

_____

One Possible Response: This multiple-choice item employs the verboten "all-of-the-above" alternative, hence should immediately be sent scurrying to a nearby paper shredder.

---

8. True or False? To avoid constructing tests that fail to discriminate among test takers, items should never be created that fail to elicit a reasonable amount of incorrect responses from students.

This item's biggest-bopper badness? _____

_____

_____

One Possible Response: There are way too many negatives in this item. Or, if you prefer, the item's absence of worth is due chiefly to its failure to incorporate sufficient numbers of non-negative words.

9. Which of the following procedures has been most widely used by those who must set passing standards (that is, cut-scores) to distinguish among students who are classified as below basic, basic, proficient, and advanced on state-level accountability tests?

   a. Judgment of seasoned teachers and curricular specialists

   b. Reliance on "impact data"—that is, the proportion of students who would fail at various cut-scores

   c. Students' own judgments about appropriate cut-scores

   d. Iterative procedures in which preliminary judgments made by individuals are discussed, then made once more after standard-setters consider actual impact data indicating how many students (total and in subgroups) would be classified at various cut-scores

This item's biggest-bopper badness? _____

_____

_____

 One Possible Response: This item clearly violates the third guideline for the creation of multiple-choice items. The length of alternatives shouldn't indicate what the correct choice is apt to be. Savvy students will opt for choice d, the correct response, because it is much more detailed.

10. Which of the following indices shouldn't be employed to gauge an item's quality?

    a. An item-discrimination index

    b. An item's congruence with the curricular aim supposedly assessed by the item

    c. The item's p value

    d. An estimate of test-retest reliability

This item's biggest-bopper badness? _____

_____

_____

One Possible Response: This item's most serious weakness is that the stem is stated negatively, but that negativity is not highlighted. On the contrary, it is sneakily nestled as a contraction (*shouldn't*). Items with negative stems need to have those negatives emphasized by italics, boldface type, or similar alerting mechanisms.

■ Glossary

binary-choice item   A test item requiring a student to select one of two presented options.

computer-adaptive assessment   Computer-adjusted presentation of test items to students so that, depending on students' responses to previous items on the test, new items can be chosen that mesh most appropriately with a student's demonstrated level of achievement.

computer-based assessment   When computers are employed not only to present assessment tasks to students, but also when those students provide their responses to such items by computers.

distractors   The wrong-answer options used in a multiple-choice test item.

item alternatives   The answer options used in a multiple-choice test item.

matching item   A test-item format that requires students to associate items, as directed, from two different lists.

multiple binary-choice item   A binary-choice item that, along with other binary-choice items, is based on a single, usually somewhat lengthy set of stimulus material.

multiple-choice test item   A test item requiring a student to choose a response from three or more presented options.

premises   A matching item's listed elements (on the left) for which a match is sought from a list of responses (on the right).

responses   In general, a student's answer to an assessment task (or test item). For matching items, responses are the listed elements (on the right) from which matching selections to premises (on the left) are made.

stem   The initial part of a multiple-choice item—that is, the stimulus to which one of the multiple-choice options serves as the best response.

true-false item   A common binary-choice item in which a student's two options regarding the accuracy of a presented statement are *true* or *false*.

Constructed-Response Tests

You're going to learn about constructed-response tests in this chapter. To be really truthful, you're going to learn about only two kinds of *paper-and-pencil* constructed-response items—namely, short-answer items and essay items (including students' written compositions). Although I suspect you already know that "you can't tell a book by its cover," now you've discovered that a chapter's title doesn't always describe its contents accurately. Fortunately, as far as I know, there are no state or federal "truth-in-chapter-entitling" laws.

You might be wondering why your ordinarily honest, never-fib author has descended to this act of blatant mislabeling. Actually, it's just to keep your reading chores more manageable. You already know that student-constructed responses can be obtained from a wide variety of item types. In this chapter, we'll be looking at two rather traditional forms of constructed-response items, both of them paper-and-pencil in nature. The focus will be on *performance tests,* such as those that arise when we ask students to make oral presentations or supply comprehensive demonstrations of complex skills in class. We'll be dealing with portfolio assessment and how portfolios are used for assessment purposes.

From Chapter 7 of *Classroom Assessment: What Teachers Need to Know,* Seventh Edition. W. James Popham.

The major payoff of all constructed-response items is they elicit student responses more closely approximating the kinds of behavior students must display in real life. After students leave school, for example, the demands of daily living almost never require them to choose responses from four nicely arranged alternatives. And when was the last time, in normal conversation, you were obliged to render a flock of true-false judgments about a set of statements? Yet, you may well be asked to make a brief oral presentation to your fellow teachers or to a parent group, or you may be asked to write a brief report for the school newspaper about your students' field trip to City Hall. Constructed-response tasks unquestionably coincide more closely with nonacademic tasks than do selected-response tasks.

As a practical matter, if the nature of a selected-response task is sufficiently close to what might be garnered from a constructed-response item, then you may wish to consider a selected-response assessment tactic to be a reasonable surrogate for a constructed-response assessment tactic. Selected-response tests are clearly much more efficient to score. And, because almost all of the teachers I know are busy folks, time-saving procedures are not to be scoffed at. Yet, there will be situations when you'll want to make inferences about your students' status when selected-response tests just won't fill the bill. For instance, if you wish to know what kind of a cursive writer Jamal is, then you'll have to let Jamal write cursively. A true-false test about *i* dotting and *t* crossing just doesn't cut it.

■ Short-Answer Items

The first kind of constructed-response item we'll look at is the *short-answer item*. Short-answer items call for students to supply a word, a phrase, or a sentence in response to either a direct question or an incomplete statement. If an item asks students to come up with a fairly lengthy response, it would be considered an essay item, not a short-answer item. If the item asks students to supply only a single word, then it's a *really* short-answer item.

Short-answer items are suitable for assessing relatively simple kinds of learning outcomes such as those focused on students' acquisition of knowledge. If crafted carefully, however, short-answer items can measure substantially more challenging kinds of learning outcomes. The major advantage of short-answer items is that students need to *produce* a correct answer, not merely recognize it from a set of selected-response options. The level of partial knowledge that might allow a student to respond correctly to a choose-the-best-response item won't be sufficient when the student is required to produce a correct answer to a short-answer item.

The major drawback with short-answer items, as is true with all constructed-response items, is that students' responses are difficult to score. The longer the responses sought, the tougher it is to score them accurately. And inaccurate scoring, leads to reduced reliability—which, in turn, reduces the validity of the test-based inferences we make about students—which, in turn, reduces the quality of the decisions we base on those inferences. Educational measurement is much like the rest of life—it's simply loaded with trade-offs. When classroom teachers choose constructed-response tests, they must be willing to trade some scoring accuracy (the kind of accuracy that comes with selected-response approaches) for greater congruence between constructed-response assessment strategies and the kinds of student behaviors about which inferences are to be made.

Here, you will find five straightforward item-writing guidelines for short-answer items. Please look them over, and then I'll briefly amplify each guideline and describe how it works.

Item-Writing Guidelines for Short-Answer Items

1. Usually employ direct questions rather than incomplete statements, particularly for young students.
2. Structure the item so that a response should be concise.
3. Place blanks in the margin for direct questions or near the end of incomplete statements.
4. For incomplete statements, use only one or, at most, two blanks.
5. Make sure blanks for all items are equal in length.

Using Direct Questions Rather than Incomplete Statements

For young children, the direct question is a far more familiar format than the incomplete statement. Accordingly, such students will be less confused if direct questions are employed. Another reason short-answer items should employ a direct-question format is that the use of direct questions typically forces the item writer to phrase the item so less ambiguity is present. With incomplete-statement formats, there's often too much temptation simply to delete words or phrases from statements the teacher finds in textbooks. To make sure there isn't more than one correct answer to a short-answer item, it is often helpful if the item writer first decides on the correct answer and then builds a question or incomplete statement designed to elicit a *unique* correct response from knowledgeable students.

Nurturing Concise Responses

Responses to short-answer items, as might be inferred from what they're called, should be *short*. Thus, no matter whether you're eliciting responses that are words, symbols, phrases, or numbers, try to structure the item so a brief response is clearly sought. Suppose you conjured up an incomplete statement item such as this: "An animal that walks on two feet is _____." There are all sorts of answers a student might legitimately make to such an item. Moreover, some of those responses could be fairly lengthy. Now note how a slight restructuring of the item constrains the student: "An animal that walks on two feet is technically classified as _____." By the addition of the phrase "technically classified as," the item writer has restricted the appropriate responses to only one—namely, "biped." If your short-answer items are trying to elicit students' phrases or sentences, you may wish to place word limits on each, or at least indicate in the test's directions that only a *short* one-sentence response is allowable for each item.

Always try to put yourself, mentally, inside the heads of your students and try to anticipate how they are apt to interpret an item. What this second guideline suggests is that you massage an item until it truly lives up to its name—that is, until it becomes a *bona fide* short-answer item.

Positioning Blanks

If you're using direct questions in your short-answer items, place the students' response areas for all items near the right-hand margin of the page, immediately after the item's questions. By doing so, you'll have all of a student's responses nicely lined up for scoring. If you're using incomplete statements, try to place the blank near the end of the statement, not near its beginning. A blank positioned too early in a sentence tends to perplex the students. For instance, notice how this too-early blank can lead to confusion: "The _____ is the governmental body which, based on the United States Constitution, must ratify all U.S. treaties with foreign nations." It would be better to use a direct question or to phrase the item as follows: "The governmental body which, based on the United States Constitution, must ratify all U.S. treaties with foreign nations is the _____."

Limiting Blanks

For incomplete-statement types of short-answer items, you should use only one or two blanks. Any more blanks and the item is labeled a "swiss-cheese item," or an item with holes galore. Here's a swiss-cheese item to illustrate the confusion that a profusion of blanks can make in what is otherwise a decent short-answer item: "After a series of major conflicts with natural disasters, in the year _____, the explorers _____ and _____, accompanied by their _____, discovered _____." The student who could supply correct answers to such a flawed short-answer item should also be regarded as a truly successful explorer.

Inducing Linear Equality

Too often in short-answer items, a beginning item writer will give away the answer by varying the length of the answer blanks so that short lines are used when short answers are correct and long lines are used when lengthier answers are correct. This practice tosses unintended clues to students and so should be avoided. In the interest of linear egalitarianism, not to mention decent item writing, keep all blanks for short-answer items equal in length. Be sure, however, the length of the answer spaces provided is sufficient for students' responses—in other words, not so skimpy that students have to cram in their answers in an illegible fashion.

In review, short-answer items are the most simple form of constructed-response items, but they can help teachers measure important skills and knowledge. Because such items seek students' constructed rather than selected responses, they can be employed to tap some genuinely higher-order skills. Although students' responses to short-answer items are more difficult to score than are their answers to selected-response items, the scoring of such items isn't impossible. That's because short-answer items, by definition, should elicit only *short* answers.

■ Essay Items: Development

The essay item is surely the most commonly used form of constructed-response assessment item. Anytime teachers ask their students to churn out a paragraph or two on what the students know about Topic X or to compose an original composition describing their "Favorite Day," an *essay item* is being used. Essay items are particularly useful in gauging a student's ability to synthesize, evaluate, and compose. Such items have a wide variety of applications in most teachers' classrooms.

A special form of the essay item is the *writing sample*—when teachers ask students to generate a written composition in an attempt to measure students' composition skills. Because the procedures employed to construct items for such writing samples and, thereafter, for scoring students' compositions, are so similar to the procedures employed to create and score responses to any kind of essay item, we'll treat writing samples and other kinds of essay items all at one time in this chapter. You'll find it helpful, however, to remember that the requirement to have students generate a writing sample is, in reality, a widely used type of *performance test*.

For assessing certain kinds of complex learning outcomes, the essay item is the hands-down winner. It clearly triumphs when you're trying to see how well students can create original compositions. Yet, there are a fair number of drawbacks associated with essay items, and if you're going to consider using essay items in your own classroom, you ought to know the weaknesses as well as the strengths of this item type.

One difficulty with essay items is they're more difficult to write—at least write properly—than is generally thought. I must confess that as a first-year high school teacher, I sometimes conjured up essay items while walking to school and then slapped them up on the chalkboard so that I created almost instant essay exams. At the time, I thought my essay items were pretty good. Such is the pride of youth and the product of ignorance. I'm glad I have no record of those items. In retrospect, I assume they were pretty putrid. I now know that generating a really good essay item is a tough task—a task not accomplishable while strolling to school. You'll see this is true from the item-writing rules to be presented shortly. It takes time to create a solid essay item. You'll need to find time to construct suitable essay items for your own classroom assessments.

The most serious problem with essay items, however, is the difficulty teachers have in reliably scoring students' responses. Let's say you use a six-item essay test to measure your students' ability to solve certain kinds of problems in social studies. Suppose that, by some stroke of measurement magic, all your students'

Decision Time

Forests or Trees?

Allison Allen is a brand-new English teacher assigned to work with seventh-grade and eighth-grade students at Dubois Junior High School. Allison has taken part in a state-sponsored summer workshop that emphasizes "writing as a process." Coupled with what she learned while completing her teacher education program, Allison is confident that she can effectively employ techniques such as brainstorming, outlining, early drafts, peer critiquing, and multiple revisions. She assumes that her students will acquire not only competence in their composition capabilities but also confidence about their possession of those capabilities. What Allison's preparation failed to address, however, was how to grade her students' compositions.

Two experienced English teachers at Dubois Junior High have gone out of their way to help Allison get through her first year as a teacher. Mrs. Miller and Ms. Stovall have both been quite helpful during the early weeks of the school year. However, when Allison asked them one day during lunch how she should judge the quality of her students' compositions, two decisively different messages were given.

Ms. Stovall strongly endorsed *holistic* grading of compositions—that is, a general appraisal of each composition as a whole. Although Ms. Stovall bases her holistic grading scheme on a set of explicit criteria, she believes a single "gestalt" grade should be given so that "one's vision of the forest is not obscured by tree-counting."

Arguing with equal vigor, Mrs. Miller urged Allison to adopt *analytic* appraisals of her students' compositions. "By supplying your students with a criterion-by-criterion judgment of their work," she contended, "each student will be able to know precisely what's good and what isn't." (It was evident during the fairly heated interchanges that Mrs. Miller and Ms. Stovall had disagreed about this topic in the past.) Mrs. Miller concluded her remarks by saying, "Forget about that forest-and-trees metaphor, Allison. What we're talking about here is clarity!"

 If you were Allison, how would you decide to judge the quality of your students' compositions?

responses could be transformed into typed manuscript form so you could not tell which response came from which student. Let's say you were asked to score the complete set of responses *twice*. What do you think is the likelihood your two sets of scores would be consistent? Well, experience suggests that most teachers aren't able to produce very consistent results when they score students' essay responses. The challenge in this instance, of course, is to *increase* the reliability of your scoring efforts so you're not distorting the validity of the score-based inferences you want to make on the basis of your students' responses.

Creating Essay Items

Because the scoring of essay responses (and students' compositions) is such an important topic, you'll soon be getting a set of guidelines on how to score responses to such items. The more complex the nature of students' constructed responses become the more attention you'll need to lavish on scoring. You can't score responses to items that you haven't written, however, so let's look at the five guidelines for the construction of essay items.

Item-Writing Guidelines for Essay Items

1. Convey to students a clear idea regarding the extensiveness of the response desired.
2. Construct items so the student's task is explicitly described.
3. Provide students with the approximate time to be expended on each item as well as each item's value.
4. Do not employ optional items.
5. Precursively judge an item's quality by composing, mentally or in writing, a possible response.

Communicating the Desired Extensiveness of Students' Responses

It is sometimes thought that if teachers decide to use essay items, students have total freedom of response. On the contrary, teachers can structure essay items so students produce (1) barely more than they would for a short-answer item or, in contrast, (2) extremely lengthy responses. The two types of essay items reflecting this distinction in the desired extensiveness of students' responses are described as restricted-response items and extended-response items.

A *restricted-response item* decisively limits the form and content of students' responses. For example, a restricted-response item in a health education class might ask students the following: "Describe the three most common ways HIV, the AIDS virus, is transmitted. Take no more than 25 words to describe each method of transmission." In this example, the number of HIV transmission methods was specified, as was the maximum length for each transmission method's description.

In contrast, an *extended-response item* provides students with far more latitude in responding. Here's an example of an extended-response item from a social studies class: "Identify the chief factors contributing to the U.S. government's financial deficit during the past two decades. Having identified those factors, decide which factors, if any, have been explicitly addressed by the U.S. legislative and/or executive branches of government in the last five years. Finally, critically evaluate the likelihood that any currently proposed remedies will bring about significant reductions in the U.S. national debt." A decent response to such an extended-response item not only should get high marks from the teacher but might also be the springboard for a successful career in politics.

One technique teachers commonly use to limit students' responses is to provide a certain amount of space on the test paper or in their students' response booklets. For instance, the teacher might direct students to "Use no more than two sheets (both sides) in your blue books to respond to each test item." Although the space-limiting ploy is an easy one to implement, it really disadvantages students who write in a large-letter, scrawling fashion. Whereas such large-letter students may only be able to cram a few paragraphs onto a page, those students who write in a small, scrunched-up style may be able to produce a short novella in the same space.

This first guideline asks you to think carefully about whether the inference at issue that you wish to make about your students is best serviced by students' responses to (1) more essay items requiring shorter responses or (2) fewer essay items requiring extensive responses. Having made that decision, then be sure to convey to your students a clear picture of the degree of extensiveness you're looking for in their responses.

Describing Students' Tasks

Students will find it difficult to construct responses to tasks if they don't understand what the tasks are. Moreover, students' responses to badly understood tasks are almost certain to yield flawed inferences by teachers. The most important part of an essay item is, without question, the description of the *assessment task*. It is the assessment task students respond to when they generate essays. Clearly, then, poorly described assessment tasks will yield many off-target responses that, had the student truly understood what was being sought, might have been more appropriate.

There are numerous labels used to represent the assessment task in an essay item. Sometimes it's simply called the *task,* the *charge,* or perhaps the *assignment.* In essay items that are aimed at eliciting student compositions, the assessment task is often referred to as a *prompt.* No matter how the assessment task is labeled, if you're a teacher who is using essay items, you must make sure the nature of the task is really set forth clearly for your students. Put yourself, at least hypothetically, in the student's seat and see if, with the level of knowledge possessed by most of your students, the nature of the assessment task is really apt to be understood.

To illustrate, if you wrote the following essay item, there's little doubt your students' assessment task would have been badly described: "In 500 words or less, discuss democracy in Latin America." In contrast, notice in the following item how much more clearly the assessment task is set forth: "Describe how the checks and balances provisions in the U.S. Constitution were believed by the Constitution's framers to be a powerful means to preserve democracy (300–500 words)."

Providing Time-Limit and Item-Value Guidance

When teachers create an examination consisting of essay items, they often have an idea regarding which items will take more of the students' time. But students don't know what's in the teacher's head. As a consequence, some students will lavish loads of attention on items the teacher thought warranted only modest effort, yet devote little time to items the teacher thought deserved substantial attention. Similarly, sometimes teachers will want to weight certain items more heavily than others. Again, if students are unaware of which items count most, they may toss reams of rhetoric at the low-value items and have insufficient time to give more than a trifling response to the high-value items.

To avoid these problems, there's quite a straightforward solution—namely, letting students in on the secret. If there are any differences among items in point value or in the time students should spend on them, simply provide this information in the directions or, perhaps parenthetically, at the beginning or end of each item. Students will appreciate such clarifications of your expectations.

Avoiding Optionality

It's fairly common practice among teachers who use essay examinations to provide students with a certain number of items and then let each student choose to answer fewer than the number of items presented. For example, the teacher might allow students to "choose any three of the five essay items presented." Students, of course, really enjoy such an assessment procedure because they can respond to items for which they're well prepared and avoid those items for which they're inadequately prepared. Yet, other than inducing student glee, this optional-items classroom assessment scheme has little going for it.

When students select different items from a menu of possible items, they are actually responding to different examinations. As a consequence, it is impossible to judge their performances on some kind of common scale. Remember, as a classroom teacher you'll be trying to make better educational decisions about your students by relying on test-based inferences regarding those students. It's tough enough to make a decent test-based interpretation when you have only one test to consider. It's infinitely more difficult to make such interpretations when you are faced with a medley of different tests because you allow your students to engage in a mix-and-match measurement procedure.

In most cases, teachers rely on an optional-items procedure with essay items when they're uncertain about the importance of the content measured by their examinations' items. Such uncertainty gives rise to the use of optional items because the teacher is not clearheaded about the inferences for which the examination's results will be used. If you spell out those inferences crisply, prior to the examination, you will usually find you'll have no need for optional item selection in your essay examinations.

Previewing Students' Responses

After you've constructed an essay item for one of your classroom assessments, there's a quick way to get a preliminary fix on whether the item is a winner or loser. Simply toss yourself, psychologically, into the head of one of your typical students and then anticipate how such a student would respond to the item. If you have time, and are inclined to do so, you could try writing a response that the student might produce to the item. More often than not, because you'll be too busy to conjure up such fictitious responses in written form, you might try to compose a mental response to the item on behalf of the typical student you've selected. An early mental run-through of how a student might respond to an item can often help you identify deficits in the item because, when you put yourself, even hypothetically, on the other side of the teacher's desk, you'll sometimes discover shortcomings in items you otherwise wouldn't have identified. Too many times I've seen teachers give birth to a set of essay questions, send them into battle on examination day, and only then discover that one or more of the items suffers severe genetic deficits. Mental previewing of likely student responses can help you detect such flaws while there's still time for repairs.

In review, we've looked at five guidelines for creating essay items. If you'll remember that all of these charming little collections of item-specific recommendations should be adhered to *in addition to* the five general item-writing commandments set forth in , you'll probably be able to come up with a pretty fair set of essay items. Then, perish the thought, you'll have to score your students' responses to those items. That's what we'll be looking at next.

Essay Items: Scoring Students' Responses

By looking at how to evaluate students' responses to performance assessments and how to judge students' portfolios, you'll be learning much more about how to evaluate your students' performances on constructed-response assessments. In this chapter we'll be looking only at how to score students' responses to essay items (including tests of students' composition skills). You'll find that many of the suggestions for scoring students' constructed responses you will encounter will also be applicable when you're trying to judge your students' essay responses. But just to keep matters simple, let's look now at recommendations for scoring responses to essay items.

Guidelines for Scoring Responses to Essay Items

1. Score responses holistically and/or analytically.
2. Prepare a tentative scoring key in advance of judging students' responses.
3. Make decisions regarding the importance of the mechanics of writing prior to scoring.
4. Score all responses to one item before scoring responses to the next item.
5. Insofar as possible, evaluate responses anonymously.

Choosing an Analytic and/or Holistic Scoring Approach

During the past decade or two, the measurement of students' composition skills by having students generate actual writing samples has become widespread. As a consequence of all this attention to students' compositions, educators have become far more skilled regarding how to evaluate students' written compositions. Fortunately, classroom teachers can use many of the procedures that have been identified and refined while educators scored thousands of students' compositions during statewide assessment extravaganzas.

A fair number of the lessons learned about scoring students' writing samples apply quite nicely to the scoring of responses to any kind of essay item. One of the most important of the scoring insights picked up from this large-scale scoring of students' compositions is that almost any type of student-constructed response can be scored either *holistically* or *analytically*. That's why the first of the five guidelines suggests you make an early-on decision whether you're going to score your students' responses to essay items using a holistic approach or an analytic approach or, perhaps, using a combination of the two scoring approaches. Let's look at how each of these two scoring strategies works.

A *holistic scoring* strategy, as its name suggests, focuses on the essay response (or written composition) as a whole. At one extreme of scoring rigor, the teacher can, in a fairly unsystematic manner, supply a "general impression" overall grade to each student's response. Or, in a more systematic fashion, the teacher can isolate, in advance of scoring, those evaluative criteria that should be attended to in order to arrive at a single, overall score per essay. Generally, a score range of four to six points is used to evaluate each student's response. (Some scoring schemes have a few more points, some a few less.) A teacher, then, after considering whatever factors should be attended to in a given item, will give a score to each student's response. Here is a set of evaluative criteria teachers might use in holistically scoring a student's written composition.

Illustrative Evaluative Criteria to Be Considered When Scoring Students' Essay Responses Holistically

For scoring a composition intended to reflect students' writing prowess:

- Organization
- Communicative Clarity
- Adaptation to Audience
- Word Choice
- Mechanics (spelling, capitalization, punctuation)

And now, here are four evaluative factors a speech teacher might employ in holistically scoring a response to an essay item used in a debate class.

Potential Evaluative Criteria to Be Used When Scoring Students' Essay Responses in a Debate Class

For scoring a response to an essay item dealing with rebuttal preparation:

- Anticipation of Opponent's Positive Points
- Support for One's Own Points Attacked by Opponents
- Isolation of Suitably Compelling Examples
- Preparation of a "Spontaneous" Conclusion

When teachers score students' responses holistically, they do *not* dole out points-per-criterion for a student's response. Rather, the teacher keeps in mind evaluative criteria such as those set forth in the previous two boxes. The speech teacher, for instance, while looking at the student's essay response to a question regarding how someone should engage in effective rebuttal preparation, will not necessarily penalize a student who overlooks one of the four evaluative criteria. The response as a whole may lack one thing, yet otherwise represent a really wonderful response. Evaluative criteria such as those illustrated here simply dance around in the teacher's head when the teacher scores students' essay responses holistically.

In contrast, an *analytic scoring* scheme strives to be a fine-grained, specific point-allocation approach. Suppose, for example, instead of using a holistic method of scoring students' compositions, a teacher chose to employ an analytic method of scoring students' compositions. Under those circumstances, a scoring guide such as the example in Figure 1 might be used by the teacher. Note, for each evaluative criterion in the guide, the teacher must award 0, 1, or 2 points. The lowest overall score for a student's composition, therefore, would be 0, whereas the highest overall score for a student's composition would be 10 (that is, 2 points times 5 criteria).

The advantage of an analytic scoring system is it can help you identify the specific strengths and weaknesses of your students' performances and, therefore, you can communicate such diagnoses to students in a pinpointed fashion. The downside of analytic scoring is that a teacher sometimes becomes so attentive to the subpoints in a scoring system that, almost literally, the forest (overall quality) can't be seen because of a focus on individual trees (the separate scoring criteria). In less metaphoric language, the teacher will miss the communication of the student's response "as a whole" because of excessive attention to a host of individual evaluative criteria.

One middle-of-the-road scoring approach can be seen when teachers initially grade all students' responses holistically and then return for an analytic scoring of only those responses that were judged, overall, to be unsatisfactory. After the analytic scoring of the unsatisfactory responses, the teacher then relays more fine-grained diagnostic information to those students whose unsatisfactory responses

figure 1 ■ An Illustrative Guide for Analytically Scoring a Student's Written Composition

Factor	Unacceptable (0 points)	Satisfactory (1 point)	Outstanding (2 points)
1. Organization		✓	
2. Communicative Clarity			✓
3. Audience Adaptation		✓	
4. Word Choice			✓
5. Mechanics		✓	

Total Score = 7

were analytically scored. The idea underlying this sort of hybrid approach is that the students who are most in need of fine-grained feedback are those who, on the basis of the holistic evaluation, are performing less well.

This initial guideline for scoring students' essay responses applies to the scoring of responses to all kinds of essay items. As always, your decision about whether to opt for holistic or analytic scoring should flow directly from your intended use of the test results. Putting it another way, your choice of scoring approach will depend on the educational decision linked to the test's results. (Is this beginning to sound somewhat familiar?)

Devising a Tentative Scoring Key

No matter what sort of approach you opt for in scoring your students' essay responses, you'll find it will be useful to develop a tentative scoring key for responses to each item *in advance* of actually scoring students' responses. Such tentative scoring schemes are almost certain to be revised on the basis of your scoring of actual student papers, but that's to be anticipated. If you wait until you commence scoring your students' essay responses, there's too much likelihood you'll be unduly influenced by the responses of the first few students whose papers you grade.

If those papers are atypical, the resultant scoring scheme is apt to be unsound. It is far better to think through, at least tentatively, what you really hope students will supply in their responses and then modify the scoring key if unanticipated responses from students suggest that alterations are requisite.

If you don't have a tentative scoring key in place, there's a great likelihood you'll be influenced by such factors as a student's vocabulary or writing style even though, in reality, such variables may be of little importance to you. Advance exploration of the evaluative criteria you intend to employ, either holistically or analytically, is a winning idea when scoring responses to essay items.

Let's take a look at what a tentative scoring key might look like if employed by a teacher in a U.S. History course. The skill being promoted by the teacher is a genuinely high-level one that's reflected in the following curricular aim:

> When presented with a description of a current real-world problem in the United States, the student will be able to (1) cite one or more significant events in American history that are particularly relevant to the presented problem's solution, (2) defend the relevance of the cited events, (3) propose a solution to the presented problem, and (4) use historical parallels from the cited events to support the proposed solution.

As I indicated, this is no rinky-dink low-level cognitive skill. It's way, way up there in its cognitive demands on students. Now, let's suppose our hypothetical history teacher routinely monitors students' progress related to this skill by having students respond to similar problems either orally or in writing. The teacher presents a real-world problem. The students, aloud or in an essay, try to come up with a suitable four-part response.

In Figure 2 you'll see an illustrative tentative scoring key for evaluating students' oral or written responses to constructed-response items measuring their mastery of this curricular aim. As you can discern, in this tentative scoring key, greater weight has been given to the fourth subtask—namely, the student's provision of historical parallels to support the student's proposed solution to the real-world problem the teacher proposed. Much less significance was given to the first subtask of citing pertinent historical events. This, remember, is a *tentative* scoring key. Perhaps when the history teacher begins scoring students' responses, it will turn out that the first subtask is far more formidable than the teacher originally thought, and the fourth subtask seems to be handled without much difficulty by students. At that point, based on the way students are actually responding, this hypothetical history teacher surely ought to do a bit of score-point juggling in the tentative scoring key before applying it in final form to the appraisal of students' responses.

Deciding Early about the Importance of Mechanics

Few things influence scorers of students' essay responses as much as the mechanics of writing employed in the response. If the student displays subpar spelling, chaotic

figure 2 ■ An Illustrative Tentative Scoring Key for a High-Level Cognitive Skill in History

Students' Subtasks	Tentative Point Allocation		
	Weak Response	*Acceptable Response*	*Strong Response*
1. Citation of Pertinent Historical Events	0 pts.	5 pts.	10 pts.
2. Defense of the Cited Historical Events	0 pts.	10 pts.	20 pts.
3. Proposed Solution to the Presented Problem	0 pts.	10 pts.	20 pts.
4. Historical Support of Proposed Solution	0 pts.	20 pts.	40 pts.

Total Points Possible = <u>90 pts.</u>

capitalization, and poor punctuation, it's pretty tough for a scorer of the student's response to avoid being influenced adversely. In some instances, of course, mechanics of writing certainly do play a meaningful role in scoring students' performances. For instance, suppose you're scoring students' written responses to a task of writing an application letter for a position as a reporter for a local newspaper. In such an instance, it is clear that mechanics of writing would be pretty important when judging the students' responses. But in a chemistry class, perhaps the teacher cares less about such factors when scoring students' essay responses to a problem-solving task. The third guideline simply suggests you make up your mind about this issue early in the process so, if mechanics aren't all that important to you, you don't let your students' writing mechanics subconsciously influence the way you score their responses.

Scoring One Item at a Time

If you're using an essay examination with more than one item, be sure to score all your students' responses to one item, then score all their responses to the next item, and so on. Do *not* score all responses of a given student and then go on to the next student's paper. There's too much danger a student's responses to early items will unduly influence your scoring of their responses to later items. If you score all responses to item number 1 and then move on to the responses to item number 2, you can eliminate this tendency. In addition, the scoring will actually go a bit quicker because you won't need to shift evaluative criteria between items. Adhering to this fourth guideline will invariably lead to more

Parent Talk

The mother of one of your students, Jill Jenkins, was elected to your district's school board two years ago. Accordingly, anytime Mrs. Jenkins wants to discuss Jill's education, you are understandably "all ears."

Mrs. Jenkins recently stopped by your classroom to say that three of her fellow board members have been complaining there are too many essay tests being given in the district. The three board members contend that such tests, because they must be scored "subjectively," are neither reliable nor valid.

Because many of the tests you give Jill and her classmates are essay tests, Mrs. Jenkins asks you if the three board members are correct.

 If I were you, here's how I'd respond to Jill's mom. (Oh yes, because Mrs. Jenkins is a board member, I'd simply ooze politeness and professionalism while I responded.)

"Thanks for giving me an opportunity to comment on this issue, Mrs. Jenkins. As you've already guessed, I truly believe in the importance of constructed-response examinations such as essay tests. The real virtue of essay tests is that they call for students to *create* their responses, not merely *recognize* correct answers, as students must with other types of tests such as multiple-choice exams.

"The three school board members are correct when they say it is more difficult to score constructed-response items consistently than it is to score selected-response items consistently. And that's a shortcoming of essay tests. But it's a shortcoming that's more than compensated for by the far greater *authenticity* of the tasks presented to students in almost all constructed-response tests. When Jill writes essays during my major exams, this is much closer to what she'll be doing in later life than choosing the best answer from four options. In real life, people aren't given four-choice options. Rather, they're required to generate a response reflecting their views. Essay tests give Jill and her classmates a chance to do just that.

"Now, let's talk briefly about consistency and validity. Actually, Mrs. Jenkins, it is important for tests to be scored consistently. We refer to the consistency with which a test is scored as its *reliability*. And if a test isn't reliable, then the interpretations about students we make based on test scores aren't likely to be valid. It's a technical point, Mrs. Jenkins, but it isn't a *test* that's valid or invalid; it's a score-based inference about students that may or may not be valid. As your board colleagues pointed out, some essay tests are not scored very reliably. But essay tests *can* be scored reliably and they *can* yield valid inferences about students.

"I hope my reactions have been helpful. I'll be happy to show you some of the actual essay exams I've used with Jill's class. And I'm sure the District Superintendent, Dr. Stanley, can supply you with additional information."

 Now, how would you respond to Mrs. Jenkins?

consistent scoring and hence to more accurate response-based inferences about your students. There'll be more paper shuffling than you might prefer, but the increased accuracy of your scoring will be worth it. (Besides, you'll be getting a smidge of psychomotor exercise.)

Striving for Anonymity

Because I've been a teacher, I know all too well how quickly teachers can identify their students' writing styles, particularly those students who have especially distinctive styles, such as the "scrawlers," the "petite letter-size crew," and those who dot their *i*s with half-moons or cross their *t*s with lightning bolts. Yet, insofar as you can, try not to know whose responses you're scoring. One simple way to help in that effort is to ask students to write their names on the reverse side of the last sheet of the examination in the response booklet. Try not to peek at the students' names until you've scored all of the exams.

I used such an approach for three decades of scoring graduate students' essay examinations at UCLA. It worked fairly well. Sometimes I was really surprised because students who had appeared to be knowledgeable during class discussions displayed just the opposite on the exams, while several Silent Sarahs and Quiet Quentins came up with really solid exam performances. I'm sure if I had known whose papers I had been grading, I would have been improperly influenced by my classroom-based perceptions of different students' abilities. I am not suggesting that you shouldn't use students' classroom discussions as part of your evaluation system. Rather, I'm advising you that classroom-based perceptions of students can sometimes cloud your scoring of essay responses. This is one strong reason for you to strive for anonymous scoring.

In review, we've considered five guidelines for scoring students' responses to essay examinations. If your classroom assessment procedures involve any essay items, you'll find these five practical guidelines will go a long way in helping you come up with consistent scores for your students' responses. And consistency is something that makes psychometricians mildly euphoric.

What Do Classroom Teachers Really Need to Know about Constructed-Response Tests?

At the close of a chapter dealing largely with the nuts and bolts of creating and scoring written constructed-response tests, you probably expect to be told you really need to internalize all those nifty little guidelines so, when you spin out your

but what does this have to do with
Teaching?

A teacher wants students to learn the stuff that's being taught—to learn it well. And one of the best ways to see if students have really acquired a cognitive skill or have truly soaked up scads of knowledge is to have them display what they've learned by *generating* answers to constructed-response tests. A student who has learned something well enough to toss it out from scratch, rather than choosing from presented options, clearly has learned it pretty darn well.

But, as this chapter points out, the creation and scoring of really first-rate constructed-response items, especially anything beyond short-answer items, requires serious effort from a teacher. And if constructed-response items aren't really first-rate, then they are not likely to help a teacher arrive at valid interpretations about students' correct knowledge and/or skills. Decent constructed-response tests take time to create and to score. And that's where this kind of classroom assessment runs smack into a teacher's instructional-planning requirements.

A classroom teacher should typically reserve constructed-response assessments for a modest number of really *significant* instructional outcomes. And, remember, a teacher's assessments typically exemplify the outcomes the teacher wants most students to master. It's better to get students to master three to five really *high-level* cognitive skills, adroitly assessed by excellent constructed-response tests, than it is to have students master a litany of low-level outcomes. In short, choose your constructed-response targets with care. Those choices will have curricular and instructional implications.

Putting it another way, if you, as a classroom teacher, want to determine whether your students have the skills and/or knowledge that can be best measured by short-answer or essay items, then you need to refresh your memory regarding how to avoid serious item construction or response scoring errors. 183, 187. Don't believe you are obligated to use short-answer or essay items simply because you now know a bit more about how to crank them out. If you're interested in the extensiveness of your students' *knowledge* regarding Topic *Z*, it may be far more efficient to employ fairly low-level selected-response kinds of items. If, however, you really want to make inferences about your students' abilities to perform the kinds of tasks represented by short-answer and essay items, then the guidelines provided in the chapter should be consulted.

own short-answer and essay items, you'll elicit student responses you can score accurately. Well, that's not a terrible aspiration, but there's really a more important insight you need to walk away with after reading the chapter. That insight, not surprisingly, derives from the central purpose of classroom assessment—namely, to draw accurate inferences about students' status so you can make more appropriate educational decisions. What you really need to know about short-answer items and essay items is that you should use them as part of your classroom assessment procedures if you want to make the sorts of inferences about your students that those students' responses to such items would support.

■ Chapter Summary

After a guilt-induced apology for the chapter's mislabeling, the chapter started off with a description of short-answer items accompanied by a set of guidelines regarding how to write short-answer items. The chapter then took up essay items and indicated that, although students' written compositions constitute a particular kind of essay response, most of the recommendations for constructing essay items and for scoring students' responses were the same, whether measuring students' composition skills or skills in subject areas other than language arts. Guidelines were provided for writing essay items and for scoring students' responses to essay items .

Self-Check

This chapter's self-check exercises will start off with a brief set of illustrative short-answer and essay items. Your task is to identify whether any of the chapter's item-writing guidelines have been violated. If so, you are to indicate what the violated guideline was or, if two or more guidelines have been flaunted, which ones those were. If not, indicate that no guidelines have been violated. Because you'll be responding with brief constructed responses, what kind of test item do you suppose you're about to mess with?

Oh yes, if you want to, you might like to engage in a quick review of the item-writing guidelines. It's not necessary, but some people are compulsive when they think their self-worth is going to be under scrutiny.

1. (The following item was written for fifth-graders.) Before the United States became an independent nation, most of the men and women who had come to settle were from which European nation or nations?

   _____ _____ _____

   Any violation(s)? _____

   _____

Constructed-Response Tests

2. (This item is for high school students.) You have just viewed a videotape containing three widely seen television commercials. What is the one classic propaganda technique present in all three commercials? _____

   Any violation(s)? _____

   _____

3. (This item is for eighth-grade students.) If a friend has asked you to engage in the use of alcohol or _____, and you wish to decline, you should _____ and _____ without delay.

   Any violation(s)? _____

   _____

4. (This item was written for eleventh-grade English students.) In the space provided below and on the attached sheet, please compose a brief 200-word editorial in favor of the school district's expanded after-school tutorial program. The intended audience for your position statement consists of those people who read the local newspaper's editorial page. Because you have the entire class period to prepare your response, please use the scratch paper provided for a first draft and then revise your draft editorial before copying it on these sheets. The editorial will contribute 40 percent to your six-week's Persuasive Writing grade.

   Any violation(s)? _____

   _____

5. (This item was written for sixth-graders.) Thinking back over the mathematics lesson and homework assignments you had during the past 12 weeks, what conclusions can you draw? Take no more than one page for your response.

   Any violation(s)? _____

   _____

6. For the chapter's final self-check exercise, please read the description of how a fictitious teacher went about scoring an essay examination in a high school class called U.S. Government Service. Then evaluate how well the teacher carried out the scoring.

   > "I was using a four-item essay examination on which my students were to spend 10 to 15 minutes per item. Before scoring students' papers, I worked up a tentative analytic scoring guide for each item. I identified

two evaluative criteria that *had* to be satisfied in each response in order for it to receive full credit. If a student satisfied a criterion fairly well, the response earned 5 points; if the criterion was satisfied really well, the response earned 10 points. In all, then, with two criteria per item, and 0 to 10 points per criterion, I could give a student 0 points up to 80 points. My scoring keys, which placed no emphasis on a student's use of mechanics, worked so well that I didn't have to revise them.

"I scored each student's response to all four items at a single sitting, and I found I could usually interpret students' responses more sensibly because, from the student's name on the first page of the response booklet, I could tell whose responses I was grading. The entire scoring operation for the 29 students in my class took somewhat less than 90 minutes."

What is your evaluation of this teacher's scoring procedures?

_____

_____

Pondertime

1. What do you think has been the *instructional* impact, if any, of the widespread incorporation of student writing samples in the high-stakes educational achievement tests used in numerous states?

2. How would you contrast short-answer items and essay items with respect to their elicited levels of cognitive behavior? Are there differences in the kinds of cognitive demands called for by the two item types? If so, what are they?

3. What do you see as the major weaknesses of short-answer and essay items? What are their major strengths?

4. What would influence you in deciding whether to use selected-response items or the kinds of constructed-response items treated in this chapter?

5. Not all of my colleagues agree with my recommendation not to allow students to choose from alternative items the ones they will answer. What is your view on this issue?

Self-Check Key

1. This item really doesn't violate any of the guidelines, but it's a weak item because it violated one of the general-purpose item-writing commandments. The item presents an ambiguous task to students insofar as it asks for a nation (or

nations) from which "most" of the settlers came and then provides three blank spaces, thereby indicating that not one, but *three* responses are sought, even though, technically, there is only one "most." An astute answer from you for this self-check item would have been something along these lines: "No violations, but cruddy nonetheless."

2. This item violates no guidelines and isn't really all that shabby.

3. This item violates a pair of guidelines. It uses too many blanks and the blanks are unequal in length. It would be difficult for students, given the nearly total ambiguity introduced by the initial blank, to know how to respond to the item. It is, in short, a loser item.

4. This item violates none of the chapter's item-writing guidelines for essay items. As you can note, the first three guidelines have all been specifically followed in the item. It's a fairly decent prompt for a persuasive writing task.

5. This item violates several of the chapter's guidelines for writing essay items. Although it limits the student's response to one page, there is substantial ambiguity about the nature of the task the teacher wants the students to undertake. Twelve weeks' worth of mathematics can add up (a mathematical operation) to a pretty hefty pile of math. The number of conclusions the student can legitimately draw are myriad. Thus, Guideline 2 is clearly violated because the student doesn't know what to do. Guideline 3 is also violated because there's no indication given regarding time limit or point value for the item. This item needs a good deal of refurbishing.

6. This fictitious teacher adhered to one of the guidelines when a tentative analytic scoring key was used dealing with the importance of a student's written mechanics. There were two serious guideline violations, however, insofar as the teacher didn't score items one at a time and also failed to score students' responses anonymously. On balance, therefore, you should have given a "thumbs-down" to this teacher's essay-scoring effort. The two serious violations are too likely to threaten the validity of any score-based inferences the teacher might wish to draw.

■ Additional Stuff

Downing, S. M., and Haladyna, T. M. (Eds.). (2006). *Handbook of test development*. Mahwah, NJ: Lawrence Erlbaum.

Miller, M. D., and Linn, R. (2013). *Measurement and assessment in teaching* (11th ed.). Columbus, OH: Pearson.

Nitko, A. J., and Brookhart, S. M. (2011). *Educational assessment of students* (6th ed.). Upper Saddle River, NJ: Prentice-Hall/Merrill Education.

Stiggins, R. J., and Chappuis, J. (2011). An Introduction to *Student-involved assessment FOR learning* (6th ed.). Upper Saddle River, NJ: Prentice-Hall.

■ Cyber Stuff

■ *Education Northwest* was initially established in 1966 as the Northwest Regional Laboratory. Much of the early work of that Laboratory focused on educational evaluation and assessment. Education Northwest now conducts more than 200 projects annually with communities, districts, and schools all across the nation. A search for "educational assessment" resources yields about 200 entries, subdividable according to such categories as news stories, resources, and events. www.educationnorthwest.org

■ Extended Applications

It is a truism that the more a person uses something, the more familiar with this something the person becomes. This self-evident notion surely applies to the assessment-related knowledge, skills, and concepts you have been reading about in the foregoing pages. Thus, to provide readers of *Classroom Assessment* with additional opportunities to apply the content contained in this text, this final section contains a variety of exercises intended to give readers an opportunity to use what they've been reading about.

In a sense, of course, the Self-Check exercises found at the close of this chapter provides an opportunity for readers to apply the chapter's content. Nonetheless, the more times you use a concept, skill, or a body of knowledge, the more likely it is that you will master this content so you can employ it in varied situations.

For each of the text, you will find an extended-application exercise calling for you to do some thinking about that chapter's content as it applies to a real-world situation. Each exercise is preceded by a brief introduction setting forth the reason that the upcoming extended-application exercise has been selected.

Because many of these exercises call on you to generate an original response rather than select a response from a set of options, it is difficult to supply an "answer key" for readers' unpredictable responses. So, what you'll find following all the exercises is One Possible Response—an indication of how I would have personally responded to the exercise if I had been asked to do so. Please don't regard my response as the only way to respond to an exercise. After all, by definition, this is only "one possible" response. Instead, please think of my response as a fairly flimsy form of feedback. You can certainly disagree with me, even emphatically, yet still profit from doing the exercise.

Remember, what is being provided in this section. The exercises deliberately intended to extend how you apply the content treated in *Classroom Assessment*. I hope you find these exercises useful in enhancing your understanding of what teachers need to know about classroom assessment.

■ Whomping Up Winning Items

Introduction

"Cruddy items create cruddy inferences." That pithy assertion, although infrequently voiced in psychometric circles, is nonetheless true. Accordingly, the Extended Applications exercise for this chapter is designed to give you practice in distinguishing between constructed-response items that are dazzling and those that are dumb. Ten such items will be plopped onto your practice plate, half of them being short-answer items and the other half being essay items. You are to imagine that a teacher-colleague of yours has asked you to look over the items to see if they have any problems.

In evaluating each item, please use not only in this chapter's guidelines for short-answer items and essay items.

Following each boxed item, you'll find the following conditional query: "Any flaws and, if so, which one(s)?" Try to respond to that question for each item, mentally or on paper, *before* considering the answer represented in One Possible Response.

 Exercise Directions: Presented here are 10 constructed-response test items. Please review each one to determine if there are any flaws in the item based either on this chapter's item-writing guidelines. One or more of the 10 items will have no flaws. If you find a deficiency in an item, indicate the nature of that flaw (or those flaws) in the space provided.

---

1. *A short-answer item for eighth-graders:* According to *Robert's Rules of Order,* a _____ motion can be _____ effectively delayed if someone introduces a motion to refer the _____ to a _____.

Any flaws and, if so, which one(s)? _____

_____

_____

One Possible Response: This item violates the fourth item-writing guideline for short-answer items because it's an incomplete statement with more than two blanks. This sort of Swiss-cheese item is certain to confuse test takers.

> **2.** *An essay item for eleventh-graders:* Based on the 10-week unit of study on the three branches of government that our class has just concluded, please indicate whether you believe the legislative, executive, or judicial branch is most powerful. Defend your choice as persuasively as you can, relying on relevant arguments and evidence. Please do so—using the paper supplied or employing one of the computers in our classroom—in 500 words or less. Your response to this item will count for one-third of this test's total points, and you should spend no more than a half hour in composing your response.

Any flaws and, if so, which one(s)? _____

_____

_____

One Possible Response: This essay item, in my estimate, looks pretty solid. I find no major flaws in the item, especially because it appears to be based on a recently concluded unit of study.

> **3.** *A short-answer item for sixth-graders:* _____ and _____ are the two least frequently used parts of speech in the English language.

Any flaws and, if so, which one(s)? _____

_____

_____

One Possible Response: Here we see a failure to follow the third of the item-writing guidelines for short-answer items—namely, the guideline indicating that the blanks for incomplete statements should be placed near the end of the statement. This item commences with a pair of blanks. It would require little effort to revise this weak item so that its blanks were near the end of the statement.

> **4.** *A short-answer item for third-graders:* In the story you read yesterday about the "Tardy Turtle," we learned that this kind of turtle usually lives for _____ years.

Constructed-Response Tests

Any flaws and, if so, which one(s)? _____

_____

_____

➤ *One Possible Response:* Because this short-answer item was written for young students (third-graders), it should have taken the form of a direct question. It would be easy to morph this item into a direct question.

---

5. *An essay item for ninth-graders:* Please choose one of the three types of map projections we have studied in this geography class, then describe the distinctive features of that map projection and, having done so, evaluate the usefulness of such maps to everyday citizens. Please devote no more than 20 minutes to this item. If you prefer, you can omit this item and respond, instead, to one of the two 20-minute questions below regarding the role of maps in geographic studies.

Any flaws and, if so, which one(s)? _____

_____

_____

➤ *One Possible Response:* The fourth item-writing guideline for essay items indicated that optional items not be used because such an approach would reduce the comparability of students' essays. This is the chief shortcoming of the geography item.

---

6. *An essay item for twelfth-graders:* Facing a quandary, being enervated by an excessive expenditure of energy, and making an irrevocable determination are all situations faced by the world's leaders. "Crossing the Rubicon" is a metaphor for one of the foregoing three situations. In fewer than 200 words, please explain which of these situations is best represented by the metaphor, whose crossing of the Rubicon is involved, and how that event actually worked out.

Any flaws and, if so, which one(s)? _____

_____

_____

One Possible Response: This item appears to flop on several courts. First off, it violates the item-writing guideline that the students' task should be explicitly described. The item also seems to sin against the first two general item-writing commandments presented. There's way too much ambiguity and opacity in this item. This item also violates the commandment calling for the avoidance of complex syntax in an item. A student would need to read the item several times and, only if quite lucky, could then figure out what sort of response is being sought. This is, clearly, a loser item.

> 7. *A short-answer item for fourth-graders:* One of America's most important documents, a document that led to the founding of this nation, was
>
> _____ _____ _____ _____.

Any flaws and, if so, which one(s)? _____

_____

_____

One Possible Response: The final item-writing guideline for short-answer items urges item-writers to make certain all of an item's blanks are equal in length. Because this item's blanks aren't equal, cunning fourth-graders will figure out that what's being sought for an answer is *The Declaration of Independence.*

> 8. *A short-answer item for a second-grader:* These letters are all vowels: A, O, U, E. What is another vowel? _____

Any flaws and, if so, which one(s)? _____

_____

_____

One Possible Response: This item looks okay. It is not clear whether the content of the item is developmentally appropriate or curricularly appropriate for second-graders. One hopes it is. The item is intended to elicit an *I* as an answer. Because of the brevity of the item's intended answer, it is almost a "shortest-answer-possible item." If some precocious second-grader tosses in a *Y* or a *W,* those two "occasional" vowels, let's hope the kid gets full credit.

9. *An essay item for tenth-graders:* In the blank (half-page) space provided below, please evaluate the rubric that we have been using for the past two months to judge the quality of students' persuasive essays. More specifically, consider each of the rubric's five evaluative criteria, then indicate which of those criteria is least important in appraising the quality of a persuasive essay. Briefly defend your choice of this criterion. You should spend no more than 15 minutes on your response to this item. Your response to this item will be weighted twice as heavily as your response to other items in the test.

Any flaws and, if so, which one(s)? _____

_____

_____

 One Possible Response: I don't see any serious flaws in this item. Perhaps you do. If I were a tenth-grader once more, I think I'd know how to respond to an item such as this.

10. *A short-answer item for eighth-graders:* What is the most blatant manifestation of a teenager's daily intake of 60 fat grams and 4,000 calories? _____

Any flaws and, if so, which one(s)? _____

_____

_____

One Possible Response: This item has a major flaw, and it stems from the item's use of "blatant manifestation." The inclusion of this unnecessarily opaque phrase violates the fifth of general item-writing commandments—specifically, avoiding the use of vocabulary terms more advanced than required. The item also has only one blank for a response space, probably not enough space for some test takers. However, many eighth-grade students simply won't know what a "blatant manifestation" really is. There are many more understandable phrases that could have been substituted. For example, "significant outcome" would do a satisfactory communication job in this instance.

■ Glossary

analytic scoring   A method of scoring a student's constructed responses involving the application of multiple evaluative criteria, one criterion at a time. After having employed the evaluative criteria separately, there may be an aggregation of these separate judgments into a final, overall evaluation.

assessment task   The part of an essay item or performance test that describes what it is the student should do to complete the assessment.

essay item   A test item eliciting a response of one or more paragraphs from a student.

extended-response item   An essay item that gives a student few constraints about how he or she is to respond, especially with respect to the length of his or her responses.

holistic scoring   The method of scoring a student's constructed responses that calls for the synthesized application of multiple evaluative criteria—that is, simultaneously using several distinguishable factors to arrive at an overall judgment about the quality of a student's response.

prompt   The assessment task, typically for a writing sample, that indicates what the focus of a student's composition should be.

restricted-response item   An essay item that markedly limits the form and content of a student's response to the item.

short-answer item   A test item eliciting a brief response, usually a word or phrase, from a student.

writing sample   A student-generated composition intended to allow inferences about a student's writing abilities.

Performance
Assessment

During the early 1990s, a good many educational policymakers became enamored with performance assessment. *Performance assessment* is an approach to measuring a student's status based on the way the student completes a specified task. Theoretically, of course, when the student chooses between *true* and *false* for a binary-choice item, the student is completing a task, although an obviously modest one. But the proponents of performance assessment have measurement schemes in mind that are meaningfully different from binary-choice or multiple-choice tests. Indeed, it was a dissatisfaction with traditional paper-and-pencil tests that caused many educators to travel eagerly down the performance-testing trail.

■ What Is a Performance Test?

Before digging into what makes performance tests tick and how you might use them in your own classroom, we'd best explore the chief attributes of such an assessment approach. Even though all educational tests, as noted earlier, require students to perform in some way, when most educators talk about performance tests, they are thinking about assessments in which the student is required to construct an original response. More often than not, an examiner (such as the teacher) *observes* the process of construction so that observation of the student's performance and judgment of that performance are required. Four decades ago, Fitzpatrick and Morrison (1971) observed that "there is no absolute distinction between performance tests and other classes of tests." They pointed out that the distinction between performance assessments and more conventional tests is chiefly the degree

From Chapter 8 of *Classroom Assessment: What Teachers Need to Know*, Seventh Edition. W. James Popham. Copyright © 2014 by Pearson Education, Inc. All rights reserved.

to which the examination simulates the criterion situation—that is, the extent to which the examination approximates the kind of student behaviors about which we wish to make inferences.

Suppose, for example, a teacher who had been instructing students in the process of collaborative problem solving wanted to see whether students had acquired this collaborative skill. The *inference* at issue centers on the extent to which each student has mastered the skill. The *educational decision* on the line might be whether particular students need additional instruction or, instead, whether it's time to move on to other curricular aims. The teacher's real interest, then, is in how well students can work with other students to arrive collaboratively at solutions to problems. In Figure 1, you will see there are several assessment procedures that could be used to get a fix on a student's collaborative problem-solving skills. Yet, note that the two selected-response assessment options (numbers 1 and 2) don't really ask students to construct anything. For the other three constructed-response assessment options (numbers 3, 4, and 5), however, there are clear differences in the degree to which the task presented to the student coincides with the class of

figure 1 ■ A Set of Assessment Options That Vary in the Degree to Which a Student's Task Approximates the Curricularly Targeted Behavior

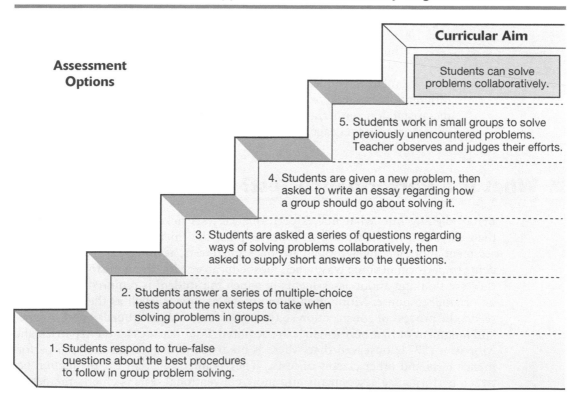

tasks called for by the teacher's curricular aim. Assessment Option 5, for example, is obviously the closest match to the behavior called for in the curricular aim. Yet, Assessment Option 4 is surely more of a "performance test" than is Assessment Option 1.

It should be apparent to you, then, that different educators will be using the phrase *performance assessment* to refer to very different kinds of assessment approaches. Many teachers, for example, are willing to consider short-answer and essay tests a form of performance assessment. In other words, those teachers essentially equate performance assessment with any form of constructed-response assessment. Other teachers establish more stringent requirements in order for a measurement procedure to be described as a performance assessment. For example, some performance-assessment proponents contend that genuine performance assessments must possess at least three features:

- *Multiple evaluative criteria.* The student's performance must be judged using more than one **evaluative criterion**. To illustrate, a student's ability to speak Spanish might be appraised on the basis of the student's accent, syntax, and vocabulary.
- *Prespecified quality standards.* Each of the evaluative criteria on which a student's performance is to be judged is clearly explicated in advance of judging the quality of the student's performance.
- *Judgmental appraisal.* Unlike the scoring of selected-response tests in which electronic computers and scanning machines can, once programmed, carry on without the need of humankind, genuine performance assessments depend on human judgments to determine how acceptable a student's performance really is.

Looking back to Figure 1, it is clear that if the foregoing three requirements were applied to the five assessment options supplied, Assessment Option 5 would qualify as a performance test, and Assessment Option 4 probably would as well, but the other three assessment options wouldn't qualify under a definition of performance assessment requiring the incorporation of multiple evaluative criteria, prespecified quality standards, and judgmental appraisals.

A good many advocates of performance assessment would prefer that the tasks presented to students represent real-world rather than school-world kinds of problems. Other proponents of performance assessment would be elated simply if more school-world measurement was constructed response rather than selected response in nature. Still other advocates of performance testing want the tasks in performance tests to be genuinely *demanding*—that is, way up the ladder of cognitive difficulty. In short, proponents of performance assessment often advocate different approaches to measuring students on the basis of how they perform.

You'll sometimes encounter educators who use other phrases to describe performance assessment. For example, they may use the phrase **authentic assessment** (because the assessment tasks more closely coincide with real-life, nonschool tasks) or *alternative assessment* (because such assessments constitute an alternative to traditional, paper-and-pencil tests). *Portfolio assessment* is a particular type of performance assessment and should not be considered a synonymous descriptor for the performance-assessment approach to educational measurement.

We now turn to the twin issues that are at the heart of performance assessments: *selecting appropriate tasks* for students and, once the students have tackled those tasks, *judging the adequacy of students' responses.*

■ Identifying Suitable Tasks for Performance Assessment

Performance assessment typically requires students to respond to a small number of more significant tasks rather than respond to a large number of less significant tasks. Thus, rather than answering 50 multiple-choice items on a conventional chemistry examination, students who are being assessed via performance tasks may find themselves asked to perform an actual experiment in their chemistry class and then prepare a written interpretation of the experiment's results and an analytic critique of the procedures they used. From the chemistry teacher's perspective, instead of seeing how students respond to the 50 "mini-tasks" represented in the

Decision Time

Grow, Plants, Grow!

Francine Floden is a third-year biology teacher in Kennedy High School. Because she has been convinced by several of her colleagues that traditional paper-and-pencil examinations fail to capture the richness of the scientific experience, Francine has decided to base almost all of her students' grades on a semester-long performance test. As Francine contemplates her new assessment plan, she decides that 90 percent of the students' grades will stem from the quality of their responses to the performance test's task; 10 percent of the grades will be linked to classroom participation and a few short true-false quizzes administered throughout the semester.

The task embodied in Francine's performance test requires each student to design and conduct a two-month experiment to study the growth of three identical plants under different conditions and then prepare a formal scientific report describing the experiment. Although most of Francine's students carry out their experiments at home, several students use the shelves at the rear of the classroom for their experimental plants. A number of students vary the amount of light or the kind of light received by the different plants, but most students modify the nutrients given to their plants. After a few weeks of the two-month experimental period, all of Francine's students seem to be satisfactorily under way with their experiments.

Several of the more experienced teachers in the school, however, have expressed their reservations to Francine about what they regard as "overbooking on a single assessment experience." The teachers suggest to Francine that she will be unable to draw defensible inferences about her students' true mastery of biological skills and knowledge based on a single performance test. They urged her to reduce dramatically the grading weight for the performance test so that, instead, additional grade-contributing examinations can be given to the students.

Other colleagues, however, believe Francine's performance-test approach is precisely what is needed in courses such as biology. They recommend she "stay the course" and alter "not one whit" of her new assessment strategy.

 If you were Francine, what would your decision be?

multiple-choice test, an estimate of each student's status must be derived from a student's response to a single, complex task. Given the significance of each task used in a performance-testing approach to classroom assessment, it is apparent that great care must be taken in the selection of performance-assessment tasks. Generally speaking, classroom teachers will either have to (1) generate their own performance test tasks or (2) select performance test tasks from the increasing number of tasks available from educators elsewhere.

Inferences and Tasks

Consistent with the frequently asserted message of this text about classroom assessment you are currently reading, the chief determinants of how you assess your
students are (1) the inference you want to make about those students and (2) the
decision that will be based on the inference. For example, suppose you're a history teacher and you've spent a summer at a lakeside cabin meditating about curricular matters (which, in one lazy setting or another, is the public's perception of
how most teachers spend their vacations). After three months of heavy curricular
thought, you have concluded that what you really want to teach your students is
for them to be able to apply historical lessons of the past to the solution of current
and future problems that, at least to some extent, parallel the problems of the past.
You have decided to abandon your week-long, 1,500-item true-false final examination that your stronger students refer to as a "measurement marathon" and your
weaker students refer to by using a rich, if earthy, vocabulary. Instead of true-false
items, you are now committed to a performance-assessment strategy and wish to
select tasks for your performance tests to help you infer how well your students
can draw on the lessons of the past to illuminate their approach to current and/or
future problems.

In Figure 2, you will see a graphic depiction of the relationships among (1)
a teacher's key curricular aim, (2) the inference that the teacher wishes to draw
about each student, and (3) the tasks for a performance test intended to secure
data to support the inference that the teacher wants to make. As you will note, the
teacher's curricular aim provides the source for the inference, and the assessment
tasks yield the evidence needed for the teacher to arrive at defensible inferences
regarding the extent to which students can solve current or future problems using

figure 2 ■ Relationships among a Teacher's Key Curricular Aim, the
Assessment-Based Inference Derivative from the Aim,
and the Performance-Assessment Tasks Providing
Evidence for the Inference

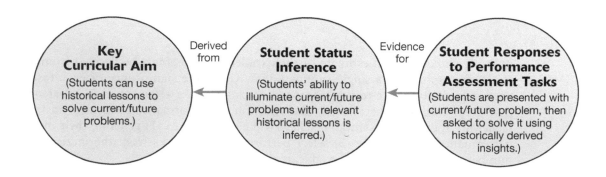

historical lessons. To the degree that students have mastered the curricular aim, the teachers will make a decision about how much more instruction, if any, is needed.

The Generalizability Dilemma

One of the most serious difficulties with performance assessment is, because students respond to fewer tasks than would be the case with conventional paper-and-pencil testing, it is often more difficult to generalize accurately about what skills and knowledge are possessed by the student.

To illustrate, let's say you're trying to get a fix on your students' ability to multiply pairs of double-digit numbers. If, because of your instructional priorities, you can devote only a half-hour to assessment purposes, you could require the students to respond to 20 such multiplication problems in the 30 minutes available. (That's probably more problems than you'd need, but I'm trying to draw a vivid contrast for you.) From a student's responses to 20 multiplication problems, you can get a pretty fair idea about what kind of double-digit multiplier the student is. As a consequence of the student's performance on a *reasonable sample* of items representing the curricular aim, you can conclude "Javier really knows how to multiply those sorts of problems," or "Fred really couldn't multiply double-digit multiplication problems if his life depended on it." It is because you have sampled well the kind of student performance (to which you wish to make an inference) that you can confidently make inferences about your students' abilities to solve similar sorts of multiplication problems. With only a 30-minute assessment period available, however, if you moved to a more elaborate kind of performance test, you might only be able to have students respond to one big-bopper item. For example, if you presented a multiplication-focused mathematics problem involving the use of manipulatives, and wanted your students to derive an original solution and then describe it in writing, you'd be lucky if your students could finish the task in a half hour. Based on this single task, how confident would you be in making inferences about your students' abilities to perform comparable multiplication tasks?

And this, as you now see, is the rub with performance testing. Because students respond to fewer tasks, the teacher is put in a trickier spot when it comes to deriving inferences about students' abilities. If you use only one performance test, and a student does well on the test, does this signify the student *really* possesses the category of skills the test was designed to measure, or did the student just get lucky? On the other hand, if a student messes up on a single-performance test, does this signify the student *really* doesn't possess the assessed skill, or was there a feature in this particular performance test that misled the student who, given other tasks, might have performed wonderfully?

As a classroom teacher, you're faced with two horns of a classic measurement dilemma. Although performance tests often measure the kinds of student abilities you'd prefer to assess (because those abilities are in line with really worthwhile curricular aims), the inferences you make about students on the basis of their responses to performance tests must be made with increased caution. As with many dilemmas, there may be no perfect way to hop this one's two horns. But there is, at least, a way of dealing with the dilemma as sensibly as you can. In this instance, the solution strategy is to devote great care to the selection of the tasks embodied in your performance tests. Among the most important considerations in selecting such tasks is to choose tasks that optimize the likelihood of accurately generalizing about your students' capabilities. If you really keep generalizability at the forefront when you select/construct performance-test tasks, you'll be able to make the strongest possible performance-based inferences about your students' capabilities.

Factors to Consider When Evaluating Performance-Test Tasks

We've now looked at what many measurement specialists regard as the most important factor you can consider when judging potential tasks for performance assessments—*generalizability*. Let's look at a list of seven such factors you might wish to consider, whether you select a performance-test task from existing tasks or, in contrast, create your own performance-test tasks.

Evaluative Criteria for Performance-Test Tasks

- *Generalizability.* Is there a high likelihood the students' performance on the task will generalize to comparable tasks?
- *Authenticity.* Is the task similar to what students might encounter in the real world as opposed to encounter only in school?
- *Multiple foci.* Does the task measure multiple instructional outcomes instead of only one?
- *Teachability.* Is the task one that students can become more proficient in as a consequence of a teacher's instructional efforts?
- *Fairness.* Is the task fair to all students—that is, does the task avoid bias based on such personal characteristics as students' gender, ethnicity, or socioeconomic status?
- *Feasibility.* Is the task realistically implementable in relation to its cost, space, time, and equipment requirements?
- *Scorability.* Is the task likely to elicit student responses that can be reliably and accurately evaluated?

Whether you're developing your own tasks for performance tests or selecting such tasks from an existing collection, you may wish to apply some but not all the factors listed here. Personally, I would usually try to apply all seven factors, although I can see how one might, on occasion, dump the *authenticity* criterion or the *multiple foci* criterion. In some instances, for example, school tasks rather than real-world tasks might be suitable for the kinds of inferences a teacher wishes to reach, hence the authenticity criterion may not be relevant. And even though it is economically advantageous to measure more than one outcome at one time, particularly considering the time and effort that goes into almost any performance test, there may be instances in which a single educational outcome is sufficiently important so it warrants a solo performance test. More often than not, though, a really good task for a performance test will satisfy most, if not all seven, of the evaluative criteria presented here.

Performance Tests and Teacher Time

I promised that if you completed this text with a reasonable degree of attentiveness, you'd become a better teacher. Now I have another promise for you. I promise to be *honest* about the measurement mysteries we're probing together. And this brings me to an important consideration regarding performance testing. In brief, it takes time!

Think for a moment about the time that you, as the teacher, need to give to (1) the selection of suitable tasks, (2) the development of an appropriate scheme for scoring students' responses, and (3) the actual scoring of students' responses. Talk to any teacher who's already used many classroom performance tests and you'll learn it takes a ton of time to use performance assessment.

So what I want to suggest is that there's one additional factor you should throw into your decision-making about performance assessment. It is the *significance of the skill* you're using the performance test to assess. Because you'll almost certainly have time for only a handful of such performance tests in your teaching, make sure that every performance test you use is linked to a truly significant skill you're trying to have your students acquire. If performance assessments aren't based on genuinely demanding skills, you'll soon stop using them because, to be truthful, they'll be more trouble than they're worth.

■ Identifying Scoring Criteria

Performance assessments invariably are based on constructed-response measurement procedures in which students generate rather than select their responses. Student-constructed responses must be scored, however, and it's clearly much tougher to score constructed responses than to score selected responses. The scoring of constructed responses centers on the *evaluative criteria* one calls on to determine the adequacy of students' responses. Let's turn our attention now to the evaluative criteria we use to decide whether students' responses to performance tests are splendid or shabby.

A *criterion*, according to *Webster's Dictionary*, is "a standard on which a judgment or decision may be based." In the case of scoring students' responses to a performance test's task, you're clearly trying to make a judgment regarding the adequacy of the student's constructed response. The specific criteria to be used in making that judgment will obviously influence the way you score a student's response. For instance, if you were scoring a student's written composition on the basis of organization, word choice, and communicative clarity, you might arrive at very different scores than if you had scored the composition on the basis of spelling, punctuation, and grammar. The evaluative criteria used when scoring students' responses to performance tests (or their responses to any kind of constructed-response item) really control the whole assessment game.

Due to my compulsion to fall back on my five years of Latin studies in high school and college, I feel responsible for explaining that the Latin word *criterion* is singular and the Latin word *criteria* is plural. Unfortunately, so many of today's educators mix up these two terms that I don't even become distraught about it anymore. However, now that you know the difference, if you find any of your colleagues erroneously saying "the criteria is" or "the criterion were," you can display an ever so subtle, yet altogether condescending, smirk.

The scoring procedures for judging students' responses to performance tests are usually referred to these days as *scoring rubrics* or, more simply, **rubrics**. A rubric that's used to score students' responses to a performance assessment has, at minimum, three important features:

- *Evaluative criteria.* These are the factors to be used in determining the quality of a student's response.
- *Descriptions of qualitative differences for the evaluative criteria.* For each evaluative criterion, a description must be supplied so qualitative distinctions in students' responses can be made using the criterion.
- *An indication of whether a holistic or analytic scoring approach is to be used.* The rubric must indicate whether the evaluative criteria are to be applied collectively in the form of *holistic* scoring or on a criterion-by-criterion basis in the form of *analytic* scoring.

The identification of a rubric's evaluative criteria, as might be guessed, is probably the most important task for rubric developers. If you're creating a rubric for a performance test you wish to use in your own classroom, be careful not to come up with a lengthy laundry list of evaluative criteria a student's response should satisfy. Personally, I think when you isolate more than three or four evaluative criteria per rubric, you've identified too many. If you find yourself facing more than a few evaluative criteria, simply *rank each criterion in order of importance* and then chop off those listed lower than the very most important ones.

The next job you'll have is deciding how to *describe in words* what a student's response must be in order to be judged wonderful or woeful. The level of descriptive detail you apply needs to work *for you*. Remember, you're devising a scoring rubric for your own classroom, not a statewide or national test. Keep the aversiveness of the work down by employing brief descriptors of quality differences you can use when teaching and, if you're instructionally astute, your students can use as well.

Performance Assessment

Finally, you'll need to decide whether you'll make a single, overall judgment about a student's response by considering all of the rubric's evaluative criteria as an amalgam (holistic scoring) or, instead, award points to the response on a criterion-by-criterion basis (analytic scoring). The virtue of holistic scoring, of course, is it's quicker to do. The downside of holistic scoring is it fails to communicate to students, especially low-performing students, what their shortcomings are. Clearly, analytic scoring yields a greater likelihood of diagnostically pinpointed scoring and sensitive feedback than does holistic scoring. Some classroom teachers have attempted to garner the best of both worlds by scoring all responses holistically and then analytically rescoring (for feedback purposes) all responses of low-performing students.

Because most performance assessments call for fairly complex responses from students, there will usually be more than one evaluative criterion employed to score students' responses. For each of the evaluative criteria chosen, a numerical scale is typically employed so that for each criterion, a student's response might be assigned a specified number of points—for instance, 0 to 6 points. Usually, these scale points are accompanied by verbal descriptors; sometimes they aren't. For instance, in a 5-point scale, the following descriptors might be used: $5 =$ Exemplary, $4 =$ Superior, $3 =$ Satisfactory, $2 =$ Weak, $1 =$ Inadequate. If no verbal descriptors are used for each score point on the scale, a scheme such as the following might be employed:

In some cases, the scoring scale for each criterion is nonnumerical; that is, it consists only of verbal descriptors such as "exemplary," "adequate," and so on. Although such verbal scales can be useful with particular types of performance tests, their disadvantage is that scores from multiple criteria cannot be added together in order to produce a meaningful overall score.

The heart of the intellectual process in isolating suitable evaluative criteria is to get to the essence of what the most significant factors are that distinguish acceptable from unacceptable responses. In this instance, as in many others, less is more. A few truly important criteria are preferable to a ton of trifling criteria. Go for the big ones. If you need help in deciding what criteria to employ in conjunction with a particular performance test, don't be reluctant to ask colleagues to toss in their ideas regarding what *significant* factors to use (for a given performance test) in order to discriminate between super and subpar responses.

In this chapter you'll be presented with scoring rubrics that can serve as useful models for your own construction of such rubrics. In those illustrative scoring rubrics, you'll see that great care has been taken to isolate a small number of instructionally addressable evaluative criteria. The greatest payoff from a well-formed scoring rubric is in its contribution to improved instruction.

students with the two aspects of the criterion—that is, overall structure and se-quence; (2) helping students identify essays in which overall structure and sequence are, or are not, acceptable; and (3) supplying students with gobs of guided and independent practice in writing narrative essays possessing the desired overall structure and sequence. The better students become in being able to employ this double-barreled criterion in their narrative essays, the better those students will be at responding to a task such as the illustrative one we just saw about the local fire-fighters' visit to the classroom. This skill-focused evaluative criterion for *organiza-tion,* in other words, can generalize to a wide variety of narrative-writing tasks, not just an essay about visiting fire-folk.

And even if teachers do not create their own rubrics—for instance, if rubrics are developed by a school district's curriculum or assessment specialists—those teachers who familiarize themselves with skill-focused rubrics in advance of in-structional planning will usually plan better instruction than will teachers who aren't familiar with a skill-focused rubric's key features. Skill-focused rubrics make clear what a teacher should emphasize instructionally when the teacher attempts to promote student mastery of the skill being measured. Remember, although stu-dents' acquisition of knowledge is an important curricular aspiration for teachers, assessment of students' knowledge can obviously be accomplished by procedures other than the use of performance tests.

Let me now set out five rubric rules I encourage you to follow if you're creat-ing your own skill-focused scoring rubric—a rubric you should generate *before* you plan your instruction.

Rule 1: Make sure the skill to be assessed is significant. It takes time and trouble to generate scoring skill-focused rubrics. It also takes time and trou-ble to score students' responses by using such rubrics. Make sure the skill be-ing promoted instructionally, and scored via the rubric, is worth all this time and trouble. Skills that are scored with skill-focused rubrics should represent demanding accomplishments by students, not trifling ones.

Teachers ought not be ashamed to be assessing their students with only a handful of performance tests, for example. It makes much more sense to measure a modest number of truly important skills properly than to do a shoddy job in measuring a shopping-cart-load of skills.

Rule 2: Make certain all of the rubric's evaluative criteria can be addressed instructionally. This second rule calls for you always to "keep your instructional wits about you" when generating a rubric. Most importantly, you must scrutinize every potential evaluative criterion in a rubric to make sure you can actually teach students to master it.

This doesn't oblige you to adhere to any particular instructional approach. Regardless of whether you are wedded to the virtues of direct instruction, indirect instruction, constructivism, or any other instructional strategy, what you must be certain of is that students can be *taught* to employ appropriately *every* evaluative criterion used in the rubric.

Rule 3: Employ as few evaluative criteria as possible.   Because people who start thinking seriously about a skill will often begin to recognize a host of nuances associated with the skill, they sometimes feel compelled to set forth a veritable litany of evaluative criteria. But for instructional purposes, as for most other purposes, less almost always turns out to be more. Try to focus your instructional attention on three or four evaluative criteria; you'll become overwhelmed if you try to promote students' mastery of a dozen evaluative criteria.

Rule 4: Provide a succinct label for each evaluative criterion.   The instructional yield of a skill-focused rubric can be increased simply by giving each evaluative criterion a brief explanatory label. For instance, suppose you were trying to improve your students' oral presentation skills. You might employ a skill-focused rubric for oral communication containing four evaluative criteria—namely, *delivery, organization, content,* and *language.* These one-word, easy-to-remember labels will help remind you *and your students* of what's truly important in judging mastery of the skill being assessed.

Rule 5: Match the length of the rubric to your own tolerance for detail.   I've spent a fair amount of time worrying about this particular rule because much of my early experience in generating skill-focused rubrics dealt with the creation of lengthy scoring rubrics for high-stakes statewide or districtwide assessments. Such detailed rubrics were intended to constrain scorers so their scores would be in agreement. But I've discovered that many classroom teachers consider fairly long, rather detailed rubrics to be altogether off-putting. Whereas those teachers might be willing to create and/or use a one-page rubric, they would regard a six-page rubric as reprehensible. More recently, therefore, I've been recommending much shorter rubrics—rubrics that never exceed one or two pages.

Of course, not all teachers are put off by very detailed rubrics. Some teachers, in fact, find that abbreviated rubrics just don't do an adequate job for them. Such detail-prone teachers would rather work with rubrics that specifically spell out just what's involved when differentiating between quality levels regarding each evaluative criterion. I've therefore come to the conclusion that rubrics should be built to match the detail preferences of the teachers involved. Teachers who believe in brevity should create brief rubrics, and teachers who believe in detail should create lengthier rubrics. If school districts (or publishers) are supplying rubrics to teachers, I recommend both a short and a long version be provided. Let teachers decide on the level of detail that best meshes with their own tolerance/need for detail.

Lights . . . Action . . . Computers!

Two major educational assessment consortia were established in 2010: the Partnership for the Assessment of Readiness for College and Careers (PARCC) and the Smarter Balanced Assessment Consortium (SBAC). Early on, both of those federally funded collaboratives promised that a meaningful number of computer-based performance tests would be included in the assessments they were developing for the 2014–15 school year. These performance tests would take full advantage of technological advances in the presentation and scoring of computer-governed test items. Leaders of both SBAC and PARCC were confident that, because they intended to employ computer-controlled items for their new assessments, and could require students to respond to those items on computers, it would be possible to present test-takers with more challenging, yet authentic, kinds of performance tests.

Not surprisingly, U.S. educators have been looking forward to scrutinizing examples of these computer-controlled performance assessments as soon as PARCC and SBAC make such prototypes available for review. Clearly, the utilization of computer-monitored items holds immense promise for the creation of subtle and sophisticated tasks for these consortia-built tests.

However, glitter alone won't help a guitar produce good music. Educators will need to apply the same levels of evaluative scrutiny to fancy computer-generated performance tests that they previously applied to performance tests served up in paper-and-ink test booklets. That is, can we base valid inferences about a student's mastery of a worthwhile curricular aim on a student's interaction with one of these glitzy, computer-governed performance tests? If the tests do, as hoped, provide evidence regarding a student's status related to a worthwhile curricular aim, can teachers determine what sort of instructional support is needed by a student whose performance-test efforts are flawed? If a computer-based performance test is loaded with sparkle and spangles, yet turns out to be merely an intelligence test, was that performance test really worth building?

When you try to decide how much confidence you should give to inferences based on your students' performance-test results, this is where good, hard thinking needs to prevail. Do not defer, automatically, to the results of assessments based on flashy, computer-managed test results. Instead, think through carefully—for yourself—just what's going on when students are asked to complete a glitzy performance test. Then, thinking about "what's going on" when arriving at a score-base inference, decide for yourself whether to trust the evidence staring you in the face.

■ Ratings and Observations

Once you've selected your evaluative criteria, you then need to apply them reliably to the judgment of students' responses. If the nature of the performance test task calls for students to create some sort of *product,* such as a written report of an experiment carried out in a biology class, then at your leisure you can rate the product's quality in relation to the criteria you've identified as important. For example, if you had decided on three criteria to use in evaluating students' reports of biology experiments, and could award from 0 to 4 points for each criterion, then you could leisurely assign from 0 to 12 points for each written report. The more clearly you understand what each evaluative criterion is, and what it means to award a different number of points on whatever scale you've selected, the more accurate your scores will be. Performance tests that yield student products are easier to rate because you can rate students' responses when you're in the mood.

It is often the case with performance tests, however, that the student's performance takes the form of some kind of *behavior.* With such performance tests, it will usually be necessary for you to observe the behavior as it takes place. To illustrate, suppose that you are an elementary school teacher whose fifth-grade students have been carrying out fairly elaborate social studies projects culminating in 15-minute oral reports to classmates. Unless you have the equipment to videotape your students' oral presentations, you'll have to observe the oral reports and make judgments about the quality of a student's performance as it occurs. As was true when scores were given to student products, in making evaluative judgments about students' behavior, you will apply whatever criteria you've chosen and assign what you consider to be the appropriate number of points on the scales you are using.

For some observations, you'll find it sensible to make instant, on-the-spot quality judgments. For instance, if you are judging students' social studies reports on the basis of (1) content, (2) organization, and (3) presentation, you might make observation-based judgments on each of those three criteria as soon as a report is finished. In other cases, your observations might incorporate a delayed evaluative approach. For instance, let's say that you are working with students in a speech class on the elimination of "filler words and sounds," two of the most prominent of which are starting a sentence with "well" and interjecting frequent "uh"s into a presentation. In the nonevaluative phase of the observation, you could simply count the number of "well"s and "uh"s uttered by a student. Then, at a later time, you could decide on a point allocation for the criterion "avoids filler words and sounds." Putting it another way, systematic observations may be set up so you make immediate or delayed allocations of points for the evaluative criteria you've chosen. If the evaluative criteria involve qualitative factors that must be appraised more judgmentally, then on-the-spot evaluations and point assignments are typically the way to go. If the evaluative criteria involve more quantitative factors, then a "count now and judge later" approach usually works better.

Sources of Error in Scoring Student Performances

When scoring student performances, there are three common sources of error that can contribute to inaccurate inferences. First, there is the *scoring scale*. Second, there are the *scorers* themselves who may bring a number of bothersome biases to the enterprise. Finally, there are errors in the *scoring procedure*—that is, the process by which the scorers employ the scoring scale.

Scoring-Instrument Flaws

The major defect with most scoring instruments is the lack of descriptive rigor with which the evaluative criteria to be used are described. Given this lack of rigor, ambiguity exists in the interpretations scorers make about what the scoring criteria mean. This typically leads to a set of unreliable ratings. For example, if teachers are to rate students on the extent to which students are "controlling," some teachers may view this as a positive quality and some may view it as a negative quality. Clearly, an inadequately clarified scoring form can lead to all sorts of "noise" in the scores provided by teachers.

Procedural Flaws

Among common problems with scoring students' responses to performance tests, we usually encounter demands on teachers to rate too many qualities. Overwhelmed scorers are scorers rendered ineffectual. Teachers who opt for a large number of evaluative criteria are teachers who have made a decisively inept opt. Care should be taken that no more than three or four evaluative criteria are to be employed in evaluations of students' responses to your performance assessments. Generally speaking, the fewer evaluative criteria used, the better.

but what does this have to do with Teaching?

Teachers are busy people. (This profound recognition will not come as a surprise to anyone who really knows what a teacher's life is like.) But busy people who are apt to survive in their task-buffeted lives will typically try to manage their multiple responsibilities efficiently. Busy people who are teachers, therefore, need to make sure they don't expend their finite reservoir of energy unwisely. And that's where caution needs to be exerted with respect to the use of performance tests. Performance testing, you see, can be so very *seductive*.

Because performance tests are typically focused on measuring a student's mastery of real-world, significant skills, such tests are appealing. If you're an English teacher, for example, wouldn't you rather see whether your students possess composition skills by having them whip out actual "written-from-scratch" compositions than having them spot punctuation problems in multiple-choice items? Of course you would.

But although the allure of performance assessment is considerable, you should never forget that *it takes time!* And the time-consumption requirements of performance testing can readily eat into a teacher's daily 24-hour allotment. It takes time for teachers to come up with defensible tasks for performance tests, to devise suitable rubrics for scoring students' responses, and to actually score those responses. Performance assessment takes time. But, of course, proper performance testing not only helps teachers aim their instruction in the right directions; it also allows students to recognize the skill(s) being promoted.

So, the trick is to select judiciously the cognitive skills you will measure via performance tests. Focus on a small number of truly significant skills. You'll be more likely to maintain your instructional sanity if you employ only a handful of high-level performance tests. Too many performance tests can quickly put a teacher over the edge.

Teachers' Personal-Bias Errors

Bias is clearly an undesirable commodity. Teachers, albeit unintentionally, are frequently biased in the way they score students' responses. Several kinds of personal-bias errors are often encountered when teachers score students' constructed responses. The first of these, known as *generosity error*, occurs when a teacher's bias leads to higher ratings than are warranted. Teachers with a proclivity toward generosity errors see good even where no good exists.

At the other extreme, some teachers display *severity errors*. A severity error, of course, is a tendency to underrate the quality of a student's work. When a pupil's product deserves a "good," a teacher suffering from this personal-bias error will award it only an "average" or even a "below average."

Another sort of personal-bias error is known as *central-tendency error*. This describes a tendency for teachers to view everything as being "in the middle of the scale." Very high or very low ratings are avoided by such folks. They prefer the warm fuzziness of the mean or the median. They tend to regard midpoint ratings as inoffensive and they therefore dispense midpoint ratings almost thoughtlessly.

A particularly frequent error arises when a teacher's overall impression of a student influences how the teacher rates that student with respect to an individual criterion. This error is known as *halo effect*. If a teacher has a favorable attitude toward a student, that student will receive a host of favorable ratings (deserved or not) on a number of individual criteria. Similarly, if a teacher has an unfavorable attitude toward a student, the student will receive a pile of unfavorable ratings on all sorts of separate criteria.

One way to minimize halo effect, at least a bit, is occasionally to reverse the order of the high and low positions on the scoring scale so the teacher cannot *unthinkingly* toss out a whole string of positives (or negatives). What you really need to do to avoid halo effect when you're scoring students' responses is to remember it's always lurking in the wings. Try to score a student's responses on each evaluative criterion using that specific criterion, not a contaminated general impression of the student's ability.

What Do Classroom Teachers Really Need to Know about Performance Assessment?

Performance assessment has been around for a long, long while. Yet, in recent years, a growing number of educators have become strong supporters of this form of assessment because it (1) represents an alternative to traditional paper-and-pencil tests and (2) is often more authentic—that is, reflective of tasks people need to perform in the real world. One of the things you need to understand about performance assessment is that it differs from more conventional assessment chiefly in the degree the assessment task matches the skills and/or knowledge about which you wish to make inferences. Because performance tasks often coincide more closely with high-level cognitive skills than do paper-and-pencil tests, more accurate inferences can often be derived about students. Another big plus for performance tests is they establish assessment targets that, because such targets often influence the teacher's instruction, have a positive impact on instructional activities.

You need to realize, however, that because performance tasks require a fair chunk of time from students, the teacher is often faced with making rather shaky generalizations on the basis of relatively few student performances. It's also important for you to recognize that the development of defensible performance tests is difficult cerebral work. It takes rigorous thinking to identify suitable tasks for performance tests and then isolate appropriate evaluative criteria and spell out the scoring scale for each criterion. And, of course, once the test and its associated scoring procedures are in place, you still have to score students' performances, an operation that invariably takes much more time than is required to score a ream of answers to selected-response items.

The chapter's final admonitions regarding the biases that teachers bring to the scoring of students' responses to performance tests should serve as a reminder. If you employ performance tests frequently in your classrooms, you'll need to be careful at every step of the process—from the original conception and birthing of a performance test down to the bias-free scoring of students' responses.

Parent Talk

The vice president of your school's Parent Advisory Council has asked you to tell him why so many of your school's teachers are now assessing students with performance tests instead of the more traditional paper-and-pencil tests.

 If I were you, here's how I'd respond:

"The reason that most of us are increasingly relying on performance tests these days is that performance tests almost always measure higher-level student skills. With traditional tests, too many of our teachers found they were assessing only the students' abilities to memorize facts.

"In recent years, educators have become far more capable of devising really *demanding* performance tests that require students to display genuinely high-level intellectual skills—skills that are way, way beyond memorization. We've learned how to develop the tests *and* how to score students' responses using carefully developed scoring rules that we refer to as *rubrics*.

"Please stop by my classroom and I'll show you some examples of these demanding performance tests. We're asking more from our students, and we're getting it."

 Now, how would you respond to the vice president of the Parent Advisory Council?

■ Chapter Summary

Although this chapter dealt specifically with performance assessment, a number of the points made in the chapter apply with equal force to the scoring of any type of constructed-response items such as those used in essay tests or short-answer tests. After defining performance tests as a measurement procedure in which students create original responses to an assessment task, it was pointed out that performance tests differ from more conventional tests primarily in the degree the test situation approximates the real-life situation to which inferences are made.

The identification of suitable tasks for performance assessments was given considerable attention in the chapter because unsuitable tasks will surely lead to unsatisfactory performance assessments. Seven evaluative criteria were supplied for performance test tasks: (1) generalizability, (2) authenticity, (3) multiple foci, (4) teachability, (5) fairness, (6) feasibility, and (7) scorability. Particular emphasis was given to selecting tasks about which defensible inferences could be drawn regarding students' generalized abilities to perform comparable tasks.

The significance of the skill to be assessed via a performance task was stressed. Next, *evaluative criteria* were defined as the factors by which the acceptability of a student's performance is judged. The evaluative criteria constitute the most important features of a *rubric* that's employed to score student responses. The significance of selecting suitable evaluative criteria was emphasized. Once the criteria have been identified, a numerical scoring scale, usually consisting of three to six score points, is devised for each evaluative criterion. The evaluative criteria are applied to student performances in the form of ratings for student products or observations for student behaviors.

Distinctions were drawn among *task-specific, hypergeneral,* and *skill-focused rubrics*. Deficits in the former two types of rubrics render them inappropriate for supporting a teacher's classroom instructional effort. A skill-focused rubric, however, can markedly enhance a teacher's instruction.

 # Self-Check

For this chapter's self-check, you'll need to respond to a bit of performance testing yourself. More specifically, you are now asked to generate a scoring guide for a fairly straightforward task requiring students to describe, in a letter to a foreign pen pal, "how a U.S. president is elected." The task is one of several such tasks in which the student is asked to describe an important procedure in U.S. government to a foreign pen pal.

Now, focusing on students at a grade level with which you are familiar, please develop a first-draft scoring guide consisting of one or more evaluative criteria and a scale for each criterion.

 # Pondertime

1. What do you personally consider to be the greatest single strength of performance assessment? How about the greatest single weakness?

2. Are there any sorts of topics or curricular aims for which you think performance assessment most appropriate?

3. What do you think the likelihood is that performance assessment will be widely used by the classroom teachers you know? Why?

4. Do you believe performance assessment is more likely to be used by individual teachers in their classrooms rather than for large-scale, statewide "educational accountability" assessments? Why?

5. Do you prefer *holistic* or *analytic* scoring of students' responses to performance tests? And, pray tell, why?

6. Assuming that one or both of the multistate assessment consortia established in 2010 can create computer-enhanced performance tests for the nation's students, what do you think will be the greatest strengths and weaknesses of such tests?

Self-Check Key

Not knowing what sort of scoring guide you would come up with, it's pretty difficult to provide very specific feedback to help you discern how suitable your scoring guide is. Ideally, you should have (1) identified evaluative criteria, (2) described the criteria, and (3) provided a point scale for each criterion with as much specificity as your energy permitted.

If you're using this text in connection with a formal class, perhaps you can get a classmate to exchange scoring guides with you for a robust co-critiquing session. If you're married or are engaged in a meaningful relationship, ask your partner to look over your scoring guide and see if that person understands how to score students' responses to the pen pal assignment. If you currently aren't involved in a significant relationship, I do *not* suggest that you try to curry favor with a prospective paramour by calling on that person to mess around with your scoring guide. Instead, try dinner and a movie.

■ Additional Stuff

Boyd-Batstone, P. (2007). *Anecdotal records assessment: An observational tool with a standards-based focus*. Norwood, MA: Christopher-Gordon Publishers.

Fitzpatrick, R., and Morrison, E. J. (1971). "Performance and product evaluation." In E. L. Thorndike (Ed.), *Educational Measurement* (pp. 237–270). Washington, DC: American Council on Education.

Glickman-Bond, J., and Rose, K. (2006). *Creating and using rubrics in today's classrooms: A practical guide*. Norwood, MA: Christopher-Gordon Publishers.

Marzano, R. J. (2008). *Vision document*. Bloomington, IN: Marzano Research Laboratory.

Waugh, C. K., and Gronlund, N. (2013). *Measurement and assessment in teaching* (10th ed.). Columbus, OH: Pearson.

Wormeli, R. (2008). "Show what you know," *Principal Leadership, 9,* no. 1 (September): 48–52.

■ Cyber Stuff

- *The Buros Institute of Mental Measurements,* now located at the University of Nebraska, has for more than 70 years provided assistance to those using commercially published tests. The Institute's *Tests In Print* serves as a comprehensive bibliography for all known commercially published tests. The Buros Institute's *Mental Measurements Yearbook,* the cornerstone of the agency's publishing activities, contains timely and consumer-oriented test reviews. More than a dozen of these periodically revised yearbooks have now been published. This website contains online test reviews and information on over 3,500 tests as well as links to myriad assessment-related sites. **www.unl.edu/buros**

■ *Performance Assessment Links in Science (PALS)* is an online, standards-based, continually updated resource bank of performance-assessment tasks indexed according to the National Science Education Standards and other standards frameworks. Developed by SRI International, PALS contains tasks, directions for students, administrative procedures, rubrics, and examples of student work. Rater-training materials are available. Many of the materials and procedures identified on this website are applicable to subject areas other than science. **www.pals.sri.com**

■ Extended Applications

It is a truism that the more a person uses something, the more familiar with this something the person becomes. This self-evident notion surely applies to the assessment-related knowledge, skills, and concepts you have been reading about in the foreging pages. Thus, to provide readers of *Classroom Assessment* with additional opportunities to apply the content contained in this text, this final section contains a variety of exercises intended to give readers an opportunity to use what they've been reading about.

In a sense, of course, the Self-Check exercises found at the close of this chapter provided an opportunity for readers to apply a chapter's content. Nonetheless, the more times you use a concept, skill, or a body of knowledge, the more likely it is that you will master this content so you can employ it in varied situations.

For each of the text, you will find an extended-application exercise calling for you to do some thinking about that chapter's content as it applies to a real-world situation. Each exercise is preceded by a brief introduction setting forth the reason that the upcoming extended-application exercise has been selected.

Because many of these exercises call on you to generate an original response rather than select a response from a set of options, it is difficult to supply an "answer key" for readers' unpredictable responses. So, what you'll find following all the exercises is One Possible Response—an indication of how I would have personally responded to the exercise if I had been asked to do so. Please don't regard my response as the only way to respond to an exercise. After all, by definition, this is only "one possible" response. Instead, please think of my response as a fairly flimsy form of feedback. You can certainly disagree with me, even emphatically, yet still profit from doing the exercise.

Remember, what is being provided in this section. The exercises deliberately intended to extend how you apply the content treated in *Classroom Assessment*. I hope you find these exercises useful in enhancing your understanding of what teachers need to know about classroom assessment.

■ Clucky-Conduct Detection

Introduction

One of education's truisms is that students who are able to accurately evaluate the performances of others are better able to evaluate their own performances. For instance, if a student recognizes when other students inappropriately use double negatives while they are speaking, then that student is more likely to be able to personally identify (and, hopefully, avoid) double negatives in the student's own utterances.

That's essentially the rationale for this Extended Applications exercise. You'll be given a description of the way a middle school teacher, Ms. Bakke, is using performance assessment in her seventh-grade English class. Your task in the exercise is to see if you can spot errors in the way Ms. Bakke is doing so. If you can discern when colleagues are engaged in clucky conduct, you'll be more likely to detect clucky conduct on your own part.

As you see how Ms. Bakke employs performance assessments in her classes, and how she relies on rubrics as she does so, please be looking for *errors of commission* rather than *errors of omission*. The reason for this is that, in most instances involving performance assessments or almost any other aspect of education, it is always possible to identify one or two extra bells-and-whistles that a teacher *could* have added to the mix. Accordingly, errors of omission are not only tough to spot but they are often also downright debatable. Thus, to keep this exercise more crisp, please consider the way Ms. Bakke plays the performance assessment game in her classes, and then identify any conduct (an error of commission) that, according to this chapter, reeks of cluckiness.

 Exercise Directions: Please review the manner in which teacher Estelle Bakke utilized performance testing in her seventh-grade English classroom. Then, if you identify any clear errors of commission in Ms. Bakke's use of performance assessment, indicate the nature of those mistakes. Please do so before consulting the One Possible Response.

Ms. Bakke's Performance Testing

Beginning a bit over a year ago, largely as a consequence of taking an educational measurement course in connection with her pursuit of a master's degree, Ms. Bakke became a proponent of performance assessment. Whenever the topic comes up in the teachers' lounge, Ms. Bakke tells her colleagues that if teachers want to arrive at accurate inferences about their students' mastery of key skills, then the tests to use are those that most closely approximate the way such skills would be used in the real world. She then argues, sometimes with more fervor than her colleagues prefer, traditional paper-and-pencil tests just aren't as powerful as performance tests. Having witnessed Ms. Bakke become quite excited when she deals with this topic, most of her fellow teachers tend to avoid the topic altogether.

The heart of Ms. Bakke's performance-assessment strategy is never to let a single month go by without gauging her students' skill mastery by using a performance assessment. For example, when her seventh-graders were studying how a business letter should be written, Ms. Bakke called for the students in all four of her seventh-grade English classes to create an actual business letter addressed to an individual in the local community. A list of 40 individuals—and a set of possible topics for each—was distributed to all students at the outset of the three-week unit on "business letters." Students were to prepare a *bona fide* business letter during the unit, make a copy for Ms. Bakke, then actually mail the letter to one of the people on Ms. Bakke's 40 "designated-persons" list.

In all, then, over the course of a full academic year, Ms. Bakke calls for her students to complete about 12 to 14 performance tests. Each of these tests focuses on measuring a student's mastery of a significant English-related skill. Students' performances are always evaluated using a scoring guide (rubric) distributed to students on the first day of a new unit of study. Every one of the rubrics is distinctive, focused on the particular skill being promoted instructionally (and being assessed via a performance test).

Because Ms. Bakke believes the most essential component of a rubric is the set of evaluative factors used when appraising a student's actual performance, she always identifies a minimum of 10 evaluative factors her students can employ when—especially during instruction itself—students judge their own work. In order to come up with a fine-grained collection of evaluative factors for each of the skills she teaches, Ms. Bakke carries out a detailed analysis of those qualities that legitimately distinguish between genuine skill mastery and skill nonmastery.

Ms. Bakke supplies these distinctive per-skill rubrics to her students at the outset of every new instructional unit, then devotes explanatory attention to the nature of each rubric's evaluative factors. Students are given practice in using every unit's rubric, usually by applying the rubrics to their own work, but often using the rubric in a peer-critiquing session in which students evaluate a classmate's work.

Ms. Bakke believes that her complete commitment to performance testing has literally transformed her instructional approach. She recommends it with enthusiasm to any teacher who'll listen, and even to those teachers who seemed disinclined to listen.

■ ■ ■

One Possible Response: There were two serious errors of commission made by Ms. Bakke, and both of them can be captured by the phrase *too many*. She used far too many performance tests in her class. Moreover, she used far too many evaluative factors in her rubrics.

Let's get real. Ms. Bakke has four classes of, say, 25 to 30 students. By trying to use 12 to 14 performance tests in a year, and constructing the tasks and the rubrics that go with them, not to mention scoring students' performances, Ms. Bakke will soon slip into a serious psychotic state. It would be far better for her to focus on only a small number of super-significant skills, then do a first-rate job of using performance tests to measure her students' mastery of those skills.

The other flaw in this teacher's approach was that she insisted on using too many evaluative factors in her rubrics. It is instructionally astute for her to distribute those rubrics to her students at the beginning of each instructional unit. This helps students understand how to judge their emerging skill mastery. But a minimum of 10 evaluative criteria per rubric is clucky indeed. Most human beings can't keep so many evaluative factors in their heads. Ms. Bakke's students probably won't be able to do so either.

It makes more sense for a rubric to be based on three or four *potent* evaluative criteria—factors that a student can master and use—than to build a rubric whose too many evaluative factors overwhelm students.

Other than these two major mistakes, Ms. Bakke's advocacy of performance testing was terrific—as was her implementation of this potent assessment procedure.

■ Glossary

authentic assessment   Performance assessment in which the student's tasks resemble real-life tasks.

evaluative criterion   A factor with which, along with other such factors, we judge the quality of a student's performance.

halo effect   The error of allowing a test-scorer's overall impression of a student to influence any criterion-by-criterion evaluations of the student's response to a test.

hypergeneral rubrics   Scoring guides whose evaluative criteria are described in excessively general—hence, dysfunctional—terms.

performance assessment   A form of testing in which a student is given a task, typically a demanding one, then asked to respond to the task orally, in writing, or by constructing a product.

rubrics   A scoring guide employed to evaluate the quality of a student's responses to performance tests, a student's portfolios, or any kind of student-generated response.

skill-focused rubrics   Scoring guides whose evaluative criteria are applicable for judging a student's responses to any suitable skill-measuring task.

task-specific rubrics   Scoring guides whose evaluative criteria deal only with scoring a student's responses to a particular task, not the full range of tasks that might represent the skill being measured.

Portfolio Assessment

"**A**ssessment should be a part of instruction, not apart from it" is a point of view most proponents of portfolio assessment would enthusiastically endorse. Portfolio assessment, a contemporary entry in the educational measurement derby, has captured the attention of many educators because it represents a clear alternative to more traditional forms of educational testing.

A *portfolio* is a systematic collection of one's work. In education, portfolios refer to systematic collections of students' work. Although the application of portfolios in education has been a relatively recent phenomenon, portfolios have been widely used in a number of other fields for many years. Portfolios, in fact, constitute the chief method by which certain professionals display their skills and accomplishments. For example, portfolios are traditionally used for this purpose by photographers, artists, journalists, models, architects, and so on. An important feature of portfolios is that they must be updated as a person's achievements and skills grow.

Portfolios have been warmly embraced by those educators who regard traditional assessment with less than enthusiasm. In Table 1, for example, a chart presented by Tierney, Carter, and Desai (1991) indicates what those three proponents of portfolios believe are the differences between *portfolio assessment* and assessment based on standardized testing.

From Chapter 9 of *Classroom Assessment: What Teachers Need to Know*, Seventh Edition. W. James Popham. Copyright © 2014 by Pearson Education, Inc. All rights reserved.

table 1 ■ Differences in Assessment Outcomes between Portfolios and Standardized Testing Practices

Portfolio	Testing
Represents the range of reading and writing students are engaged in	Assesses students across a limited range of reading and writing assignments which may not match what students do
Engages students in assessing their progress and/or accomplishments and establishing ongoing learning goals	Mechanically scored or scored by teachers who have little input
Measures each student's achievement while allowing for individual differences between students	Assesses all students on the same dimensions
Represents a collaborative approach to assessment	Assessment process is not collaborative
Has a goal of student self-assessment	Student assessment is not a goal
Addresses improvement, effort, and achievement	Addresses achievement only
Links assessment and teaching to learning	Separates learning, testing, and teaching

Source: Material from *Portfolio Assessment in the Reading-Writing Classroom,* by Robert J. Tierney, Mark A. Carter, and Laura E. Desai, published by Christopher-Gordon Publishers, Inc. © 1991, used with permission of the publisher.

■ Classroom Portfolio Assessment versus Large-Scale Portfolio Assessment

Classroom Applications

Most advocates of portfolio assessment believe the real payoffs for such assessment approaches lie in the individual teacher's classroom, because the relationship between instruction and assessment will be strengthened as a consequence of students' continuing accumulation of work products in their portfolios. Ideally, teachers who adopt portfolios in their classrooms will make the ongoing collection and appraisal of students' work a central focus of the instructional program rather than a peripheral activity whereby students occasionally gather up their work to convince a teacher's supervisors or students' parents that good things have been going on in class.

Here's a description of how an elementary teacher might use portfolios to assess students' progress in social studies, language arts, and mathematics. The teacher, let's call him Phil Pholio, asks students to keep three portfolios, one in each of those three subject fields. In each portfolio, the students are to place their early and revised work products. The work products are always dated so Mr. Pholio, as well as the students themselves, can see what kinds of differences in quality take place over time. For example, if effective instruction is being provided, there should be discernible improvement in the caliber of students' written compositions, solutions to mathematics problems, and analyses of social issues.

Three or four times per semester, Mr. Pholio holds 15- to 20-minute portfolio conferences with each student about the three different portfolios. The other, non-conferencing students take part in small-group and independent learning activities while the portfolio conferences are conducted. During a conference, the participating student plays an active role in evaluating his or her own work. Toward the close of the school year, students select from their regular portfolios a series of work products that not only represent their best final versions but also indicate how those final products were created. These selections are placed in a display portfolio featured at a spring open-school session designed for parents. Parents who visit the school are urged to take their children's display portfolios home. Mr. Pholio also sends portfolios home to parents who are unable to attend the open-school event.

There are, of course, many other ways to use portfolios effectively in a classroom. Phil Pholio, our phictitious (sic) teacher, employed a fairly common approach, but a variety of alternative procedures could also work quite nicely. The major consideration is that the teacher uses portfolio *assessment* as an integral aspect of the *instructional* process. Because portfolios can be tailored to a specific student's evolving growth, the ongoing diagnostic value of portfolios for teachers is immense.

Who Is Evaluating Whom?

Roger Farr, a leader in language arts instruction and assessment, contends that the real payoff from proper portfolio assessment is that students' *self-evaluation* capabilities are enhanced. Thus, during portfolio conferences the teacher encourages students to come up with personal appraisals of their own work. The conference, then, becomes far more than merely an opportunity for the teacher to dispense an "oral report card." On the contrary, students' self-evaluation skills are nurtured not only during portfolio conferences but also throughout the entire school year. For this reason, Farr strongly prefers the use of **working portfolios** instead of **showcase portfolios** because he believes self-evaluation is nurtured more readily in connection with ongoing reviews of products not intended to impress external viewers.

For self-evaluation purposes, it is particularly useful to be able to compare earlier work with later work. Fortunately, even if a teacher's instruction is downright abysmal, students grow older and, as a consequence of maturation, tend to get better at what they do in school. If a student is required to review three versions of a student's written composition (a first draft, a second draft, and a final draft), self-evaluation can be fostered by encouraging the student to make comparative judgments of the three compositions based on appropriate evaluative criteria. As anyone who has done much writing knows, written efforts tend to get better with time and revision. Contrasts of later versions with earlier versions can prove illuminating from an appraisal perspective and, because students' self-evaluation is so critical to their future growth, from an instructional perspective as well.

Large-Scale Applications

It is one thing to use portfolios for classroom assessment; it is quite another to use portfolios for large-scale assessment programs. Several states and large school districts have attempted to install portfolios as a central component of a large-scale accountability assessment program—that is, a program in which student performances serve as an indicator of an educational system's effectiveness. To date, the results of efforts to employ portfolios for accountability purposes have not been encouraging.

In large-scale applications of portfolio assessments for accountability purposes, students' portfolios are judged either by the students' regular teachers or by a cadre of specially trained scorers (often teachers) who carry out the scoring at a central site. The problem with specially trained scorers and central-site scoring is that it typically costs much more than can be afforded. Some states, therefore, have opted to have all portfolios scored by students' own teachers who then relay such scores to the state department. The problem with having regular teachers score students' portfolios, however, is that such scoring tends to be too unreliable for use in accountability programs. Not only have teachers usually not been provided with thorough training about how to score portfolios, but there is also a tendency for teachers to be biased in favor of their own students. To cope with such problems, sometimes teachers in a school or district evaluate their students' portfolios, but then a random sample of those portfolios are scored by state officials as an "audit" of the local scoring's accuracy.

One of the most visible of the statewide efforts to use portfolios on every pupil has been a performance assessment program in the state of Vermont. Because substantial national attention has been focused on the Vermont program, and because it has been evaluated independently, many policymakers in other states have drawn on the experiences encountered in the Vermont Portfolio Assessment Program. Unfortunately, independent evaluators of Vermont's statewide efforts to use portfolios found that there was considerable unreliability in the appraisals given to students' work. It's tough to draw valid inferences about students' achievements if the assessments of those achievements are not made with consistency.

But, of course, this is a text about classroom assessment, not large-scale assessment. It certainly hasn't been shown definitely that portfolios do *not* have a place in large-scale assessment. What has been shown, however, is that there are significant obstacles to be surmounted if portfolio assessment is going to make a meaningful contribution to large-scale educational accountability testing.

Decision Time

Does Self-Evaluation Equal Self-Grading?

After a midsummer, schoolwide three-day workshop on the Instructional Payoffs of Classroom Portfolios, the faculty at Rhoda Street Elementary School have agreed to install student portfolios in all classrooms for one or more subject areas. Maria Martinez, an experienced third-grade teacher in the school, has decided to try out portfolios only in mathematics. She admits to her family (but not to her fellow teachers) that she's not certain she'll be able to use portfolios properly with her students.

Because she has attempted to follow the guidelines of the National Council of Teachers of Mathematics, Maria stresses mathematical problem solving and the integration of mathematical understanding with content from other disciplines. Accordingly, she asks her students to place in their mathematics portfolios versions of their attempts to solve quantitative problems drawn from other subjects. Maria poses these problems for her third-graders and then requires them to prepare an initial solution strategy and to revise that solution at least twice. Students are directed to put all solutions (dated) in their portfolios.

Six weeks after the start of school, Maria sets up a series of 15-minute portfolio conferences with her students. During the three days on which the portfolio conferences are held, students who are not involved in a conference move through a series of learning stations in other subject areas where they typically engage in a fair amount of peer critiquing of each others' responses to various kinds of practice exercises.

Having learned during the summer workshop that the promotion of students' self-evaluation is critical if students are to get the most from portfolios, Maria devotes the bulk of her 15-minute conferences to students' personal appraisals of their own work. Although Maria offers some of her own appraisals of most students' work, she typically allows the student's self-evaluation to override her own estimates of a student's ability to solve each problem.

Because it will soon be time to give students their 10-week grades, Maria doesn't know whether to base the grades on her own judgments or on students' self-appraisals.

 If you were Maria, what would you decide to do?

■ Key Ingredients in Classroom Portfolio Assessment

Although there are numerous ways to install and sustain portfolios in a classroom, you will find that the following seven-step sequence provides a reasonable template for getting under way with portfolio assessment. Taken together, these seven activities capture the key ingredients in classroom-based portfolio assessment.

Portfolio Assessment

1. *Make sure your students "own" their portfolios.* In order for portfolios to represent a student's evolving work accurately, and to foster the kind of self-evaluation so crucial if portfolios are to be truly educational, students must perceive portfolios to be collections of their own work and not merely temporary receptacles for products you ultimately grade. You will probably want to introduce the notion of portfolio assessment to your students (assuming portfolio assessment isn't already a schoolwide operation and your students aren't already familiar with the use of portfolios) by explaining the distinctive functions of portfolios in the classroom.

2. *Decide on what kinds of work samples to collect.* Various kinds of work samples can be included in a portfolio. Obviously, such products will vary from subject to subject. In general, a wide variety of work products is preferable to a limited range of work products. Ideally, you and your students can collaboratively determine what goes in the portfolio.

3. *Collect and store work samples.* Students need to collect the designated work samples as they are created, place them in a suitable container (a folder or notebook, for example), and then store the container in a file cabinet, storage box, or some suitably safe location. You may need to work individually with your students to help them decide whether particular products should be placed in their portfolios. The actual organization of a portfolio's contents depends, of course, on the nature of the work samples being collected.

4. *Select criteria by which to evaluate portfolio work samples.* Working collaboratively with students, carve out a set of criteria by which you and your students can judge the quality of your students' portfolio products. Because of the likely diversity of products in different students' portfolios, the identification of evaluative criteria will not be a simple task. Yet, unless at least rudimentary evaluative criteria are isolated, the students will find it difficult to evaluate their own efforts and, thereafter, to strive for improvement. The criteria, once selected, should be described with clarityregarding how to employ a rubric's evaluative criteria when judging students' responses to performance test tasks.

5. *Require students to evaluate continually their own portfolio products.* Using the agreed-on evaluative criteria, be sure your students routinely appraise their own work. Students can be directed to evaluate their work products holistically, analytically, or using a combination of both approaches. Such self-evaluation can be made routine by requiring each student to complete brief evaluation slips on 3" × 5" cards on which they identify the major strengths and weaknesses of a given product and then suggest how the product could be improved. Be sure to have your students date such self-evaluation sheets so they can keep track of modifications in their self-evaluation skills. Each completed self-evaluation sheet should be stapled or paper-clipped to the work product being evaluated.

6. *Schedule and conduct portfolio conferences.* Portfolio conferences take time. Yet, these interchange sessions between teachers and students regarding

students' work are really pivotal in making sure portfolio assessment fulfills its potential. The conference should not only evaluate your students' work products but should also help them improve their self-evaluation abilities. Try to hold as many of these conferences as you can. In order to make the conferences time efficient, be sure to have students prepare for the conferences so you can start right in on the topics of most concern to you and the student.

7. *Involve parents in the portfolio assessment process.* Early in the school year, make sure your students' parents understand what the nature of the portfolio assessment process is you've devised for your classroom. Insofar as is practical, encourage your students' parents/guardians periodically to review their children's work samples as well as their children's self-evaluation of those work samples. The more active parents become in reviewing their children's work, the stronger the message will be to the child that the portfolio activity is really worthwhile. If you wish, you may have students select their best work for a showcase portfolio or, instead, simply use the students' working portfolios.

These seven steps reflect only the most important activities teachers might engage in when creating assessment programs in their classrooms. There are obviously all sorts of variations and embellishments possible.

There's one situation in which heavy student involvement in the portfolio process may not make instructional sense. This occurs in the early grades when, in the teacher's judgment, those little tykes are not developmentally ready to take a meaningful hand in a full-blown portfolio self-evaluation extravaganza. Any sort of educational assessment ought to be *developmentally appropriate* for the students who are being assessed. Thus, for students who are in early primary grade levels, a teacher may sensibly decide to employ only *showcase* portfolios to display a child's accomplishments to the child and the child's parents. *Working* portfolios, simply bristling with student-evaluated products, can be left for later. This is, clearly, a teacher's call.

Purposeful Portfolios

There are numerous choice-points you'll encounter if you embark on a portfolio assessment approach in your own classroom. The first one ought to revolve around *purpose.* Why is it that you are contemplating a meaningful prance down the portfolio pathway?

Assessment specialists typically identify three chief purposes for portfolio assessment. The first of these is *documentation of student progress* wherein the major function of the assembled work samples is to provide the student, the teacher, and the student's parents with evidence about the student's growth—or lack of it. These are the *working* portfolios that provide meaningful opportunities for self-evaluation by students.

Pointing out that students' achievement levels ought to influence teachers' instructional decisions, Anderson (2003, p. 44) concludes that "the information should be collected as near to the decision as possible (e.g., final examinations are administered in close proximity to end-of-term grades). However, if decisions are to be based on learning, then a plan for information collection over time must be developed and implemented." The more current any documentation of students' progress is, the more accurate that documentation is apt to be.

A second purpose of portfolios is to provide an opportunity for *showcasing student accomplishments.* Stiggins (2007) describes portfolios that showcase students' best work as *celebration portfolios,* and he contends celebration portfolios are especially appropriate for the early grades. In portfolios intended to showcase student accomplishments, students typically select their best work and reflect thoughtfully on its quality.

One midwest teacher I know always makes sure students include the following elements in their showcase portfolios:

- A letter of introduction to portfolio reviewers
- A table of contents
- Identification of the skills or knowledge being demonstrated
- A representative sample of the student's best work
- Dates on all entries
- The evaluative criteria (or rubric) being used
- The student's self-reflection on all entries

The inclusion of student self-reflections about ingredients of portfolios is a pivotal ingredient in showcase portfolios. Some portfolio proponents contend a portfolio's self-evaluation by the student helps the learner to learn better and permits the reader of the portfolio to gain insights about how the learner learns.

A final purpose for portfolios is *evaluation of student status*—that is, the determination of whether students have met previously determined quality levels of performance. McMillan (2011) points out that when portfolios are used for this purpose, there must be greater standardization about what should be included in a portfolio and how the work samples should be appraised. Typically, teachers select the entries for this kind of portfolio, and considerable attention is given to scoring so any rubrics employed to score the portfolios will yield consistent results even if different scorers are involved. For portfolios being used to evaluate student status, there is usually less need for self-evaluation of entries—unless such self-evaluations are themselves being evaluated by others.

Well, we've peeked at three purposes underlying portfolio assessment. Can one portfolio perform all three functions? My answer is a somewhat shaky *yes*. But if you were to ask me whether one portfolio can perform all three functions *well,* you'd get a rock-solid *no*. The three functions, though somewhat rather related— like second cousins—are fundamentally different.

That's why your very first decision if you're going to install portfolios in your classroom is to decide on the *primary purpose* of the portfolios. You can then determine what the portfolios should look like and how students should prepare them.

Scripture tells us that "no man can serve two masters." (The authors of that scriptural advice, clearly insensitive to gender equality, were not implying that females are more capable of double-master serving.) Similarly, one kind of portfolio cannot blithely satisfy multiple functions. Some classroom teachers rush into portfolio assessment because they've heard about all of the enthralling things that portfolios can do. But one kind of portfolio cannot easily fulfill all three functions. Pick your top-priority purpose and then build your portfolio assessment to satisfy this purpose.

Work-Sample Selection

For a teacher just joining the portfolio party, another key decision hinges on the identification of the work samples to be put into the portfolios. All too often, teachers who are novices at portfolio assessment will fail to think divergently enough about the kinds of entries that should constitute a portfolio's chief contents.

But divergency is not necessarily a virtue when it comes to the determination of a portfolio's contents. You shouldn't search for varied kinds of work samples simply for the sake of variety. What's important is that the particular kinds of work samples to be included in the portfolio will allow you to derive valid inferences about the skills and/or knowledge you're trying to have your students master. It's far better to include a few kinds of *inference-illuminating* work samples than to include a galaxy of work samples, many of which do not contribute to your inferences about students' knowledge or skills.

Appraising Portfolios

As indicated earlier in the chapter, students' portfolios are almost always evaluated by the use of a scoring rubric. The most important ingredients of such a rubric are its evaluative criteria—that is, the factors to be used in determining the quality of a particular student's portfolio. If there's any sort of student self-evaluation to be done, and such self-evaluation is almost always desirable, then it is imperative that students have access to, and thoroughly understand, the rubric that will be used to evaluate their portfolios.

For certain applications of formative assessment, students must definitely understand the rubrics (and those rubrics' evaluative criteria). However, for *all* forms of portfolio assessment, students' familiarity with rubrics is imperative.

Here's one quick-and-dirty way to appraise any sort of portfolio assessments you might install in your classroom. Simply ask yourself whether your students' portfolios have substantially increased the accuracy of the inferences you make regarding your students' skills and knowledge. If your answer is *yes*, then portfolio assessment is a winner for you. If your answer is *no*, then pitch those portfolios without delay—or guilt. But wait! If your answer resembles "I'm not sure," then you really need to think this issue through rigorously. Classroom assessment is supposed to contribute to more valid inferences from which better instructional decisions can be made. If your portfolio assessment program isn't *clearly* doing those things, you may need to make some serious changes in that program.

■ The Pros and Cons of Portfolio Assessment

You must keep in mind that portfolio assessment's greatest strength is that it can be tailored to the individual student's needs, interests, and abilities. Yet, portfolio assessment suffers from the drawback faced by all constructed-response measurement. Students' constructed responses are genuinely difficult to evaluate, particularly when those responses vary from student to student.

As was seen in Vermont's Portfolio Assessment Program, it is quite difficult to come up with consistent evaluations of different students' portfolios. Sometimes the scoring guides devised for use in evaluating portfolios are so terse and so general as to be almost useless. They're akin to Rorschach inkblots in which different scorers see in the scoring guide what they want to see. In contrast, some scoring guides are so detailed and complicated that they simply overwhelm scorers. It is difficult to devise scoring guides that embody just the right level of specificity. Generally speaking, most teachers are so busy they don't have time to create elaborate scoring schemes. Accordingly, many teachers (and students) find themselves judging portfolios by using fairly loose evaluative criteria. Such criteria tend to be interpreted differently by different people.

Portfolio Assessment

Not of time required

Another problem with portfolio assessment is it takes time—loads of time—to carry out properly. Even if you're very efficient in reviewing your students' portfolios, you'll still have to devote many hours both in class (during portfolio conferences) and outside of class (if you also want to review your students' portfolios by yourself). Proponents of portfolios are convinced the quality of portfolio assessment is worth the time such assessment takes. You at least need to be

but what does this have to do with Teaching?

Portfolio assessment almost always fundamentally changes a teacher's approach to instruction. A nifty little selected-response test, or even a lengthy constructed-response exam, can usually be tossed into a teacher's ongoing instructional program without significantly altering how the teacher goes about teaching. But that's not so with portfolio assessment. Once a teacher hops aboard the portfolio bus, there's a long and serious ride in the offing.

Portfolio assessment, if it's properly focused on helping children improve by being able to evaluate their own work samples, becomes a continuing and *central* component of a teacher's instructional program. Work samples have to be chosen, scoring rubrics need to be developed, and students need to be taught how to use those rubrics to monitor the evolving quality of their efforts. Portfolio assessment, therefore, truly dominates most instructional programs in which it is employed.

The first thing you need to do, therefore, is decide whether the knowledge and skills you are trying to have your students master (especially the skills) lend themselves to portfolio assessment. Will there be student work samples that, because they permit you to make inferences about your students' evolving skill mastery, could provide the continuing focus for portfolio assessment?

Some content lends itself delightfully to portfolio assessment. Some doesn't. During my first year as a high school teacher, I taught two English courses and a speech class. Because my English courses focused on the promotion of students' composition skills, I think that a portfolio assessment might have worked well in either English course. My students and I could monitor their improvements in being able to write.

But I don't think I would have been able to use portfolios effectively in my speech class. At that time, television itself had just arrived on the West Coast, and videotaping was unknown. Accordingly, my speech students and I wouldn't have had anything to toss in their portfolios.

The first big question you need to ask yourself when it comes to portfolio assessment is quite simple: Is this powerful but time-consuming form of assessment right for what I'm trying to teach?

prepared for the required investment of time if you decide to undertake portfolio assessment. And teachers will definitely need to receive sufficient training to learn how to carry out portfolio assessment well. Any teachers who set out to do portfolio assessment by simply stuffing student stuff into folders built for stuff stuffing will end up wasting their time and their students' time. Meaningful professional development is a must if portfolio assessment is to work well. If several teachers in a school will be using portfolio assessment in their classes, this would be a marvelous opportunity to establish a *teacher learning community* in which, on a continuing basis during the year, portfolio-using teachers meet to share insights and work collaboratively on common problems.

On the plus side, however, most teachers who have used portfolios agree portfolio assessment provides a way of documenting and evaluating growth happening in a classroom in ways standardized or written tests cannot. Portfolios have the potential to create authentic portraits of what students learn. I agree with Stiggins (2007) when he points out that for portfolios to merge effectively with instruction, they must have a story to tell. Fortunately, this story can be made compatible with improved student learning.

Most of the teachers I've talked with who use portfolio assessments are primarily enamored with two payoffs. They believe that the *self-evaluation* it fosters in students is truly important in guiding students' learning over time. They also think the *personal ownership* students experience regarding their own work, and the progress they experience, makes the benefits of portfolio assessment outweigh its costs.

What Do Classroom Teachers Really Need to Know about Portfolio Assessment?

The more familiar you are with different kinds of test items, the more likely you will be to select an item type that best provides you with the information you need in order to draw suitable inferences about your students. Until recently, portfolios haven't been viewed as a viable assessment option by many teachers. These days, however, portfolio assessment clearly is a legitimate weapon in a teacher's assessment arsenal.

You need to realize, if portfolio assessment is going to constitute a helpful adjunct to your instructional program, portfolios will have to become a central, not tangential, part of what goes on in your classroom. The primary premise in portfolio assessment is that a particularized collection of a student's *evolving* work will allow both the student and you to determine the student's progress. You can't gauge the student's progress if you don't have frequent evidence of the student's efforts.

It would be educationally unwise to select portfolio assessment as a one-time measurement approach to deal with a short-term instructional objective. Rather, it makes more sense to select some key curricular aim, such as the student's ability to write original compositions, and then monitor this aspect of the student's learning throughout the entire school year. It is also important for you to recall that although portfolio assessment may prove highly valuable for classroom instruction and measurement purposes, at this juncture there is insufficient evidence it can be used appropriately for large-scale assessment.

A number of portfolio assessment specialists believe the most important dividend from portfolio assessment is the increased abilities of students to evaluate their own work. If this becomes one of your goals in a portfolio assessment approach, you must be certain to nurture such self-evaluation growth deliberately via portfolios instead of simply using portfolios as convenient collections of work samples.

The seven key ingredients in portfolio assessment that were identified in the chapter represent only one way of installing this kind of assessment strategy. Variations of those seven suggested procedures are not only possible but also to be encouraged. The big thing to keep in mind is that portfolio assessment offers your students and you a way to particularize your evaluation of each student's growth over time. And, speaking of time, it's only appropriate to remind you it takes substantially more time to use a portfolio assessment approach properly than to score a zillion true-false tests. If you opt to try portfolio assessment, you'll have to see whether, *in your own instructional situation,* it yields sufficient educational benefits to be worth the investment you'll surely need to make in it.

Parent Talk

Suppose that Mr. and Mrs. Holmgren, parents of your student, Harry, stopped by your classroom during a back-to-school night to examine their son's portfolio. After spending almost 30 minutes going through the portfolio and skimming the portfolios of several other students, they speak to you—not with hostility, but with genuine confusion. Mrs. Holmgren sums up their concerns nicely with the following comments: "When we stopped by Mr. Bray's classroom earlier this evening to see how our daughter, Elissa, is doing, we encountered a series of extremely impressive portfolios. Elissa's was outstanding. To be honest, Harry's portfolio is a lot less polished. It seems that he's included everything he's done in your class, rough drafts as well as final products. Why is there this difference?"

 If I were you, here's how I'd respond to Harry's parents:

"It's really good that you two could take the time to see how Harry and Elissa are doing. And I can understand why you're perplexed by the differences in Elissa's and Harry's portfolios. You see, there are *different* kinds of student portfolios, and different portfolios serve different purposes.

"In Mr. Bray's class, and I know this because we often exchange portfolio tips with one another during regular meetings of our teacher learning community, students prepare what are called *showcase* portfolios. In such portfolios, students pick their very best work to show Mr. Bray and their parents what they've learned. I think Mr. Bray actually sent his students' showcase portfolios home about a month ago so you could see how well Elissa is doing. For Mr. Bray and his students, the portfolios are collections of best work that, in a very real sense, celebrate students' achievements.

"In my class, however, students create *working* portfolios in which the real emphasis is on getting students to make progress and to evaluate this progress *on their own*. When you reviewed Harry's portfolio, did you see how each entry is dated and how he had prepared a brief self-reflection of each entry? I'm more interested in Harry's seeing the improvement he makes than in anyone seeing polished final products. You, too, can see the striking progress he's made over the course of this school year.

"I'm not suggesting that my kind of portfolio is better than Mr. Bray's. Both have a role to play. Those roles, as I'm sure you'll see, are quite different."

 Now, how would you respond to Mr. and Mrs. Holmgren?

■ Chapter Summary

After defining portfolios as systematic collections of students' work, contrasts were drawn between portfolio assessment and more conventional testing. It was suggested that portfolio assessment was far more appropriate for an individual teacher's classroom assessment than for large-scale accountability assessments.

An emphasis on self-assessment was suggested as being highly appropriate for portfolio assessment, particularly in view of the way portfolios can be tailored to an *individual* student's evolving progress. Seven steps were then suggested as key ingredients for classroom teachers to install and sustain portfolio assessment in their classroom: (1) establish student ownership, (2) decide on what work samples to collect, (3) collect and score work samples, (4) select evaluative criteria, (5) require continual student self-evaluations, (6) schedule and conduct portfolio conferences, and (7) involve parents in the portfolio assessment process.

Three different functions of portfolio assessment were identified—namely, documentation of student progress, showcasing student accomplishments, and evaluation of student status. Teachers were urged to select a primary purpose for portfolio assessment.

The chapter was concluded with an identification of plusses and minuses of portfolio assessment. It was emphasized that portfolio assessment represents an important measurement strategy now available to today's classroom teachers.

 # Self-Check

The self-check for this chapter will be somewhat different because it has been stressed that teachers who install portfolio assessment systems in their own classes will undoubtedly devise procedures to mesh with their own subject-matter emphases and the abilities, interests, and maturity of the students they teach. Nonetheless, to give you a bit of practice in using the seven key ingredients of classroom performance assessments presented in the chapter, you'll be reading a pair of scenarios about fictitious teachers who are installing and operating portfolio assessment programs in their mythical classrooms. Your task, as a compliant self-checker, is to read each scenario and then decide if one or more of the seven key ingredients are missing or have been violated. If you want to review the seven ingredients before you tackle these two self-check exercises, there are no prohibitions to your returning to the respective text.

Scenario One

Having decided to adopt a portfolio assessment approach for the composition segment of her junior high school English classes, Maria Flores introduces her students to the new assessment scheme by asking a commercial-artist friend of hers to speak to each class. The artist brings his own portfolio and shows students how the portfolio allows prospective clients to judge his work. Ms. Flores tells her students that her friend's portfolio is called a "showcase portfolio" and that students will be preparing both a showcase portfolio to periodically involve their parents in reviewing work products, as well as a "working portfolio" to keep track of *all* of their composition drafts and final products. Ms. Flores and her friend emphasize that both kinds of portfolios must be owned by the students, not the teacher.

Because all of their drafts and final versions are to be collected, students simply place copies of all such products in folders and, when finished, in a designated file drawer. Early in the academic year, Ms. Flores works with each of her classes to decide collaboratively on the criteria to be used on judging the composition efforts for a given class. Although there are slight differences in the criteria decided on for each class, the criteria for all of her classes are fairly similar.

Ms. Flores makes sure to review all students' portfolios at least once a month. Typically, she devotes one preparation period a day to a different class's portfolios. Because the portfolios are readily available in a file cabinet in her classroom, Ms. Flores finds it convenient and time efficient to evaluate students' progress in this manner. She provides a brief (dated) "teacher's evaluation" for students to consider when they work with their own portfolios.

At least twice every term, Ms. Flores selects what she considers to be the students' best finished works from their working portfolios. She places such work products in a showcase portfolio. Students are directed to take these showcase portfolios home to let their families see what kinds of compositions they have been creating. Parents are enthusiastic about this practice. A number of parents have told the school principal that Ms. Flores's "take-home" portfolio system is the way they would like to see other aspects of their children's performances evaluated.

Now, please critique Ms. Flores's efforts in relation to the seven key ingredients of portfolio assessment supplied in the chapter.

Scenario Two

A third-grade teacher, Gary Gately, has just completed a summer staff-development workshop on portfolio assessment. He and a number of the teachers at his school have decided to try out performance assessment in at least limited parts of their instructional and assessment programs. Gary has also decided to use portfolios with his students' mathematics work.

He introduces students to the activity by stressing the importance of their personal ownership of the portfolios and the significance of their own evaluations of the kinds of mathematics work they put in their portfolios. Gary suggests to the class that students include only problem-solution mathematics work in their portfolios. Thus, all drill work and simple computational work is not to be put in the portfolios. The students discuss this suggestion and readily agree.

Gary works with students for two full days to decide on the evaluative criteria they, and he, will use to evaluate the mathematics work in the portfolios. They decide that the major criteria will be (1) selection of proper solution strategies, (2) accurate completion of selected solution procedures, and (3) arrival at the correct solution to the problem.

Students routinely collect their work and place it for safekeeping in specially marked cardboard boxes that Gary has placed on the "Portfolio Shelf." Every two months, Gary holds an individual portfolio conference with each student during which he supplies the student with a "teacher's appraisal" of the portfolio's work.

It is clear to Gary that his students' ability to solve mathematics problems has improved substantially. Although it took students several weeks to get used to the process, they now seem to thoroughly enjoy Gary's version of portfolio assessment in mathematics.

Conjure up a critique of Mr. Gately's approach to portfolio assessment.

Pondertime

1. What do you personally believe is the most important strength of portfolio assessment? What about the most important weakness of this form of assessment?

2. Three purposes of portfolio assessment were described in the chapter: documentation of student progress, showcasing student accomplishments, and evaluation of student status. Which of these three purposes do you believe to be most meritorious? And, of course, why?

3. What subjects, if any, do not lend themselves to some form of portfolio assessment?

4. If it is true that portfolios need to be personalized for particular students, is it possible to devise one-size-fits-all criteria for evaluating classroom portfolio work products? Why or why not?

5. How can the substantial time demands of portfolio assessment be most effectively addressed by classroom teachers?

Self-Check Key

Scenario One

Ms. Flores's approach to portfolio assessment had much to commend it. Indeed, if the approach is really working, she probably shouldn't tinker with it. There were, however, two ingredients Ms. Flores overlooked that some proponents of portfolio assessment consider important. First, she didn't push students very hard in the direction of self-evaluation. Second, she didn't hold any one-on-one portfolio conferences. During such conferences, of course, Ms. Flores could nurture students' self-evaluation skills. For a first try at performance assessment, however, our fictitious Ms. Flores did a rather nifty job.

Scenario Two

Gary missed out on only two of the chapter's seven key ingredients. He didn't involve parents in the process and, although he made some early noise about promoting self-evaluation on the part of the students, he really didn't push students' self-evaluation during the portfolio conferences or apart from those conferences.

◼ Additional Stuff

Anderson, Lorin W. (2003). *Classroom assessment: Enhancing the quality of teacher decision making.* Mahwah, NJ: Lawrence Erlbaum.

Andrade, H. (2007/2008). "Self-assessment through rubrics," *Educational Leadership, 65,* no. 4 (December/January): 60–63.

McMillan, J. H. (2011). *Classroom assessment: Principles and practice for effective standards-based instruction* (5th ed.). Boston: Allyn and Bacon.

Miller, M. D., and Linn, R. (2013). *Measurement and assessment in teaching* (11th ed.). Columbus, OH: Pearson.

Niguidula, D. (2005). "Documenting learning with digital portfolios," *Educational Leadership, 63,* no. 3 (November): 44–47.

Sadler, P. M., and Good, E. (2006). "The impact of self- and peer-grading on student learning," *Educational Assessment, 11,* no. 1: 1–32.

Stiggins, Richard J. (2007). *Student-involved classroom assessment for learning* (5th ed.). Upper Saddle River, NJ: Prentice-Hall.

Stiggins, Richard J., and Chappuis, J. (2011). *An introduction to student-involved classroom assessment for learning* (6th ed.). Boston: Pearson.

Tierney, R. J., Carter, M. A., and Desai, L. E. (1991). *Portfolio assessment in the reading-writing classroom.* Norwood, MA: Christopher-Gordon Publishers.

◼ Cyber Stuff

- *Edutopia* is a project of the George Lucas Educational Foundation. The group makes available a website often presenting innovative uses of classroom educational assessments such as portfolio assessments and performance assessments. One of the organization's core strategies is comprehensive assessment, so a search of "assessment articles" yielded about 800 resources. This site contains a delightful mix of theoretically sound and eminently practical ideas about assessment. **www.edutopia.org**

Extended Applications

It is a truism that the more a person uses something, the more familiar with this something the person becomes. This self-evident notion surely applies to the assessment-related knowledge, skills, and concepts you have been reading about in the foreging pages. Thus, to provide readers of *Classroom Assessment* with additional opportunities to apply the content contained in this text, this final section contains a variety of exercises intended to give readers an opportunity to use what they've been reading about.

In a sense, of course, the Self-Check exercises found at the close of this chapter provided an opportunity for readers to apply a chapter's content. Nonetheless, the more times you use a concept, skill, or a body of knowledge, the more likely it is that you will master this content so you can employ it in varied situations.

For each of the text, you will find an extended-application exercise calling for you to do some thinking about that chapter's content as it applies to a real-world situation. Each exercise is preceded by a brief introduction setting forth the reason that the upcoming extended-application exercise has been selected.

Because many of these exercises call on you to generate an original response rather than select a response from a set of options, it is difficult to supply an "answer key" for readers' unpredictable responses. So, what you'll find following all the exercises is One Possible Response—an indication of how I would have personally responded to the exercise if I had been asked to do so. Please don't regard my response as the only way to respond to an exercise. After all, by definition, this is only "one possible" response. Instead, please think of my response as a fairly flimsy form of feedback. You can certainly disagree with me, even emphatically, yet still profit from doing the exercise.

Remember, what is being provided in this section. The exercises deliberately intended to extend how you apply the content treated in *Classroom Assessment*. I hope you find these exercises useful in enhancing your understanding of what teachers need to know about classroom assessment.

Portfolio Procedures: Fine and Flawed

Introduction

This exercise is based on the same rationale as was the exercise for the chapter: If teachers can spot flawed conduct by colleagues, then those observant teachers will be more likely to discern similar mistakes in their own conduct.

Because an important feature of this chapter's treatment of portfolio assessment is its isolation of seven key ingredients associated with classroom portfolio assessment, you're now going to be given two fictional vignettes describing two teachers who—for the very first time—are carrying out portfolio assessment in their own classrooms. Your task in this two-part exercise is to see whether each teacher either omits or messes up one or more of the chapter's seven key ingredients.

This exercise is similar to the Self-Check that's found at the close of this chapter where two fictional teachers were, in a somewhat flawed fashion, employing portfolio assessment. I assure you that the two pretend teachers in the upcoming exercise are different from the two Self-Check teachers. Actually, they've never met.

 Exercise Directions: Please read each of the following two vignettes, then—for each—identify any omitted or distorted activities identified in this Chapter's Key Ingredients in Classroom Portfolio Assessment.

Vignette One: Fourth-Grade Composition

Mark Jones has been teaching fourth-graders for three years and enjoys his teaching tremendously. This year, however, he has decided to install a portfolio assessment system to help students become more skilled in writing the sorts of rudimentary compositions required of such youngsters. Officials in his state have only recently required fourth-grade students to provide original on-demand writing samples during the state's annual spring accountability tests for all students in grades 3 through 8 and 11. Here's how Mark used portfolio assessment in his class.

At the beginning of the school year, Mark introduced himself to his new students and indicated that in his class, students would be keeping portfolios of their written compositions as a way of helping them learn how to become better writers. He provided each student with a cardboard expandable folder on which each student's name was printed. Mark pointed out that whatever went into those folders belonged to the student whose name was on the folder. He stated that the contents of each folder were *private property,* and only the folder's owner could make available to others the written compositions that, over time, would be collected. Most importantly, Mark continued, "These portfolios are being used *not to grade you* but to *improve your composition skills.*"

Mark then told his students he wants them to place in their portfolios certain selections from the once-a-week compositions that he will ask them to write. After discussing the number of compositions to place in the portfolios, Mark and his students agreed that any composition of two paragraphs or more in length will be placed in the portfolios, but only from the first and third weeks of each month. Approximately, then, 18 compositions are to be placed in each student's expandable folder. The folders are going to be stored in three file cabinets designated for that purpose.

During the second week of the school year, Mark described to his students what a "rubric" is and how it was to be the chief way that he (and they) would be evaluating their written work. He placed six evaluative criteria on the chalkboard—for example, "a composition's organization"—then explained and discussed each criterion with his students. Because the evaluative criterion of "voice" proved too unclear to the class, and because students strongly preferred that it be dropped, Mark acceded. The rubric for judging students' compositions, then, featured the following five evaluative criteria: organization, content, mechanics, word choice, and clarity. To help his students see how the criteria were to be used, he distributed several particularly strong and several particularly weak compositions from previous students, then showed his class how these compositions did or did not satisfy the rubric's evaluative criteria.

Mark urged his students to employ their five-criterion rubric throughout the school year to monitor what he was sure would be their evolving ability to write first-rate compositions. As the months went by, Mark was quite pleased with the way that portfolio assessment seemed to be rolling along in his fourth-grade class.

Any missing/messed up activities by Mark? _____

_____

_____

 One Possible Response: Mark's portfolio procedure can be characterized in one simple phrase as "Super Start: Subsequent Stumble." He really hit the ground galloping and did a great job in employing activities consistent with the chapter's seven key ingredients. But then, other than urging his students to use the class-determined rubric to evaluate their own work, he failed to capitalize on the real payoff of portfolio assessment—namely, getting students to become skilled self-evaluators. That sort of self-evaluation is best accomplished by *requiring* students to appraise their own efforts. Self-evaluation can also be nurtured by frequent portfolio conferences with the teacher and, insofar as is practical, by involving parents in the evaluative process.

Mark seems to have established a sensible structure for classroom portfolio assessment, but he failed to take advantage of the most significant reason portfolio assessment has prospered in our schools—that is, increasing students' abilities to judge the quality of their own work.

■ ■ ■

Vignette Two: High School General Science

Jolene Jergins is an experienced high school science teacher who has, over the years, taught chemistry, biology, and physics. For the past two years, in the large urban high school where Jolene teaches, she has been teaching general science courses that draw on all three of those content areas—as well as some material based on earth and space science.

During the past year, Jolene employed a portfolio assessment approach in two of her four general science classes—primarily to see if, in her judgment, it helped or hurt students' learning. Here's how she did it:

In the two portfolio-assessment classes (about 30 students in each), Jolene opened each class by pointing out that she would be using portfolio assessment, for the first time in any of her classes, to improve students' "investigative skills." She admitted, quite candidly, that she was not sure about whether portfolio assessment was going to be effective. However, if it was going to work at all, students would need to recognize that the portfolios belonged to the students who created them—not to her. The purpose of portfolio assessment, she continued, is to foster each student's skills by relying on self-evaluation, not teacher evaluation. Thus, whether a student would benefit from this assessment approach, she concluded, would be based on whether each student truly owned what was in that student's portfolio.

Because there were to be eight small-scale, student-conducted investigations carried out during the year, Jolene decided that a student's write-up of each investigation should include a description of the study's procedures, any resultant data, and the conclusions drawn by the student.

Jolene then described four criteria to be used in judging a student's investigative efforts. These four criteria, when combined, constituted the rubric by which students were to judge their own work and, on a number of occasions, the work of other students during each month's "peer-critiquing" sessions. The rubric was to be applied to each required investigation so that all students not only appraised their investigations using the four-criterion rubric, but identified the investigation's chief weakness they needed to address during their next investigations.

Four times each term, Jolene held brief conferences with her students, typically focusing on the most recently completed investigations and, in particular, on ways to strengthen future investigations. While these portfolio conferences were going on, students not involved in a conference were directed to work on their next investigation. Her students seem to enjoy these conferences.

At the end of a full year of trying out portfolio assessment in two of her general science classes, Jolene concluded that next year she would employ this classroom assessment approach in all of her classes.

Any missing/messed up activities by Jolene? _____

_____

_____

 One Possible Response: Jolene did a solid job of playing the portfolio assessment game properly. She seemed to focus on the big dividend from this assessment approach—namely, the promotion of students' self-evaluation skills—in this instance dealing with the skills needed to carry out a small-scale scientific investigation.

In truth, we don't know how she scored students' work samples, but that's usually not a big deal. Nor did Jolene involve parents in the portfolio process. But remember that Jolene teaches in a high school, and parents of high school students are notoriously disinclined to get very involved in their teenagers' school endeavors. It surely wouldn't hurt to send home an occasional working portfolio or a showcase portfolio, but Jolene should not get too optimistic about the likely payoffs of such parent overtures.

On balance, Jolene did a good job of bringing portfolio assessment to her classroom. Maybe she can enlist next year's students to carry out an investigation dealing with "the effectiveness of Jolene's version of portfolio assessment."

■ Glossary

portfolio assessment An assessment approach centered on the systematic appraisal of a student's collected work samples.

showcase portfolios Collections of a student's "best work"—that is, the work samples deemed to be of the highest quality. Such portfolios are typically used for celebrating students' accomplishments with parents, policymakers, and so on.

working portfolios Ongoing collections of a student's work samples focused chiefly on the improvement, over time, in a student's self-evaluated skills.

Affective Assessment

Affective variables, most educators concede, are important. Students' attitudes toward learning, for example, play a major role in how much learning those students subsequently pursue. The values students have regarding truthfulness and integrity shape their daily conduct. And students' self-esteem, of course, influences almost everything they do. There's little doubt that the affective status of students should concern all educators.

In truth, however, few classroom teachers give explicit attention to influencing their students' attitudes and values. Even fewer classroom teachers actually try to assess the affective status of their students. Certainly, a teacher may observe a student's sour demeanor and conclude he's "out of sorts" or she's "a mite depressed," but how many times have you heard about a teacher who tried to gather *systematic* evidence regarding students' attitudes and interests? Unfortunately, systematic assessment of affect is pretty uncommon.

This chapter will address the issue of affective assessment by providing you with general insights regarding the assessment of students' attitudes, interests, and values. Thereafter, the chapter will give you some practical, step-by-step procedures for gauging students' status regarding a number of educationally important affective variables.

Why Assess Affect?

One question you might be asking yourself is, Why assess attitudes at all? Many teachers, particularly those who teach older students, believe that their only educational mission is to increase students' knowledge and skills. Affect, such teachers believe, simply doesn't fall into their proper sphere of influence. However, students who learn to do mathematics like magicians yet abhor mathematics certainly aren't apt to apply the mathematics they've learned. Students who can compose outstanding essays but believe they are "really rotten writers" won't spend much time volitionally churning out essays.

The Importance of Affect

I'd like to get my own bias regarding this issue out on the table so you don't think I'm trying to subliminally influence you. I personally believe affective variables are often more significant than cognitive variables. How many times, for example, have you seen people who weren't all that intellectually "gifted" still succeed because they were highly motivated and hard working? Conversely, how many times have you seen truly able people simply veer away from challenges because they did not consider themselves worthy? Day in and day out, we see the enormous impact people's affective status has on them. Affect is every bit as important as cognitive ability.

Have you ever seen a group of kindergarten students troop off to school loaded with enthusiasm and gumption, only to encounter those same students a few years later and see that a fair number were disenchanted with school and

Decision Time

Where Went Wonder?

Lance Larson has decided to try to get an accurate reading of his kindergarten students' attitudes toward school. Although he has worked with kindergartners for the past four years, only recently has Lance become convinced of the importance of student affect.

Because he is dealing with very young children, most of whom can't read when they arrive at Mission Elementary School, Lance uses an orally administered, anonymously completed inventory for which he reads a question to the students and they are to respond by circling either a smiling face or a frowning face. Students respond to one question, and then another, after Lance tells them to "Answer by the bird," "Answer by the star," and so on.

At the end of the first week of school, students' responses to Lance's inventory indicated they really liked school. In fact, 100 percent of the children responded that they couldn't wait to find out what new things they would learn at school each day. However, three months later, a readministration of the same inventory showed students' attitudes toward school seemed to have taken a nosedive. Well over half of his kindergartners indicated they no longer looked forward to coming to school. Almost 75 percent, in fact, indicated they were often bored in class. Lance was alarmed.

 If you were Lance, what would you decide to do?

down on themselves? Well, I have. And what's going on with such children is surely taking place in the affective realm. When most kindergartners start school, they are enthused about school and themselves. However, after failing to be successful for a year or two, many of those formerly upbeat children carry around decisively lowered self-concepts. They've tried and been found wanting. Such negative attitudes about self and school will typically influence all of a child's subsequent education. Yet, because few teachers try to assess their students' affective status, most teachers don't know what their students' attitudes, interests, and values really are. This situation, I believe, needs to change.

Spurring Affectively Focused Instruction

Even if there were no such thing as externally imposed "educational accountability" whereby students' performances on high-stakes tests serve as indicators of educational effectiveness, what's on achievement tests would still influence the stuff teachers teach. When I was a high school teacher, I knew what kinds of items I had on my final exams. (That is, I knew in the second year of teaching, after I'd whipped out my first-year final exams only minutes before my students needed to take those exams.) Because I wanted my students to do well on my final exams, I made reasonably sure I spent at least some instructional time on the content covered by the final examinations.

It's the same with affective assessment. Let's say you've installed a fairly straightforward pretest-posttest evaluation design to assess changes in your students' responses to an affective inventory regarding whether they are interested in the subject(s) you're teaching. Your recognition that there will be a formal pretest-posttest assessment of students' subject-matter interest will, as surely as school buses run late, influence you to provide instruction so your students will, in fact, become more positive about the subject(s) you're teaching.

In other words, the presence of affective postinstruction measurement will incline you to include affectively focused activities in your instruction. In a sense, you're saying to yourself—and anyone else you care to have understand your instructional planning—that affective outcomes are important enough for you to formally assess. You can be assured that what's important enough to be assessed, even if it's measured in your classroom and nowhere else in the world, is likely to influence your instruction. As I confessed earlier, I think affectively focused instruction deals with the kinds of outcomes that are some of the most important we teach.

It has been said *we measure what we treasure*. Well, if we really think affective outcomes are worth promoting, we darn well ought to measure them.

Monitoring Students' Status

In addition to serving as an end-of-instruction target, affective assessment devices, if administered regularly, help teachers determine if modifications in their instructional program are warranted. For example, let's say you're a physics teacher and you want to get a fix on how enthused your students are about continuing their study of physics in college. Ideally, you'd like a fair number of your students to get fairly ecstatic over the raptures of future physics coursework. Suppose each month you employ a brief self-report attitudinal inventory focused on the likelihood of students' pursuing future physics instruction. For illustrative purposes, let's assume that in September, 60 percent of your students registered an interest in taking college physics courses and in October about 65 percent indicated such an interest. In November, however, interest in future physics courses plummeted so only 25 percent of your students signified any interest in college physics. This is a clear message to you that something went on in late October or early November to really turn off your budding Nobel Laureates. A review of your instructional program during that period and some serious effort on your part to generate more interest in postsecondary physics would seem to be warranted. As you can see, periodic monitoring of your students' affective status can assist you in seeing what sorts of shifts in your instructional program might be needed.

In review, there are a number of reasons classroom teachers should devote at least a segment of their assessment program to the measurement of students' affect. If you don't believe your students' attitudes, interests, and values are important, of course, you'll not agree with the views I've expressed. But if you do think student affect is significant, you'll want to learn what kinds of affective variables to assess and how to assess them. That's coming up shortly.

■ The Other Side of the Argument

Before turning to the nuts and bolts of affective assessment, I need to point out that not all citizens share my view regarding the importance of affective assessment and instruction. Particularly during the past decade we have seen the emergence of vocal individuals who have taken strong positions against public schools' offering anything other than traditional academic (cognitive) education. Usually representing religious or conservative constituencies, these critics have argued it is the job of the family and church to promote values in children, and any attempt by the schools to systematically modify students' attitudes or values should cease.

I agree with these critics that if any attention to affective outcomes is to be given, it must be focused only on those affective consequences that would be close to universally approved. For example, I regard the promotion of students' positive attitudes toward learning as an affective aspiration almost everyone would support. Similarly, I can't really imagine there are too many people who wouldn't want the schools to nurture students' self-esteem. Yet, I would hate to see educators dabbling with any controversial attitudes or values—those that a vast majority of parents wouldn't want their children to possess.

If you decide to devote some of your classroom assessment/instruction time to affective targets, you'll clearly need to consider carefully the legitimacy of the targets you select. And even if you do so, you should recognize there will be some people who may disapprove of such affective education regardless of the care with which you select your affective curricular aims.

Which Affective Variables Should Be Assessed?

A Closer Look at Affect

Before discussing the sorts of variables that you, as a classroom teacher, might wish to assess, let's spend just a moment looking at the nature of *affect* itself. The reason such affective variables as students' attitudes, interests, and values are important to us is that those variables typically influence students' future behavior. If you think about this for a bit, you'll realize we don't really care very much, in the abstract, whether students' attitudes toward learning are positive. The reason we want to promote positive attitudes toward learning is because students who have positive attitudes toward learning today will be inclined to pursue learning in the future.

The affective status of students lets us see how students are predisposed to behave subsequently. If we find that students believe healthy bodies are important, those students will be predisposed to maintain their own bodily health in the future. If we find that students have positive attitudes toward persons from other ethnic groups, then in the future such students will be predisposed to behave appropriately toward persons from other ethnic groups. As seen in Figure 1, current affective status predicts future behavior.

Do attitudes predict future behavior perfectly? Of course not. But suppose there are 100 third-graders who display very negative attitudes toward violence as a way of settling disputes, and there are 100 third-graders who believe violence is an altogether suitable way of resolving disputes. Probabilistically, in the future there are likely to be fewer violent dispute-resolution behaviors from the first 100 third-graders than from the second. Affective assessment, therefore, allows teachers to get a far-better-than-chance fix on the behavioral dispositions of their students. That's why affective assessment is so important.

figure 1 ■ The Relationship between Current Affect and Future Behavior Wherein an Individual's Affective Status Predicts That Individual's Future Behavior

As you know, schools have historically focused on cognitive variables. And that's probably the way it's always going to be. Thus, if you are interested in giving some attention to affect in your own classroom, you'll need to select your affective foci judiciously. That's what we'll deal with next. We'll look at attitudes first and then consider interests and values.

Potential Attitudinal Targets

There are all sorts of possible attitudinal targets for a teacher's instruction. Here are a few of the attitudes most commonly endorsed by teachers as reasonable attitudinal targets:

- *Positive attitudes toward learning.* Students should regard the act of learning positively. Students who are positive today about learning will tend to be tomorrow's learners.
- *Positive attitudes toward self.* Self-esteem is the attitude on which most people's personal worlds turn. Although children's self-esteem is probably influenced more by parents and nonschool events than by teachers, what happens in the classroom can have a significant impact on children's self-esteem.
- *Positive attitudes toward self as a learner.* Self-esteem as a learner is an affective variable over which educators have substantial influence. If students believe they are capable of learning, they will tend to learn.
- *Appropriate attitudes toward those who differ from us.* The more tolerant and accepting students are toward members of other ethnic, gender, national, racial, or religious groups, the more likely those students will behave properly toward such individuals in the future.

There are numerous other subject-specific kinds of attitudes teachers will want to foster. For example, many teachers who deal with language arts will want to enhance students' heightened confidence as writers—that is, students' more positive attitudes toward their own composition capabilities. Science teachers will want to foster students' curiosity. Health education teachers will wish to promote students' accurate perceptions of their vulnerability to health risks such as sexually transmitted diseases. Depending on your own instructional responsibilities, you'll discover there are usually several attitudinal assessment contenders you'll want to consider.

Potential Interest Targets

Students' interests represent another set of potential targets. Clearly, if you're a high school chemistry teacher, you'd like at least some of your students to develop an interest in chemistry. Similarly, teachers of U.S. government would prefer that their students become interested in governmental affairs rather than regard such topics as repugnant. Here, then, are a few illustrations of the kinds of interest targets teachers might consider for possible assessment:

- *Subject-related interests.* Students should regard the subject matter taught (for example, mathematics) as more interesting at the end of instruction than they did when instruction began. At the very least, students should be no less interested in the subject being taught as a consequence of the teacher's instruction.
- *Interest in reading.* Because of the enormous impact students' reading prowess has on their subsequent lives, we'd like students to be interested in reading and, indeed, enjoy it. Children who read because of their interest will—almost whether they want to or not—become good readers.
- *Interest in emerging technology.* As the world becomes increasingly dependent on technological advances, students who are interested in these sorts of technological improvements are more apt to learn about computers and, as a consequence, be able to utilize such technological tools.

To get a fix on possible interest-focused affective targets that might be suitable for assessment in your particular teaching situation, simply give a good, hard think to the things you'd like to see your students, as a consequence of what goes on in your classroom, become more interested in. It's just that straightforward.

Potential Value Targets

There are all sorts of values to which people subscribe that the schools should have nothing to do with. Most educators agree that political values and religious values, for example, should not be dealt with instructionally in the schools. Whether students turn out to be liberals or conservatives is really none of a teacher's business. And, historically, there's been a long tradition in the United States of separating church and state. Teachers, therefore, certainly shouldn't be advocating acceptance of particular religions or rejection of others. Well, then, what sorts of values are sufficiently meritorious and noncontroversial so they could serve as the targets for classroom attention? Here are a few to consider:

- *Honesty.* Students should learn to value honesty in their dealing with others.
- *Integrity.* Students should firmly adhere to their own code of values—for example, moral or artistic values.
- *Justice.* Students should subscribe to the view that all citizens should be the recipients of equal justice from governmental law enforcement agencies.
- *Freedom.* Students should believe that democratic nations must provide the maximum level of freedom to their citizens.

Although these kinds of values may seem to be little more than lofty, flag-waving endorsements of goodness, you may still wish to consider them and similar values for potential effective assessment in your own classroom. If there really are significant values you would like your students to embrace, and those values fall properly in the sphere of what schools should be about, then the possibility of including such values in a classroom assessment program may have real appeal for you.

Don't try to assess too many affective variables. You'd be surprised how quickly you can become overwhelmed with the time required to gather such data, and the time needed to make sense of the data you collect. This is another "less is more" setting in which you should try to get a fix on only a few of the affective dimensions you regard as most important for your students.

How Should Affect Be Assessed in Classrooms?

The assessment of affect can be carried out at varying levels of complexity and sophistication. To illustrate, in psychological experiments designed to get a fix on children's honesty, researchers have utilized trained accomplices who contrive elaborate situations in which a child can or cannot cheat; then the researchers observe the child's behavior through one-way mirrors in order to draw inferences about the child's tendencies to be honest or dishonest in situations where the attractiveness of the temptations vary. I know few teachers who have the time or inclination to engage in very elaborate assessment of their students' affective status, although I suspect those teachers would know how to use one-way mirrors advantageously.

As a practical matter, the classroom assessment of student affect must be relatively easy to pull off, or it simply isn't going to happen. Teachers are too busy to carry out the galaxy of responsibilities they already face each day. Accordingly, in this chapter I'm only going to set out for you a single, readily accomplishable procedure to assess your students' attitudes and values. If you wish to consider more elaborate and time-demanding ways of measuring your students' affect, there are several excellent volumes cited in the Additional Stuff section at the end of the chapter. The books by Anderson and Bourke (2000) and by Webb and others (1981) are particularly thought provoking.

Self-Report Assessment

You can get a decent fix on students' affective status by asking them to complete *self-report inventories.* If you set up the assessment situation so students can respond in a truly anonymous fashion, the data derived from self-report instruments can really be useful to you. Just as importantly, the use of straightforward self-report devices won't be so onerous you become disenchanted with such measurement. Anderson and Bourke (2000) provide a compelling argument in favor of self-report affective measurement by educators.

Likert Inventories

Because of its ready applicability to a variety of affective assessment targets, the approach to attitudinal measurement introduced many years ago by Rensis Likert (1903–1981) is the most widely used. You've probably responded to **Likert inventories** many times in your life. They consist of a series of statements to which you register your agreement or disagreement. For example, you are given a statement such as "Reading this text about classroom assessment represents one of the finest professional experiences of my career." You then choose from a set of options to decide whether you agree or disagree with the statement. The usual options, at least for adults, are *strongly agree, agree, uncertain, disagree,* and *strongly disagree.* (I am altogether confident you would have opted for the *strongly agree* response regarding the previous illustrative statement about this text's impact on your professional life.)

Clearly, depending on the age of the students you're teaching, you'll need to make adjustments in the statements used and in the number and/or phrasing of the response options. For example, with very young children you might need to use brief statements containing very simple words. You might even have to read the statements aloud. Older students might be able to handle the five-choice agreement scale just described, but for younger students you'll most likely want to drop down to three response options (for instance, *agree, don't know,* and *disagree*) or even two response options (perhaps *yes* and *no*). You'll be the best judge of the language level to be used with the students you teach. In general, err in the direction of less-demanding rather than more-demanding language. Incidentally, you could probably win a few faculty-lounge trivia contests by quizzing your colleagues about Likert's first name. Face it, Rensis is not a widely used moniker!

The essence of this sort of measurement, of course, boils down to the way students who complete an inventory respond to a collection of negative and positive statements about the same affective variable. This being so, the statements in a Likert inventory or, indeed, any affective inventory, must be created with considerable care. To illustrate, dare not be *too* positive or *too* negative so no student will ever agree (or disagree) with it. Take a look at the two statements about school given below and then decide which statement would elicit a greater *range* of agreement in students' responses:

- *Every day in every way, school is always the most enjoyable part of my day.* (Strongly Agree, Agree, Not Sure, Disagree, Strongly Disagree)
- *Even though I occasionally find school disagreeable, most of the time I enjoy it.* (Strongly Agree, Agree, Not Sure, Disagree, Strongly Disagree)

The initial statement is so "goody-goody" that few students are apt to agree with it. In contrast, the second statement has sufficient qualifiers ("occasionally" and "most of the time") so there will most likely be students who will agree with it and also students who will disagree with it. You need to be certain your inventory's statements are constructed so they are neither *too* positive nor *too* negative.

Even though Likert inventories have been around for more than three-quarters of a century (Likert, 1932), I rarely recommend a traditional Likert inventory these days to assess students' affect. As you now see, a Likert inventory is focused on a *single* affective variable. Thus, Likert inventories require a substantial amount of inventory-development energy from the teacher, and I find most teachers are interested in several, rather than only one, affective variable. Accordingly, I urge teachers to employ assessment devices that can simultaneously get at several affective variables, not just one. Let me describe how to build the kind of affective inventory I think will have the most utility for you in your own classroom. As you will see, the assessment strategy being used in this procedure is essentially the same as the one used in a traditional Likert inventory, but focused on more than a solitary affective variable.

Multifocus Affective Inventories

A *multifocus affective inventory* is an assessment device that attempts to collect information about a number of students' affective dispositions. Such inventories must, therefore, reduce the number of statements (items) dealing with a particular affective variable. So, whereas a traditional Likert inventory might devote 10 to 20 items to a single affective dimension, a multifocus affective inventory might contain items measuring only five or six affective dimensions, but assess each one of those with just a few items.

The trade-off is obvious. Will two items dealing with, for example, a student's "interest in science" yield inferences as accurate as a 10-item inventory devoted only to that same affective dimension? Of course not. The key question, however, is the following: Does a teacher really *require* 10 items on an inventory in order to arrive at a sufficiently valid inference regarding a classroom full of students' interest in history? I don't think so.

Remember, all educational measurement devices are much less precise than typically thought by educators and noneducators alike. Affective assessment is no exception. This issue boils down to the following question: If you're trying to get a fix on the affective status of an entire class of students, what's the minimum number of items (statements) you'll be willing to rely on? Having dealt with this issue in my own classes more than a few times, for me the answer turns out to be *two*. That's right; I think I can garner sufficient insights from my students' responses to two affect-related items—one stated positively and one stated negatively—to come up with an actionable inference about my students' affect.

If you regard two items per affective focus as being too skimpy, then you might bump that number up to four items per affective focus. By doing so, of course, this will either (1) reduce the number of affective dimensions you can address in an inventory or (2) make your inventory so long that students, having seen the numerous upcoming responses they must supply, will often race rapidly through such a lengthy inventory and, thereby, reduce the thoughtfulness of their responses to all of the items. You'll get a better idea about how to create a multifocus affective inventory if I supply you with a step-by-step construction procedure—along with an illustrative inventory of this type.

Building a Multifocus Affective Inventory

Here, then, is a five-step process for creating multifocus affective inventories suitable for classroom use.

1. *Select the affective variables to measure.* In recognition that you will be devoting only a small number of items to each affective variable you choose, you'll need to identify the educationally significant attitudes, interests, or values about which you will ask students to respond.

2. *Determine how many items to allocate to each affective variable.* You must include an equal number of positive *and* negative statements for each affective variable you choose. For openers, start with a minimum of two items per variable. Then, if you decide you need to add more items per variable, increase the number of items in multiples of two. For instance, with two items per affective variable, you would use one positively phrased statement and one negatively phrased statement. For four items per affective variable, you would use two positive statements and two negative statements. In a given affective

inventory, incidentally, there is no need to devote an identical number of items to each affective variable being assessed. So you might attempt to measure several variables with two items per variable, but allocate four items to other variables being measured in the same inventory. The choice regarding numbers of items you'll need hinges on your judgment regarding the minimum number of items necessary to yield reasonably accurate inferences about a student group's affective status with respect to a particular affective variable.

3. *Create a series of positive and negative statements related to each affective variable.* The statements in a multifocus affective inventory are similar to those used in Likert inventories. Yet, because you are attempting to gauge your students' affective dispositions with only a few items, even greater care should be taken to craft the statements so they are apt to elicit differential responses from students. All of these statements (items) should be scattered randomly throughout the inventory—that is, not placed in any sort of identifiable groups related to a particular affective dimension.

4. *Determine the number and phrasing of students' response options.* At this point you need to determine whether you'll use three, four, or five response options for students to register agreement/disagreement with the inventory's statements. You'll also need to decide whether you're using the traditional Likert responses (such as "strongly agree") or some sort of alternative responses (such as "true for me").

5. *Create clear directions for the inventory and an appropriate presentation format.* Directions for affective inventories should be given more attention than is usually allotted by those who develop typical classroom achievement tests. Students are often unfamiliar with these sorts of affective assessment devices and, therefore, need to understand what they're being asked to do. Be certain to include (a) lucid directions about how to respond; (b) at least one sample item; (c) a request for students to supply anonymous, honest responses; and (d) a reminder there are no right or wrong answers to the inventory's items.

Please refer to the illustrative multifocus affective inventory presented in Figure 2. This inventory was developed for use with students in grades 4 through 6 and was intended to allow teachers to get a fix on students' sentiments regarding three subject areas (science, mathematics, and social studies) as well as three important skills students need to acquire (reading, writing, and making oral presentations). In addition, the inventory seeks students' responses regarding school in general. In all, then, the 14-item inventory in Figure 2 tries to tap seven affective variables by using two items per variable.

Spend just a few moments looking at the items in the Figure 2 inventory. Note, for instance, each positively phrased statement regarding a particular variable is balanced by a counterpart statement that's phrased negatively. To illustrate, Statement 5 is a negative statement about giving oral reports, but Statement 11 is a positive statement regarding that same skill. Note also the two statements for each

figure 2 ■ An Illustrative Multifocus Affective Inventory for Students in Grades 4–6

SCHOOL AND ME

Directions: Please indicate how much the statements in this inventory are true for you. Some of the statements are positive and some are negative. Decide whether each statement is true *for you*. There are no right or wrong answers, so answer honestly. Do not write your name on the inventory. Only make X marks.

Here is a sample:

Response (one per statement)

	True for me.	Not true for me.	I'm not sure.
I like to go to the movies.	☒	☐	☐

When you are finished, a student will collect your inventory and place it and all other completed inventories in a sealed envelope that will be taken by the student directly to the principal's office. Thank you for your help.

Response (one per statement)

Statements	True for me.	Not true for me.	I'm not sure.
1. In general, I like school a lot.	☐	☐	☐
2. I like to learn about scientific things.	☐	☐	☐
3. I can write good reports and stories.	☐	☐	☐
4. I don't like to read.	☐	☐	☐
5. I don't like to speak in front of the class.	☐	☐	☐
6. I think that doing mathematics is fun.	☐	☐	☐
7. I like when we learn about social studies.	☐	☐	☐
8. I don't want to grow up to be a scientist.	☐	☐	☐
9. I really don't like to write very much.	☐	☐	☐
10. I like to read books when I have the time.	☐	☐	☐
11. I usually enjoy speaking in front of other students.	☐	☐	☐
12. I don't like to do mathematics problems.	☐	☐	☐
13. When we do social studies in school, I don't like it.	☐	☐	☐
14. Overall, I don't enjoy school very much.	☐	☐	☐

variable need *not* be mirror-image contradictions such as "I like school" versus "I don't like school."

Multifocus affective inventories are scored in the same way Likert inventories are scored: Points are awarded for students' agreement with positive statements and also for students' disagreement with negative statements. So, for example, if there were five level-of-agreement options available ranging from strong agreement to strong disagreement in an inventory using only two items per affected variable, you would assign a maximum of five points per item (for strong agreement with a positive item or strong disagreement with a negative item) and a minimum of one point per item (for strong agreement with a negative item or strong disagreement with a positive item). Thus, focusing on a pair of items dealing with, for instance, students' interest in science, the scores on this two-item pair could range from a high of 10 to a low of 2.

Perhaps you are uncomfortable about arriving at inferences for an entire class of students based on only two items. But the purpose of this sort of assessment is to give *you* insights regarding your students' affect. If the inference you come up with based on only a pair of items is way out of whack with your own best judgment about your students' affective learnings, then treat the two-item data with a slug of suspicion. *You* are always the decision-maker in your class. I promise you that insights based even on two-item inventories—administered to a whole group of students—will often prove useful to you.

The Importance of Genuine Anonymity

In order for you to draw accurate inferences about your students' affective status based on their responses to self-report inventories, it is clearly necessary for students to *respond truthfully* to your affective inventories. Unfortunately, many students tend to provide what are referred to as **socially desirable responses** to affective self-report devices. In other words, many students are inclined to respond in the way they think society (in this case, you) wants them to respond. Students are particularly apt to provide socially desirable responses if they believe the teacher can trace their responses. Consequently, to increase the likelihood that students will respond honestly to your affective inventories, it is imperative you not only make all students' responses anonymous but you also employ as many procedures as possible so most students regard their responses as truly untraceable.

Among the more simple but effective **anonymity-enhancement procedures** you might want to consider are these:

1. *Directions.* Make sure the directions for your affective inventories stress the importance of honest answers and that students are not to put their names on their inventories.
2. *Response restrictions.* Set up your inventories so the *only* form of student response is to be check marks, circling of preferred answers, and so on. Because students believe the teacher may figure out who supplied which

inventory by recognizing students' handwriting, don't permit any handwriting whatsoever on affective inventories. If you are desperate to give students an opportunity to supply written comments, then supply your students with totally separate forms on which they can make written comments.

3. *Collection.* Install a procedure whereby students deposit their completed inventories in a collection box, or have a student (not one thought to be your "pet" student) collect the completed inventories. Announce *before* students start to fill out the inventories that one of these collection methods will be employed.

As you can see, you must try to make sure your students really don't think there's any way to trace their responses back to them. Even under those circumstances, this doesn't ensure that students will respond truthfully. However, well-

Parent Talk

"You're messing with my child's head," was the first comment you heard from Mrs. Jillian, Paul's mother, when she telephoned you at school during your after-school planning period. Mrs. Jillian then continued by saying she had heard from Paul that you were getting students to fill out "attitude tests" that try to find out "whether kids have the right attitudes." Mrs. Jillian concluded by asking, "How dare you delve into Paul's value and attitudes! Isn't this something his dad and I should be influencing?"

 If I were you, here's how I'd respond to Mrs. Jillian:

"I agree completely with you, Mrs. Jillian, about whose right it is to influence Paul's values and attitudes. That responsibility is yours and Mr. Jillian's. But I have a hunch you may not have a clear picture of what I'm trying to do in Paul's class. Let me explain.

"As you may know, children at Paul's age often become disinterested in certain subjects, especially mathematics and science. What I've been trying to do is determine ways I can help improve or sustain my students' interest in science and mathematics. I've been administering *anonymous* attitude inventories related to math and science on a pretest and posttest basis—that is, in the fall and in the spring. But I'm not using the results of those anonymous inventories to influence the attitudes or values of Paul or any other child. What I'm trying to do is figure out how my own teaching can engender more interest, from the entire class, in science and mathematics.

"I would *never* try to influence a value or attitude that falls within your family's purview. But I'm sure you'd like Paul, and the other students in his class, to regard science and mathematics positively, not negatively. Whether the children eventually pursue careers related to science or mathematics will, of course, be up to them and their families."

 Now, how would you respond to Mrs. Jillian?

conceived anonymity-enhancement techniques increase the odds that students will respond honestly.

When to Assess Affect

When should classroom teachers assess their students' affective status? Well, for openers, it seems important to set up at least a preinstruction and a postinstruction measure of students' attitudes, interests, and/or values. Thus, for elementary teachers teaching students in self-contained classrooms, an affective assessment at the start of the school year and again at its close will allow teachers to discern any meaningful changes in students' affect. Ideally, however, teachers can engage in occasional "affective dip sticking" to monitor students' affect. For example, every couple of months, a teacher might measure students' self-esteem as learners as well as their attitudes regarding learning. If these occasional assessments suggest inappropriate affective changes are occurring, the teacher may wish to modify affect-related aspects of the instructional program.

In the next section of the chapter, you'll discover that you can often *sample* your students' affective status rather than measure all students' affective status. Thus, some of the suggested affective dip sticking might be carried out only with a portion of your students.

What Kinds of Inferences Are at Stake in Affective Assessment?

When teachers use cognitively oriented tests, they typically make inferences about individual students. If, for instance, Harvey Haley earns a high score on a mathematics test, the teacher makes an inference about Harvey's possession of certain mathematics skills and knowledge. Teachers need to make inferences about individual students in order to make decisions about how to provide suitable instruction for those students.

Teachers also aggregate students' individual scores on achievement tests to arrive at group-focused inferences. For instance, if most students in a history class performed poorly on a start-of-the-term achievement pretest, yet most students earned top scores on a comparable posttest administered near the term's conclusion, the teacher would conclude that the students, as a group, had learned substantially more about history.

It's different with affect. Whereas cognitive tests (and, in most cases, psychomotor tests) are measures of students' *optimum performance,* affective inventories strive to measure students' *typical performance.* Remember that when students complete most affective devices, those results don't count toward the students' grade, so self-report assessment offers students a wonderful opportunity to distort their responses. Thus, there's a strong likelihood that at least some students won't respond honestly. As a consequence, inferences about the affective status of *individual* students (based on a student's responses to an affective inventory) are risky.

Besides, instructional decisions about individual students based on affective assessment devices are rare. If Harry Helms knows history well, but happens to hate it, few teachers would give Harry a low grade in history based on his disdain for "dead folks' foolishness."

In contrast, however, teachers often make *instructional* decisions about what goes on in class based on aggregated affective data. Assuming that there will be a small number of students who supply inaccurate responses, it is still reasonable to assume that the total collectivity of students' responses will permit meaningful *group-focused inferences*. And those are the kinds of inferences you should be making when you use affective assessment instruments. Because I've already pointed out that affective inventories must be administered anonymously, you've

but what does this have to do with Teaching?

I know very few teachers who don't believe, at some level, that student affect is important. Most teachers realize that if students learn to detest schooling, it's unlikely those students will wind up near the top of any academic sweepstakes. Most chemistry teachers want their students to groove on chemistry. Most math teachers want their students to get mildly ecstatic over the relationships nestled in the theorem tumbled onto by Pythagoras some 2,500 years ago. Yet, although most teachers recognize that students' interests, attitudes, and values are important, few teachers deliberately strive to promote appropriate affect in their students.

One of the reasons for this neglect of affect is that students' affective dispositions often get lost in the curricular roads today's teachers must travel. There is so much knowledge and so many skills that society wants today's students to master. And the current accountability pressures for teachers to boost students' test scores have made it even less likely teachers will have time to promote positive student affect. It's easy to see how affect gets overlooked, even by teachers who recognize its importance. And that's where affective assessment arrives to save the day. Even if a teacher uses only one self-report inventory, at the start of a term and at its conclusion, the *presence* of this assessment instrument will almost certainly incline the teacher to think about the degree to which any classroom activities are being directed toward the promotion of appropriate affective outcomes.

Affective assessment instruments, even a 10-item self-report inventory, will sensitize the teacher to affect's importance. And such sensitized teachers will typically devote at least *some* effort to the promotion of the kinds of student attitudes, interests, and values that—far more than the cognitive content we cram into their heads—will surely influence their lives.

Affective Assessment

surely recognized that getting a fix on a particular student's affective status is literally impossible. Anonymity is, after all, anonymity.

However, there's another good reason for arriving at only group-focused affective inferences. Even if you were to use all sorts of anonymity-enhancement procedures when you administer any affective inventory, some students will *still* not respond honestly. Certain students will be fearful of offending you in any way, even though cloaked by anonymity, and thus will respond more positively than they would if they were being completely truthful. Interestingly, however, there are also some students who will use their anonymity cloaks as an opportunity to "get even" with you for your real or imagined shortcomings. Such students will then toss more negativity your way than they really feel. Will these too-positive or too-negative responses cancel each other out perfectly? Of course not. But they will do at least some cancelling out and, as a consequence, should allow you to put greater confidence in your students' *average* response as a reflection of the entire group's affective status.

Affective assessment devices are simply too crude to permit individual-focused inferences. In aggregate, however, you ought to be able to make some very solid judgments about how your students, as a group, are affectively disposed. This is why, in some cases, you can collect affective data from only, say, half of your class yet still make a fairly accurate inference about the group based on responses from that 50-percent sample. Sample-based, en route affective assessment of your students, especially as a way of coming up with dip-stick inferences about that group of students, really works quite well.

What Do Classroom Teachers Really Need to Know about Affective Assessment?

The most important thing you need to know about affective assessment is that if you don't measure your students' affective status in a systematic fashion, you're far less likely to emphasize affect instructionally. Moreover, without systematic affective assessment, you're not apt to have a very decent fix on the affective consequences, possibly unintentional, that you're having on your students.

If you do decide to engage in some affective measurement in your own classes, you'll be much better off if you rely on fairly straightforward self-report instruments (Likert inventories or multifocus affective inventories) rather than trying to employ some exotic affective measurement strategies that are both time-consuming and, at the same time, yield inferences of arguable validity. You also need to know affective assessment devices are too imprecise to allow you to make inferences about individual students. Group-focused inferences are as far as you should go in the affective realm.

There's one other thing teachers ought to recognize about the assessment of affect—namely, that most teachers do not possess even a foggy notion about how to promote affect *instructionally*. If teachers actually decide to measure important student affect, they'll typically need some solid professional-development support to learn how to alter students' attitudes, values, and interests. There are a number of instructional techniques for doing so, but most teachers are unaware of those affective-focused instructional procedures. Here's where a *professional learning community*—that is, a group of educators who meet periodically to deal with topics such as "affective instructional techniques"—would be especially useful.

■ Chapter Summary

The chapter was initiated by an unabashed endorsement of the instructional importance of affect and, as a consequence, the importance of assessing students' affective status. It was suggested that the use of affective assessment in classrooms would incline teachers to address affective goals instructionally. It was also argued that if teachers monitor their students' affective status, instructional modifications can be made whenever inappropriate or insufficient affective shifts in students are occurring. Affective variables were described as important predictors of individuals' future behaviors because people's affective status reveals their behavioral dispositions. It was also pointed out, however, that there are vocal groups whose members oppose instructional attention to affect.

Regarding the kinds of affective variables to assess in one's classroom, a series of potential attitudinal, interest, and value foci were presented. Teachers were urged to select only a few highly meaningful affective variables rather than so many as to induce affective overwhelm.

Self-report assessment procedures were recommended as the most practical way to gather affective data in classrooms. Multifocus affective inventories were recommended over Likert inventories on the practical ground that Likert inventories assess only a single affective dimension. Teachers are, it was argued, usually interested in more than one affective variable. A five-step process for constructing multifocus affective inventories was described. Anonymity was identified as an indispensable component of appropriate affective assessment. Several anonymity-enhancement procedures were presented. It was also suggested that affective assessments be made prior to and at the conclusion of instruction as well as in the form of occasional affective dip sticking.

Finally, the nature of affective inferences was explored. It was argued the imprecision of affective assessment devices should incline teachers to make group-focused inferences rather than inferences about individual students.

 # Self-Check

For this chapter's self-check exercises, you'll be presented with descriptions of fictitious teachers engaged in some form of affective assessment. Based on what you've read in the chapter, critique the actions of the teachers described in the following scenarios.

Affective Assessment

Scenario One

Molly Muggins, having read a chapter such as the one you've just about finished, has jumped into affective assessment with both feet. She measures her third-grade students' attitudes toward reading, writing, mathematics, science, and social studies every month. Molly's students are asked to complete the following sentence for each of the five subjects: My current opinion of (*name of subject*) is:

The monthly affective assessment takes only about 10 minutes. Molly has identified certain students who have particularly negative reactions toward particular subject areas. She intends to work individually with these students in an attempt to foster more positive attitudes.

What do you think of Molly's affective assessment efforts?

Scenario Two

Having decided to employ a multifocus Likert-like inventory for his affective assessments, Alex Allen, an English teacher, decided to focus on his students' confidence regarding three significant language arts skills: the students' ability to (1) communicate orally, (2) compose written compositions, and (3) comprehend what they have read. What Alex hopes to do is use students' levels of confidence regarding each of these key skills as, in a sense, surrogates for students' actual competence in those three arenas.

Alex decides to allocate four items for each of these three variables, thereby ending up with a 12-item affective inventory. He phrases the four statements for each of these three variables so that two of the statements represent how a student would feel if the student were reasonably confident in displaying that skill. Alex also provides two statements representing the opposite—that is, little confidence. He spends considerable time in crafting the 12 statements so that it seems likely his students will supply different responses. Indeed, Alex asks two other English teachers in his school to review his items to make sure those statements are focused on the appropriate affective variable and also seem likely to elicit varied responses from students.

Alex opts to use a fairly traditional five-option response scheme for his new inventory whereby students respond to each item by indicating *strongly agree, agree, uncertain, disagree,* or *strongly disagree.* He will score each response from 1 to 5, depending on the way a student responds, so that for each of the three skills about which he is securing confidence evidence, a student's score can range from 4 points to 20 points—with higher scores reflecting greater confidence about the skill that's the focus of the four statements.

Finally, Alex carefully works out a set of explanations for his new inventory. It is to be completed anonymously, and because his students are unfamiliar with this sort of affective inventory, Alex provides two examples

228

of how students are to respond to each item. He also asks his two teacher colleagues to review his directions for clarity.

Alex intends to employ this new inventory at the beginning of the school year, midpoint, and at the close of the year. He is enthusiastic about the new inventory, and has been thinking of instructional tactics to enhance his students' confidence with regard to all three of the key language arts skills he will be addressing.

What do you think of Alex's efforts to create an affective inventory?

Scenario Three

Carl Klevins, a woodshop instructor, is immensely interested in affect. Because fewer and fewer students are signing up for his woodshop classes, Carl strives to promote subject-approaching tendencies on the part of his students. "I want my students, boys and girls alike, to become truly enthralled with the feel of sawdust in their pockets and the sound of other students using the woodshop's lathe." Carl spends at least five minutes per week jotting down in his notebook the behaviors that indicate to him that certain students are responding positively to woodshop activities.

What do you think of Carl's way of getting a fix on his students' attitudes?

 # Pondertime

1. Some citizens are adamantly opposed to having the schools engage in any kind of systematic effort to influence students' attitudes or values. What do you suppose might be the reasons for their resistance to affective instruction and, most probably, to affective assessment as well?

2. Suppose you are an elementary teacher and you've decided to use a multi-focus affective inventory on a pretest-posttest basis for that school year. Assuming that you will measure each affective variable you assess with either two items or four items, and you want to assess only a half-dozen affective variables, what variables would you choose to include in your inventory?

3. Throughout the chapter, a strong preference for self-report assessment devices was registered in contrast to more elaborate exotic assessment schemes. Do you agree with that position? Why or why not?

4. Can you think of procedures, other than those cited in the chapter, to enhance students' perceptions that their responses are truly anonymous?

5. How do you suggest that teachers, once they decide to assess students' affect, should learn how to promote changes in students' affect?

Self-Check Key

Scenario One

Molly messed up on a monthly basis. By requiring students to write out their responses, anonymity was blown. It's not even clear that students weren't supposed to put their names on their responses. In addition, Molly appears to be making individually focused inferences about how much certain subjects are liked. At best, even if she cleaned up her measurement act, Molly should only draw group-focused inferences. Molly's affective assessment efforts were simply not stellar.

Scenario Two

Alex was pretty much on target the whole way through. Indeed, he so compliantly adhered to the five steps suggested earlier in the chapter for creating multifocus affective inventories that you might conclude he had read this chapter.

Scenario Three

There are some teachers who can make extremely insightful judgments about students' unobservable affective status based on certain observable acts of students. Unfortunately, there are probably just as many teachers who are likely to make the wrong inferences about students' affect based on their observed behaviors. One of the more vexing difficulties to be coped with when using observation-based assessments of affect is that people often see what they want to see in a given situation. Teachers are no different. Thus, although we're glad to see Carl's attentiveness to affect, his assessment approach leaves a load to be desired.

■ Additional Stuff

Anderson, L. W., and Bourke, S. F. (2000). *Assessing affective characteristics in the schools* (2nd ed.). Mahwah, NJ: Lawrence Erlbaum.

Chamberlin, S. A. (2010). "A review of instruments created to assess affect in mathematics," *Journal of Mathematics Education, 3,* no. 1 (June): 167–182.

Likert, R. (1932). "A technique for the measurement of attitudes," *Archives of Psychology, 140*: 1–55.

Preble, B., and Taylor, L. (2008/2009). "School climate through students' eyes," *Educational leadership, 66,* no. 4 (December/January): 35–40.

Webb, E. J., Campbell, D. T., Schwartz, R. D., Sechreat, L., and Grove, J. B. (1981). *Nonreactive measures in the social sciences* (2nd ed.). Boston: Houghton Mifflin.

■ Extended Applications

I t is a truism that the more a person uses something, the more familiar with this something the person becomes. This self-evident notion surely applies to the assessment-related knowledge, skills, and concepts you have been reading about in the foregoing pages. Thus, to provide readers of *Classroom Assessment* with additional opportunities to apply the content contained in this text, this final section contains a variety of exercises intended to give readers an opportunity to use what they've been reading about.

In a sense, of course, the Self-Check exercises found at the close of this chapter provided an opportunity for readers to apply a chapter's content. Nonetheless, the more times you use a concept, skill, or a body of knowledge, the more likely it is that you will master this content so you can employ it in varied situations.

For each of the text, you will find an extended-application exercise calling for you to do some thinking about that chapter's content as it applies to a real-world situation. Each exercise is preceded by a brief introduction setting forth the reason that the upcoming extended-application exercise has been selected.

Because many of these exercises call on you to generate an original response rather than select a response from a set of options, it is difficult to supply an "answer key" for readers' unpredictable responses. So, what you'll find following all the exercises is One Possible Response—an indication of how I would have personally responded to the exercise if I had been asked to do so. Please don't regard my response as the only way to respond to an exercise. After all, by definition, this is only "one possible" response. Instead, please think of my response as a fairly flimsy form of feedback. You can certainly disagree with me, even emphatically, yet still profit from doing the exercise.

Remember, what is being provided in this section. The exercises deliberately intended to extend how you apply the content treated in *Classroom Assessment*. I hope you find these exercises useful in enhancing your understanding of what teachers need to know about classroom assessment.

■ An Affective Assessment Potpourri

Introduction

In this exercise you'll be encountering 10 descriptions of fictional teachers doing things related to affective assessment. Because what these 10 teachers are up to covers a wide range of affect-relevant stuff, all of which teachers ought to know, this Extended Applications exercise can be characterized as an affective assessment potpourri. *Potpourri* is one of those French words that ends up being pronounced nothing like it looks. What sensible Yankee could conclude that potpourri is pronounced as "po poo re," with the accent on *either* the first or last syllable? The French are so flexible.

Anyway, for each teacher whose actions will be described, you are to decide whether the teacher behaved appropriately from an affective assessment perspective and, if not, what the teacher did wrong. Make up your own mind before peeking at what's contained in the One Possible Response.

 Exercise Directions: In each of the following 10 descriptions of a teacher's actions, please indicate whether the action is okay or, if not, why. Some of the actions, all of which are related to affective assessment, will be okay. Some won't.

1. Mrs. Bevins wants to build a Likert-like affective inventory but decides to measure five attitudinal variables of her sixth-grade students using only two statements per variable—one positive and one negative.

Okay? If not, why? _____

_____

_____

One Possible Response: Because Mrs. Bevins is interested in five affective variables, she is sensibly reducing the number of items per variable. What she's up to is okay if she just wants to use a 10-item inventory. A 20-item inventory for sixth-graders containing four items per variable (two positives and two negatives) would be equally okay.

2. When Lance Potter tries to get a fix on his U.S. History students' attitude toward the study of history, although he employs an anonymous self-report inventory, he does allow students to add written comments if they wish to do so.

Okay? If not, why? _____

_____

_____

One Possible Response: Lance has a good focus for his affective self-report inventory, and it surely should be completed anonymously. But having students write comments obliterates anonymity because teachers can identify students' writing, or at least students think teachers can spot "who wrote what."

3. Miss Thane has created a brief affective inventory for her second-graders in which those students are to respond to a series of 10 statements related to reading by circling a "smiley" face or a "frowny" face. The following is one of the statements Miss Thane has included in the inventory: "I like to read much more than watching TV, going to movies, or playing."

Okay? If not, why? _____

_____

_____

One Possible Response: The problem with this statement in Miss Thane's affective inventory is not that it is equivocal (indeterminately positive *or* negative). No, the problem is that the statement is too extreme. It's doubtful that many second-graders are so enamored of reading that they'd rather read than play, watch TV, or go to a movie. Sometimes, a bit of equivocality is desirable. Ask any career diplomat.

> 4. Ruby Thornton believes that her seventh-grade students should become more clearheaded about the values they hold, especially important values. Accordingly, she has developed an anonymous affective inventory asking students to indicate the degree to which they agree with 15 statements regarding the proper place of religion in public schooling.

Okay? If not, why? _____

_____

_____

One Possible Response: Although Ruby's motive is commendable, teachers ought not be dabbling in the assessment of values thought by most to be the province of the family and/or church. Affective assessments focused on controversial values are inappropriate.

> 5. Although Jed Jenkins routinely assesses his fifth-graders' status with respect to educationally relevant affective variables, he only attempts to arrive at inferences about his entire class and never about the affective status of individual students.

Okay? If not, why? _____

_____

_____

One Possible Response: What Jed is doing, deriving group-focused inferences rather than individual-focused inferences, is quite appropriate. This is precisely the way that sensible inference-making should take place when teachers assess their students' affect.

> 6. Mr. Spivey assesses his mathematics students' affect at the close of each school year with anonymous self-report inventories. He often compares the responses of one year's students with the responses of students he taught in earlier years.

Okay? If not, why? _____

_____

_____

One Possible Response: Mr. Spivey needs to assess affect more frequently, at least at the beginning and end of each school year. Ideally, some along-the-way assessment of his students' affect would let him know whether instructional modifications are warranted. Beyond that problem, when Mr. Spivey compares the responses from different groups of students, he is apt to come up with some seriously specious mistakes in judgments. Groups of students may differ dramatically from year to year. Comparisons between different collections of students should be made with great caution.

7. Lori Lee gives her fourth-grade students an anonymous self-report attitudinal inventory on the first day of school. As soon as all students have completed their inventories, she tells them they are to place their completed inventories in a collection box near the classroom door when they exit for recess.

Okay? If not, why? _____

_____

_____

 One Possible Response: Lori Lee is too late. If her intention is to get students to perceive that their responses to this kind of inventory are truly anonymous, particularly when (on the first day of school) students are not familiar with Lori or her assessment approaches, the collection-box approach should be announced *before* students begin completing their self-report inventories.

8. Ms. Akido wants to have the sophomores and juniors in her English classes help her improve instructionally. In an affective inventory she has created especially for that purpose, students are to anonymously register agreement or disagreement with instructionally relevant statements such as: "I feel I can ask Ms. Akido questions without being embarrassed" and "Ms. Akido moves through much of the content for our course too rapidly." However, in an attempt to secure pointed improvement suggestions from students, she urges students to suggest ways she could do a better teaching job. These suggestions are to be written on the back of the inventories and are not to be signed.

Okay? If not, why? _____

_____

_____

One Possible Response: When Ms. Akido allows students to write additional comments on the inventories, albeit without students' signatures, the cloak of anonymity is instantly removed. If she is desperate to snare such suggestions, she should collect them separately—and thus not contaminate students' responses to her affective inventory. Even with anonymity in play, Ms. Akido is apt to get some seriously inflated responses from her students. After all, she is asking students to engage in evaluating her performance, and even high school students will be inclined to supply socially desirable responses in such situations.

9. During her fourth year as a first-grade teacher, Mrs. Tubbs decides to periodically gauge her students' interest in all of the subjects she teaches. Mrs. Tubbs reads

aloud a series of statements such as, "I like it when we study mathematics" and "I don't enjoy social studies in our class." Students circle a positive, negative, or neutral representation of a child's face. After each of these administrations, she arrives at class-focused interpretations about her first-graders' interests in various subjects.

Okay? If not, why? _____

_____

_____

 One Possible Response: Mrs. Tubbs is playing the affective assessment game properly with her first-graders. By gauging her students' interests in various subjects with a multifocus affective inventory, Mrs. Tubbs can decide if altered instructional activities are necessary.

10. In the process of creating a Likert-like inventory to measure his Spanish students' attitudes toward certain aspects of Latin cultures, Mr. Juarez asks a group of six colleagues to independently review all of his draft statements to classify them as "way too positive," "way too negative," or "somewhere in the middle." Any statements seen by three or more of his colleagues as "way too positive" or "way too negative" are removed from the self-report inventory that Mr. Juarez is developing.

Okay? If not, why? _____

_____

_____

One Possible Response: Mr. Juarez is clearly trying to include only statements in his new inventory that are not too blatantly positive or negative. He has made a good decision to secure collegial reactions to the under-development items in his new inventory, and to dump any statements that are not "somewhere in the middle."

■ Glossary

anonymity-enhancement procedures The steps a teacher takes so that a student accurately perceives his or her responses to self-report affective assessment inventories are truly untraceable.

Likert inventories Affective assessment devices organized around a respondent's self-reported degree of agreement with a series of presented statements.

professional learning community A group of educators who meet periodically, over an extended period of

time, to enhance their competencies related to one or more particular topics.

self-report inventories An assessment tool, often completed anonymously, wherein a student's responses reveal his or her values, behaviors, attitudes, and so on.

socially desirable responses Responses of a student that do not represent the student's actual sentiments but, instead, reflect how the student believes he or she *should* respond.

Improving Teacher-Developed Assessments

I f you've ever visited the manuscript room of the British Museum, you'll recall seeing handwritten manuscripts authored by some of the superstars of English literature. It's a moving experience. Delightfully, the museum presents not only the final versions of famed works by such authors as Milton and Keats but also the early drafts of those works. It is somewhat surprising and genuinely encouraging to learn those giants of literature didn't get it right the first time. They had to cross out words, delete sentences, and substitute phrases. Many of the museum's early drafts are genuinely messy, reflecting all sorts of rethinking on the part of the author. Well, if the titans of English literature had to revise their early drafts, is it at all surprising that teachers usually need to spruce up their classroom assessments?

This chapter is designed to provide you with several procedures by which you can improve the assessment instruments you develop. I can promise that if you use the chapter's recommended procedures, your tests will get better. Yet, they'll probably never make it to the British Museum—unless you carry them in when visiting.

There are two general improvement strategies to be described in this chapter. First, you'll learn about *judgmental item-improvement* procedures in which the chief means of sharpening your tests is human judgment—your own and that of others. Second, you'll be considering *empirical item-improvement* procedures based on students' responses to your assessment procedures. Ideally, if time permits and your motivation abounds, you can use both forms of test-improvement procedures for your own classroom assessment devices.

But I really need to give you a heads-up regarding the upcoming *empirical* item-repair procedures. What you'll recognize when you get into that section,

From Chapter 11 of *Classroom Assessment: What Teachers Need to Know*, Seventh Edition. W. James Popham. Copyright © 2014 by Pearson Education, Inc. All rights reserved.

276is there are *numbers* in it. (There's even a formula or two.) Upon encountering this material, perhaps you'll conclude I've tricked you—lulled you into a sense of nonnumeric complacency then blindsided you with a quagmire of quantitative esoterica. But that's not so. Don't be intimidated by the last half of the chapter's quantitative stuff. It truly constitutes a fairly Mickey-Mouse level of number-nudging. Just take it slow and easy. You'll survive surprisingly well. I promise.

■ Judgmentally Based Improvement Procedures

Human judgment, although it sometimes gets us in trouble, is a remarkably useful tool. Judgmental approaches to test improvement can be carried out quite systematically or, in contrast, rather informally. Judgmental assessment-improvement strategies differ chiefly according to who is supplying the judgments. There are three sources of test-improvement judgments you should consider—those supplied by (1) yourself, (2) your colleagues, and (3) your students. We'll consider each of these potential judgment sources separately.

Judging Your Own Assessment Instruments

Let's suppose you've created a 70-item combination short-answer and multiple-choice examination for a U.S. government class and, having administered it, you want to improve the examination for your next year's class. We'll assume that during item development you did a reasonable amount of in-process sharpening up of the items so they represented what, at the time, was your best effort. Now, however, you have an opportunity to revisit the examination to see if its 70 items are all that marvelous. It's a good thing to do.

Let's consider another kind of assessment. Suppose you have devised what you think are pretty decent directions for your students to follow when preparing portfolios or when responding to tasks in a performance test. Even if you regard those directions as suitable, it's always helpful to review such directions after a time to see if you can now detect shortcomings that, at the time you originally prepared the set of directions, escaped your attention.

As you probably know from other kinds of writing, it is almost always the case that if you return to one of your written efforts after it has had time to "cool off," you're likely to spot deficits that, in the heat of the original writing, weren't apparent to you. However, beyond a fairly casual second look, you will typically be able to improve your assessment procedures even more if you approach this test-improvement task systematically. To illustrate, you could use specific review criteria when you judge your earlier assessment efforts. If a test item or a set of directions falls short on any criterion, you should obviously do some modifying.

Presented here are five review criteria you might wish to consider if you set out systematically to improve your classroom assessment procedures:

- *Adherence to item-specific guidelines and general item-writing commandments.* When you appraise your assessment procedures, it will be useful to review briefly the general item-writing commandments as well as the particular item-writing guidelines provided for the specific kind of item(s) you've developed. If you now see violations of the principles set forth in either of those two sets of directives, fix the flaws.

- *Contribution to score-based inference.* Recall that the real reason teachers assess students is in order to arrive at score-based inferences about the status of students. Therefore, it will be helpful for you to reconsider each aspect of a previously developed assessment procedure to see whether it does, in fact, really contribute to the kind of inference about your students you wish to draw.

- *Accuracy of content.* There's always the possibility that previously accurate content has now been superseded or contradicted by more recent content. Be sure to see if the content you included earlier in the assessment instrument is still accurate and that your answer key is still correct.

- *Absence of content lacunae.* This review criterion gives me a chance to use one of my favorite words, the plural form of *lacuna* which, incidentally, means a *gap*. Although *gaps* would have done the job in this instance, you'll admit *gaps* look somewhat tawdry when stacked up against *lacunae*. (This, of course, is a norm-referenced contrast.)

  Hindsight is a nifty form of vision. Thus, when you take a second look at the content coverage represented in your assessment instrument, you may discover you originally overlooked some important content. This review criterion is clearly related to an earlier review criterion regarding the assessment's contribution to the score-based inference that you want to make. Any meaningful lacunae in content will obviously reduce the accuracy of your inference.

- *Fairness.* Although you should clearly have tried to eradicate any bias in your assessment instruments when you originally developed them, there's always the chance you overlooked something. Undertake another bias review just to make certain you've been as attentive to bias elimination as you possibly can be.

I can personally attest to a case of bias blindness when I authored a textbook on educational evaluation in the seventies. Recognizing that a number of women at the time were beginning to take offense at authors' use of masculine pronouns when referring to unnamed individuals (for example, "The student lost *his* lunch"), I had assiduously written the textbook so that all my illustrative make-believe people were plural. I never had to use *his* or *her* because I could always use *their*. I was smugly proud of my pluralization prowess. Yet, having been so attentive to a pronoun issue that might offend some women,

I blithely included a cartoon in the book that showed scantily clad females cavorting before male members of a school board. Talk about dumb! If only I'd taken a serious second look at the book before it hit the presses, I might have spotted my insensitive error. As it was, because the cartoon appeared in all copies of the first edition (not the second!), I received more than a few heated, and quite deserved, complaints from readers—both male and female!

I'm not suggesting you fill out an elaborate rating form for each of these five review criteria—with each criterion requiring a numerical rating. Rather, I'm recommending that you seriously think about these five criteria before you tackle any judgmental review of a previously developed assessment instrument.

Collegial Judgments

If you are working with a colleague whose judgment you trust, it's often helpful to ask this person to review your assessment procedures. To get the most mileage out of such a review, you'll probably need to provide your co-worker with at least a brief description of review criteria such as the five previously cited ones—that is, (1) adherence to item-specific guidelines and general item-writing commandments, (2) contribution to score-based inference, (3) accuracy of content, (4) absence of content lacunae, and (5) fairness. You will need to describe to your colleague the key inference(s) you intend to base on the assessment procedure. It will also be useful to your colleague if you identify the decisions that will, thereafter, be influenced by your inferences about students.

I've found that collegial judgments are particularly helpful to teachers who employ many performance tests or who use portfolio assessments. Most of the empirically based improvement procedures you'll be learning about later in the chapter are intended to be used with more traditional sorts of items such as those found in multiple-choice exams. For portfolio assessment and performance tests, judgmental approaches will often prove more useful.

Remember, if *you* are the creator of the portfolio assessment or performance tests you're setting out to improve, you're apt to be biased in their favor. After all, parents usually adore their progeny. What you need is a good, hard, *nonpartisan* review of what you've been up to assessment-wise.

To do a thorough job of helping you review your assessment approaches, of course, your colleague will need to put in some time. In fairness, you'll probably feel obliged to toss in a *quid pro quo* or two whereby you return the favor by reviewing your colleague's tests (or by resolving a pivotal personal crisis in your colleague's private life). If your school district is large enough, you might also have access to some central-office supervisorial personnel who know something about assessment. Here's a neat opportunity to let them earn their salaries—get them to review your assessment procedures. It is often asserted that another pair of eyes can help improve almost any written document. This doesn't necessarily mean the other pair of eyes see accurately while yours are in need of contact lenses. You should listen to what other reviewers say, but be guided by your own judgments about the virtues of their suggestions.

Student Judgments

When teachers set out to improve assessment procedures, a rich source of data is often overlooked because teachers typically fail to secure advice from their students. Yet, because students have experienced test items in a most meaningful context, more or less as an executionee experiences a firing squad, student judgments can provide useful insights. Student reactions can help you spot shortcomings in particular items and in other features of your assessment procedures such as a test's directions or the time you've allowed for completing the test.

The kinds of data secured from students will vary, depending on the type of assessment procedure being used, but questions such as those on the item-improvement questionnaire in Figure 1 can profitably be given to students after they have completed an assessment procedure. Although the illustrative questionnaire in Figure 1 is intended for use with a selected-response type of test, only minor revisions would be needed to make it suitable for a constructed-response test, a performance test, or a portfolio assessment system.

It is important to let students finish a test prior to their engaging in such a judgmental exercise. If students are asked to *simultaneously* play the roles of test takers and test improvers, they'll probably botch up both tasks. No student should be expected to serve two such functions, at least at the same time.

Simply give students the test as usual, collect their answer sheets or test booklets, and provide them with new, blank test booklets. *Then* distribute a questionnaire, such as the one seen earlier. In other words, ask students to play examinees and item reviewers, but to play these roles consecutively, not simultaneously.

Now, how do you treat students' reactions to test items? Let's say you're a classroom teacher and a few students come up with a violent castigation of one of your favorite items. Do you automatically buckle by scrapping or revising the item? Of course not; teachers are made of sterner stuff. Perhaps the students were miffed about the item because they didn't know how to answer it. One of the best ways for students to escape responsibility for a dismal test performance is to assail the test itself. Teachers should anticipate a certain amount of carping from low-scoring students.

figure 1 ■ An Illustrative Item-Improvement
Questionnaire for Students

Item-Improvement Questionnaire for Students

1. If any of the items seemed confusing, which ones were they?

2. Did any items have more than one correct answer? If so, which ones?

3. Did any items have no correct answers? If so, which ones?

4. Were there words in any items that confused you? If so, which ones?

5. Were the directions for the test, or for particular subsections, unclear? If so, which ones?

Yet, after allowing for a reasonable degree of complaining, student reactions can sometimes provide useful insights for teachers. A student-castigated item may, indeed, deserve castigation. To overlook students as a source of judgmental test-improvement information, for either selected-response or constructed-response items, would clearly be an error.

To review, then, judgmentally based test-improvement procedures can rely on the judgments supplied by you, your colleagues, or your students. In the final analysis, you will be the decision-maker regarding whether to modify your assessment procedures. Nonetheless, it is typically helpful to have others react to your tests.

■ Empirically Based Improvement Procedures

In addition to judgmentally based methods of improving your assessment procedures, there are improvement approaches based on the empirical data students supply when they respond to the assessment instruments you've developed. Let's turn, then, to the use of student-response data in the improvement of assessment procedures. A variety of empirical item-improvement techniques have been well honed over the years. We will consider the more traditional item-analysis procedures first, turning later to a few more recent wrinkles for using student data to improve a teacher's classroom assessments procedures.

Most of the procedures employed to improve classroom assessments on the basis of students' responses to those assessments rely on numbers. And I recognize there are some readers of this text (*you* may be one) who are definitely put off by numbers. I sometimes believe there is a secret cult among teachers and prospective teachers who have taken a "tremble pledge"—that is, a vow to tremble when encountering any numerical value larger than a single digit (a number larger than 9). If you are one of these mathphobics, I beg you to stay calm because the numbers you'll be encountering in this chapter will really be Simple-Simon stuff. Tremble not. It'll be pain free. Just work through the easy examples and you'll survive with surprising ease.

Difficulty Indices

One useful index of an item's quality is its *difficulty*. The most commonly employed item-difficulty index, often referred to simply as a *p value*, is calculated as follows:

$$\text{Difficulty } p = \frac{R}{T}$$

where R = the number of students responding correctly (right) to an item.

T = the total number of students responding to the item.

To illustrate, if 50 students answered an item, and only 37 of them answered it correctly, then the p value representing the item's difficulty would be

$$\text{Difficulty } p = \frac{37}{50} = .74$$

It should be clear that such p value can range from 0 to 1.00, with higher p values indicating items that more students answered correctly. For example, a p value of .98 would signify an item answered correctly by almost all students. Similarly, an item with a p value of .15 would be one that most students (85 percent) missed.

The p value of an item should always be viewed in relationship to the student's chance probability of getting the correct response. For example, if a binary-choice item is involved, *on the basis of chance alone,* students should be able to answer the item correctly half of the time, and thus the item would have a p value of .50. On a four-option multiple-choice test, a .25 p value by chance alone would be expected.

Educators sometimes err by referring to items with high p values (for instance, p values of .80 and above) as "easy" items, while items with low p values (of, say, .20 and below) are described as "difficult" items. Those descriptions may or may not be accurate. Even though we typically refer to an item's p value as its *difficulty* index, the actual difficulty of an item is tied to the instructional program surrounding it. If students are especially well taught, they may perform excellently on a complex item that, by anyone's estimate, is a tough one. Does the resulting p value of .95 indicate the item is easy? No. The item's complicated content may have simply been taught effectively. For example, almost all students in a pre-med course for prospective physicians might correctly answer a technical item about the central nervous system that almost all "people off the street" would answer incorrectly. A p value of .96 based on the pre-med students' performances would not render the item intrinsically easy.

Item-Discrimination Indices

For tests designed to yield norm-referenced inferences, one of the most powerful indicators of an item's quality is the **item-discrimination index**. In brief, an *item-discrimination index* typically tells us how frequently an item is answered correctly by those who perform well on the total test. Fundamentally, an item-discrimination index reflects the relationship between students' responses for the total test and their responses to a particular test item. One approach to computing an item-discrimination statistic is to calculate a correlation coefficient between students' total test scores and their performance on a particular item.

A *positively discriminating item* indicates an item is answered correctly more often by those who score well on the total test than by those who score poorly on the total test. A *negatively discriminating item* is answered correctly more often by those who score poorly on the total test than by those who score well on the total test. A *nondiscriminating item* is one for which there's no appreciable difference in the correct response proportions of those who score well or poorly on the total test. This set of relationships is summarized in the following chart. (Remember that < and > signify *less than* and *more than,* respectively.)

Type of Item	Proportion of Correct Responses on Total Test
Positive Discriminator	High Scorers > Low Scorers
Negative Discriminator	High Scorers < Low Scorers
Nondiscriminator	High Scorers = Low Scorers

In general, teachers would like to discover that their items are positive discriminators because a positively discriminating item tends to be answered correctly by the most knowledgeable students (those who scored high on the total test) and incorrectly by the least knowledgeable students (those who scored low on the total test). Negatively discriminating items indicate something is awry, because the item tends to be missed more often by the most knowledgeable students and answered correctly more frequently by the least knowledgeable students.

Now, how do you go about computing an item's discrimination index? The following four steps can be employed for the analysis of classroom assessment procedures:

1. *Order the test papers from high to low by total score.* Place the paper having the highest total score on top, and continue with the next highest total score sequentially until the paper with the lowest score is placed on the bottom.
2. *Divide the papers into a high group and a low group, with an equal number of papers in each group.* Split the groups into upper and lower halves. If there is an odd number of papers, simply set aside one of the middle papers so the number of papers in the high and low groups will be the same. If there are several papers with identical scores at the middle of the distribution, then randomly assign them to the high or low distributions so the number of papers in the two groups is identical. The use of 50-percent groups has the advantage of providing enough papers to permit reliable estimates of upper and lower group performances.
3. *Calculate a p value for each of the high and low groups.* Determine the number of students in the high group who answered the item correctly and then divide this number by the number of students in the high group. This provides you with p_h. Repeat the process for the low group to obtain p_l.
4. *Subtract p_l from p_h to obtain each item's discrimination index (D).* In essence, then, $D = p_h - p_l$.

Suppose you are in the midst of conducting an item analysis of your midterm examination items. Let's say you split your class of 30 youngsters' papers into two equal upper-half and lower-half papers. All 15 students in the high group answered item 42 correctly, but only 5 of the 15 students in the low group answered it correctly. The item discrimination index for item 42, therefore, would be $1.00 - .33 = .67$.

Now, how large should an item's discrimination index be in order for you to consider the item acceptable? Ebel and Frisbie (1991) offer the experience-based guidelines in Table 1 for indicating the quality of items to be used for making

table 1 ■ Guidelines for Evaluating the Discriminating Efficiency of Items

Discrimination Index	Item Evaluation
.40 and above	Very good items
.30–.39	Reasonably good items, but possibly subject to improvement
.20–.29	Marginal items, usually needing improvement
.19 and below	Poor items, to be rejected or improved by revision

Source: Ebel and Frisbie (1991).

norm-referenced interpretations. If you consider their guidelines as approximations, not absolute standards, they'll usually help you decide whether your items are discriminating satisfactorily.

An item's ability to discriminate is highly related to its overall difficulty index. For example, an item answered correctly by all students has a total p value of 1.00. For that item, the p_h and p_l are also 1.00. Thus, the item's discrimination index is zero ($1.00 - 1.00 = 0$). A similar result would ensue for items in which the overall p value was zero—that is, items no student had answered correctly.

With items that have very high or very low p values, it is thus less likely substantial discrimination indices can be obtained. Later in the chapter you will see this situation has prompted proponents of criterion-referenced interpretations of tests (who often hope almost all postinstruction responses from students will be correct) to search for alternative ways to calculate indices of item quality.

Decision Time

To Catch a Culprit: Teacher or Test?

Susan Stevens teaches sixth-grade social studies in Exeter Middle School. During the seven years she has taught at Exeter, Susan has always spent considerable time in developing what she refers to as "credible classroom assessments." She really has put in more than her share of weekends working to create crackerjack examinations.

This last spring, however, Susan completed an extension course on educational testing. In the course she learned how to compute discrimination analyses of her test items. As a consequence, Susan has been subjecting all of her examinations to such analyses this year.

On one of her examinations containing mostly selected-response items, Susan discovered to her dismay that 4 of the test's 30 items turned out to have negative discriminators. In other words, students who performed well on the total test answered the 4 items incorrectly more often than students who didn't do so well on the total test. To her surprise, all 4 negatively discriminating items dealt with the same topic—that is, relationships among the legislative, judicial, and executive branches of the U.S. government.

Susan's first thought was to chuck the 4 items because they were clearly defective. As she considered the problem, however, another possibility occurred to her. Because all 4 items were based on the same instructional content, perhaps she had confused the stronger students with her explanations.

 If you were Susan and wanted to get to the bottom of this issue so you could decide whether to overhaul the items or the instruction, how would you proceed?

table 2 ■ A Typical Distractor-Analysis Table

Item No. 28	Alternatives				
$(p = .50, D = -.33)$	A	B*	C	D	Omit
Upper 15 students	2	5	0	8	0
Lower 15 students	4	10	0	0	1

Distractor Analyses

For a selected-response item that, perhaps on the basis of its p value or its discrimination index, appears to be in need of revision, it is necessary to look deeper. In the case of multiple-choice items, we can gain further insights by carrying out a *distractor analysis* in which we see how the high and low groups are responding to the item's distractors.

Presented in Table 2 is the information typically used when conducting a distractor analysis. Note that the asterisk in Table 2 indicates that choice B is the correct answer to the item. For the item in the table, the difficulty index (p) was .50 and the discrimination index (D) was $-.33$. An inspection of the distractors reveals there appears to be something in alternative D that is enticing the students in the high group to choose it. Indeed, while over half of the high group opted for choice D, not a single student in the low group went for choice D. Alternative D needs to be reviewed carefully.

Also note that alternative C is doing nothing at all for the item. No student selected choice C. In addition to revising choice D, therefore, choice C might be made a bit more appealing. It is possible, of course, particularly if this is a best-answer type of multiple-choice item, that alternative B, the correct answer, needs a bit of massaging as well. For multiple-choice items in particular, but also for matching items, a more intensive analysis of student responses to individual distractors can frequently be illuminating. In the same vein, careful scrutiny of students' responses to essay and short-answer items can typically supply useful insights for revision purposes.

■ Item Analysis for Criterion-Referenced Measurement

When teachers use tests intended to yield criterion-referenced interpretations, they typically want most students to score well on those tests after instruction has occurred. In such instances, because postinstruction p values may approach 1.0, traditional item-analysis approaches will often yield low discrimination indices. Accordingly, several alternative approaches to item analysis for criterion-referenced measurement have been devised in recent years.

Parent Talk

Suppose a parent of one of your students called you this morning, before school, to complain about his son's poor performance on your classroom tests. He concludes his grousing by asking you, "Just how sure are you the fault is in Tony and not in your tests?"

If I were you, here's how I'd respond to the parent:

"I'm glad you called about your son's test results because I'm sure we both want what's best for Tony, and I want to be sure I'm making the instructional decisions that will be best for him.

"The way I use my classroom tests is to try to arrive at the most accurate conclusion I can about how well my students have mastered the skills and knowledge I'm trying to teach them. It's very important; therefore, the conclusions I reach about students' skill levels are valid. So, every year I devote systematic attention to the improvement of each of my major exams. You'll remember that it was on the last two of these exams that Tony scored so badly.

"What I'd like to do is show you the exams I've been giving my students and the data I use each year to improve those exams. Why don't we set up an after-school or, if necessary, an evening appointment for you and your wife to look over my classroom assessments and the evidence I've been compiling over the years to make sure my tests help me make valid inferences about what Tony and the rest of my students are learning."

Now, how would you respond to this parent?

Two general item-analysis schemes have been employed thus far, depending on the kinds of student groups available. Both of these item-analysis schemes are roughly comparable to the item-discrimination indices used with tests that yield norm-referenced inferences. The first approach involves the administration of the test to *the same group of students* prior to and following instruction. A disadvantage of this approach is that the teacher must wait for instruction to be completed before securing the item-analysis data. Another problem is that the pretest may be *re-active,* in the sense that its administration sensitizes students to certain items so students' posttest performance is actually a function of the instruction *plus* the pretest's administration.

Using the strategy of testing the same groups of students prior to and after instruction, we can employ an item discrimination index calculated as follows:

$$D_{ppd} = p_{post} - p_{pre}$$

where p_{post} = proportion of students answering the item correctly on posttest.

p_{pre} = proportion of students answering the item correctly on pretest.

The value of D_{ppd} (discrimination based on the pretest-posttest difference) can range from -1.00 to $+1.00$, with high positive values indicating an item is sensitive to instruction.

For example, if 41 percent of the students answered item 27 correctly in the pretest and 84 percent answered it correctly on the posttest, then item 27's D_{ppd} would be $.84 - .41 = .43$. A high positive value would indicate the item is sensitive to the instructional program you've provided to your students. Items with low or negative D_{ppd} values would be earmarked for further analysis because such items are not behaving the way one would expect them to behave if instruction were effective. (It is always possible, particularly if many items fail to reflect large posttest-minus-pretest differences, that the instruction being provided was not so very wonderful.)

The second approach to item analysis for criterion-referenced measurement is to locate two *different groups of students,* one of which has already been instructed and one of which has not. By comparing the performance on items of instructed and uninstructed students, you can pick up some useful clues regarding item quality. This approach has the advantage of avoiding the delay associated with pretesting and posttesting the same group of students and also of avoiding the possibility of a re-active pretest. Its drawback, however, is that you must rely on human judgment in the selection of the "instructed" and "uninstructed" groups. The two groups should be fairly identical in all other relevant respects (for example, in intellectual ability) but different with respect to whether or not they have been instructed. The isolation of two such groups sounds easier than it usually is. Your best bet would be to prevail on a fellow teacher whose students are studying different topics than yours.

If you use two groups—that is, an instructed group and an uninstructed group—one of the more straightforward item discrimination indices is D_{uigd} (discrimination based on uninstructed versus instructed group differences). This index is calculated as follows:

$$D_{uigd} = p_i - p_u$$

where p_i = proportion of instructed students answering an item correctly.

p_u = proportion of uninstructed students answering an item correctly.

The D_{uigd} index can also range in value from -1.00 to $+1.00$. To illustrate its computation, if an instructed group of students scored 91 percent correct on a particular item, while the same item was answered correctly by only 55 percent of an uninstructed group, then D_{uigd} would be $.91 - .55 = .36$. Interpretations of D_{uigd} are similar to those used with D_{ppd}.

but what does this have to do with

Teaching?

Because of the demands on most teachers' time, the typical teacher really doesn't have time to engage in unbridled test-polishing. So, as a practical matter, very few teachers spend *any* time trying to improve their classroom assessments. It is all too understandable.

But there are two approaches to item improvement described in this chapter, one of which, a judgmentally based strategy, doesn't burn up much time at all. It's a judgmental approach to item improvement that represents a realistic item-improvement model for most classroom teachers.

Whereas teachers should understand the basics of how a test can be made better by using empirical data based on students' responses, they'll rarely be inclined to use such data-based strategies for improving items unless a test is thought to be a super-important one.

During the 29 years that I taught courses in the UCLA Graduate School of Education, the *only* tests that I ever subjected to empirical item-improvement analyses were my midterm and final exams in courses I taught year after year. Oh, to be sure, I applied judgmental improvement techniques to most of my other tests, but the only tests I did a full-throttle, data-based improvement job on were the one or two most important tests for an oft-taught course.

My fear is that the apparent complexity of empirical item-improvement efforts might even dissuade you from routinely employing *judgmental* item-improvement procedures. Don't let it. Even if you *never* use students' data to sharpen your classroom tests, those tests will almost surely still need sharpening. Judgmental approaches will help do the job.

As suggested earlier, clearly there are advantages associated with using both judgmental and empirical approaches to improving your classroom assessment procedures. Practically speaking, classroom teachers have only so much energy to expend. If you can spare a bit of your allotted energy to spiff up your assessment instruments, you'll usually see meaningful differences in the quality of those instruments.

■ What Do Classroom Teachers Really Need to Know about Improving Their Assessments?

You ought to know that teacher-made tests can be improved as a consequence of judgmental and/or empirical improvement procedures. Judgmental approaches work well with either selected-response or constructed-response kinds of test items. Empirical item-improvements have been used chiefly with selected-response tests and hence are more readily employed with such test items. You should realize that most of the more widely used indices of item quality, such as discrimination indices, are intended for use with test items in norm-referenced assessment approaches, and may have less applicability to your tests if you employ criterion-referenced measurement strategies. Finally, you must understand that because educators have far less experience in using (and improving) performance assessments and portfolio assessments, there isn't really a delightful set of improvement procedures available for those assessment strategies—other than good, solid judgment.

■ Chapter Summary

A focus on two strategies for improving assessment procedures was seen in this chapter. It was suggested that, with adequate time and motivation, teachers could use judgmental and/or empirical methods of improving their assessments.

Judgmentally based improvement procedures were described for use by teachers, teachers' colleagues, and students. Five review criteria for evaluating assessment procedures were presented for use by teachers and their colleagues: (1) adherence to item-specific guidelines and general item-writing commandments, (2) contribution to score-based inferences, (3) accuracy of content, (4) absence of content lacunae, and (5) fairness. A set of possible questions to ask students about test items was also provided.

Two empirical item-improvement indices described in the chapter were p values and item-discrimination indices. A step-by-step procedure for determining item-discrimination values was described. Designed chiefly for use with norm-referenced measurement, item-discrimination indices do not function well when large numbers of students respond correctly (or incorrectly) to the items involved. Distractor analyses have proven highly useful in the improvement of multiple-choice items because the effectiveness of each item's alternatives can be studied. Finally, two indices of item quality for criterion-referenced measurement were described. Although roughly comparable to the kind of item-discrimination indices widely used with norm-referenced measurement, the two indices for criterion-referenced assessment can be used in settings where many effectively taught students perform well on examinations.

Self-Check

For the first five exercises on this chapter's self-check, see if you can determine whether the item-improvement scheme described is primarily a *judgmental* or an *empirical* item-improvement approach.

1. A mathematics teacher (wouldn't you know?) improves her test items by modifying those items that fail to correlate highly with students' total test scores.

2. At the end of his major examinations, a chemistry teacher requires his students to critique a blank copy of a test they just completed in order to identify any confusing items.

3. Because he has learned that very difficult or very easy items don't discriminate among students, a sixth-grade teacher discards any test items having p values less than .10 or more than .90.

4. Groups of high school science teachers interested in "alternative assessment in the sciences" regularly exchange newly developed performance tests with one another for purposes of evaluation and to secure test-improvement suggestions. Accompanying each performance test is a set of information indicating how students appraised the test after completing it.

5. An art teacher rejects the idea that his fellow art teachers' appraisals of test items are meritorious and hence scrutinizes all his criterion-referenced test items using a discrimination index based on pretest-to-posttest differences in p values.

For the last five self-check exercises, you'll be presented with a brief description of a teacher's actions or a set of data from an analysis of a classroom assessment item. Then you'll be asked a parenthetical question. See how well you can answer each parenthesized question.

6. A music teacher has analyzed her History of Music final examination and discovered that for 5 of the 35 short-answer items, the p values were .95 or above.

   (Should this music teacher delete the five items the next time she uses the test?)

7. Here's a distractor analysis for a multiple-choice item in a social studies teacher's geography test:

Item No. 10	Alternatives			
$(p = .50, D = .50)$	A	B	C	$D*$
Upper 12 students	2	0	1	9
Lower 12 students	1	6	2	3

*Correct answer

   (Is there anything present in these data to suggest serious item deficits?)

8. A teacher reports to her principal that almost all of her items she has studied based on the D_{uigd} index have values well in excess of .50.

   (Should the teacher toss these items out?)

9. Now check out this distractor analysis from a multiple-choice item in a physical education instructor's examination on Sports Safety Rules:

Response Options						Item No. 27
A	B*	C	D	F	Omit	(p = .62, D = .15)
1	15	1	1	2	0	Top 20 students
2	12	2	1	3	0	Bottom 20 students

*Correct answer

(If the teacher is using the test to select the very best students, is this item acceptable?)

10. Mr. Philips, a health education teacher, analyzes his tests using empirical data from students' performances. He tries to reuse items that have discrimination indices below .20 and p values between .23 and .75. If he gets a negatively discriminating item, he is elated.

(Is Mr. Philips making sensible decisions?)

Pondertime

1. Why is it difficult to generate discrimination indices for performance assessments consisting of only one or two fairly elaborate tasks?

2. If you found there was a conflict between judgmental and empirical evidence regarding the merits of a particular item, which form of evidence would you be inclined to believe?

3. Why do you suppose relatively few classroom teachers attempt systematically to improve their assessment procedures?

4. Why is it usually true that when teachers review tests they've written earlier, the teachers can often spot deficits not previously discerned?

5. Why is it that many teachers who employ criterion-referenced assessment strategies tend to place little emphasis on traditional item discrimination indices?

Self-Check Key

1. Empirical

2. Judgmental

3. Empirical

4. Judgmental

5. Empirical

6. Not necessarily. The students' high performances may simply indicate superb instruction.

7. No, the item is a pretty tough one, but it discriminates well. The distractor analysis suggests the three distractors (Choices *A, B,* and *C*) appear to be doing their jobs. It seems to be an okay item.

8. Again, a negative answer wins here. The whopping difference between the performance of instructed versus uninstructed students most likely attests to the teacher's potent instruction.

9. The physical education teacher appears to be using the test in order to make norm-referenced interpretations (selecting "the very best students"). In this case, the discrimination index (.15) is too low for the item to be acceptable.

10. Unfortunately, Mr. Philips is shooting for lower discrimination indices than he should. There's nothing wrong with choosing middle difficulty items, but he should be distressed, not jubilant, when his items discriminate negatively. Such negative discriminators arise when more of the most capable students miss an item while more of the least capable answer it correctly. Unless Mr. Philips is truly perverse, he should be chagrined when such items are encountered in his tests.

■ Additional Stuff

Downing, Steven M., and Haladyna, T. M. (Eds.). (2006). *Handbook of test development.* Mahwah, NJ: Lawrence Erlbaum.

Ebel, R. L., and Frisbie, D. A. (1991). *Essentials of educational measurement* (5th ed.). Englewood Cliffs, NJ: Prentice-Hall.

Leighton, J. P., and Gokiert, R. J. (2008). "Identifying potential test item misalignment using student verbal reports," *Educational Assessment, 13,* no. 4: 215–242.

Miller, M. D., and Linn, R. (2013). *Measurement and assessment in teaching* (11th ed.). Columbus, OH: Pearson.

Thorndike, Robert M., and Thorndike-Christ, T. (2010). *Measurement and evaluation in psychology and education* (8th ed.). Boston: Allyn and Bacon.

Waugh, C. K., and Gronlund, N. (2013). *Measurement and assessment in teaching* (10th ed.). Columbus, OH: Pearson.

■ Extended Applications

It is a truism that the more a person uses something, the more familiar with this something the person becomes. This self-evident notion surely applies to the assessment-related knowledge, skills, and concepts you have been reading about in the foregoing pages. Thus, to provide readers of *Classroom Assessment* with additional opportunities to apply the content contained in this text, this final section contains a variety of exercises intended to give readers an opportunity to use what they've been reading about.

In a sense, of course, the Self-Check exercises found at the close of this chapter provided an opportunity for readers to apply a chapter's content. Nonetheless, the more times you use a concept, skill, or a body of knowledge, the more likely it is that you will master this content so you can employ it in varied situations.

For each of the text, you will find an extended-application exercise calling for you to do some thinking about that chapter's content as it applies to a real-world situation. Each exercise is preceded by a brief introduction setting forth the reason that the upcoming extended-application exercise has been selected.

Because many of these exercises call on you to generate an original response rather than select a response from a set of options, it is difficult to supply an "answer key" for readers' unpredictable responses. So, what you'll find following all the exercises is One Possible Response—an indication of how I would have personally responded to the exercise if I had been asked to do so. Please don't regard my response as the only way to respond to an exercise. After all, by definition, this is only "one possible" response. Instead, please think of my response as a fairly flimsy form of feedback. You can certainly disagree with me, even emphatically, yet still profit from doing the exercise.

Remember, what is being provided in this section. The exercises deliberately intended to extend how you apply the content treated in *Classroom Assessment*. I hope you find these exercises useful in enhancing your understanding of what teachers need to know about classroom assessment.

■ Decisions, Decisions!

Introduction

If teachers set out to shape up their classroom tests, then those teachers will need to be making a flock of decisions, usually on an item-by-item basis. Although it is impossible to foresee all of the many item-specific decisions that will need to be made in such instances, a fair number of those decisions are anticipatable. Accordingly, in this exercise you'll be given 10 terse assessment-improvement situations along with a teacher's subsequent decision. It will be your task to discern whether the teacher's decision is *deft* (that's good) or *dimwitted* (that's the opposite of good). As usual, you'll have one opinion to contrast with your own—in the form of One Possible Response. But you should make up your own mind *before* seeing what it says.

 Exercise Directions: Please consider the caliber of the teacher's decision in each of the 10 briefly described situations below. Then indicate, by choosing *Deft* or *Dimwitted,* whether you believe the teacher's decision was sound or unsound.

1. Because Mr. Guertiza believes his instructional-unit pretests should help him see what his students *do not* know, he wants to revise all of the pretests for his instructional-unit pretests to eliminate items on which students score too well. Consequently, he decides to excise all items which, in the past, typically have p values of .25 or less. Was that decision deft or dimwitted? (Choose one.)

DEFT   DIMWITTED

 One Possible Response: In this situation, Mr. Guertiza's intention was sensible, but he is mixed up on what a p value signifies: He should be dumping items from his pretests that have high values, not low ones.

2. Mrs. Hallett teaches all of her high school's health education classes. To make sure her advice to students is accurate, she does a monthly Internet search to see if there are new research findings she should incorporate in her instruction. This month's search revealed that two key studies had invalidated a set of previously accepted notions about the way several serious contagious diseases are transmitted among teenagers. So, without seeking any agreement from her colleagues or her school's administrators, Mrs. Hallett decides to immediately change her tests—and her instruction—to represent the new research findings. Was that decision deft or dimwitted? (Choose one.)

DEFT   DIMWITTED

 One Possible Response: Mrs. Hallett should get all sorts of applause for keeping her teaching and her testing up to date. Teachers, especially teachers who are responsible for content apt to be modified, definitely need to keep up with late-breaking developments in their fields, then make suitable alterations in their assessments and their instruction. (Latin teachers, most likely, shouldn't worry about this issue.) Mrs. Hallett need not seek concurrence from her colleagues or administrators. Her decision was simply dripping with deftness.

3. Mr. Chen has built a series of new tests for a two-unit combined course in social studies and language arts. The course will be taught for the first time next school year to his school district's eleventh-graders. Mr. Chen has asked two colleagues to review his newly devised tests because both of those teachers recently completed a doctoral-level course in educational measurement. Although both of his colleagues urge him to collect empirical data regarding his items, about a dozen of the items in his tests were identified by those two teachers as having violated one or more experience-based item-construction rules. So, even without reliance on empirical data—because the new course won't be offered until the

upcoming fall—Mr. Chen decides to revise or remove the offending items. Was that decision deft or dimwitted? (Choose one.)

DEFT   DIMWITTED

 One Possible Response: Mr. Chen was delightfully deft in his decision. We can assume the two teacher-colleagues he asked to review his items were fairly sharp folks. So, if Mr. Chen believes his colleagues' reactions make sense, he is wise to jiggle or jettison the miscreant items.

4. A fifth-grade teacher, Mr. Digby, relies exclusively on four-option multiple-choice tests for his key end-of-unit exams. He tries to carry out distractor analyses for his tests' items whenever he has time (which, he recounts with feeling, is almost never these days). He recently arrived at the following distractor analysis for one of his mathematics items. Based on students' performances on other items, Mr. Digby believes the instruction related to this item was reasonably effective.

Item No. 11	Answer Choices				
p value = .5 D = −.1	A*	B	C	D	Omit
Upper Half-Class	4	0	5	1	0
Lower Half-Class	6	1	1	0	2

*Correct Answer

Based on this information, Mr. Digby decides to retain Item No. 11 as it is, thus making it available for use in his subsequent math tests. Was that decision deft or dimwitted? (Choose one.)

DEFT   DIMWITTED

 One Possible Response: Mr. Digby needs to work on his interpretation of such distractor analyses. Not only is the item a negative discriminator but there also seems to be something in Choice *c* that's tantalizing the higher-scoring students. This item either needs work or a quick trip to the shredder. Mr. Digby's decision to retain the item as it is was decidedly dimwitted.

5. Ms. Mallon teaches high school physics, usually to eleventh-graders, and works hard on her end-of-semester exams so that those exams yield sensible criterion-referenced interpretations. She persuades an English teacher who instructs tenth-graders to administer a 25 percent sample of her end-of-course physics exam to that teacher's tenth-graders, none of whom has ever taken a course in physics. A comparison of Ms. Mallon's students' end-of-year performances and the tenth-graders' performances reveals that there is an enormous difference between the scores of the two groups of students—decisively in favor of Ms. Mallon's physics students. She decides to leave her tests unaltered. Was that decision deft or dimwitted? (Choose one.)

DEFT   DIMWITTED

 One Possible Response: This is precisely the way that you'd like to see a contrast between instructed and uninstructed students turn out. Ms. Mallon's decision not to tinker with her test was deft indeed. The English teacher who agreed to require her students to take a physics test they knew nothing about, however, might need a dose of psychotherapy.

6. Even though Mr. Peavy, a high school chemistry teacher, wants his important tests to yield criterion-referenced interpretations, he still needs those tests to be "psychometrically sound." Accordingly, when he reviews his recently administered exams, he decides to delete all items that do not discriminate positively, even if such items' *p* values are quite high. Was that decision deft or dimwitted? (Choose one.)

DEFT   DIMWITTED

 One Possible Response: Well-taught content often leads to many students' high-level performances on tests. When almost all students answer an item correctly, this item rarely discriminates, so Mr. Peavy's decision to dump nondiscriminating items is, especially from a criterion-referenced perspective, dimwitted. Criterion-referenced inferences are usually corrupted when items covering well-taught content are eliminated.

7. Mrs. Jorgenson asks her fifth-graders to appraise the important exams they take in social studies, English, and mathematics. On the social studies exams, even though her test's items display satisfactory empirical indices, quite a few students complain the items are so lengthy that the tests are "only reading exams." Despite the positive empirical evidence, Mrs. Jorgenson decides to appreciably shorten the amount of reading required in her social studies tests. Was that decision deft or dimwitted? (Choose one.)

DEFT   DIMWITTED

 One Possible Response: The issue in this instance deals with the validity of score-based inferences. It seems Mrs. Jorgenson has realized her students' concerns about "too much reading" may decrease the validity of her inferences about their social studies achievement. Psychometrics aside, Mrs. Jorgenson's decision was appropriate. Students' reviews of the items on classroom tests can be genuinely illuminating. Mrs. Jorgenson, in this instance, was deft as deft can be.

8. Mr. Childers teaches Algebra I in an urban high school, and has been doing so for a good many years. He has developed an end-of-course exam in collaboration with Mrs. Evans, who teaches his school's Algebra II class. An important purpose of this Algebra I end-of-course exam is to predict which students will be successful in Algebra II. Mr. Childers and Mrs. Evans often discuss this exam, describing it as "a sort of aptitude test intended to yield norm-referenced interpretations about Algebra I students' likelihood of success in Algebra II." Both of the teachers have spent some time considering the following

item-analysis information for one of the multiple-choice items in the Algebra I "predictor" test:

Test		Item #6	Answer Options				
Difficulty	Discrimination						
p Value = 70	D = .40	A	B	C	D*	Omitted
Top 1/3 of Class		0	1	0	9	0
Bottom 1/3 of Class		1	3	0	5	1

*Correct Answer

Although Mrs. Evans believes the item should be revised, Mr. Childers decides to keep it as is. Was that decision deft or dimwitted? (Choose one.)

DEFT   DIMWITTED

 One Possible Response: Because this exam is aimed at norm-referenced interpretations, and because it seems to discriminate satisfactorily, Mr. Childers's decision was a good one. Mrs. Evans, perhaps because of having to solve too many simultaneous equations over the years, was off-base in her thinking about this item. Deft is the verdict on Mr. Childers's decision.

9. Mr. Rodriguez works with a group of his district's teachers as they develop an examination to identify the most skilled geometry students in the district. The exam is to be presented via computers, and all 120 of its early-version items have been tried out with a group of volunteer seniors, each of whom not only took the district's geometry course but also passed it with an A or B.

   When all the participating teachers in the work group are given printouts presenting psychometric data for the 120 items, Mr. Rodriguez decides to argue for the elimination of any item that has a positive discrimination index of .35 or higher. Was that decision deft or dimwitted? (Choose one.)

DEFT   DIMWITTED

 One Possible Response: This collaboratively developed geometry exam is intended to identify the most capable of the district's geometry students. Thus, it is an exam patently intended to yield norm-referenced interpretations. With such a comparatively oriented exam, what's sought are items that can discriminate efficiently among test takers. So, when Mr. Rodriguez decided to argue for dumping the most discriminating of the 120 try-out items, his was definitely a dimwitted decision. For the measurement mission that the district's educators have chosen, test developers want items with high, not low, discrimination indices.

10. Miss Smothers has recently been elected to her middle school's Classroom Assessment Committee. For the last month, the committee's members have been sharply divided over the importance of determining an item's quality via empirical or judgmental means. Proponents of the empirical side of the argument argue that data-derived indicators of an item's quality are quantitative and objective, whereas judgmentally based appraisals of an

item's quality can suffer the well-known shortcomings associated with human judgment. At the next scheduled meeting of the school's Classroom Assessment Committee, its members must vote to support one of the following two policies:

Policy No. 1: The quality of test items for this school's classroom assessments will be determined *exclusively* on the basis of well-established, empirical indices of an item's psychometric caliber.

Policy No. 2: Test-item quality for this school's classroom assessments will be based on *both* empirical indices of quality and judgmental estimates of an item's merits.

Miss Smothers, after devoting considerable thought to the pros and cons of the two propositions, has decided to vote for Policy No. 2. Was that decision deft or dimwitted? (Choose one.)

DEFT   DIMWITTED

 One Possible Response: Miss Smothers may have read this chapter in *Classroom Assessment* and understood it! Both judgmental and empirical approaches can make contributions to making the items on classroom tests sparkle. Not to use both of these approaches would be dimwitted. Miss Smothers's decision, in contrast, was decisively deft.

◼ Glossary

distractor analysis Scrutiny of a student's empirical performances on the different answer options contained in multiple-choice and matching items.

empirical item improvement Improving an item's quality based on a student's performance on the item.

item-discrimination index A numerical indicator contrasting, on a particular test item, the proportion of high total-test performers and the proportion of low total-test performers.

judgmental item improvement Improving an item's quality based on the opinions of student and/or non-student reviewers.

p value An indicator of an item's difficulty based on the percent of students who answer the item correctly. Thus, an item answered correctly by 67 percent of students would have a *p* value of .67.

Formative Assessment

S uppose there were a really convincing collection of research evidence showing that a particular *assessment-based* instructional strategy helped students learn more and learn it better. Suppose further, because this assessment-based instructional strategy helped students learn more and learn it better, teachers who used this research-supported strategy became demonstrably more successful.

Because both of those two suppositions are stone-cold true, wouldn't it seem that most of today's teachers would be using this assessment-based instructional strategy in their classrooms? Yet, at the moment, most teachers aren't. In this chapter, you'll discover why.

■ Assessment That Transforms Teaching

The assessment-based instructional strategy to be treated in this chapter is *formative assessment*, and you'll learn what it is and what it isn't. You'll also learn why, when abundant evidence is at hand indicating formative assessment works—and works well—this potent process is not more widely employed by teachers. As you read further in the chapter, see if you can figure out—on your own—why far fewer teachers are currently employing formative assessment than one might think. That's right, think of the chapter as a condensed mystery novel in which your task is to understand what formative assessment is, discover how it can improve a teacher's effectiveness, and then come up with an accurate answer to the following question: *Why is formative assessment, a research-ratified instructional strategy, not more widely used in our schools?*

From Chapter 12 of *Classroom Assessment: What Teachers Need to Know*, Seventh Edition. W. James Popham. Copyright © 2014 by Pearson Education, Inc. All rights reserved.

Early on, however, I want to get my personal preference out there in plain sight so you can interpret my chapter-chatter accurately. I am a definite believer in formative assessment. I think research evidence aplenty exists showing us that formative assessment, if used by teachers, helps kids learn better. Based on this belief, I desperately want to see formative assessment used more extensively in our schools. As you read the chapter, whether you are an experienced teacher or an in-preparation teacher, you'll sometimes find me touting the merits of formative assessment. This is because I think formative assessment constitutes a potent process that *all* educators should be touting.

What Is Formative Assessment?

Let's look at the definition of formative assessment and then poke briefly into this definition's key elements:

> *Formative assessment is a planned process in which assessment-elicited evidence of students' status is used by teachers to adjust their ongoing instructional procedures or by students to adjust their current learning tactics.*

A process, not a test. Perhaps what's most important in this definition is that formative assessment is a *process* rather than a *test*. Moreover, it is a *planned* process. So, during a teachers' lounge conversation, if one of your colleagues were to describe a particular test as "a formative test," you now know that, according to the above definition, your colleague would be mistaken. Formative assessment is not a test but, instead, a carefully conceived process wherein the results of assessments are used by teachers or students to improve what they are doing. The process of collecting such assessment-based evidence, and then using this evidence to make adjustments, is at the very heart of the formative-assessment process. If you prefer, you can accurately think of formative assessment as an *instructional strategy.* It's a strategy for using assessment-elicited evidence to enhance teachers' instruction and to improve students' learning. It is, most definitely, not a particular type of test.

As you will soon see, thoughtful planning needs to take place early in the formative-assessment process—a process that's definitely not a spur-of-the-moment undertaking. Teachers, of course, make on-the-spot changes all the time. For example, in the midst of what a teacher believes will be a lucid explanation of a particular concept, if the teacher sees that most students look totally confused, the teacher might sensibly make an instant decision to start the explanation over again, and try to improve its clarity. On-the-spot instructional changes of this sort are fine, and they'll often improve instruction. Such on-the-spot instructional changes should be encouraged. They just aren't formative assessment. Formative assessment is a process requiring some serious up-front planning if it is going to work as well as the research evidence says it can work.

Terminological Lineage The "formative" part of the formative-assessment label traces its ancestry to a distinction first drawn by Scriven (1967) more than four decades ago. Scriven's separation of formative and summative functions, however, was related to educational *evaluation,* not to assessment. As you will see, the gist of that evaluation-related distinction has been retained when today's educators contrast formative and summative *assessment.* Scriven argued that *summative evaluation* took place when educators appraised the worth of a fully mature, completed instructional program such as a published collection of self-study history booklets. In contrast, *formative evaluation* occurred when educators appraised the worth of a yet malleable instructional program—for example, a set of under-construction instructional materials still in the tryout-and-revision stage of development. Summative evaluation is employed to inform *go/no-go decisions* about a program, whereas formative evaluation is used to make *improvement decisions* regarding a program. These evaluation-related meanings of the adjectives *formative* and *summative* have carried over to today when those two labels are applied to the use of educational assessments.

Summative assessment takes place when educators collect test-based evidence to inform decisions about already completed instructional activities such as when statewide accountability tests are administered each spring to determine the instructional effectiveness of a state's schools during the soon-to-be-completed school year. As another example of summative assessment, we can think of the final examination a teacher administers to her students, the purpose of that exam being chiefly to help the teacher assign an appropriate grade to her students based on how much those students have learned during a semester or school year. The decision riding on results of the student's performance on the final exam is not an instructional-improvement decision but, rather, a decision about what grade the teacher should dispense to her students.

In contrast to summative assessment, formative assessment focuses on improving the way teachers are teaching something and the way students are learning something. Formative assessment has a "make-better" measurement mission, whereas summative assessment tries to answer the "instructional-quality" question.

Although a given test may be employed in connection with a summative assessment function, it is possible (if the test is properly crafted) for this very same test to be used also as part of the formative-assessment process. In other words, *tests,* all by themselves, are neither formative nor summative. It is the *use* to which a given test's results are put that makes the assessment part of the formative-assessment process or, instead, finds it contributing to a summative-assessment decision. Of course, if educators specifically build a test to fulfill a particular function, such as the improvement of a teacher's instruction, then the test will more likely be suited for a formative measurement mission than for a summative measurement mission. You'll soon see examples of how to build tests so they contribute optimally to the formative-assessment process.

Assessment-Based Evidence   Getting back to the definition of formative assessment, a central feature of the formative-assessment process is the collection of *evidence* from students via some sort of assessment procedure. This evidence-gathering activity need not rely on formal exams such as paper-and-pencil tests or, these days, computer-presented tests. Although time-honored test tactics are typically time honored because, over time, they have worked well enough to be retained, you will soon be seeing several more innovative ways of collecting evidence regarding students' mastery of particular skills or knowledge. The assessment-elicited evidence referred to in the definition of formative assessment can be obtained by a wide variety of assessment ploys, not merely traditional assessment procedures.

Adjustments   If you take a careful look at the definition of formative assessment, you'll see that the evidence elicited by assessment procedures is used either by *teachers* to adjust their ongoing *instruction* or by *students* to adjust their current *learning tactics* (that is, the procedures students are using in an effort to learn what they are supposed to be learning). Formative assessment, therefore, is a process involving teachers and/or students—not merely teachers. Instructional adjustments are made by teachers regarding their ongoing, that is, *current*, instruction, not instruction aimed at a subsequent group of students. Similarly, the adjustments by students in how they're trying to learn something are those adjustments made with respect to their current learning tactics, not those learning tactics to be used in later classes. Formative assessment, although planned in advance, is a "right now" process focused on shaping up what's currently being taught and learned.

It is not a silly idea, of course, for teachers to assess their current students at the close of instruction to see how well those students have learned, and then for those teachers to make changes in next year's or next term's instruction. No, making such changes represents instructional savvy. Assessing the impact of this year's instruction on students in order to make improvement-focused adjustments in next year's instruction is a smart way for teachers to operate. But those make-better adjustments, if they do not center on a teacher's *current* collection of students, are not part of the formative-assessment process.

A Distinctive Way of Thinking about Instruction   Definitions, even carefully crafted ones, often can't capture the richness of what's being defined. As you look again at the definition of formative assessment, what may not come through is that the formative-assessment process represents a decidedly *distinctive* instructional strategy, a strategy in which teachers and students routinely employ assessments to come up with the evidence to let them know whether adjustments are called for in what's going on in class. Formative assessment is, at bottom, a strategy in which the most important decisions about instruction or learning are made based on students' current *assessed* achievement status. If you, as a teacher-in-training or an already experienced teacher, decide to employ formative assessment in your own classes, I promise that you'll end up thinking about instruction in a manner profoundly different from the way most teachers have traditionally conceived of teaching. Formative assessment can, indeed, transform the way a teacher teaches.

Is Formative Assessment the Same as "Assessment *for* Learning"?

In the past several years, some educators have become excited about the potential instructional dividends of swapping a three-letter preposition for a two-letter preposition. I know it's difficult to imagine any sort of preposition-exchanging that's capable of generalizing even a tiny bit of educational excitement but, trust me, it has.

I'm referring to the notion of assessment *for* learning that's being recommended instead of the more traditional way of thinking about assessment—namely, assessment *of* learning. You see, when most educators have thought about assessment in years past, those educators saw assessment chiefly as a way of figuring out how much their students have learned. Clearly, the time-honored way of regarding testing was to conceive of it as assessment *of* learning. But, increasingly, we find prominent instructional specialists arguing that if teachers are ever to get the most instructional mileage out of their classroom testing, then the way to regard such testing is to view it as a vehicle to enhance instructional effectiveness or, with only a simple preposition-flip, to view it as assessment *for* learning.

Incidentally, assessment *for* learning is not supposed to replace all instances of assessment *of* learning. There are many situations in education when we really do want to find out what kids know and what they don't know. That's assessment *of* learning, and it's not a bad thing. However, there should be many more occasions when we see assessment *for* learning dominating an instructional scene. But before getting into some of the ways assessment *for* learning can be installed in a teacher's classroom, let me clarify for you where this feisty little phrase came from in the first place.

In the United States, the expression "assessment *for* learning" is often mistakenly attributed to Richard Stiggins (2007) or to Paul Black and Dylan Wiliam (1998a), even though all three of these individuals always deny paternity regarding their fathering of the phrase. Because Dylan Wiliam is an able colleague and a good friend, and is associated with the Assessment Reform Group in England where many people think the phrase emerged, I asked Dylan if he would be willing to sleuth the origin of assessment *for* learning. (Sherlock Holmes, after all, was British.) Dylan agreed, and what he came up with you'll find in the following paragraph.

The earliest use of the phrase "assessment for learning" appears to have been in a paper presented by a Brit, Mary James (1992), at a New Orleans conference of the Association for Supervision and Curriculum Development. Three years later, the phrase was used by Ruth Sutton of England as the title of a book she wrote (Sutton, 1995). However, the first explicit contrast of assessment *for* learning with assessment *of* learning seems to have occurred in the third edition of a book by Gipps and Stobart (1997) where their first chapter is entitled "Assessment of Learning" and their second chapter is entitled "Assessment for Learning." This prepositional distinction was brought to a wider audience two years later by England's Assessment Reform Group in a guide for policymakers (Broadfoot et al., 1999).

So, thanks to Dylan's dogged Sherlocking, we now have an idea where this fine formulation came from. It is apparent that most, if not all, of the early thinking on this issue came to the United States from Great Britain. So, in addition to the debt we owe the Brits for tea, scones, and the Beatles, we now have something in the assessment realm for which we should be grateful.

For all practical purposes, the phrases *formative assessment* and *assessment for learning* can be seen as essentially interchangeable. However, not everyone who employs either one of these two descriptors always does so properly. As you'll see in a moment, the research evidence supporting the use of formative assessment is compelling. But that evidence does not support *any old* approach that someone decides to label as either formative assessment or assessment for learning.

Regrettably, we now find test publishers hawking all sorts of assessment products using the label "formative assessment." Lorrie Shepard, a leading U.S. assessment expert, has become particularly vexed with what she regards as test vendors' corruption, for marketing purposes, of an otherwise powerful assessment concept. As Shepard (2006) points out:

> *The research-based concept of formative assessment, closely grounded in classroom instructional processes, has been taken over (hijacked) by commercial test publishers and used instead to refer to formal testing systems called benchmark or interim assessment systems.*

What Formative Assessment Isn't

As you look back at the definition of formative assessment, you can discern that some applications of educational assessment would obviously not satisfy the definition's requirements. For instance, when annual accountability tests are administered at the close of a school year to evaluate a state's schools, this would clearly not be an instance of formative assessment.

And you've already learned that a test itself is not formative assessment. Tests are used to collect information that can lead teachers or students to adjust what they are currently doing. But tests, all by themselves, are not formative assessment.

You've also seen that formative assessment is a *planned* process, not a collection of off-the-cuff alterations in what's going on in class. Although teachers make instant, unplanned changes in their instructional activities, such changes do not make what's going on formative assessment. Careful thought must be given to what sorts of changes might be made, what sorts of evidence might be collected related to those changes, and what kinds of assessment devices might be used to secure this evidence. Don't let a colleague tell you, "I already use formative assessment because I can tell from my students' comments and their facial expressions whether I need to make any instructional adjustments." Such adjustments simply aren't formative assessment.

Moreover, as you saw earlier from Shepard's comment, formative assessment is most definitely *not* what commercial companies happen to call their products. As she noted, some vendors are now peddling assessment materials they describe by using labels such as the following: "interim assessments" and "benchmark assessments." Other vendors are calling the very same types of tests "formative." Commercial companies, of course, can call their products pretty much what they want to—barring violations of registered trademarks. But, as you'll soon see, just because a commercial product is called *formative assessment* by vendors, or even by a group of well-intentioned educators who have built their own test, this mislabeling does not make that product automatically mesh with the kind of empirical research evidence undergirding the formative-assessment process.

When does a teacher use formative assessment? Is it a once-in-a-while activity or an every-single-minute activity? Well, different educators may have different answers to such questions, but I hope most teachers will use the formative-assessment process selectively. To be blunt, properly conceived formative assessment demands a heap of hard thinking on the teacher's part, not to mention the necessary collection of assessment evidence from students. Formative assessment has the clear potential to prove burdensome to teachers and, therefore, dissuade them from using it. But, as you'll soon see, formative assessment helps students learn. If it's not used, then students will be instructionally short-changed. Accordingly, teachers should use formative assessment judiciously—not constantly—as they promote students' mastery of truly significant curricular aims.

What this judicious use of formative assessment would translate to, in practice, is that teachers will typically be using the formative-assessment process as they pursue students' attainment of really challenging outcomes. Such outcomes, because they tend to be higher-order cognitive competencies, will typically take some time to teach, perhaps several weeks or even a full semester or school year. It just doesn't make much sense for teachers to direct the powerful formative-assessment process at a student's mastery of, say, a set of memorized information that can be taught successfully in a couple of days. I am not knocking the importance of students' acquisition of knowledge. Possession of knowledge is a marvelous accomplishment for a student. But, more often than not, one's knowledge is employed in that person's use of higher-order cognitive skills. Because such skills take a hefty hunk of time to teach, formative assessment often works best when it is employed by teachers as they promote their students' mastery of these really significant curricular aims.

As I indicated, not everyone may agree with me on this issue, and some proponents of formative assessment would prefer that the process be used by teachers day-in and day-out. If you decide to employ formative assessment in your own classes, this will be your choice. I urge you not to overuse it—that is, not to use it so much that you become disinclined to use it at all.

■ Formative Assessment Research Support

Certain actions should be taken whether or not there is research evidence supporting those actions. A mother should protect her child even if she has not read a definitive research-rooted article in *Pediatrics* attesting to the wisdom of a particular protective action. Similarly, we hold the door open for an overloaded supermarket shopper because it's the proper thing to do—despite our not having reviewed empirical evidence supporting the positive consequences of such door-opening behavior. Common sense, not research evidence, often inclines people to do the right thing.

Let's think for a moment about formative assessment, an approach to instructional decision-making in which a teacher uses along-the-way assessment evidence from students as a guide to whether any instructional adjustments are needed. Formative assessment is an instructional strategy that, on the face of it, makes a sack full of sense. Because teachers are human beings, and human beings often make mistakes, formative assessment simply asks a teacher to monitor students' progress to see whether the teacher's instructional decisions were good ones. Thus, if instructional changes are needed, those changes can be made. Teachers invariably try to "get it right the first time." But, of course, many times an original instructional design will be substantially less than perfect. By monitoring students' status to see how instruction is working, less than wonderful instruction can be altered so it becomes more wonderful. Similarly, if students are given evidence regarding their own progress in learning whatever they're supposed to be learning, then those students can determine whether their learning tactics need to be adjusted. In almost any sort of instructional setting, formative assessment would make sense even if not one dollop of empirical research were at hand to support its effectiveness.

But such research has, in fact, been carried out. It's much more than a dollop, and it's quite persuasive. So, in addition to a common-sense rationale supporting formative assessment as a classroom instructional strategy, teachers now have ample empirical evidence on hand to confirm the commonsensical.

The Black and Wiliam Research Review

Paul Black and Dylan Wiliam are two British researchers who, in 1998, published a remarkably important review of almost 10 years' worth of empirical research dealing with classroom assessment (Black and Wiliam, 1998a). Entitled "Assessment and Classroom Learning," their rather technical review appeared in the March 1998 issue of the journal *Assessment in Education* and, frankly, attracted only modest attention from U.S. educators. However, in October of the same year, these two authors published a follow-up article in the more widely read *Phi Delta Kappan* (Black and Wiliam, 1998b) not only summarizing their earlier review of research evidence but also describing policy implications of that evidence. In contrast to the March article's almost nonexistent impact on the thinking of American educators, the October essay in the *Kappan* garnered considerable attention. It was Black and Wiliam's March review of classroom assessment research, however, that provided the chief empirical underpinnings of today's formative assessment. As a consequence, let's first look at how these two British researchers went about their review, and then see what they concluded from their analyses.

Basing their review on almost 10 years of research about classroom assessment, Black and Wiliam used two earlier extensive reviews (Crooks, 1988; Natriello, 1987) as the springboards for their own work. Employing a conception of formative assessment essentially similar to the definition presented earlier in this chapter, Black and Wiliam first identified more than 680 research publications appearing to be potentially relevant to their inquiry. From those possibilities, they isolated approximately 250 reports as suitable for further scrutiny and, having reviewed each one carefully, incorporated its results in their synthesis of this considerable body of research.

What is particularly refreshing in this review is the transparency with which the two reviewers describe the criteria they used to decide whether or not to include a specific investigation in their conclusions and, if so, how much weight to ascribe to its results. To be candid, in research reviews of this sort, attention must always be given to the stringency of the analytic procedures employed by the reviewers. The Black and Wiliam 1998 review of classroom assessment research is impressive not only for its analytic rigor but also for its forthright description of the many interpretative quandaries faced during the review, and the procedures chosen to deal with those issues.

Based on the comprehensive study of published research, what did these two British investigators conclude? Well, the quotation below is, for all current teachers and all prospective teachers, worth at least two or three re-readings:

> *The research reported here shows conclusively that formative assessment does improve learning. (Black and Wiliam, 1998a, p. 61)*

Are those learning improvements something substantial or something trifling? Black and Wiliam (1998a) concluded that the student gains in learning triggered by formative assessment were "amongst the largest ever reported for educational interventions" (p. 61). Let's look at this last conclusion for a moment. First off, we need to take seriously any assertion containing the term *amongst*. (Even in print, British people seem so convincingly credible.) But, more importantly, please note that formative assessment, when used by teachers in their classrooms, is capable of causing student gains as great as any ever reported for educational interventions. We are not talking here about tiny improvements in kid learning. No, on the contrary, these are whopping gains that formative assessment can bring about in students' achievement.

One conclusion reached by Black and Wiliam that makes their work especially relevant to teachers' day-to-day instruction is their finding that formative assessment is truly robust. In other words, if formative assessment is installed by teachers, *it is nearly certain to work*. As Black and Wiliam observe, "Significant gains can be achieved by many different routes, and initiatives here are not likely to fail through neglect of delicate and subtle features" (1998a, p. 61). In their review, Black and Wiliam supply numerous examples of research investigations in which it is apparent that formative assessment makes a meaningful contribution to students' learning. Sometimes the studies being reviewed focused on teachers' adjustments of their instruction; sometimes the reviewed reports dealt with students' adjustments of their own learning tactics. As Black and Wiliam observe:

> *However, the consistent feature across the variety of these examples is that they all show that attention to formative assessment can lead to significant learning gains. Although there is no guarantee that it will do so irrespective of the context and the particular approach adopted, we have not come across any report of negative effects following on an enhancement of formative practice (1998a, p. 17).*

It is apparent that the 1998 research review by Black and Wiliam placed a potent pedagogical truth smack in the hands of educators: Formative assessment works, and it works big time! Moreover, the formative-assessment process seems to work particularly well for low-performing learners (who, because of their lower levels of performance, have greater room for growth).

But even though there was some interest in the 1998 *Kappan* summary of the March 1998 research review, it was not until the enactment of NCLB that U.S. educators turned their attention seriously to the instructional recommendations provided by these two British scholars. This was because NCLB's 2002 enactment called for American educators to boost students' scores on accountability tests substantially, moving toward a point where, in 2014, all students in U.S. public schools would achieve "proficient or better" scores on NCLB-required state exams. Faced with this nontrivial challenge, many American educators recalled the 1998 *Kappan* article in which it had been pointed out that formative assessment could boost students' achievement, and by a lot—not just a little.

Well, it did not require a huge inferential leap for numerous U.S. educators to conclude that if students' in-classroom learning could be improved by formative assessment, why would not those same improvements splash over onto students' performances on NCLB accountability tests? And thus was ushered in what soon became a sometimes frenzied advocacy of formative assessment by certain educational leaders. Formative assessment was being touted as an NCLB salvation-strategy. Numerous educational administrators really believed that if they could only get enough of their teachers to use formative assessment ("whatever 'formative assessment' is"), then students' scores on NCLB tests would go up sufficiently for educators to dodge NCLB failure. It should be noted that in their review of the 250 classroom assessment studies, Black and Wiliam do not indicate formative assessment will boost students' scores on external accountability tests sufficiently for educators to avoid accountability-test failures.

Wrapping up this quick look at the empirical evidence underlying formative assessment, it is difficult to consider the Black and Wiliam synthesis of classroom assessment research without concluding that the formative-assessment process represents a particularly potent way for assessment to bolster the caliber of teachers' instruction. Even reviewers (for example, Kingston and Nash, 2011) who urge caution in our interpretation of relevant research conclude that the positive effects of the formative-assessment process are both clear and practically meaningful. Let's now look at the fundamental framework around which formative assessment can be carried out.

Learning Progressions as Frameworks

We can begin by turning to what some readers might regard as a topic more suited for a book about instruction than a book about assessment. But don't forget that the text you're currently reading is about *classroom* assessment, and the major activity that goes on in classrooms is *instruction*. Indeed, it is because formative assessment is an assessment-based way of making a teacher's *instruction* better that I hope you'll find the upcoming topic particularly pertinent to what might go on in your own classroom.

What Is a Learning Progression?

You've seen that formative assessment is basically a process in which assessment evidence is used by teachers or students to adjust what they are doing. Well, when is this assessment evidence to be collected? Clearly, teachers can't be collecting assessment evidence from kids every few minutes. After all, the really big job facing teachers is to *teach* students, not *test* students. At what points, then, during an instructional sequence should students be assessed so teachers (or the students themselves) can decide whether adjustments are in order? The answer to this significant question revolves around teachers' reliance on a **learning progression**. Here's what a learning progression is:

A learning progression is a sequenced set of building blocks—that is, subskills or bodies of enabling knowledge—it is thought students must master en route to mastering a more remote, target curricular aim.

In plain language, a learning progression is an ordered sequence of the stuff a student must learn in order to achieve a significant curricular outcome. Because the construction of a learning progression requires an expenditure of time and energy from a teacher, the "significant curricular outcome" being sought will typically deal with students' mastery of a high-level cognitive skill, the kind of skill apt to take a meaningful amount of time to teach. Examples of such skills might be a student's ability to (1) design a defensible scientific investigation, (2) write a powerful persuasive essay, or (3) select and compute the most effective statistical indicators to accurately represent a set of empirical data. Thus, the use of learning progressions and, indeed, the use of the formative-assessment process itself, is often focused on the pursuit of significant curricular aims.

Let's briefly consider the key components of the preceding definition of learning progressions. First off, the purpose of a learning progression is to identify what students need to master on their way to mastering a more remote, *target curricular aim*. This aim, as already noted, is usually a higher-order cognitive skill. In order for students to master such a target curricular aim, students will almost always first need to master one or more en route, lesser curricular aims. These lesser aims are called *building blocks,* and they consist either of *bodies of enabling knowledge* or *cognitive subskills*.

To illustrate, if the target curricular aim being sought were for students to be able to write a clear expository (explanatory) essay, then one building block might be for the student to know (that is, to have memorized) the important mechanical conventions of spelling, punctuation, and grammar. By knowing and adhering to those conventions, the student's essay is more likely to be clear than if the student's essay were laden with errors of spelling, punctuation, and grammar. So, an *enabling knowledge* building block in a learning progression aimed at a student's skill in writing clear expository essays might be the student's knowledge of mechanical conventions.

Another building block in this instance might be a cognitive *subskill*. Such a subskill might be the student's ability to effectively organize the information to be presented in an expository essay so the essay's readers would most readily understand what was being explained. The appropriate organization of an essay's content, then, might be a second building block for this learning progression.

One of the most common errors teachers make in developing a learning progression is to include too many building blocks. That's right, the more conversant a teacher becomes with the subskills and knowledge a student must possess in order to master a target curricular aim, the greater is the teacher's tendency to toss in more and more building blocks. This is surely understandable, for the more we know about something, the more attentive we become to its nuances. Yet, as you will soon see, students' mastery of *each* building block in a learning progression must be assessed. With too many building blocks in a learning progression, this assessment obligation often gets out of hand. It makes more sense to focus on a modest number of building blocks that are *truly requisite* for a student's mastery of the target curricular aim than to focus on a larger number of building blocks that are *arguably* requisite. In learning progressions, as in many realms of life, less is most definitely more.

Finally, the building blocks in a learning progression should be sequenced in the order it is believed students can most effectively master those building blocks on the way to mastering the target curricular aim. This sequence of building blocks is the one that the persons who are developing a learning progression believe is the most sensible. Although there are several intuitively reasonable guidelines for this sequencing of building blocks, such as "transmit knowledge before asking students to apply such knowledge," the actual sequence of building blocks in a learning progression is really up to the persons who are building the progression. Here's where a teacher's pedagogical prowess comes into play, for a teacher must analyze the *optimal* order in which students should try to master en route knowledge and subskills.

Consider Figure 1 for a moment and you will see one way a learning progression can be represented graphically. Note that, in this instance, the target curricular aim is represented by a rectangle, the two bodies of enabling knowledge are signified by squares, and the solo subskill is depicted by a circle. If you generate your own learning progressions, of course, you can employ any symbols that suit you. Learning progressions can be displayed horizontally as well as vertically, of course. Again, graphic representations are up to those who are trying to represent the learning progression. But most educators report that having access to some sort of graphic depiction of a learning progression helps them comprehend the relationships among the progression's building block and its target curricular aim.

Recalling that formative assessment rests on the use of assessment-elicited evidence for teachers (or students) to make adjustment decisions, when teachers identify the key building blocks they believe their students must master en route to the attainment of a target curricular aim, those teachers have thereby determined *when to assess* their students. If every building block is regarded as genuinely requisite for the student's advancement toward curricular-aim mastery, then

figure 1 ■ Graphic Depiction of a Typical Learning Progression

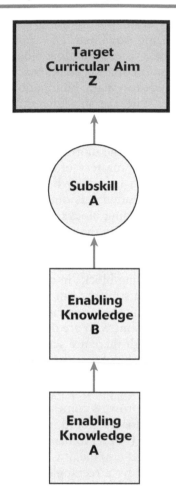

it is apparent a teacher will need to see if each building block has, in fact, been mastered. The formative-assessment process revolves around assessments and the adjustment decisions associated with every building block in a learning progression. Clearly, this is why learning progressions are regarded as the guiding framework for formative assessment.

Teachers should know, however, that a learning progression is *not* unerringly accurate. In few instances are we are able to subject learning progressions to the tryout-revision cycles that would empirically confirm their accuracy. Rather, learning progressions usually represent the best estimate that educators have made about what things students must master on their way to mastery of a significant curricular aim—and what constitutes a sensible instructional sequence for those things. Most learning progressions undergo a good many modifications as they are developed, then used. And, finally, a particular learning progression is unlikely to work well for all students. Some students learn in different, seemingly mysterious ways. A learning progression that might function marvelously for most students will often flop for a few. For those few students, meaningful modifications in "their" learning progression will be needed.

Building a Learning Progression

How does a teacher, or a group of teachers, build a learning progression? In a moment I will lay out a four-step process that you might try, but when it comes to learning progressions, I personally lean toward lean. That is, I prefer only a small number of building blocks in any learning progression. This means that the grain-size of the target curricular aim, as well as the grain-size of the learning progression's building blocks, must be fairly large. A *grain-size* refers to the scope of a curricular aim or building block. Large grain-size building blocks (or curricular aims) are broader and take more time to teach. Large grain-size building blocks (or curricular aims) sometimes subsume smaller chunks of knowledge or lesser subskills. Because too many building blocks can clutter up the formative-assessment process so it becomes unmanageable, I encourage you to opt for fairly large grain-size building blocks and, as a result, create a learning progression that doesn't contain too many building blocks.

Here, then, are fours steps to be followed in creating the kind of learning progression to serve as the formative-assessment framework for a fairly significant target curricular aim—typically a powerful cognitive skill students are supposed to master.

Step 1: Acquire a thorough understanding of the target curricular aim. Don't even think about building a learning progression unless you first have a fuzz-free fix on the nature of the target curricular aim itself. You can't come up with appropriate building blocks unless you completely comprehend the essence of the outcome being sought. One of the best ways to understand the nature of that target curricular aim is to become familiar with the assessment procedure (or procedures) to be employed in measuring students' mastery of the aim. If you are the person who will build that assessment procedure (or has already built it), then you surely have a good idea of what the target curricular aim actually consists of. If, however, others have built the end-of-instruction assessment(s), be sure you understand it (them) completely. Tests "operationalize" curricular aims—that is, tests constitute the operations that students must display in order to convince us they've mastered a curricular aim.

Step 2: Identify all requisite precursory subskills and bodies of enabling knowledge. This second step is really the toughest of our four-step process.

In this second step, you need to think through what students really must know and be able to do if they are going to be successful in mastering the target curricular aim. The most influential word in this second step is *requisite*. This second step is an effort to isolate all "must-know" subskills and knowledge. This second step is not a time to identify "nice-to-know" subskills and knowledge. To keep the number of building blocks manageable, it is sometimes necessary for several lesser subskills or bodies of enabling knowledge to be coalesced into larger grain-sizes. But the focus in this second step must be the isolation of what is truly *necessary* for students to have mastered on their way to mastery of the target curricular aim.

Step 3: Determine the measurability of each preliminarily identified building block. So far, you will have identified—in Step 2—the building blocks you deem to be necessary precursors to a student's mastery of the target curricular aim. In this third step, you must make certain that you can realistically collect evidence of students' mastery of each building block. The heart of the formative-assessment process is to find out how students are progressing with respect to each building block, and this means measuring students' status with respect to all the building blocks in the learning progression. Thus, if you can't—in a practical manner—assess students' mastery of each building block, then you ought to dump the unmeasurable ones. We'll consider several informal ways of assessing students' building-block mastery later in the chapter.

Step 4: Arrange all the building blocks in an instructionally sensible sequence. This final step calls for you to think through what sort of sequence makes the most sense from an instructional perspective and then place the learning progression's building blocks in that order. As noted before, teachers rarely have time to try these sequences out to make sure a given sequence is working properly, and it is often necessary to rearrange the sequences after the learning progression has been used a time or two. However, this is the point at which a teacher's instructional acumen is needed. Simply sequence the learning progression's building blocks in the order that a teacher should most appropriately tackle each of those building blocks.

Because formative assessment is a planned process in which students are periodically assessed and, if necessary, adjustments are made, the importance of learning progressions cannot be overestimated. If you decide to employ formative assessment in your own classes, devoting time to the generation of a defensible learning progression for your most significant curricular aims will be time well spent.

I should note that in certain other nations—for instance, Australia and New Zealand—most educators think of learning progressions as much more elongated sequences of students' likely learning sequences. For example, a group of educators might describe the step-by-step progression of skills and knowledge over a course of several years that a student would typically accomplish en route to a sophisticated mastery of a given subject. Such long-term views of learning progressions can be useful to teachers, particularly in devising the kinds of shorter-duration learning progressions described in this chapter.

So far, in this chapter's look at formative assessment, we've considered what formative assessment is, its research base, and the role of learning progressions as frameworks for formative assessment. Now it's time to see how formative assessment can work in classrooms.

Alternative Implementation Approaches

One of the most encouraging conclusions emerging from Black and Wiliam's (1998a) influential review of classroom assessment studies is that the formative-assessment process is remarkably robust. That is, a teacher who uses it is likely to boost students' learning, irrespective of the particular manner in which the teacher employs formative assessment. As long as the teacher focuses on the collection of assessment evidence from students so that, based on such evidence, either the teacher or the teacher's students can make decisions about adjusting what they're doing, formative assessment works.

But, realistically, many teachers will need more fine-grained guidance regarding how to play the formative assessment game successfully. Thus, in this section different approaches to the implementation of formative assessment will be briefly described. If you are interested in learning more about any of these three approaches, separate books are available about all three. Hopefully, from the next few pages you will recognize that formative assessment is akin to a cake capable of being sliced successfully—that is, implemented successfully, in several different ways. As long as formative assessment's implementation centers on assessed evidence of students' status, and the appropriateness of making adjustments based on this evidence, almost any reasonable approach to formative assessment is likely to work well.

A Four-Levels Approach

Remember: Formative assessment is a process that can be used either by teachers to adjust how they're teaching or by students to adjust how they're trying to learn something. Having two potential sets of actors in the formative-assessment drama can, as you might guess, engender confusion. Moreover, because different teachers will surely be using formative assessment in a variety of ways and at varying levels of intensity, this too can cause a clump of confusion.

So, in a head-on assault against confusion for those who try to implement formative assessment, one way for you to think about formative assessment is not as a single entity but, rather, as a *Levels Approach*. Here, then, are brief descriptions of four distinguishable variations of formative assessment:

Four Levels of Formative Assessment

Level 1: Teachers' Instructional Adjustments

In this first level of formative assessment, teachers collect assessment-elicited evidence that they use when deciding whether to adjust their current or immediately upcoming instructional activities.

Level 2: Students' Learning-Tactic Adjustments

A second level of formative assessment takes place when students use assessment-elicited evidence about their own skills or knowledge to decide whether to adjust how they're currently trying to learn something.

Level 3: Classroom Climate Shift

In a melding of Level 1 formative assessment and Level 2 formative assessment, we see a fundamental transformation so that a traditional, comparison-oriented classroom becomes a learning-dominated classroom in which the chief purpose of classroom assessment is not to grade students but, rather, to improve the quality of both teachers' instruction and students' learning.

Level 4: Schoolwide Implementation

In this level of implementation, the expanded use of formative assessment is promoted at the school or district level—chiefly through professional development strategies and/or teacher learning communities. Level 4 formative assessment can be employed to encourage teachers' use of one (or more) of the other three levels of formative assessment.

Although these four levels are meaningfully distinctive, they are not necessarily incremental. In other words, it is possible (but rather unlikely) for a teacher to adopt Level 2 formative assessment (where students are adjusting their own learning tactics) without the teacher's having already adopted Level 1 formative assessment (where teachers are adjusting their instruction). And, realistically, Level 3 formative assessment, where there is a substantial change in the atmosphere of a classroom, would be impossible to pull off if the teacher does not install Level 1 *and* Level 2 formative assessment. This is because Level 3 formative assessment requires substantial shifts in the conduct of *both* teachers and students. But Level 4 formative assessment (schoolwide implementation) definitely doesn't require the installation of all three of the other levels.

What actually goes on in classrooms where each of these four levels of formative assessment is being used? Well, one way for you to understand the nature of the Levels Approach is to consider Figure 2 in which the different levels are depicted along with the chief activities typically taking place within each level. (In passing, I should note that although I find most educators in North America concerned with the Level 1 aspects of formative assessment—that is, the teacher's instructional adjustments—in many other parts of the world, greater attention is given to Level 2 formative assessment—that is, helping students take greater responsibility for their own learning.)

figure 2 ■ Four Levels of Formative Assessment

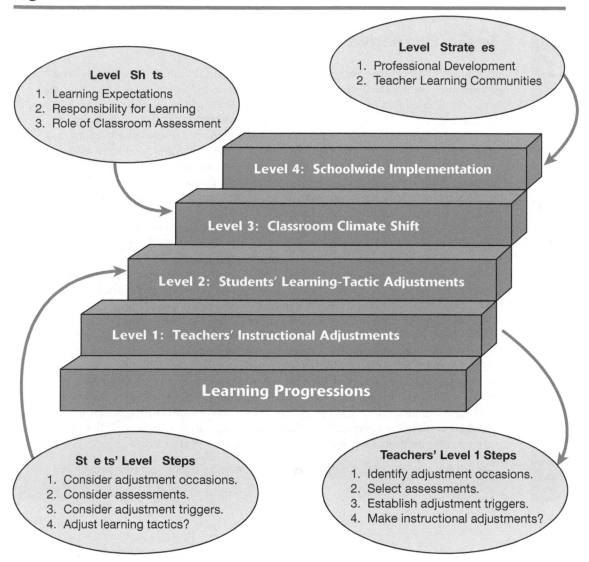

Please note in Figure 2 that below the four levels of formative assessment, learning progressions underlie the whole works. This is because the four levels are carried out against a guiding framework in which a learning progression's sequenced building blocks help the teacher decide *when* to collect assessment evidence from students. A well-conceived learning progression, as indicated earlier, is integral to the effective implementation of formative assessment.

In a separate book about formative assessment (Popham, 2008), I have presented—for teachers' consideration—the formative-assessment process as this

Decision Time

To Go Formative or Not?

Reggie Rawlins teaches fifth-grade students in a rural county school in an eastern Washington county fairly close to Spokane. He has recently completed an online master's degree in educational leadership, and found one of the more interesting courses in that program was, to his surprise, a class dealing with educational measurement.

In that course, Reggie acquired two insights that have caused him more than a little discomfort. One of those insights was that the classroom formative-assessment process, when used by teachers, will help students learn what they are supposed to be learning. Although Reggie does not currently use formative assessment with his fifth-graders, he realizes that if he chose to do so, he could employ at least some level of it in his class for the upcoming school year.

On the other hand, he also learned that certain statewide accountability tests, because of the way they have been constructed, are unlikely to detect even substantial improvements in students' classroom learning. Indeed, one of Reggie's online classmates presented an oral report near the end of the measurement class indicating that the specific accountability test then used in his own midwest state would not reveal when classroom instructional improvements were actually occurring.

As Reggie ponders the situation, he sees that if he were to implement formative assessment in his class, then his students would surely be likely to learn more. However, those improvements in students' learning might not show up on the state's annual accountability tests. Moreover, Reggie learned—especially from the anecdotal accounts of teachers who had used formative assessment themselves—that adoption of this approach invariably requires a meaningful expenditure of energy on the teacher's part. Given that, if he used formative assessment with his fifth-graders, his anticipated classroom improvements might not show up on "the big tests." Reggie is not sure whether he should use formative assessment next year or not.

 If you were Reggie and were faced with this situation, what would your decision be?

four-levels approach. If you think you wish to explore in more detail how these four levels of formative assessment actually function, you might wish to explore what's in that analysis. With the Levels Approach to formative assessment, as will be true of other ways of tackling formative assessment, a teacher may choose to use one or more segments of the approach.

A Five-Applications Approach

This second approach to formative assessment hinges heavily on timing—that is, *when* a teacher collects assessment evidence regarding students' status and *when* a teacher or student makes adjustment decisions. I've written a second book about formative assessment structured around this *applications approach* to formative assessment (Popham, 2011). You may wish to consider that text if you regard this way of thinking about formative assessment as potentially useful. Here, then, are descriptions of five applications of the formative-assessment process.

Five Applications of Formative Assessment

1. *Immediate Instructional Adjustments* In this initial application of formative assessment, a teacher collects assessment evidence, analyzes this evidence, and then decides on the spot—immediately—whether to alter instruction in the next few moments. Two ways for the teacher to collect assessment evidence for this application are available: (1) *teacher-administered assessments* such as brief during-lesson quizzes wherein students supply answers to multiple-choice questions by displaying lettered cards or (2) *student-reported levels of understanding* such as when students signify how well they comprehend a topic by the use of green/yellow/red cards or plastic cups. For this particular application of formative assessment, the teacher needs to have an instructional adjustment standing "at the ready" in case students' assessment data indicate an immediate alteration in instruction is needed.

2. *Near-Future Instructional Adjustments* A near-future instructional adjustment involves the teachers' collecting assessment evidence, perhaps via during-lesson tests or end-of-lesson "exit tickets" by which students display on slips of paper (handed to the teacher on the way out of the classroom) what they learned during a class session. If the assessment evidence indicates that an instructional adjustment is warranted, the teacher delivers such an adjustment during the next few class sessions. One advantage of this formative-assessment application is that a teacher need not have an "at the ready" instructional adjustment on hand. Thus, if the assessment evidence collected from students indicates no instructional adjustment is needed, the teacher will not have wasted time preparing an instructional approach that's destined to languish—unused. Conversely, if it turns out that students' assessment evidence indicates an instructional adjustment appears to be necessary, the teacher will have a day or two to prepare what will, with forethought, be an *effective* instructional adjustment.

3. *Last-Chance Instructional Adjustments* This third formative-assessment application is employed only when students are about to be administered a particularly high-stakes examination of some sort, such as a high school graduation test, a grade-to-grade promotion test, or an especially significant accountability test on which a school staff's competence will be evaluated. While there is still sufficient time to install some meaningful final-hours of instruction for students, instruction can be more effectively targeted because of the diagnostic information obtained from the administration of an exam that is sufficiently similar to the upcoming test to be accurately characterized as a "dress-rehearsal exam." Based on the instructional insights about students' weaknesses yielded by the dress-rehearsal exam, more tailored instruction focused on students' shortcomings can precede the approaching high-stakes test, thereby leading to students' improved performances.

4. *Learning-Tactic Adjustments* This fourth application of formative assessment is essentially identical to Level 2 in the previously described Levels Approach to formative assessment. Assessment evidence is collected from students and then made available to those students so that, if the students wish to do so, they can alter their learning tactics—in other words, the ways they are trying to learn whatever they are supposed to be learning. As in Level 2 of the Levels Approach, the thrust of this application is to transform students into more autonomous learners than we typically see in our classrooms. Because most students will have scant experience in monitoring their own learning status, and making decisions about whether to (and how to) adjust their learning tactics, students will need substantial support in their use of this formative-assessment application.

5. *Classroom Climate Shifts* In this fifth application we see a formative-assessment application that is the same as the third level of the Levels Approach—namely, an implementation procedure where both the teacher and the students are relying on evidence collected from ongoing classroom assessments to decide whether any adjustments (either in a teacher's instructional procedures or in students' learning tactics) are warranted. Because of a concerted "everyone participates" strategy, changes in the classroom orientation are sought so that (1) responsibility for learning is shared by all, (2) there is an expectation that every student will be a successful learner, and (3) classroom assessments will be used chiefly for learning enhancement rather than for student grading.

The five applications just described are displayed graphically in Figure 3.

As when teachers implement formative assessment by employing the previously described Levels Approach, a teacher need not use all five variations of the Applications Approach. Indeed, a teacher might give formative assessment a try by using only one version of the very first application—that is, by making immediate instructional-adjustment decisions employing students' self-reported levels of understanding as represented by their use of colored cups or cards. The advantage of both the Levels Approach and the Applications Approach is that they provide teachers with options regarding the fervor with which they wish to embrace formative assessment. Teachers' "baby steps" are usually welcomed by proponents of these approaches to formative assessment. Let's turn, now, to a final implementation approach whereby teachers can, ever so gingerly, give formative assessment a ride around the block.

A Five-Strategies Approach

A third way of splitting up the formative-assessment process as seen in Figure 3, has been introduced by Dylan Wiliam and his colleagues (Leahy et al., 2005). That's right, Wiliam is the same British bloke who, along with his countryman Paul Black, set the formative-assessment bonfire afire with their 1998 review of

figure 3 ■ Five Applications of Formative Assessment

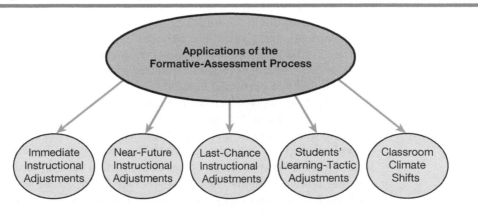

classroom assessment research (Black and Wiliam, 1998). In contrast to the two previously described implementation models—the Levels Approach and the Applications Approach—we can characterize this third conceptualization of formative assessment as a *Strategies Approach*. Wiliam has refined this approach, and he described its nuances in a volume devoted to his view of the formative-assessment process (Wiliam, 2011). If you wish to learn more about this Strategies Approach, be sure to refer to that book. It is loaded with particularly practical implementation procedures.

Wiliam believes that all teaching boils down to three essential *processes* and three *roles* by the individuals involved. As he sees it, the three key processes are (1) finding out where students are in their learning, (2) finding out where they are going, and (3) finding out how to get there. The three roles involved in this enterprise are those of (1) teacher, (2) learner, and (3) peer. When Wiliam crosses the three processes with the three roles, he arrives at a three-by-three, nine-cell matrix. By doing a deft bit of coalescing to those nine cells, he ends up with five key strategies of formative assessment that constitute this third attempt to subdivide the formative-assessment process into more teacher-palatable clumps. Here, briefly, is a description of each of the five strategies in this approach, first described by Leahy and associates in 2005.

Five Strategies of Formative Assessment

1. *Clarifying, sharing, and understanding learning intentions and criteria for success* Wiliam believes it incontestable that if students understand the nature of what they are intended to learn, they will learn it better than if they had no idea about what learning is being sought. Communicating a set of learning intentions to students, however, is often more reflective of the teacher's artistry than a teacher's adherence to a set of scientifically validated communication techniques regarding how to get students to understand

what's being asked of them. Wiliam thinks learning intentions should be stated in language comprehensible to the student, not in the sorts of "official language" that might be found in formal curricular documents. Moreover, when students are given the criteria by which the success of their performances will be judged, those success criteria should be applicable to the full range of tasks a student might be asked to accomplish, not merely the specific task included in a particular examination.

2. *Engineering effective classroom discussions, activities, and learning tasks that elicit evidence of learning*   Because eliciting evidence of students' learning is a quintessential element of the formative-assessment process, this second strategy in Wiliam's approach is particularly important, and he describes a wide array of both formal and informal techniques by which teachers (and students themselves) can gather evidence about students' learning. Such evidence, then, can be used to make inferences—hopefully valid ones—regarding students' learning status. For example, by including in classroom discussions a number of key questions that, when responded to by all students as part of an en route ungraded quiz, the teacher can discern how well students have mastered significant knowledge or subskills that are precursive to students' mastery of a major curricular aim. Teachers must possess a wide array of evidence-eliciting techniques to make this second strategy effective.

3. *Providing feedback that moves learning forward*   Providing students with feedback based on their performances on assessments is widely regarded as an instructionally useful activity. However, as Wiliam makes clear, not all feedback has a positive impact on students' learning. Indeed, ill-conceived feedback can harm, not help, students' learning. Wiliam, who has reviewed research evidence regarding feedback through the years, concluded, "If I had to reduce all of the research on feedback into one simple overarching idea, at least for academic subjects in school, it would be this: feedback should cause thinking" (2011, p. 127). In about 40 percent of empirical studies, as he points out, feedback has a negative effect on learning. This suggests, clearly, that feedback must be carefully conceived; it must direct students' attention to "what's next" rather than how well a student performed on an already completed assessment. Well-designed feedback, an imperative for successful formative assessment, must engender in students a cognitive reaction rather than an emotional reaction—and this cognitive response must be aimed at the student's future activities.

4. *Activating learners as instructional resources for one another*   Although substantial research evidence attests to the power of collaborative and cooperative learning, such procedures are encountered far less frequently in today's classrooms than one would expect. In this fourth strategy, activating students as learning resources for one another is regarded as a remarkably important way to enhance the potency of formative assessment. Almost always involving some form of peer assessment or peer tutoring, a wide range of these techniques should be in the teacher's tool kit. Peer assessment, geared toward

improvement rather than evaluation, can be especially powerful. However, both peer assessment and peer tutoring can have considerable benefits for the students who are *supplying* the assistance rather than *receiving* it, for those students providing assistance are obliged to internalize learning intentions and success criteria in the context of another student's work.

5. *Activating students as the owners of their own learning*   Although teachers have a significant role to play in structuring the situations in which learning takes place, it is only learners who create learning. This final strategy is based on the premise that, to the extent students are better able to manage their own learning, the more likely is it that they will learn well. A teacher who sets out to help students reflect critically on their own learning will discover that this aspiration, although difficult, is attainable for all students. But because reflecting on one's own learning is often emotionally charged, developing students' management skills for fostering *genuine* ownership of their learning takes time—particularly with students who have a history of failing.

As you can see, the Wiliam's Strategy Approach shares features of the two implementation models described earlier—the Levels Approach and the Applications Approach. What all three approaches are intended to do is provide a framework for teachers who wish to employ the formative-assessment process. If you wish to consider doing so, you will find the following treatments of formative assessment useful: For the Levels Approach, see Popham (2008); for the Applications Approach, see Popham (2011); and for the Strategies Approach, see Wiliam (2011). Because there is nothing inherently contradictory among all three of these implementation models, some teachers might find it useful to choose elements of two, or even all three, of the approaches.

◼ Why the Delay?

At the outset of this chapter, you were asked to figure out why formative assessment, an assessment-based instructional strategy boasting all sorts of research support, is not more widely used in our schools. Now it's time to come up with an answer to that question. Why do *you* think we don't currently see formative assessment flourishing in most of the nation's classrooms?

There is no right answer to this important question, but I think I can identify at least three reasons why we seem to be dawdling in the implementation of formative assessment. Let's see how my answers mesh with those you may have come up with on your own as you were reading the chapter.

One deterrent to our greater use of formative assessment is educators' *considerable misunderstanding about the nature of formative assessment.* Large numbers of educators think of formative assessment as a test, not a process. It's tough

Parent Talk

Suppose one of your better students, Mary Ruth Green, brings in a note from her parents, expressing concern that your classes seem to be organized to "teach to the test, not educate students." Mr. and Mrs. Green ask you to call them at home so they can, using their speaker phone, both discuss this concern with you.

 If I were you, here's what I'd say on the phone to Mary Ruth's parents:

"Thanks for raising this issue. It's an important concern, and because we all want what's best for Mary Ruth, I'm pleased to be able to explain how we're using tests in my class.

"Actually, I do use tests to influence my instruction. But the tests really only *represent* the skills and knowledge I'm trying to get Mary Ruth and her classmates to learn. I use the tests to help me plan my instruction and to make an interpretation about whether students are mastering what the test represents. In this way, I'll know whether more instruction is needed on particular topics.

"Please be assured, I am definitely not teaching to particular test items. All of the items on my tests, in fact, have never been seen before by the students. But those items do reflect the knowledge and skills my class is supposed to promote.

"You'll also realize that half of Mary Ruth's grade is based on the portfolio assessment system we use. I think the portfolio work samples, when blended with the test results, give me an even better picture of my students' progress."

Now, how would you respond to Mr. and Mrs. Green?

to get substantial benefits in kid learning if teachers think some sort of magic-bullet test is going to help them transform a tawdry instructional sequence into a terrific one. Another form of misunderstanding occurs when educators believe formative assessment is intended to help only *teachers* adjust what they are up to, not to help *students* alter their learning tactics. The Black and Wiliam research review (1998a) makes it clear that if students are actively involved in the learning process, and are given the assessment data to manage their own learning tactics, those students will display superior achievements to those displayed by students who are uninvolved in the learning process and who do not monitor their own ongoing progress. A misunderstood formative-assessment process is unlikely to be widely adopted because those educational leaders who are encouraging teachers to employ formative assessment will end up advocating with imprecision that which they themselves do not understand.

Nor do most of the nation's assessment companies help out in this regard. Many, but certainly not all, testing vendors have developed their own for-purchase assessment products they hawk as the way to boost students' scores on high-stakes accountability tests. Such companies have no interest in helping teachers understand that, according to the research evidence now at our disposal, it is formative assessment *as an evidence-informed, classroom monitoring/adjustment process* that has been shown to be effective—not a collection of prefabricated, off-the-shelf assessment systems. Thus, some self-interested assessment firms are contributing directly to misunderstandings about formative assessment on the part of many educators.

A second roadblock to educators' greater use of formative assessment is the inherent difficulty of getting people to change their ways. Most of today's educators have been educating students for more than a few minutes. And, during the years those educators have been doing their jobs, they have adopted certain instructional behaviors that, in their estimate, work! Almost all teachers think what they're doing helps their students. Otherwise, most teachers would not be doing those things. Now, because of most teachers' firm beliefs that what they have been doing will benefit students, you can see how difficult it is to get those teachers to adopt something fundamentally different. And, be assured, even Level 1 formative assessment is fundamentally different from the way most teachers typically approach their instruction. Moreover, both Level 2 and Level 3 formative assessment constitute particularly dramatic breaks from instruction as usual. So, another factor slowing down teachers' acceptance of a research-proven classroom strategy that works is, simply, human beings' reluctance to alter their established behavior.

Finally, despite the fact that formative assessment can improve students' achievement, and improve it dramatically, this improved achievement may not show up on many external accountability tests. Certain kinds of external accountability tests are basically unable to accurately measure the quality of instruction students receive. Insofar as this is true, teachers who might be doing a crackerjack instructional job by using formative assessment may discover that, despite what their classroom tests demonstrate is considerable improvements in their students' achievements, those improvements simply don't show up on the high-stakes tests being used in that locale to evaluate schools. Disillusioned with such results, some teachers will understandably back away from using what seems to be an ineffectual formative-assessment process.

These, then, are three reasons I believe formative assessment is not more widely employed in our schools: (1) misunderstandings regarding formative assessment, (2) teachers' tendencies to resist altering their current conduct, and (3) the failure of many external accountability tests to accurately mirror the improvements occurring in the classrooms of teachers who use formative assessment. You may arrive at different conclusions about why we are not currently surrounded by swarms of teachers who rely on formative assessment to deliver the best possible instruction to their students. But these are my best guesses.

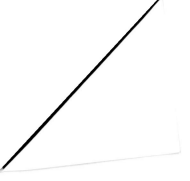

Whatever obstacles exist to the greater use of formative assessment, we need to overcome those impediments. We must do whatever is necessary so that formative assessment will be used far more widely in our nation's classrooms. Formative assessment works, and it works to help students learn. Accordingly, we need much more of it.

■ What Do Classroom Teachers Really Need to Know about Formative Assessment?

What a teacher really needs to know about formative assessment depends almost completely on what the teacher intends to do with formative assessment. If teachers don't intend to use formative assessment in their own classrooms, then there's much less such teachers must know about it. A "non-user" teacher, however, should still know what formative assessment is—and what it isn't. It's especially important these days, even for non-using teachers, to understand the essential nature of formative assessment. This is because, as a member of a school's faculty, such teachers can help forestall their colleagues' sometimes unthinking adoption of commercial products that, though praised by those products' publishers, have essentially no evidence to support their use. If a non-user teacher has a general understanding of what the research basis underlying formative assessment actually is, then research-free claims of effectiveness for commercial products can be contrasted with the kind of evidence Black and Wiliam (1998a) have assembled to show that classroom assessment, if used formatively, can benefit students. Summing up, even teachers who don't intend to use formative assessment should know what it is, what it isn't, and the nature of its research support.

On the other hand, if a teacher intends to actually use formative assessment, then what that teacher needs to know is substantially greater. For openers, a would-be user of formative assessment must obviously understand what formative assessment is and what it isn't. Any prospective user of formative assessment must surely grasp the nature of formative assessment as a process in which assessment-elicited evidence allows teachers to adjust their instruction and students to adjust their learning tactics. Potential users of formative assessment must also recognize how, by dividing formative assessment into different levels or applications, teachers can understand this potent process more accurately.

Teachers who intend to use formative assessment must be thoroughly conversant with the structure of learning progressions, and the role those progressions play in the formative-assessment process. Unless a teacher is fortunate enough to stumble onto an already-developed learning progression for the same target curricular aim a teacher has chosen, then the teacher should be able to build a brand-new learning progression from scratch.

Finally, depending on the level(s) or application(s) of formative assessment a teacher hopes to employ, a prospective user of formative assessment ought to be reasonably conversant with the major activities associated with those approaches.

but what does this have to do with
Teaching?

Formative assessment is not the same thing as teaching. On the contrary, formative assessment is an assessment-rooted process capable of making teaching better. It may be useful for educators to think of formative assessment as a *companion activity* whose one and only *raison d'être* is to improve the quality of teaching. It does so by providing the assessment-based evidence that informs selected instructional decisions a teacher should make.

Accordingly, formative assessment must, of necessity, be a *classroom-based* process. Formative assessment doesn't take place in a principal's office or at a school district's central offices. Formative assessment occurs in a particular classroom taught by a particular teacher, and it is based on assessment evidence collected from that teacher's current students. To the extent that anyone tries to make formative assessment an activity occurring outside what goes on in a given teacher's classroom, those efforts really cannot be supported by the existing research base that so strongly undergirds the use of classroom-based formative assessment.

Teaching consists of the instructional activities a teacher chooses to employ, and those activities are chosen on the basis of conscious decisions made by the teacher. One category of such instructional decisions can be accurately characterized as *adjustment decisions*—that is, decisions regarding whether preplanned instruction should be adjusted by a teacher and, if so, in what ways. Well, those adjustment decisions are precisely the ones that the formative-assessment process is intended to inform. If formative assessment is employed properly, teachers' adjustment decisions will be better and, as a consequence, kids will be better educated.

What does formative assessment have to do with teaching? *Everything!*

■ Chapter Summary

Formative assessment was defined, at the chapter's outset, as a planned process in which assessment-elicited evidence of students' status is used by teachers to adjust their ongoing instructional procedures or by students to adjust their current learning tactics. Because a teacher's understanding of this conception of formative assessment is essential, considerable attention was given to describing the key components of the definition.

The second emphasis of the chapter was on the research evidence underlying the formative-assessment process. The Black and Wiliam (1998a) review of almost a decade's worth of classroom assessment investigations currently supplies the bulk of evidence usually called on to support the effectiveness of formative assessment. Based on 250 solid studies drawn from almost 700 such studies, Black and Wiliam concluded the empirical evidence they studied "shows conclusively

formative
assessment
improves
learning

that formative assessment does improve learning." Moreover, the improvements in students' learning attributed to formative assessment were among the largest ever reported for educational interventions. Finally, Black and Wiliam pointed out that the formative-assessment process is so robust it can be employed by teachers in diverse ways, yet still work well.

Considerable attention was given in the chapter to learning progressions—the sequenced sets of building blocks students must master en route to mastering a more remote, target curricular aim. The building blocks in a learning progression are either (1) bodies of enabling knowledge or (2) cognitive subskills. Learning progressions function as the frameworks for the formative-assessment process because assessments of students' building-block mastery supply the evidence for teachers (or students) to decide whether to make adjustments. Suggestions were provided regarding how to build a learning progression for a selected curricular aim.

Three alternate ways of conceptualizing the formative-assessment process were then presented. A *four-application approach* consisted of the following levels: 1: Teachers' Instructional Adjustments; 2: Students' Learning-Tactic Adjustments; 3: Classroom Climate Shift; and 4: Schoolwide Implementation. A *five-applications approach* featured 1: Immediate Instructional Adjustments; 2: Near-Future Instructional Adjustments; 3. Last-Chance Instructional Adjustments; 4: Learning-Tactic Adjustments; and 5: Classroom Climate Shifts. Finally, a *five-strategies approach* was set forth featuring the following strategies: 1: Clarifying, sharing, and understanding learning intentions and criteria for success; 2: Engineering effective classroom discussions, activities, and learning tasks that elicit evidence of learning; 3: Providing feedback that moves learning forward; 4: Activating learners as instructional resources for one another; and 5: Activating students as the owners of their own learning.

The chapter was concluded with some speculation regarding why it is that this research-supported, assessment-rooted process is not more widely used by teachers. It was contended that the reluctance of many teachers to adopt formative assessment is due to (1) educators' misunderstandings about formative assessment, (2) teachers' natural reluctance to alter their current behaviors, and (3) the inability of many accountability tests to accurately measure classroom improvements attributable to formative assessment.

 # Self-Check

For this chapter about formative assessment, you can think of the self-check exercises as a sort of "Vignette Village." You'll be presented with five brief vignettes describing common behaviors engaged in by educators. Each vignette deals with one of the topics in the chapter. Preceding each vignette, you'll be informed (via an italicized statement) what you are to decide about in the upcoming vignette.

Vignette 1: Quentin, the Quiz Whiz

In the following vignette, please decide whether the teacher is or isn't using formative assessment as defined in the chapter.

Quentin Ives teaches fifth-grade students at Emerson Elementary School. His daily mathematics lessons are almost always concluded by a five-item quiz because Quentin believes the prospect of these end-of-lesson quizzes motivates his students to pay closer attention during the lesson. Quentin uses an items-correct grading system whereby his students' final grade in mathematics is based on each student's average score on these per-lesson quizzes. Because Quentin's students invariably score well on the mathematics section of the state's annual accountability tests, his principal often expresses delight with Quentin's frequent use of daily quizzes. (*Is Quentin using formative assessment? YES or NO*)

Vignette 2: Carrie's Math Kids

In the following vignette, please decide which level *of the four-level formative-assessment process the teacher is using.*

Carrie Klevens teaches general mathematics in a large inner-city high school. Because many of the students she teaches typically have trouble with any sort of standardized achievement test in math, and particularly the state's yearly accountability tests, Carrie decides to embark on what is, for her, a dramatically atypical approach to instruction. She informs all her students, at the beginning of each Friday's class, that she will be giving an exam covering what was taught during that week's first four days. The exams, however, will be immediately scored by a parent volunteer who has agreed to assist with the general mathematics course and return exams to students before that Friday's class is finished. The exams will, however, not be graded. The only purpose of giving the exams and returning them rapidly to students is for the students to reach a personal judgment about how well their study strategies are working. Carrie announces this new procedure to her classes, and promises to describe different sorts of learning procedures that her students might wish to consider using. However, the students are to decide themselves, on the basis of each Friday's nongraded tests, whether to stay with their current learning approaches or, instead, try something new. (*Which* level *of formative assessment is Carrie using?*)

Vignette 3: Alicia's "Older" Students

In the following vignette, please decide which application *of the five-application formative-assessment process the teacher is using.*

Alicia's first three years of teaching were all carried out with students in kindergarten or first grade. This year, however, reduced enrollments have limited the number of primary-grade assignments in her school, so she was assigned to teach a class of fifth-graders. Although Alicia has read about the payoffs of formative assessment, she never actually used it during her previous teaching assignments. However, during the current year with her fifth-grade class, she has been applying the formative-assessment process in a manner that she believes will benefit her new students. She just completed a six-week unit in language arts dealing with "Organization of Presentations." Her chief curricular target of this unit was to help her students become skilled in the way they organized content for their reports, either written presentations or oral presentations. As she analyzed what students needed to learn during the unit, Alicia identified two major building blocks to be accomplished by her students. Accordingly, she administered two during-class exams along the way to see how well her students had mastered each of these building blocks.

Because she had not previously taught fifth-grade students, and was unsure about her students' likely language arts skills, Alicia waited until she had scored all their exams to decide if any instructional adjustments were needed. Happily, her students did so well on each exam that Alicia concluded no modifications in her instructional plans were necessary. She was convinced, however, that if an instructional adjustment had been required, she could have prepared one and delivered it in a day or so following the two exams. (*Which* application *of formative assessment was Alicia using?*)

Vignette 4: Peter Peer-Prep Prowlers

In the following vignette, please decide which strategy *of the five-strategy approach to the formative-assessment process is being used.*

Peter Ames almost literally worships at the altar of collaborative learning. During the first few sessions of his middle school mathematics classes, he informs his students that his class motto is always "Collaboration crushes ignorance!" Every two weeks, almost without exception, he gives students a brief nongraded (but scored) quiz intended chiefly to give students a better fix on how well they are mastering what's recently been taught. Roughly half of the quizzes are scored by Peter, particularly those involving the use of many constructed-response items, but the other half of the quizzes are scored by other students. Scores for all quizzes are posted on the classroom's bulletin board along with a designation of which students are, for that quiz, supposed to be PPPs—that is, Peer-Prep Prowlers.

These designated PPPs are supposed to meet briefly, caucus about what to emphasize instructionally during some "Round Two" peer tutoring, and then spend the initial half of the class working with students whose scores on the quizzes indicate the need for additional instruction either from the teacher or from a classmate. These PPP sessions are always governed by students' scores on the nongraded quizzes, and during a semester, all students in a class will become a PPP on at least one occasion. The students in Peter's classes invariably increase their peer-tutoring skills as the course progresses. (*Which* strategy *of formative assessment is Peter using?*)

Vignette 5: Lydia's Learning Progression

In the following vignette, decide if the teacher has made any major mistakes in building a learning progression.

Lydia Larsen teaches fifth-graders in a rural midwest school district. Her state has recently adopted the "Heartland Core Curriculum" that sets forth what students at each grade are to learn. One of the mathematics skills to be taught in the fifth grade is a skill that, up until this time, Lydia has not been obliged to teach. To get a solid understanding of the skill, Lydia decides to build a learning progression leading up to students' skill mastery. Here is the sequence she follows.

Initially, Lydia tries to acquire a thoroughgoing understanding of the math skill itself by reading what is described in the Heartland Core Curriculum documents. Then, from her state's Department of Education website, she gets copies of sample items that can be employed by the state's teachers to measure this math skill. After studying both of these sources of information, she thinks she knows what the skill entails. Lydia then identifies the building blocks she believes her students must master on their way to acquiring the new math skill. She finds that, after conversations with other teachers about the skill, there appear to be two pivotal building blocks students absolutely need to achieve if they are to have any hope of mastering the new math skill. One of the building blocks is a body of enabling knowledge describing the step-by-step order in which key parts of the skill must be used. The other building block is a cognitive subskill focused on a student's actual application of the knowledge contained in the other building block. Lydia plans to assess students' mastery of both building blocks by using fairly conventional classroom assessments containing both selected-response and constructed-response items. She sequences the two building blocks so that she will first teach the knowledge building block and, thereafter, the subskill building block.

Her fellow teachers think Lydia's learning progression makes great instructional sense, and two of them ask if they can use her learning progression in their own classes. (*Did Lydia make any major mistakes in building a learning progression for the new math skill? YES or NO*)

 # Pondertime

1. At the moment, in comparing the frequency with which we see Level 1, Level 2, and Level 3 formative assessment actually used in classrooms, by far the most commonly encountered is Level 1 formative assessment. Why do you think this is so? Which application of the five-applications approach and which strategy of the five-strategies approach is most likely to be used by teachers? Why?

2. What do you believe would be most effective in encouraging more teachers to adopt the formative-assessment process in their own classrooms?

3. If you were trying to explain to a parent, using only a sentence or two, the "true essence of formative assessment," what would you say to that parent?

4. The chapter was concluded with some speculation about why it is that formative assessment is not used more widely. If you had to choose the single-most important impediment that prevents more teachers from employing formative assessment, what would this one impediment be? Do you think it is possible to remove this impediment?

Self-Check Key

Vignette 1
Quentin's frequent quizzes seem to be used exclusively for grading and motivation, not as evidence for him to make instructional adjustments or for his students to make adjustments in their learning tactics. This, therefore, would not be an instance of formative assessment as defined in the chapter.

Vignette 2
Carrie is clearly attempting to move into a new way of trying to get her students to make friends with general mathematics. Because there is little evidence that Carrie is using students' test performances to make adjustments in her own instruction, and a clear plan to allow students to use their own test performances to adjust their learning tactics, Carrie is not engaged in Level 3 or, for that matter, Level 1 formative assessment. This is a fairly clear-cut instance of Level 2 formative assessment.

Vignette 3
Alicia played it safe—and smart—by holding off on devising new instructional procedures until she had discerned whether her fifth-graders were going to need any altered instructional activities. The more familiar she becomes with students of this age, the more confidence she will acquire regarding the likelihood that instructional adjustments are going to be needed for particular topics. This, then, is an instance of near-future instructional adjustment. Had Alicia readied instructional activity for an immediate instructional adjustment, that preparation would have been wasted because her initial instruction seemed to do the needed job satisfactorily.

Vignette 4
This is a pretty apparent instance of the fourth of Wiliam's strategies focused on activating learners as instructional resources for one another. Whether students are serving as peer assessors or peer tutors, in most instances they will need guidance from their teacher about how to deliver such support for classmates successfully. Rarely, during their school careers, have today's students learned how to function as instructional resources for one another. Teachers who opt for this formative-assessment strategy must make sure to provide support for students as they assume these new roles.

Vignette 5
It is always possible to find flaws in the way another person tackles a complex task, and it would be possible in this vignette to nit-pick at Lydia's approach to building a

learning progression. But, by and large, she touched all the progression-building bases as she generated her learning progression for the new mathematics skill. Would you expect any less from a midwestern teacher?

■ Additional Stuff

Black, P., and Wiliam, D. (1998a). "Assessment and classroom learning," *Assessment in Education: Principles, Policy and Practice, 5,* no. 1: 7–73.

Black, P., and Wiliam, D. (1998b). "Inside the black box: Raising standards through classroom assessment," *Phi Delta Kappan, 80,* no. 2: 139–148.

Crooks, T. (1988). "The impact of classroom evaluation practices on students," *Review of Educational Research, 58,* no. 4: 438–481.

Gipps, C. V., and Stobart, G. (1997). *Assessment: A teacher's guide to the issues* (3rd ed.). London, UK: Hodder and Stoughton.

Heritage, M. (2010). *Formative assessment: Making it happen in the classroom.* Thousand Oaks, CA: Corwin.

James, M. (1992). *Assessment for learning.* Paper presented at the Annual Conference of the Association for Supervision and Curriculum Development.

Kingston, N., and Nash, B. (2011). "Formative assessment: A meta-analysis and a call for research," *Educational Measurement: Issues and Practice, 30,* no. 4 (Winter): 28–37.

Leahy, S., Thompson, C. L. M., and Wiliam, D. (2005). "Classroom assessment—Minute by minute, day by day," *Educational Leadership, 63,* no. 3 (November): 18–24.

Masters, G., and Forster, M. (1996). *Progress maps.* Melbourne: Australian Council for Educational Research.

Natriello, G. (1987). "The impact of evaluation processes on students," *Educational Psychologist, 22,* no. 2: 155–175.

Popham, W. J. (2008). *Transformative assessment.* Alexandria, VA: ASCD.

Popham, W. J. (2011). *Transformative assessment in action.* Alexandria, VA: ASCD.

Scriven, M. (1967). "The methodology of evaluation." In R. W. Tyler, R. M. Gagne, and M. Scriven (Eds.), *Perspectives of curriculum evaluation,* Volume I (pp. 39–83). Chicago: Rand McNally.

Shepard, L. (2006). *Can benchmark assessments be formative? Distinguishing formative assessment from formative program evaluation.* A presentation during the National Large-Scale Assessment Conference, Council of Chief State School Officers, San Francisco, CA.

Stiggins, R. J. (2007). *Student-involved classroom assessment for learning* (5th ed.). Upper Saddle River, NJ: Prentice-Hall.

Stiggins, R., and Popham, W. J. (2008). *Assessing students' affect related to assessment for learning.* Washington, DC: The Council of Chief State School Officers.

Sutton, R. (1995). *Assessment for learning.* Salford, UK: RS Publications.

Wiliam, D. (2011). *Embedded formative assessment.* Bloomington, IN: Solution Tree.

Wiliam, D., and Thompson, M. (2008). "Integrating assessment with learning: What will it take to make it work?" In C. A. Dwyer (Ed.), *The future of assessment: Shaping teaching and learning* (pp. 53–82). New York: Lawrence Erlbaum.

Wylie, E. C. (Ed.). (2008). *Tight but loose: Scaling up teacher professional development in diverse contexts* (ETS Research Report No. RR-08-29). Princeton, NJ: Educational Testing Service.

■ Cyber Stuff

- *Dylan Wiliam's Website* is a site apt to be of particular interest to any educator concerned with formative assessment. The website contains a charming mix of information regarding one of the leading proponents of formative assessment or, as Dylan usually refers to it, as assessment *for* learning. In addition to many downloadable papers and presentations, Dylan (whose follicle-free skull resembles my own), includes a dozen photos useful for his upcoming presentations. I found the head shot "in orange" to be particularly fetching. **www.dylanwiliam.net/**

- *Te Kete Ipurangi* is a bilingual website (English and Māori) provided by the New Zealand Ministry of Education. It is intended to function as an online learning center providing quality-assured materials for that nation's educators. A section of the website, dealing with assessment for learning, contains an excellent set of descriptions regarding the key principles associated with formative assessment. And, let's face it, how many times do people living in this hemisphere have an opportunity to interact with a *bona fide* Māori website? **www.tki.org.nz/e/tki/**

- *The Association for Achievement and Improvement through Assessment* was founded in 1990 in order to promote student achievement through the development of effective practice, recording, and reporting. This United Kingdom group's website contains a host of assessment resources and links to assessment websites and organizations, many of which focus much of their energies on formative assessment (assessment *for* learning). The site, however, also identifies resources associated with assessment *of* learning. **www.aaia.org.uk/**

■ Extended Applications

It is a truism that the more a person uses something, the more familiar with this something the person becomes. This self-evident notion surely applies to the assessment-related knowledge, skills, and concepts you have been reading about in the foregoing pages. Thus, to provide readers of *Classroom Assessment* with additional opportunities to apply the content contained in this text, this final section contains a variety of exercises intended to give readers an opportunity to use what they've been reading about.

In a sense, of course, the Self-Check exercises found at the close of this chapter provided an opportunity for readers to apply a chapter's content. Nonetheless, the more times you use a concept, skill, or a body of knowledge, the more likely it is that you will master this content so you can employ it in varied situations.

For each of the text, you will find an extended-application exercise calling for you to do some thinking about that chapter's content as it applies to a real-world situation. Each exercise is preceded by a brief introduction setting forth the reason that the upcoming extended-application exercise has been selected.

Because many of these exercises call on you to generate an original response rather than select a response from a set of options, it is difficult to supply an "answer key" for readers' unpredictable responses. So, what you'll find following all the exercises is One Possible Response—an indication of how I would have personally responded to the exercise if I had been asked to do so. Please don't regard my response as the only way to respond to an exercise. After all, by definition, this is only "one possible" response. Instead, please think of my response as a fairly flimsy form of feedback. You can certainly disagree with me, even emphatically, yet still profit from doing the exercise.

Remember, what is being provided in this section. The exercises deliberately intended to extend how you apply the content treated in *Classroom Assessment*. I hope you find these exercises useful in enhancing your understanding of what teachers need to know about classroom assessment.

■ Understandings/Misunderstandings about Formative Assessment

Introduction

The setting for this exercise about formative assessment is a middle school cafeteria where about two dozen of the school's teachers are attending an exploratory meeting to see if any of them wish to take part in a teacher learning community (TLC) focused on the topic of formative assessment. It is the second week of the school year, and most teachers are trying to determine what sorts of professional development activities they will take part in during the next nine months. This exploratory meeting is a 60-minute, after-school session, and you are to play a central role in these teachers' deliberations for the next 60 minutes.

Please assume you are a teacher from another middle school in the same district, and that you and several of your fellow teachers took part during the previous school year in an eight-month TLC about formative assessment. Assume also that you have read numerous materials such as what's found, and that you have had the benefit during the previous school year of discussing with your own school's TLC colleagues a variety of issues related to formative assessment. For this Extended Applications exercise, you are to function as a formative-assessment "expert" who can help these teachers decide whether they will take part in their own school's formative-assessment TLC.

Formative Assessment

There are 10 statements in this exercise, each of them made by one of the teachers in the exploratory meeting. As an ice-breaker, you have asked each of those teachers to start off the meeting by describing what they regard as "One understanding I have about formative assessment." Your task is to distinguish between these teachers' statements that are *understandings* versus those statements that are *misunderstandings*. For any *misunderstanding* you identify, you should also correct that teacher's misperception.

The rationale for this exercise, of course, is that the more adept you become at recognizing colleagues' cloudy understandings regarding formative assessment, the more able you will be to correct such misunderstandings. As usual, try to come up with your own judgments before consulting the One Possible Response segments.

 Exercise Directions: Please consider, in turn, each of the following 10 statements about formative assessment made by teachers during an exploratory meeting regarding a potential teacher learning community. For each statement, decide whether the statement represents an understanding or a misunderstanding. For each misunderstanding that you identify, please indicate briefly how you could tactfully correct the speaker's misconception.

1. An English teacher starts off with the following comment: "If I understand formative assessment accurately, it is not a particular kind of test. On the contrary, formative assessment is a *process* wherein the results of assessments are used to make adjustments in what's taking place in class. Am I correct?"

Does this teacher's statement represent an *understanding* or a *misunderstanding*? And, if the latter, can you correct it?

_____

_____

_____

 One Possible Response: This English teacher, happily, has voiced what is perhaps the most important understanding teachers must possess about formative assessment: It is a process rather than a test, and the main mission of this process is to use assessment-elicited evidence to help teachers and/or students adjust what they are doing. The English teacher's statement is definitely an understanding, and the significance of this understanding should be emphasized to other teachers in the meeting.

2. One of the three social studies teachers in the group then makes the following assertion: "Based on what I have heard about formative assessment, it sounds like a sensible approach, but there is no evidence to support its use! Is this right?"

Does this teacher's statement represent an *understanding* or a *misunderstanding*? And, if the latter, can you correct it?

_____

_____

_____

One Possible Response: This is a definite misunderstanding. We have, in truth, relatively few procedures in education that teachers can say with confidence are "research proven," so it would be a serious mistake to overlook the very solid empirical evidence supporting the effectiveness of the formative-assessment process. Here's what you might have replied to the social studies teacher: "Actually, formative assessment has one of the most solid research bases of any instruction ploys we use in teaching. The research review reported by Paul Black and Dylan Wiliam in 1998 provides convincing evidence that formative assessment works. If you have an opportunity, and if your school chooses to have a TLC on formative assessment this year, I would urge your group to spend a couple of your sessions on the Black and Wiliam review. The TLC at our school did that last year, and it was time really well spent."

3. Belinda, a first-year science teacher, then says, "I think formative assessment is only intended to help teachers improve their instructional procedures, and really has little to do with kids adjusting how they are trying to learn things."

Does this teacher's statement represent an *understanding* or a *misunderstanding*? And, if the latter, can you correct it?

_____

_____

_____

 One Possible Response: This statement represents a serious misunderstanding of the formative-assessment process because the focus of formative assessment can be *either* on teachers' adjusting their instructional procedures *or* on students' adjusting their learning tactics. You might tell Belinda something such as, "Although in North America many educators tend to think of formative assessment as you've described it, in other nations—especially in Europe and Australasia—educators seem more attentive to the way formative assessment helps students do a better job at learning what they are supposed to be learning. Teachers in your school, Belinda, could decide to focus on assessment-based *teacher* adjustments, *student* adjustments, or *both*."

4. A math teacher then asks, "If I am making on-the-spot adjustments in my teaching based on my observations of my students' reactions to what I'm saying, doesn't this make what I'm doing formative assessment?"

Does this teacher's statement represent an *understanding* or a *misunderstanding*? And, if the latter, can you correct it?

_____

_____

_____

One Possible Response: This is a definite misunderstanding. You might say to the math teacher something along these lines: "It is often an instructionally astute thing for teachers to make on-the-spot adjustments in their teaching activities. But that doesn't make what they do 'formative assessment.' Formative assessment is a *planned* process that revolves around students' assessment performances, not their facial expressions."

5. A physical education teacher, Janet, then says, "I think formative assessment is remarkably akin to coaching. We watch how students are able to perform in a particular sport, then make our coaching adjustments based on the level of competence a student displays."

Does this teacher's statement represent an *understanding* or a *misunderstanding*? And, if the latter, can you correct it?

_____

_____

_____

 One Possible Response: Janet's comparison of formative assessment is right on the mark. She recognizes that the evidence-based approach to teaching used by those who effectively employ formative assessment is almost identical to the evidence-based approach to coaching displayed by good coaches. In most instances, of course, the evidence on which coaches rely is based on their observations of a student's athletic behavior in what might be characterized as a series of "performance tests."

6. A history teacher then makes a comment: "I've read that really sensible formative assessment is always based on a carefully identified series of building blocks that students need to master on their way to achieving a more distant curricular goal. I think these are called 'learning progressions.' We don't have those learning progressions in history; and I'm not even sure that they can be built in history. I guess that means, at least for history teachers, formative assessment is a no-no!"

Does this teacher's statement represent an *understanding* or a *misunderstanding*? And, if the latter, can you correct it?

_____

_____

_____

 One Possible Response: The history teacher makes an interesting point. Part of what he said represented a solid understanding about formative assessment—namely, that an effective use of formative assessment is almost always based on well-devised learning progressions. However, the part of the teacher's statement that is off base is when he opines that, at least in history, such progressions can't be built. Here's what might be said to the teacher regarding this misunderstanding: "Although it might be true that there are no elaborate learning progressions in history with which you are familiar, it is nonetheless possible for all teachers, history teachers included, to design 'bare-bones' learning progressions that identify a very few must-be-mastered building blocks. For example, a one-month unit on some aspect of history might lend itself to the identification of one or two bodies of enabling knowledge and one or two cognitive subskills. These sorts of rudimentary learning progressions are all that's needed to make formative assessment work well."

7. Toby, another English teacher, says, "Our school is under a pile of pressure to boost our students' scores on the state's accountability tests in math and reading. If we carry out a teacher learning community on formative assessment in this school, and then start to use it widely in the school, I assume our students' scores will rise on the state tests."

Does this teacher's statement represent an *understanding* or a *misunderstanding*? And, if the latter, can you correct it?

_____

_____

_____

 One Possible Response: Regrettably, Toby's assumption is unwarranted. This makes Toby's view a definite misunderstanding. You might say something like this to Toby and the other teachers at the meeting: "Although there is abundant evidence that students' in-class achievement will improve, these in-class gains often fail to transfer to statewide accountability tests. This is because state accountability tests are often insensitive to detection of instructional quality. So, if teachers in your school actually use formative assessment appropriately, you may see some modest improvement by your students on the state tests, but the level of those improvements will depend chiefly on the instructional sensitivity of your state tests—not the effectiveness with which you taught. If those state tests are not able to distinguish between successfully taught and unsuccessfully taught students, then your school is not likely to see a big jump in scores on the state tests."

8. Another mathematics teacher, Greta, comments, "In the math department, we've been almost deluged by advertisements of 'formative-assessment' testing systems produced by some of the nation's largest testing companies. I think these systems seem very far removed from the sort of research evidence indicating formative assessment works. They seem to be based on gigantic collections of test items, many of which do not mesh well with our state's curricular aims. As far as I can see, these companies are trying to cash in on the positive press that formative assessment has received but are not really instances of *bona fide* formative assessment."

Does this teacher's statement represent an *understanding* or a *misunderstanding*? And, if the latter, can you correct it?

_____

_____

_____

One Possible Response: Greta's got it. She seems to understand what's going on in the commercial world of selling products to educators. At the moment, there is no compelling evidence that any of the so-called formative-assessment systems being peddled by commercial firms actually improve students' achievement. And, based on the review of classroom formative assessment by Black and Wiliam in 1998, it is quite inaccurate to even characterize most of these item-laden systems as "formative assessment" in the sense that Black and Wiliam use that phrase.

9. A biology teacher, Mario, opines, "It makes for confusion when teachers try to bundle teacher-focused formative assessment with student-focused formative assessment. Although there are similarities between the two formative-assessment strategies, there are meaningful differences between them. I think we should deal with the two types of formative assessment separately rather than trying to mush them together."

Does this teacher's statement represent an *understanding* or a *misunderstanding*? And, if the latter, can you correct it?

_____

_____

_____

 One Possible Response: The biology teacher, Mario, has it just right. Many educators become seriously confused by lumping together teacher-focused formative assessment and student-focused formative assessment. It makes much more sense, both in terms of the supporting research and the implementation of the two approaches, to keep them separated as distinctive categories or decisively different levels of formative assessment.

10. Finally, a foreign-language instructor says, "Why do we need a year-long teacher learning community on formative assessment? If this assessment-based approach is so very effective, why don't we just get a guest speaker in for one of the school's ever fewer professional development days, listen to what he or she has to say, and then get on with using formative assessment in our classes. The sooner we all understand formative assessment, the quicker we can install it in the school."

Does this teacher's statement represent an *understanding* or a *misunderstanding*? And, if the latter, can you correct it?

_____

_____

_____

 One Possible Response: Most of the research bearing on the best way to get a school's faculty to adopt a new practice suggests that an approach almost certain to fail is reliance on a one-shot visiting wizard. One-shot presentations, even if delivered by a skillful speaker, rarely have the long-term impact on actual practice it is hoped they

302

will. Accordingly, this teacher has voiced a clear misunderstanding about the potency of one-shot presentations. The evidence is that extended-duration learning communities do a much better job of getting teachers to actually use the skills and knowledge addressed during a teacher learning community.

◼ Glossary

formative assessment   A planned process in which assessment-elicited evidence of students' status is used by teachers to adjust their ongoing instructional procedures or by students to adjust their current learning tactics.

learning progression   A sequenced set of building blocks—that is, subskills or bodies of enabling knowledge—it is thought students must master en route to mastering a more remote target curricular aim.

summative assessments   Tests used to make final judgments about students or the quality of a teacher's instruction.

Making Sense Out of Standardized Test Scores

Classroom teachers need to be able to interpret the results not only of their own assessment procedures but also of the various kinds of standardized tests that are frequently administered to students. Teachers need to be able to interpret such test results so they can base classroom instructional decisions on those results and also be able to respond accurately when students' parents raise such questions as, "What does my child's grade-equivalent score of 7.4 really mean?" or "When my child's achievement test results are at the 97th percentile, is that three percentiles from the top or the bottom?"

This chapter focuses on the task of making sense out of students' performances on standardized achievement and aptitude tests. One of the kinds of tests under consideration will be the achievement tests (for instance, in mathematics or reading) developed and distributed by commercial testing companies. Achievement tests are also developed and administered by state departments of education in connection with statewide assessment programs in such subjects as social studies, sciences, mathematics, reading, and writing. These state tests often employ reporting procedures akin to those used with commercially distributed standardized achievement tests.

And, even though I've desperately tried to avoid numbers larger than 9, in this chapter you'll encounter a few that are, indeed, larger. Don't be dismayed. Simply go through the examples, one step at a time, and you'll emerge from the chapter a finer human being. The numbers in this chapter will be easier to deal with than might be thought at first glance.

These days, standardized tests (especially standardized *achievement* tests) are often misused. You'll learn why it is unwise to try to evaluate educators' effectiveness on the basis of students' scores on many such tests. Nonetheless, standardized tests *do* have an important, educationally useful role to play. This chapter focuses on the appropriate uses of standardized tests.

From Chapter 13 of *Classroom Assessment: What Teachers Need to Know*, Seventh Edition. W. James Popham. Copyright © 2014 by Pearson Education, Inc. All rights reserved.

The chapter will be wrapped up with a consideration of two aptitude tests that have a whopping impact on students' lives. You'll be looking at the two examinations that often become determiners to a student's continued education. That's right, we'll be dealing with the two most widely used college entrance exams: the SAT and the ACT.

If you're a current or would-be secondary school teacher, you'll immediately recognize the need for you to know about the SAT and the ACT. After all, many of your students will soon be taking one or both of these tests. But if you're an elementary teacher, or are preparing to be one, you might be thinking, "What do college entrance exams have to do with me?" Well, all teachers—elementary and secondary—ought to understand at least the most significant facts about these two examinations. Even teachers of primary-grade kids will find parents asking questions such as, How can we get our child really ready for those in-the-future, important college entrance tests? Every teacher should be familiar with any really significant information associated with the teaching profession. Thus, because most students and their parents will, at some point, want to know more about college entrance exams, I think every single teacher—and even married ones—should know the basic SAT and ACT facts you'll learn about in this chapter.

■ Standardized Tests

A *standardized test* is a test, designed to yield either norm-referenced or criterion-referenced inferences, that is administered, scored, and interpreted in a standard, predetermined manner. Almost all *nationally* standardized tests are distributed by commercial testing firms. Most such firms are for-profit corporations, although there are a few not-for-profit measurement organizations, such as the Educational Testing Service (ETS), that distribute nationally standardized tests. Almost all nationally standardized tests, whether focused on the measurement of students' aptitude or achievement, are chiefly intended to provide norm-referenced interpretations.

Standardized achievement tests have also been developed in a number of states under the auspices of state departments of education. These statewide tests (clearly intended to be administered, scored, and interpreted in a standard, predetermined fashion) have usually been installed to satisfy a legislative mandate that establishes an educational accountability program of some sort. In certain instances, important decisions about individual students are made on the basis of a student's test performance. In many states, for example, if a student does not pass a prescribed statewide basic skills examination by the end of high school, the student is not awarded a diploma, even though the student has satisfied all other curricular requirements. In other cases, although no contingencies for individual students depend on how a student performed on a test, results of student tests are publicized by the media on a district-by-district or school-by-school basis. The test results thus serve as an indicator of local educators' effectiveness, at least in the perception of many citizens. These state-sired standardized achievement tests are generally intended to yield criterion-referenced interpretations. Educational aptitude tests are rarely, if ever, developed by state departments of education.

Although standardized tests have traditionally consisted almost exclusively of selected-response items, in recent years the developers of standardized tests have attempted to incorporate a certain number of constructed-response items in their tests. Standardized tests, because they are intended for widespread use, are developed with far more care (and cost) than is possible in an individual teacher's classroom. Even so, the fundamentals of test development are routinely employed when standardized tests are developed. In other words, the people who create the items for such tests attempt to adhere to the same kinds of item-writing and item-improvement precepts you've learned about. The writers of multiple-choice items for standardized tests worry, just as you should, about inadvertently supplying students with clues that give away the correct answer. The writers of short-answer items for standardized tests try to avoid, just as you should, the inclusion of ambiguous language in their items.

There are, of course, staggering differences in the level of effort associated with the construction of standardized tests and the construction of classroom tests. A commercial testing agency may assign a flotilla of item writers and a fleet of item editors to a new test-development project, whereas you'll be fortunate if you have a part-time teacher's aide or, possibly, a malleable spouse to proofread your tests to detect typographical errors.

Decision Time

Which Test to Believe

Each spring in the Big Valley Unified School District, students in grades 5, 8, 10, and 12 complete nationally standardized achievement tests in reading and mathematics as well as a nationally standardized test described by its publishers as "a test of the student's cognitive aptitude." Because William White teaches eighth-grade students in his English classes, he is given the task of answering any questions raised by his eighth-graders' parents about the test results.

He is faced with one fairly persistent question from most parents, particularly those parents whose children scored higher on the aptitude test than on the achievement test. For example, Mr. and Mrs. Wilkins (Wanda's parents) put the question like this: "If Wanda scored at the 90th percentile on the aptitude test and only at the 65th percentile on the achievement test, does that mean she's not logging enough study time? Putting it another way," they continued, "should we really believe the aptitude tests results or the achievement test's results? Which is Wanda's 'true' test performance?"

 If you were William, and had to decide how to answer the questions posed by Wanda's parents, what would your answers be?

◼ Group-Focused Test Interpretation

Although the bulk of this chapter will be devoted to a consideration of score-reporting mechanisms used to describe an individual student's performance, you'll sometimes find you need to describe the performance of your students as a group. To do so, you'll typically compute some index of the group of scores' *central tendency,* such as when you determine the group's ***mean*** or ***median*** performance. For example, you might calculate the *mean raw score* or the *median raw score* for your students. A *raw score* is simply the number of items a student answers correctly. The *mean,* as you probably know, is the arithmetic average of a set of scores. For example, the mean of the scores 10, 10, 9, 8, 7, 6, 3, 3, and 2 would be 6.4 (that is, summing the nine scores and then dividing that sum by 9). The *median* is the midpoint of a set of scores. For the nine scores in the previous example, the median would be 7 because this score divides the group into two equal parts. Means and medians are useful ways to describe the point at which the scores in a set of scores are centered.

In addition to describing the central tendency of a set of scores (via the mean and/or median), it is also helpful to describe the *variability* of the scores—that is, how spread out the scores are. One simple measure of the variability of a set of students' scores is the ***range***. The range is calculated by simply subtracting the lowest student's score from the highest student's score. To illustrate, suppose the highest test score by students in your class was a 49 correct out of 50 earned by Hortense (she always tops your tests; it is surprising she missed one). Suppose further that the lowest score of 14 correct was, as usual, earned by Ed. The range of scores would be 35—that is, Hortense's 49 minus Ed's 14.

Because only two scores influence the range, it is less frequently used as an index of test score variability than is the standard deviation. A ***standard deviation*** is a kind of average. More accurately, it's the average difference between the individual scores in a group of scores and the mean of that set of scores. The larger the size of the standard deviation, the more spread out are the scores in the ***distribution***. (That's a posh term to describe a set of scores.) Presented here is the formula for computing a standard deviation for a set of scores:

$$\text{Standard Deviation (S.D.)} = \sqrt{\frac{\Sigma(X - M)^2}{N}}$$

where: $\Sigma(X - M)^2$ = the sum of the squared raw scores *(X)* – the mean *(M)*

N = number of scores in the distribution

Here's a step-by-step description of how you compute a standard deviation using this formula. First, compute the mean of the set of scores. Second, subtract the mean from each score in the distribution. (Roughly half of the resulting values, called *deviation scores,* will have positive values and half will have negative values.) Third, square each of these deviation scores. This will make them all positive. Fourth, add

figure 1 ■ Two Fictitious Sets of Tests Scored with Equal Means but Different Standard Deviations

More Homogeneous Scores:

3, 4, 4, 5, 5, 5, 5, 6, 6, 7

Mean = 5.0

$S.D. = \sqrt{\dfrac{12}{10}} = 1.1$

More Heterogeneous Scores:

0, 1, 2, 4, 5, 5, 6, 8, 9, 10

Mean = 5.0

$S.D. = \sqrt{\dfrac{102}{10}} = 3.2$

the squared deviation scores together. Fifth, divide the resulting sum by the number of scores in the distribution. Sixth, and last, take the square root of the results of the division you did in the fifth step. The square root that you get is the standard deviation. Not too tough, right?

To illustrate the point that larger standard deviations represent more spread in a distribution of scores than smaller standard deviations, take a look at the two fictitious sets of scores on a 10-item short-answer test presented in Figure 1. Both sets of scores have a mean of 5.0. The distribution of scores at the left is much more homogeneous (less spread out) than the distribution of scores at the right. Note the standard deviation for the more homogeneous scores is only 1.1, whereas the standard deviation of the more heterogeneous scores is 3.2. The larger the standard deviation, therefore, the more distant, on average, will be the distribution's scores from the distribution's mean.

You may have occasions to describe the scores of an entire group of the students you teach. Those descriptions might portray your students' performances on standardized tests or on teacher-made tests. If you get at all comfortable with means and standard deviations, those two indices usually provide a better picture of a score distribution than do the median and range. But if you think means and standard deviations are statistical gibberish, then go for the median (midpoints are easy to identify) and range (ranges require only skill in subtraction). With group-based interpretations out of the way, let's turn now to interpreting individual students' scores from the kinds of standardized tests commonly used in education.

Individual Student Test Interpretation

Two overriding frameworks are generally used to interpret students' test scores. Test scores are interpreted in *absolute* or *relative* terms. When we interpret a student's test score *absolutely,* we infer from the score what it is that the student can or cannot do. For example, based on a student's performance on test items dealing with mathematics computation skills, we make an inference about the degree to which the student has mastered such computation skills. The teacher may even boil the interpretation down to a dichotomy—namely, whether the student should be classified as having mastered or not having mastered the skill or knowledge being assessed. A mastery versus nonmastery interpretation represents an *absolute* interpretation of a student's test score. Classroom teachers often use this absolute interpretive approach when creating tests to assess a student's knowledge or skills based on a particular unit of study.

When we interpret a student's test score *relatively*, we infer from the score how the student stacks up against other students who are currently taking the test or have already taken the test. For example, when we say that Johnny's test score is "above average" or "below average," we are making a relative test interpretation because we use the average performance of other students to make sense out of Johnny's test score.

As pointed out earlier, this chapter focuses on how teachers and parents can interpret scores on standardized tests. Because almost all standardized test scores require relative interpretations, the three interpretive schemes to be considered in the chapter are all relative score-interpretation schemes. The vast majority of standardized tests, whether achievement tests or aptitude tests, provide relative interpretations. Accordingly, teachers need to be especially knowledgeable about relative score-interpretation schemes.

Percentiles

The first interpretive scheme we'll consider, and by all odds the most commonly used one, is based on **percentiles** or, as they are sometimes called, *percentile ranks*. Percentiles are used most frequently in describing standardized test scores because percentiles are readily understandable to most people.

A percentile compares a student's score with those of other students in a *norm group*. A student's percentile indicates the percent of students in the norm group that the student outperformed. A percentile of 60, for example, indicates the student performed better than 60 percent of the students in the norm group.

Let's spend a moment describing what a norm group is. As indicated, a percentile compares a student's score with scores earned by those in a norm group. This comparison with the norm group is based on the performances of a group of individuals who have already been administered a particular examination. For instance, before developers of a new standardized test publish their test, they will administer the test to a large number of students who then become the norm group for the test. Typically, different norm groups of students are assembled for all the grade levels for which percentile interpretations are made.

Figure 2 shows a graphic depiction of a set of 3,000 students' scores such as might have been gathered during the norming of a nationally standardized achievement test. Remember, we refer to such students as the norm group. The area under the curved line represents the number of students who earned scores at that point on the baseline. You'll notice, for a typical norm group's performance, most students score in the middle while only a few students earn very high or very low scores.

In fact, *if* the distribution of test scores in the norm group is *perfectly* normal, then, as you see in Figure 3, over two-thirds of the scores (represented by the area under the curved line) will be located relatively close to the center of the distribution—that is, plus or minus one standard deviation (S.D.) from the mean.

Not all norm groups are national norm groups. Sometimes test publishers, at the request of local school officials, develop local norms. These local norms can be either state norms or school-district norms. Comparisons of students on the basis of local norms are sometimes seen as being more meaningful than are comparisons based on national norms.

figure 2 ■ A Typical Norm Group

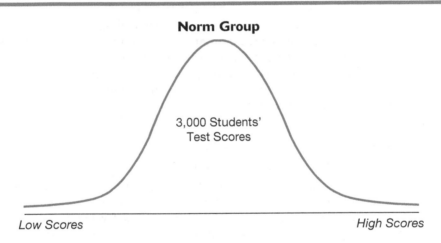

figure 3 ■ A Normally Distributed Set of Norm Group Scores

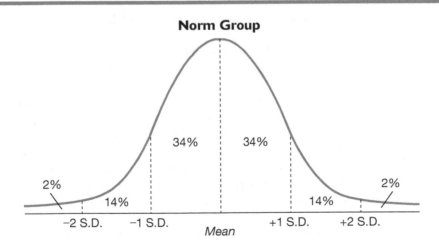

In many instances, local norms are different from national norms because the students in a particular locality are not representative of the nation's children as a whole. If there is a difference between local and national norms, then there will be a difference in a student's percentile scores. A student's raw score—that is, the number of test items answered correctly—might be equal to the 50th percentile based on *national* norms, but be equal to the 75th percentile based on *local* norms. This kind of situation would occur if the students in the local group hadn't performed as well as had students in the nation at large. National and local norms provide decisively different frameworks for interpreting standardized test results. When reporting test scores to parents, make sure you communicate clearly whether a child's percentiles are based on national or local norms.

It's also true that some norm groups have been more carefully constituted than others. For example, certain national norm groups are more representative of the nation's population than are other national norm groups. There are often large differences in the representativeness of norm groups based on such variables as gender, ethnicity, geographic region, and socioeconomic status of the students in the groups. In addition, many standardized tests are renormed only every 5 to 10 years. It is important to make sure the normative information on which percentiles are based is both representative and current.

Grade-Equivalent Scores

Let's turn from percentiles to look at a *grade equivalent* or, as they're often called, **grade-equivalent scores**. Grade-equivalent scores constitute another effort to provide a relative interpretation of standardized test scores. A *grade equivalent* is an indicator of student test performance based on grade level and months of the school year. The purpose of grade equivalents is to transform scores on standardized tests into an index reflecting a student's grade-level progress in school. A grade-equivalent score is a *developmental* score in the sense that it represents a continuous range of grade levels.

Let's look at a grade-equivalent score of 4.5:

A Grade-Equivalent Score:

Grade $\rightarrow 4.5 \leftarrow$ Month of School Year

The score consists of the grade, a decimal, and a number representing months. The number to the left of the decimal point represents the grade level, in this example, the fourth grade. The number to the right of the decimal point represents the month of the school year, in this example, the fifth month of the school year.

Some test publishers, using statistical schemes, convert raw scores on standardized tests to grade-equivalent scores. These grade-equivalent scores often appear on students' score reports. Grade-equivalent scores are most appropriate for basic skills areas such as reading and mathematics where it can be assumed the degree of instructional emphasis given to the subject is fairly uniform from grade to grade.

The appeal of grade-equivalent scores is they appear to be readily interpretable to both teachers and parents. However, many teachers and parents actually have an incorrect understanding of what grade-equivalent scores signify. To see why these scores are misunderstood, it's necessary to understand a bit about where they come from in the first place.

And Now the *Really* "Big" Tests!

Students' performances on classroom assessments are often overshadowed by students' results on the "big" tests—in other words, each state's annual accountability tests. Indeed, for almost two decades U.S. educators have seen headlines plastered atop their local newspapers either damning or praising particular schools and school districts on the basis of students' scores on that year's accountability tests. Even students who sparkled on a teacher's classroom assessments are apt to be regarded negatively if they flop on a statewide accountability test. Clearly, the "big" tests trump teacher-made assessments.

Well, if you think a state's annual accountability tests command public attention, wait until you see what's slated to be available during the 2014–15 school year! During that school year, two multistate consortia are scheduled to make available sets of assessments intended to measure students' mastery of the Common Core State Standards (CCSS) released in mid-2010 by the Council of Chief State School Officers and the National Governors Association. Because these new assessments will be essentially the same across states, no longer can state officials of a low-performing state claim, "The accountability tests of those other (higher-performing) states were tougher than our accountability tests." *The tests will be the same!* No longer can state officials of a low-performing state claim, "The passing standards of those other (higher-performing) states were higher than our state's passing standards." *The passing standards will be the same!* In short, because identical tests and identical passing standards will be used, educators in low-performing states will have few legitimate excuses to dodge the almost certain judgment that their schools were ineffective.

The two assessment consortia, both heavily funded by federal dollars, are committed to providing the nation's educators with "next generation" tests that will give accurate inferences about students' mastery of the skills and knowledge that are the focus of the CCSS. One of these consortia is the Partnership for the Assessment of Readiness for College and Careers (PARCC); the other is the Smarter Balanced Assessment Consortium (SBAC). Each consortium currently has more than two dozen states as members. The PARCC has chosen the Achieve organization to coordinate its efforts; the SBAC has selected the WestEd group to perform the same coordinating function.

(Continued)

When this manuscript was turned into the publisher, both consortia had moved forward with many of their original plans. Some serious changes were seen, however, as the two groups encountered the realities of creating assessments that will not only serve as legitimate evaluation instruments but will also stimulate improved instruction on the part of the states who choose these assessments. To illustrate, the PARCC officials have been committed to the view that their participating states must share a fundamental goal—namely, building a capacity to dramatically increase the rates at which students are successfully prepared for college and the workplace by the time they graduate from high school. The PARCC group intends to rely heavily on computer-administered assessments. Although SBAC has a similar commitment to enhancing students' career and college readiness, the SBAC leaders seem more committed to supplying a balanced set of assessments (for example, tests and tools suitable for both formative and summative functions). The SBAC members will rely heavily on computer-adaptive assessments by which computers can adjust the items students receive after tailoring those items based on students' performances on earlier items.

Given the enormity of the test-building tasks facing the PARCC and the SBAC consortia, it is more than likely we shall see more than a few alterations in their plans. It is clearly foreseeable that what was originally contemplated in the way of the CCSS-based assessments may need refinement as the 2014–15 school year careens toward both consortia. Thus, given the enormous potential significance of these two sets of assessments, any sensible U.S. educator whose state chooses to use one or both of the new tests (a handful of states have chosen not to do so) should most definitely seek information on the final nature of these two assessments. Consulting the SBAC and the PARCC websites to learn about these tests is not merely a good idea—it just might be a career-saving idea.

To determine the grade-equivalent scores that will be hooked up with particular raw scores, test developers typically administer the same test to students in several grade levels, then establish a trend line reflecting the raw score increases at each grade level. Typically, the test developers then *estimate* at other points along this trend line what the grade equivalent for any raw score would be.

Let's illustrate this important point. In Figure 4, you will see the respective performance of students at three grade levels. The same 80-item test has been given to students at all three grade levels: grades 4, 5, and 6. A trend line is then established from the three grades where the test was actually administered. The result of that estimation procedure is seen in Figure 5.

In order for these estimated grade-equivalent scores to be accurate, several assumptions must be made. First, it must be assumed the subject area tested is emphasized equally at each grade level. It must also be assumed students' mastery of the tested content increases at a reasonably constant rate at each grade level over

figure 4 ■ Student Performances at Three Grade Levels

figure 5 ■ A Trend Line Used to Estimate Average Performance of Students at Nontested Grades

an extended period of time. The assumption that the mastery of the test's content increases consistently over time is particularly difficult to support in subject areas other than reading and mathematics. And even in those two bread-and-butter subjects, students' consistent increases in mastery of content are definitely debatable.

The implied precision associated with a grade-equivalent score of 6.2, therefore, is difficult to defend. A 6.2 grade-equivalent score suggests a degree of accuracy that's simply not warranted. An unskilled interpreter of a standardized achievement test results may think a 6.2 grade-equivalent score indicates the student's raw score represents a performance equal to that of a sixth-grade pupil in the second month of the sixth-grade year. Remember, most grade-equivalent scores are created on the basis of estimation, not real test-score data. Because substantial sampling and estimation errors are apt to be present, grade-equivalent scores should always be taken with several grains of salt.

Now that you understand grade-equivalent scores to be, at best, rough estimates, let's return to the potential misinterpretations teachers and parents often make regarding grade-equivalent scores. Let's say a third-grade student makes a grade-equivalent score of 5.5 in reading. What does this grade-equivalent score mean? Here's a wrong answer: "The student can do fifth-grade work." Here's a *really* wrong answer: "The student should be promoted to the fifth grade." The right answer, of course, is that the third-grader understands those reading skills the test covers about as well as an average fifth-grader does at midyear. A grade-equivalent score should be viewed as the point where a student is along a developmental continuum, not as the grade level in which the student should be placed.

If standardized tests are used in your school district, and if those tests yield grade-equivalent scores, it is important to provide parents with an accurate picture of what a grade-equivalent score means. Parents who have not been given an accurate description of such scores frequently think a high grade-equivalent score means their child is capable of doing work at the grade level specified. Some parents even use high grade-equivalent scores as a basis for arguing their child should be advanced to a higher grade. Because many parents have a misconception of what a grade-equivalent score means, some parents may have an inflated estimate of their child's level of achievement. The high frequency of parental (and teacher) misinterpretations is the reason some districts have, as a matter of policy, eliminated grade-equivalent scores when reporting standardized test results.

Remember, if a fourth-grade student gets a grade equivalent of 7.5 in mathematics, it is *not* accurate to say the fourth-grader is doing well in seventh-grade mathematics. It is more appropriate to say a grade-equivalent score of 7.5 is an estimate of how an average seventh-grader might have performed *on the fourth-grader's mathematics test*. Obtaining a 7.5 grade-equivalent score doesn't mean the fourth-grader has any of the mathematics skills taught in the fifth, sixth, or seventh grade because those mathematics skills were probably not even measured on the fourth-grade test.

But what happens when grade-equivalent scores are *below* the actual grade level tested? Let's say a fifth-grader earns a mathematics grade-equivalent score of 2.5. It doesn't make much sense to say the fifth-grader is doing fifth-grade mathematics work as well as a second-grader, because second-graders obviously aren't given fifth-grade mathematics work. About the best you can say is that, in mathematics achievement, the fifth-grader appears to be lagging several years behind grade level.

Given the shortcomings of grade-equivalent scores, most measurement specialists are delighted that the use of these scores is diminishing.

Scale Scores

Let's move, now, to the last of our three score-interpretation schemes: *scale scores*. A scale score constitutes yet another way to give relative meaning to a student's standardized test performances. Scale scores are being employed with increasing frequency these days to report results of national and state-level standardized programs.

Although scale scores are sometimes not used in reporting standardized test results to parents, scale-score reporting systems are often employed in describing group test performances at the state, district, and school levels. Because of the statistical properties of scale scores, they can be used to permit longitudinal tracking of students' progress. Scale scores can also be used to make direct comparisons among classes, schools, or school districts. The statistical advantages of scale scores are considerable. Thus, we see scale-score reporting systems used with more frequency in recent years. As a consequence, you need to become familiar with the main features of scale scores because such scores are likely to be used when you receive reports of your students' performances on standardized tests.

A *scale* used for reporting test scores typically refers to numbers assigned to students on the basis of their test performances. Higher numbers (higher scores) reflect increasing levels of achievement or ability. Thus, such a scale might be composed of a set of raw scores where each additional test item correctly answered yields one more point on the raw-score scale. Raw scores, all by themselves, however, are difficult to interpret. A student's score on a raw-score scale provides no idea of the student's *relative* performance. Therefore, measurement specialists have devised different sorts of scales for test interpretation purposes.

Scale scores are *converted raw scores* that use a new, arbitrarily chosen scale to represent levels of achievement or ability. Shortly, you'll be given some examples to help you understand what is meant by converting scores from one scale to another. In essence, a scale-score system is created by devising a brand-new numerical scale that's often very unlike the original raw-score scale. Students' raw scores are then converted to this brand-new scale so, when score-interpretations are to be made, those interpretations rely on the converted scores based on the new scale. Such converted scores are called *scale scores*.

For example, in Figure 6, you see a range of raw score points from 0 to 40 for a 40-item test. Below the raw-score scale, you see a new, converted scale ranging from 500 to 900. For a number of reasons, to be described shortly, it is sometimes preferable to use a scale-score reporting scheme rather than a raw-score reporting scheme. Thus, a student who achieved a raw score of 30 items correct might be assigned a scale score of 800, as shown in Figure 7.

One of the reasons scale scores have become popular in recent years is the necessity to develop several equidifficult forms of the same test. For example, a

figure 6 ■ A Raw-Score Scale and a Converted-Score Scale

Raw-Score Scale	0	10	20	30	40
Converted-Score Scale	500	600	700	800	900

figure 7 ■ An Illustration of a Raw-Score Conversion to a Scale Score

Raw-Score Scale	0	10	20	30 ✕	40
Converted-Score Scale	500	600	700	800 ✕	900

basic skills test must sometimes be passed before high school diplomas are awarded to students. Those students who initially fail the test are, typically, given other opportunities to pass it. The different forms of the test used for such retake purposes should, for the sake of fairness, represent assessment challenges for students that are equivalent to those represented by the initial form of the test. However, because it is next to impossible to create test forms that are absolutely identical, scale scores can be used to help solve the problem. Scores on two test forms of differing difficulty levels can be statistically adjusted so, when placed on a converted score scale, the new scale scores represent students' performances as if the two test forms had been completely equidifficult.

Most of the more popular types of scale-score systems are based on what statisticians refer to as *item response theory*, or IRT. These types of scale-score reporting systems are distinctively different from raw-score reporting systems because IRT scale-score schemes take into consideration the difficulty and other technical properties of every single item on the test. Thus, some test publishers have produced IRT-based scale scores for their tests ranging from 0 to 1,000 across an entire K–12 grade range. For each grade level, there is a different average scale score. For example, the average scale score for third-graders might be 585 and the average scale score for the tenth-graders might be 714.

These IRT-based scale scores can, when constructed with care, yield useful interpretations if one can reference them back to some notion of relative performance such as percentiles. If average scale scores are provided at different grade levels, this also can aid in the interpretation of scale scores. Without such interpretation crutches regarding a scale score's *relative* meaning, however, scale scores cannot be meaningfully interpreted by either educators or parents.

Item response theory scales are often employed by psychometricians in an effort to devise a *vertical scale* that will allow students' test performances to be tracked across a number of grade levels. Clearly, especially in an accountability context where educators are often eager to show students' growth from year to year, such vertical scales have a special appeal. But they also have a serious drawback. In order for a vertical scale to do its job across many grade levels, it is necessary for the test items being used to correlate well with a single trait—for instance, a unitary trait such as "students' mathematical comprehension." It is this global unitary trait that permits a vertical scale to do its job properly. However, because the test's items must be linked to the unitary trait on which the vertical scale is based, those items are unable to yield meaningful diagnostic information to teachers about students' differing mathematics skills and knowledge. Legitimate diagnosticity must be jettisoned when a test's developers are preoccupied with making all their items hook into the unitary trait chosen for their vertical scale. It is impossible, for example, for a test to contain a cluster of items distinctively focused on a student's geometric skills or algebra insights if all the test's items are first required to link up with the unitary mathematical trait being assessed.

So, if officials in your school or district are considering adoption of a standardized test whose chief virtue is that it supplies a meaningful vertical scale for cross-grade comparisons of students' scores, even if the test is accompanied by marketing assertions about the test's diagnostic dividends, don't be fooled. The cost of a vertical scale is the sort of diagnostic evidence that teachers need for sensible instructional decision-making.

Errors are often made in interpreting scale scores because teachers assume all scale scores are somehow similar. For example, when initially administered over 80 years ago, the mean scale score on the verbal section of the Scholastic Assessment Test was 500. This does not signify the mean score on that test today is 500 or that other tests using scale scores will always have mean scores of 500. Scale-score systems can be constructed so the mean score is 50, 75, 600, 700, 1,000, or any number the scale's constructor has in mind.

One kind of scale score you may encounter when you work with your students' scores on standardized tests is the **normal curve equivalent**. A normal curve equivalent, usually referred to as an NCE, represents an attempt to use a student's raw score to arrive at a percentile for a raw score as if the distribution of scores on the test had been a perfectly symmetrical, bell-shaped normal curve. So, one of your students might get an NCE score indicating the student was performing at or near the top of a norm group's performance. Sometimes, unfortunately, neither the norm group's performance nor that of subsequent test takers is distributed in a normal fashion, so the meaningfulness of the student's NCE evaporates. Normal curve equivalents were originally created in an attempt to amalgamate students' performances from *different* standardized tests, perhaps none of which yielded normal distributions. As might be suspected, NCEs failed to solve this problem satisfactorily.

A final kind of scale score you should know about is called a **stanine**. Stanines are somewhat like normal curve equivalents in the sense that they assume a normal distribution for a set of scores. And this assumption, as you just read, runs counter to reality. But, as you'll soon see, a stanine score is a more gross score, so it can more easily tolerate a score distribution's departure from a normal shape.

A stanine scale divides a score distribution into nine segments that, although equal along the baseline of a set of scores (actually one-half standard deviation in distance), contain differing proportions of the distribution's scores. As you can see in Figure 8, the fifth stanine is at the center of a score distribution and contains about 20 percent of the scores. A ninth stanine score, however, contains only about 4 percent of the scores.

One advantage of stanines is they are *approximate* scale scores, and their very inexact nature conveys more clearly to everyone that educational measurement is not a superprecise assessment enterprise. As with most hierarchical classification systems, of course, a student may be *almost* at the next higher (or lower) stanine, yet may miss out by only a point or two. Such is the imprecision of measurement, even if you're using a deliberately approximation-engendering scoring system.

figure 8 ■ Stanine Units Represented in Approximate Percentages of the Normal Curve

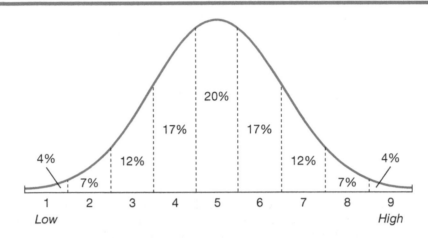

Contrasting Common Interpretive Options

We've now considered several types of score-interpretation schemes, the most frequently used of these being percentiles, grade-equivalent scores, and scale scores. (Stanines and NCEs tend to be used less frequently.) It's time to review and summarize what's really important about the three most popular ways of making sense out of standardized test scores.

We first considered percentiles. A *percentile* indicates a student's standing in relationship to that of a norm group. If a student's test score is equal to the 25th percentile, the student's performance exceeds the performances of 25 percent of the individuals in the norm group. One advantage of percentiles is they're easy to interpret. And, for the most part, people's interpretations of percentiles are accurate. A disadvantage of percentiles is the defensibility of the interpretation is totally dependent on the nature of the normative data on which the percentiles are based. Unrepresentative or out-of-date norm data yield inaccurate percentile interpretations. As pointed out earlier, because percentile interpretations are so widely used, it's imperative for teachers to be knowledgeable about such interpretations.

Percentiles

Advantage: readily interpretable

Disadvantage: dependent on quality of norm group

Next, we considered grade-equivalent scores. A *grade equivalent* indicates the nature of a student's test performance in terms of grade levels and months. Thus, a grade equivalent of 3.7 would indicate the student's test score was estimated to be the same as the average performance of a third-grader during the seventh month of the school year. One advantage of grade-equivalent scores is, because they are based on grade levels and months of the school year, they can be readily communicated to parents. A significant disadvantage associated with grade-equivalent scores, however, is they're frequently misinterpreted.

Grade Equivalents

Advantage: readily communicable

Disadvantage: often misinterpreted

Finally, scale scores were described. *Scale scores* are interpreted according to a converted numerical scale that allows us to transform raw scores into more statistically useful scale-score units. A student who gets a raw score of 35 correct out of 50 items, for example, might end up with a converted scale score of 620. An advantage of scale scores is they can be used to create statistically adjusted equidifficult test forms. Scale-score schemes based on *item response theory (IRT)* do this by weighting individual test items differently based on an item's difficulty and other technical properties in relation to those same properties for all of a test's items. A disadvantage of scale-score reporting schemes is, with the possible exception of stanines, they're almost impossible to interpret all by themselves. Unless we mentally reference scale scores back to percentiles or average grade-level scale scores, such scores are essentially uninterpretable.

Scale Scores

Advantage: useful in equalizing difficulties of different test forms

Disadvantage: not easily interpretable

It should be clear to you that each of these three score-interpretation schemes has some potential virtues as well as some potential vices. You probably realize, even if you understand the general nature of each of these three interpretation schemes, it may be necessary to secure additional technical information to interpret each reporting scheme with confidence. Such information is usually found in the technical manuals that accompany standardized tests. For example, what was the nature of the norm group on which a test's percentiles were based? What sort of mathematical operations were used in generating a scale-score reporting scheme? Is a score distribution sufficiently normal to warrant the use of NCEs? To interpret a particular standardized test's results sensibly, teachers sometimes need to do a bit of homework themselves regarding the innards of the reporting scheme being used.

The Instructional Yield from Standardized Achievement Tests

Nationally standardized achievement tests, as noted previously, are developed and sold by commercial testing companies. The more tests those companies sell, the more money those companies make. Accordingly, the representatives of commercial testing companies usually suggest that their standardized achievement tests will not

but what does this have to do with Teaching?

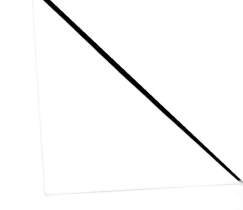

Depending on the grade levels at which elementary teachers teach, or the subjects secondary teachers teach, many teachers these days find their attention focused on their students' scores on standardized achievement tests. That's because students' scores on such tests are increasingly used as an indicator of educators' instructional success. So, if you're a teacher whose state (or school district) requires that standardized achievement tests be administered at the end of school for a grade level you teach, you can be assured there will be plenty of attention given to your students' standardized test performances. You'll learn why this practice is inappropriate when certain types of standardized tests are employed.

But even if you're a teacher whose students are at grade levels or in classes where standardized tests don't play a major role, you need to become familiar with the way teachers and parents should interpret such test performances. And that's because, as a professional, a teacher is supposed to know such things. Parents will sometimes ask you what is meant by a percentile or an NCE. You don't want to blubber forth, "Beats me!"

And, of course, if your students *are* assessed with a standardized achievement test, such as statewide accountability exams, you'll want to be able to interpret what students' scores signify, because this information will help you instructionally. Suppose, for example, it is the first week of school and you're reviewing your new fifth-grade students' end-of-year *fourth*-grade test performances. You discover that Martha Childs earned a 94th percentile in mathematics, but only a 43rd percentile in reading. This information should give you some insights about how you'll approach Martha instructionally.

And if Billy Jenkins's fourth-grade test scores gave him a seventh stanine in language arts, but a first stanine in math, I suggest you don't ask Billy to keep track of your students' lunch money.

The better fix you get on your students' relative achievement levels, the more appropriately you can teach them. Proper interpretations of standardized test scores will often help you do so.

only yield valid norm-referenced interpretations about the students who take the tests but will also provide classroom teachers with a galaxy of useful information for instructional decision-making. In my experiences, the *instructional* payoffs of standardized achievement tests are more illusory than real. More often than not, claims for the instructional dividends of such achievement tests reflect the zeal of a testing firm's sales force, not the reality of how teachers can actually use the results of standardized tests for instructional purposes.

Are standardized achievement tests better than no tests at all? Of course they are. But will standardized tests provide the instructionally sensible, fine-grained diagnostic data teachers need for accurate decisions? My answer, based on many years of using these tests, is decisively negative.

■ The SAT and the ACT: Three-Letter, High-Import Exams

Each year, millions of students put their futures on the line when they sit down to take the SAT and ACT exams, the nation's college entrance tests. Because not only students, but also students' parents, are understandably apprehensive about one or both of these college admission tests, teachers at all grade levels are apt to be questioned about the SAT or the ACT. Therefore, in the next few paragraphs I'll be describing the general nature of both exams, how they came into existence, and what their scale scores look like. I'll close out this treatment of the two tests with a candid look at the accuracy with which those tests predict a high school student's academic success in college.

The SAT

First administered in 1926, the SAT was initially called the *Scholastic Aptitude Test,* and its function was to assist admissions officials in a group of elite Northeastern universities to determine which applicants should be admitted. The original name of the test really reveals what the test's developers were up to—namely, they wanted their tests to measure the largely inborn academic *aptitudes* of high school students. Because, much later, the idea of a test's measuring innate, genetically determined aptitudes became unappetizing to many educators, the Scholastic Aptitude Test became known only as the SAT. (One wonders if the developers of the SAT took their cues from the purveyors of Kentucky Fried Chicken who, recognizing the public's concern about the health risks of fried foods, morphed their famous label into KFC. It is, of course, difficult to become genuinely negative toward any three-letter label—with the possible exception of the IRS.)

The SAT was originally conceived of as a group-administrable intelligence test designed to compare test-takers according to their inherited verbal, quantitative,

Parent Talk

Suppose that one of your students' parents, Mr. Lopez, visits your classroom during a back-to-school evening and raises a series of questions about his daughter, Concepción. Most prominently, Mr. Lopez is concerned with Concepción's scores on the nationally standardized achievement tests administered each spring in your district. Mr. Lopez is troubled by spring-to-spring changes in Concepción's percentiles. As he says, "For the last three springs, her percentile scores in language arts have been the 74th, the 83rd, and the 71st. What's going on here? Is she learning, then unlearning? What accounts for the differences?"

 If I were you, here's how I'd respond to Mr. Lopez:

"You are certainly wise to look into what appears to be inconsistent measurement on Concepción's standardized achievement tests. But what you need to understand, Mr. Lopez, is that these sorts of tests, even though they are nationally standardized, developed by reputable testing firms, and widely used, are not all that precise in how they measure students. Many parents, of course, recognize that their children's test scores are often reported numerically in the form of national percentiles. But this does *not* signify a given child's national percentile is unerringly accurate.

"The kinds of year-to-year shifting you've seen in Concepción's language arts percentiles is quite normal because a given year's test result is not unerringly accurate. Assessment specialists even admit the *anticipated* amount of flip-flop in students' scores when they talk about each test's 'standard error of measurement.' It's something like the sampling errors we hear about for national surveys—you know, 'plus or minus so many percentage points.' Well, measurement error is similar to sampling error. And let me assure you that Concepción's scores will, quite predictably, vary from spring to spring.

"What we do see in her language arts performances over the last three years is a consistently high, well above average achievement level. When her performance is compared to that of a representative, nationally normed sample, Concepción is doing very well, indeed."

 Now, how would you respond to Mr. Lopez?

and spatial aptitudes. For many years, the SAT functioned in precisely that way, although during the last few decades we have seen less attention given to the *inherited* nature of what's being assessed.

Currently, the SAT is divided into 10 separately timed sections. Three sections test critical reading (70 minutes total); three sections test mathematics (70 minutes total); three sections test writing (60 minutes total); and one unscored section tests critical reading, mathematics, or writing (25 minutes total). Over the years, the specific makeup of the SAT has been periodically altered, so if teachers and students wish to remain abreast of the latest configurations of this exam, it would be wise to consult the SAT website cited at the chapter's conclusion.

Three kinds of items are included in the SAT: multiple-choice questions, student-produced responses (in mathematics only), and an essay question. Designers of the SAT believe that it assesses students' knowledge of subject matter learned in high school as well as problem-solving skills in the three measured areas—namely, critical reading, mathematics, and writing. SAT scores are reported on a scale from 200 to 800, with additional subscores reported for the essay and the multiple-choice writing items. Because the mean score on both the critical reading and the mathematics sections is roughly 500, it is possible to obtain a quick impression of the extent to which a given student's score is at, above, or below the average score of other test-takers.

Although the 2005 addition of an essay-writing task to the SAT attracted substantial media attention, students' essay scores do not contribute heavily to their overall SAT scores—or even to their scores on the Writing section.

The test is still owned by the College Board, the group that originally created the test, but since 1947 the SAT has been developed and administered for the College Board by the Educational Testing Service (ETS). Both organizations are not-for-profit entities. A less demanding version of the test, referred to most often as the PSAT, is administered once each year in October—typically to high school students in their sophomore or junior years. Recently, the College Board introduced *Readi Step,* a standardized test for middle-school students. This two-hour test, consisting exclusively of multiple-choice items, assesses students' achievement in reading, writing, and mathematics during fall and spring testing windows. The SAT itself is administered throughout the nation on several preannounced occasions during the year.

The ACT

Although both the SAT and the ACT are typically characterized as *aptitude* exams because they are employed in an effort to predict a high-schooler's subsequent academic performance in college, the ACT's lineage makes it a decisively different kind of "aptitude" test than the SAT. Following World War II, and the subsequent enactment of the G.I. Bill of Rights (a federal law providing college tuition for returning military personnel), many more American men and women wanted to secure a college education. There was, therefore, a substantially increased need for college entrance exams.

At the University of Iowa, a gifted professor named E. F. Lindquist believed the SAT, given its ancestry as an aptitude test designed for students attending elite colleges, was not a suitable exam for many of these post-WWII college applicants. Thus, in 1959 Lindquist and his colleagues established the American College

Testing Program as a not-for-profit testing company which, in 1996, changed its official name to ACT.

From the very outset, the ACT was intended to be an unabashed *achievement* test. Architects of the ACT certainly wanted their new test to be predictive of a high school student's academic success in college, but they conceived of their new test chiefly as a measure of a student's "educational development."

The ACT is made up of separate tests in essentially the same four content areas it initially assessed: English, mathematics, reading, and science. An optional writing test is now available in which the student has 30 minutes to write an essay supporting one of two positions presented in a writing "prompt," or a task. As is true with the SAT, the ACT takes about four hours to complete.

Developers of the ACT routinely solicit content suggestions, in each of the content areas tested, from large samples of secondary teachers and curriculum coordinators as well as from college professors in the four core subject areas. Secondary-school educators are asked to identify the skills and content that students in their school or district have an option to learn by the end of their junior year in high school. College professors are asked what skills or knowledge acquired at the secondary-school level are essential for students to be academically successful during their first year of college. Based on a combination of what's taught in secondary schools and what's considered requisite for first-year success in college, items are then developed for the ACT.

Every ACT item is multiple-choice in nature, and a student gets one point for every correct answer with no subtraction of points (or partial points) for a wrong answer—as is the case in the SAT. Number-correct scores are then converted to a new 1–36 point scale for each of the separate tests from which an overall (composite) score is derived that represents the *average* of the four separate-tests' 1–36 points (unlike the SAT, where scores from its three sections are added together). The optional writing test, equivalent to the SAT's essay test, is scored on the basis of a 2–12-point scale using the judgments of two scorers who can each award 1–6 points to a student's essay. Additional information about many aspects of the SAT can be secured from the ETS website listed at the close of this chapter.

As with the SAT, there are variations of the ACT available to be used with younger students. EXPLORE is aimed at eighth- and ninth-grade students, and PLAN is available for tenth-graders. More information about these three tests is available on the ACT website listed at the chapter's conclusion.

Predictive Accuracy—And Its Implications

Because of the important decisions linked to secondary students' scores on the SAT and the ACT, test-preparations options abound for each test. These test-prep possibilities range from low-cost printed and online Internet materials all the way up to very pricy in-person preparation classes and tutorials. Although there are exceptions, the more money that's spent on a preparation activity for either of these two tests, the more effective such preparation is apt to be. This is a troubling reality, of course, because children from more affluent families have greater access to the most costly preparation options, hence tend to score better than do their less affluent classmates who can't afford high-cost preparation alternatives.

But, as important as it is, let's put test-prep bias aside for a moment. There is one, overridingly important realization all teachers must arrive at regarding the predictive accuracy of the SAT and the ACT. Here it is, all gussied up in italics:

> *Only about 25% of academic success in college is associated with a high school student's performance on the SAT or ACT.*

To calculate how well a high school student's scores on a college entrance test accurately predict his or her academic success in college, a correlation is computed between high school students' scores on the SAT (or the ACT) and their subsequent college grades—for instance, their first-year college grade-point averages. With few exceptions, the resulting correlation coefficients turn out to be approximately .50. A predictive coefficient of .50 is statistically significant, hence certainly reflects a *bona fide* relationship between students' scores on college entrance tests and their subsequent college grades.

However, to determine the practical meaningfulness of that relationship, what we must do is *square* the .50 coefficient so it becomes .25 (.50 × .50 = .25). This tells us that 25 percent of students' college grades can be linked to their performances on college admission tests. In other words, fully 75 percent of a student's college grades are due to factors *other* than students' scores on the SAT or the ACT. Such factors would include a student's motivation, study habits, and other variables over which a student has substantial control.

Now, if you are not a numerical ninny, you'll realize a student's college grades are three times more dependent on nontest factors than they are on test factors—that is, 75 percent (test-unrelated) versus 25 percent (test-related). And yet we find hoards of students who earn only "so-so scores" on the SAT or the ACT simply writing themselves off as "not smart enough" to succeed in college. College success, and success in life, is unarguably dependent on much more than a test score. Unfortunately, because the nation's educators are often unfamiliar with the predictive *imprecision* of college entrance tests, they don't do enough to dissuade students from prematurely foreclosing their college aspirations.

Over the years, a student's SAT or ACT scores have become, to many educators, and to students themselves, an unalterable definition of one's ability. That's simply not true. And teachers need not only to know it, but to make sure their students (and students' parents) know it too.

The SAT and the ACT help college officials distinguish among applicants in the common fixed-quota setting where there are more applicants for admission to a college than there are openings to that college. But the *general* predictive power of the SAT and the ACT doesn't transform those exams into definitively accurate assessment tools for *any particular* student. Teachers at all levels need to help students recognize what the SAT and the ACT exams can do—and what they can't.

What Do Classroom Teachers Really Need to Know about Interpreting Standardized Test Scores?

Because results of standardized tests are almost certain to come into your professional life, at least in some manner, you need to have an intuitive understanding of how to interpret those results. The most common ways of describing a set of scores is to provide an index of the score distribution's central tendency (usually the mean or median) and an index of the score distribution's variability (usually the standard deviation or the range). There will probably be instances in which you either must describe the performances of your students or understand descriptions of the performances of other groups of students (such as all students in your school or your district).

To make accurate interpretations of standardized test scores for your own students, and to help parents understand how to make sense of their child's standardized test scores, you need to comprehend the basic meaning of percentiles, grade-equivalent scores, and scale scores. You also ought to understand the major advantage and disadvantage of each of those three score-interpretation schemes. You'll then be in a position to help parents make sense out of their children's performances on standardized tests.

Two of the more influential tests many students will ever take are the SAT and the ACT, the most widely used college entrance tests. Classroom teachers need to know that, because of their differing lineages, the SAT and the ACT represent somewhat overlapping but fundamentally different assessment strategies. Whereas the SAT's focus is more heavily on assessing students' academic aptitudes, the ACT's focus is on measuring the kinds of skills and knowledge that, having been previously learned, are necessary in college. Although both tests are predictive of a student's college grades, only about 25 percent of students' college grades are associated with students' SAT or ACT scores.

Chapter Summary

Standardized tests were defined as assessment instruments administered, scored, and interpreted in a standard, predetermined manner. Standardized tests are used to assess students' achievement and aptitude. Tests of student achievement are developed by large testing companies as well as by state departments of education (usually to satisfy a legislatively imposed educational accountability requirement). Although most standardized tests feature the use of selected-response items, many developers of such tests attempt to incorporate modest numbers of constructed-response items in their assessment devices.

For describing a distribution of test scores, two indices of central tendency—the mean and the median—were described as well as two indices of variability—the range and the standard deviation.

Several ways of interpreting results of standardized tests were discussed: percentiles, grade-equivalent scores, scale scores, stanines, and normal curve equivalents (NCEs). The nature of each of these interpretation procedures, as well as the strengths and weaknesses of the three most popular interpretation procedures, were described.

The SAT and the ACT are, by far, America's most widely used college entrance tests. Because of its history, the SAT (originally known as the Scholastic Aptitude Test) aims to assess students' academic aptitudes—for example, a student's innate verbal, quantitative, and spatial aptitudes. The ACT attempts to function as an achievement test that, albeit predictive of students' college success, measures high school students' mastery of the skills and knowledge needed in college. Although predictive criterion-related validity coefficients of approximately .50 indicate students' SAT and ACT scores are certainly correlated with students' college grades, fully 75 percent of a student's academic success in college is linked to factors *other* than scores on either of these two tests.

 Self-Check

It's time for a good, old-fashioned true-false test to sharpen your conversance with all these exotic notions about score-interpretations. Give the following true-or-false statements your best shot:

(T or F) 1. Most standardized aptitude tests have been developed by state departments of education to implement legislatively enacted accountability laws.

(T or F) 2. One of the shortcomings of the range as an index of variability is that it is derived from only two raw scores.

(T or F) 3. If a distribution of test scores were particularly heterogeneous, it would have a larger standard deviation than if it were particularly homogeneous.

(T or F) 4. The ACT is, at bottom, an aptitude test, whereas the SAT is fundamentally an achievement test.

(T or F) 5. Locally devised norms based on the performance of local students are almost always lower than nationally devised norms based on the performance of students nationally.

(T or F)   6. Percentiles are the most commonly used way of describing students' performances on standardized tests.

(T or F)   7. Whereas percentiles represent a *relative* scheme for interpreting standardized test results, grade-equivalent scores represent an *absolute* scheme for interpreting standardized test results.

(T or F)   8. Fifty percent of a college student's grades can be linked back to that student's score (in high school) on the SAT or the ACT.

(T or F)   9. For grade-equivalent scores to function properly, it is assumed the subject area tested is emphasized about equally at each grade level tested.

(T or F)   10. A grade-equivalent score of 6.2 for a fifth-grader indicates the fifth-grader is performing six months and two weeks ahead of expectations.

(T or F)   11. Scale scores, although increasingly used to describe results of standardized tests, are difficult to interpret all by themselves.

(T or F)   12. Scale-score interpretations of standardized aptitude tests are almost always based on a mean score of 500.

(T or F)   13. One advantage of the scale scores derived from item response theory is their use permits the presentation of equidifficult challenges to students when different test forms are used.

(T or F)   14. Although grade-equivalent scores are readily communicable, they are often misinterpreted.

(T or F)   15. Empirical research shows test-preparation activities associated with getting students ready for the SAT and the ACT are essentially ineffective.

Pondertime

1. If you had to use only *one* of the three individual student interpretation schemes treated in the chapter (percentiles, grade-equivalent scores, and scale scores), which one would it be? Why did you make that choice?

2. It is sometimes argued that testing companies and state departments of education adopt scale-score reporting methods simply to make it more difficult for everyday citizens to understand how well students perform. (It's easier for citizens to make sense out of "65 percent correct" than "an IRT scale score of 420.") Do you think there's any truth in this criticism?

3. There are meaningful geographic differences in the use of the SAT and the ACT as college admissions tests. Why do you suppose this is?

4. If you were trying to explain to a group of parents how to make sense out of percentiles, grade equivalents, and scale scores, how would you go about it so that the parents would really grasp the rudiments of these three score-interpretation procedures?

5. Twenty years ago, it was much less difficult to get district educational officials to require their students to participate in the renorming of standardized tests than it is today. What factors account for that difference? What effect might this situation have on a recently renormed standardized test?

Self-Check Key

1. F	4. F	7. F	10. F	13. T
2. T	5. F	8. F	11. T	14. T
3. T	6. T	9. T	12. F	15. F

You'll note that there are seven true statements and eight false statements.

Notice the 15 items you just completed deal largely with knowledge. Yet, I'll wager the readers who performed well on this little excursion into knowledge assessment also have a pretty fair general understanding of the content addressed in the chapter. That's the reason many teachers, over the years, have been willing to use selected-response sorts of tests as stand-ins for higher-level constructed-response assessments. I'm not recommending such a practice, because I really believe loftier assessment targets spur loftier instructional approaches. I simply wanted you to see why large numbers of teachers may be inclined to reject many of the "new-fangled" assessment approaches currently being touted. Such teachers tend to believe traditional ("old-fangled"?) selected-response tests allow them to get a sufficiently accurate fix on their students' abilities.

■ Additional Stuff

Miller, M. D., and Linn, R. (2013). *Measurement and assessment in teaching* (11th ed.). Columbus, OH: Pearson.

Nitko, A. J., and Brookhart, S. M. (2011). *Educational assessment of students* (6th ed.). Boston: Pearson.

Phelps, R. P. (Ed.). (2005). *Defending standardized testing*. Mahwah, NJ: Lawrence Erlbaum.

Tankersley, K. (2007). *Tests that teach: Using standardized tests to improve instruction*. Alexandria, VA: Association for Supervision and Curriculum Development.

Waugh, C. K., and Gronlund, N. (2013). *Assessment of student achievement* (10th ed.). Columbus, OH: Pearson.

■ Cyber Stuff

- *ACT*, an independent, not-for-profit organization provides more than 100 assessment, research, information, and program management services in the arenas of education and workforce development. Founded in 1959 as the American College Testing Program, the organization changed its name to ACT in 1996. The ACT is, along with the SAT, one of the most widely used college admissions exams in the United States. As with the ETS website and its suggestions regarding appropriate preparation for its SAT, this website provides ideas about how prospective examinees can ready themselves for the ACT. **www.act.org**

- *CTB-McGraw-Hill* is one of the nation's leading publishers of standardized achievement tests, and has been so for over 85 years. This website contains a complete description of the company's tests and services. In addition, visitors to the site will find a first-rate assessment glossary, guidelines for effective assessment, products related to the company's approach to formative assessment, and a variety of other assessment-related resources. **www.ctb.com**

- *Educational Records Bureau (ERB)* is a membership organization composed of about 2,000 independent and public schools and districts in the United States and in more than 50 other countries. The ERB publishes achievement (grades 1–12) and aptitude tests (grades 3–12) chiefly for independent schools. Its tests attempt to differentiate among the most able test takers. This website, divided between the interests of teachers/administrators and parents/students, describes ERB products and services. **www.erbtest.org**

- *The Educational Testing Service (ETS)* is the world's largest private educational organization. Its website contains a wide range of content related to assessment. Many visitors to the ETS site will be interested in its description of the College Board SAT program because of the SAT's widespread use as a college admission examination. The ETS website contains a substantial amount of information dealing with how one can prepare for the SAT. Site visitors will find it interesting to see how a major publisher of educational aptitude tests deals with the issue of test preparation for its own examinations. **www.ets.org**

- *Pearson Assessment* is a major provider of educational, clinical, and psychological assessments. As one of the organizations supplying America's nationally standardized educational achievement tests, and as the leading provider of customized accountability assessments to states and districts, a reader's time spent on this website can be particularly informative. A website visitor can soon grasp the full range of Pearson's remarkable array of assessment-related initiatives. One of those initiatives is to make this organization a leader in the promotion of assessment literacy among all educators, not only users of Pearson products. **www.pearsonassessments.com**

- *Riverside Publishing* is, along with CTB-McGraw-Hill and Pearson Assessment, the remaining member of the "big three" publishers of U.S. standardized achievement tests. On this website there are the customary listings of the company's tests and other products under 15 separate assessment categories. A history of the company is provided that traces its origins to the creation of the Stanford-Binet Intelligence Scale during World War I. **www.riversidepublishing.com/**

■ Extended Applications

I t is a truism that the more a person uses something, the more familiar with this something the person becomes. This self-evident notion surely applies to the assessment-related knowledge, skills, and concepts you have been reading about in the foregoing pages. Thus, to provide readers of *Classroom Assessment* with additional opportunities to apply the content contained in this text, this final section contains a variety of exercises intended to give readers an opportunity to use what they've been reading about.

In a sense, of course, the Self-Check exercises found at the close of this chapter provided an opportunity for readers to apply a chapter's content. Nonetheless, the more times you use a concept, skill, or a body of knowledge, the more likely it is that you will master this content so you can employ it in varied situations.

For each of the text, you will find an extended-application exercise calling for you to do some thinking about that chapter's content as it applies to a real-world situation. Each exercise is preceded by a brief introduction setting forth the reason that the upcoming extended-application exercise has been selected.

Because many of these exercises call on you to generate an original response rather than select a response from a set of options, it is difficult to supply an "answer key" for readers' unpredictable responses. So, what you'll find following all the exercises is One Possible Response—an indication of how I would have personally responded to the exercise if I had been asked to do so. Please don't regard my response as the only way to respond to an exercise. After all, by definition, this is only "one possible" response. Instead, please think of my response as a fairly flimsy form of feedback. You can certainly disagree with me, even emphatically, yet still profit from doing the exercise.

Remember, what is being provided in this section. The exercises deliberately intended to extend how you apply the content treated in *Classroom Assessment*. I hope you find these exercises useful in enhancing your understanding of what teachers need to know about classroom assessment.

Teachers' Lounge Q&A

Introduction

Classroom Assessment's in this chapter covers a hefty chunk of content ranging from the computation of a standard deviation all the way to arriving at accurate score interpretations from standardized achievement tests—including the SAT and ACT. Teachers really need to know most of the stuff in this chapter because they'll often find it relates to a decision they'll need to make about a particular student or about an entire class.

So, to cover the full range of the chapter's content, this Extended Applications exercise assumes that you not only know what's in the chapter, but that you're willing to answer colleagues' questions about the topics covered in that chapter. If you can come up with accurate answers to the questions posed in this exercise.

 Exercise Directions: Please imagine you are a teacher, relaxing in your school's teachers' lounge, and the word has gotten around that you know something about standardized tests and the scores they yield. Presented here are 10 questions, each of which was raised by a different teacher. For the sake of realism, let's assume that the questions were asked over a period of several weeks, not one after another. Simply indicate how you would answer each of the questions. Your responses can, if you wish, attempt to clarify the concepts involved.

1. *Question:* "Why is it that percentiles are such a popular way to report students' scores on standardized tests?"

Your answer: _____

_____

_____

One Possible Response: "Percentiles, in contrast to all other ways of reporting students' test performances, are the most intuitively understandable to just about everyone. Despite several important shortcomings—especially when used for statistical analyses—percentiles just make sense to most people."

2. *Question:* "I'm trying to get my students to *uniformly* do really well on my exams. Should I be hoping their scores will yield a smaller or a larger standard deviation?"

Your answer: _____

_____

_____

One Possible Response: "Because you are attempting to get all your students to earn high scores on your tests, you'll be hoping your students' distributions of test scores would be quite compact, and thus reflect smaller rather than larger standard deviations. Smaller standard deviations represent sets of test scores that are homogeneous. You are striving for homogeneously *high* student performances as reflected by high mean scores and small standard deviations."

3. *Question:* "Our district stopped using grade-equivalent scores last year. Why do you suppose that happened?"

Your answer: _____

_____

_____

One Possible Response: "The problem with grade equivalents is they seem so easy to understand, but they're almost always misinterpreted. Because, in most instances, grade-equivalent scores are derived from estimates, there's substantial imprecision associated with these scores. The most egregious kind of misinterpretation of grade-equivalent scores arises when parents think their children should be placed in whatever grade level is represented by a grade-equivalent score."

4. *Question:* "I've heard that the SAT is more of an aptitude test, whereas the ACT is more of an achievement test. Several of my students' parents have asked whether, as a practical matter, this difference is important. Is it?"

Your answer: _____

_____

_____

➤ One Possible Response: "One place where this difference in the orientation of these two college entrance exams can have an impact is in the way students prepare for the tests. Because the ACT is focused on reasonably well-defined subject areas, students' test-preparation efforts can concentrate on becoming knowledgeable in those subjects. Because the SAT is based more on students' generalized verbal and quantitative aptitudes, SAT preparation programs are often discernibly different from ACT preparation programs."

5. *Question:* "All the reports we seem to receive these days about our students' performances are in the form of scale scores. Why have scale scores become so darn fashionable?"

Your answer: _____

_____

_____

➤ One Possible Response: "The reason scale scores are used so often these days is that such scores can be statistically treated in ways not possible with percentiles or even raw scores. Unfortunately, scale scores are not intuitively interpretable, so it is helpful if students' score reports can include some interpretation-aid approximations to help those who receive students' test-score reports. For instance, if there's a scale-scores-to-percentiles conversion chart, even if it is only based on approximations, this can be a big help."

6. *Question:* "Is it possible to adjust different forms of a test so students have an equally difficult challenge—irrespective of which test form they receive?"

Your answer: _____

_____

_____

➤ One Possible Response: "Yes, that's one of the big payoffs of using scale scores to report students' test performances. By relying on item-response theory (IRT) techniques, students' scale scores can be statistically massaged so students do, indeed, get an equidifficult challenge even from forms that—in raw-score terms—differ dramatically in their difficulty."

7. *Question:* "Is it true that about 67 percent of students' test scores will always fall within a test-score range of plus *and* minus one standard deviation distance from the mean?"

Your answer: _____

_____

_____

One Possible Response: "This is true *only* if a set of test scores is distributed in an approximately normal shape. If a distribution of test scores departs in any meaningful way from a normal, bell-shaped form, then there's no certainty that about two-thirds of the scores will fall plus and minus one standard deviation from the mean."

8. *Question:* "I've heard that the correlation between high school students' scores on college admission tests, such as the SAT or ACT, and the grades those students subsequently earn in college is about .50. Does this size correlation coefficient signify that we can explain half of students' college grades by considering their SAT or ACT scores?"

Your answer: _____

_____

_____

One Possible Response: "To find out how much of the variation in one variable can be accounted for by a second variable (to which that first variable is correlated), we need to *square* the correlation coefficient. Thus, by squaring a coefficient of .50, we end up with a figure of .25. So, 25 percent is actually how much of the variation in students' college grades can be explained based on high school students' scores on college entrance exams."

9. *Question:* "We hear a good deal these days about the two new sets of large-scale tests being built by the two assessment consortia—I think they are called Smarter Balanced and PARCC. Can we be assured that when these two collections of tests finally are available, because they were well funded by gobs of federal bucks, they will be suitable tests?"

Your answer: _____

_____

_____

One Possible Response: "Educational tests, whether they are classroom quizzes whomped up by teachers or large-scale examinations built by established test-development organizations, need to be scrutinized using all of the evaluative factors traditionally employed to judge educational tests. Despite the number of dollars that were used in the creation of the two sets of consortium-built tests, we must await their release and the release of accompanying technical reports dealing with evidence related to reliability, validity, and absence of bias—then judge the merits of the consortia tests. Moreover, if the tests begin to be used to evaluate schools and teachers, then we need solid evidence attesting to the instructional sensitivity of the tests. Putting it simply, then, it may be too soon to tell about the quality of these significant new tests. However, given their potential importance, educators must give really close evaluative scrutiny to the PARCC and Smarter Balanced tests once they actually wander into the world."

10. *Question:* "Our state, as you know, has adopted as its annual accountability exams one of the nation's most widely used standardized achievement tests. I've been reading the promotional literature accompanying the test and it certainly seems the test will have all sorts of diagnostic payoffs for teachers. Do you agree?"

Your answer: _____

_____

_____

 One Possible Response: "I wish I could agree, but I can't. In my view, traditionally constructed nationally standardized tests have very little yield instructionally, based on their diagnostic dividends. Remember, these tests are chiefly intended to permit educators (and parents) to make comparative interpretations about a student's test score, typically comparing a student's performance to those of students in a norm group. Despite this dominating measurement mission, such tests still try to do as much as they can to provide diagnostic information for teachers. But this information is pretty paltry. I think there is a definite role for nationally standardized achievement tests in the field of education. Parents, teachers, and students (if they are mature enough) can benefit from seeing how a student's score compares to scores of students in a national comparison group. But I'd give those tests only a few times during the years that students complete a K–12 education. More frequent administration of nationally standardized achievement tests, in my view, is a waste of both dollars and students' time."

■ Glossary

distribution   A term used to describe a set of test scores, such as when one says, "The final exam score distribution from the students in Ms. Hill's class was very homogeneous."

grade-equivalent scores   An often misinterpreted estimated score based on the grade level and months of the school year represented by a student's test performance.

item response theory (IRT)   This scale-score approach to reporting a student's test performances takes into consideration not only a student's raw score but also other factors such as item difficulty, the guessability of items, and so on. The computation of IRT scale scores requires considerable computer-based statistical analysis.

mean   The arithmetic average of a set of scores.

median   The midpoint in a set of scores when the scores are ranked from lowest to highest.

normal curve equivalent   Often referred to as an NCE, a normal curve equivalent is a scale score representing a raw score's relative position in a distribution of scores that is assumed to be normally distributed. The meaningfulness of this scale-score approach, of course, depends on the degree to which the score distribution involved is, in fact, normal.

percentiles   An interpretive score based on the percent of students in the norm group outperformed by a given student. For example, a student whose raw score exceeded the performance of 84 percent of norm group students would have earned an 84th percentile score.

range   An infrequently used measure of a score distribution's variability that is calculated simply by subtracting the value of the lowest test score from the value of the highest test score.

raw score   The number of items, without any sort of numerical transformation, answered correctly by a student.

scale scores   Converted raw scores that employ a new, arbitrarily chosen scale to represent a student's performance. A considerable number of scale scores are used in education. (See *normal curve equivalent, stanine.*)

standard deviation   A statistical index revealing the degree to which the scores in a group of scores are spread out from the group's mean score, larger standard deviations reflecting more score-spread than smaller standard deviations.

standardized test   Any test that is administered, scored, and interpreted in a standard, predetermined manner.

stanine   A scale score based on the division of test scores into nine units of one-half standard deviation distances (on the score distribution's baseline). The highest stanine, number 9, contains about 4 percent of the scores—as does the lowest stanine, number 1. The middle stanine, number 5, contains about 20 percent of the scores if the distribution is fairly normal in shape.

Appropriate and Inappropriate Test-Preparation Practices

T his chapter deals with an important assessment-related issue that never really troubled teachers a few decades ago. Unfortunately, it is a problem today's classroom teachers have to confront seriously. Faced with growing pressures to increase students' scores on achievement tests, pressures that have been ratcheted up dramatically because of today's accountability requirements, some teachers have responded by engaging in test-preparation practices that are highly questionable. In recent years, for example, a number of reports have been made of teachers and administrators who deliberately coached students with actual copies of a supposedly "secure" examination. There are even reports of educators' erasing students' incorrect answers and substituting correct answers in their place. Teachers caught cheating on high-stakes tests have lost both their teaching licenses and their jobs. Rather than a few isolated instances, such violations of test security have become, sadly, quite common.

■ High-Stakes Assessment Arrives

The preoccupation with student test scores as the definitive indicator of educational effectiveness first surfaced in the 1980s. Although attention had been given to the quality of student test performances prior to that decade, it was in the 1980s that attentiveness to student test performance became pervasive. In large measure, the focus on pupils' test scores stemmed from increasing incredulity on the part of citizens about whether public education was performing properly. Taxpayers, and their elected representatives, registered serious doubts that educational tax dollars were being well spent. Spawned by such doubts, the era of educational accountability became a reality in the 1980s when state after state enacted laws requiring students to be assessed by annually administered achievement tests. Students' performances on such tests were used not only to determine the quality of statewide schooling but also (because of the widespread practice of publishing such test scores in local newspapers) to mirror the effectiveness of individual school districts and schools.

In every sense of the expression, these legislatively mandated achievement tests were *high-stakes tests* because there were significant contingencies associated with the test results. The contingencies were experienced either by the students who took the tests or by the educators who administered the tests. To students, the tests were significant because test scores were often linked to high school graduation or to grade-level promotion. To educators, because of the manner in which test results were publicized by the local media, high test scores were viewed as indicating an effective instructional program and, of course, low test scores were seen to indicate the opposite. Because of these contingencies, teachers and administrators found themselves frequently called on to raise test scores. Candid educators will agree that pressures to boost students' test scores are still widespread.

When NCLB was enacted in 2002, high-stakes testing in America became the law of the land. Not surprisingly, a good many educators regarded federal accountability with both fear and loathing. Some protesters came up with a variety of arguments and slogans against such testing. My favorite was "High stakes are for tomatoes!" But protesters notwithstanding, the enactment of NCLB elevated our test-related stakes to previously unforeseen heights.

Discussions with classroom teachers regarding what sorts of test-preparation practices they view as appropriate and inappropriate have led to one inescapable conclusion: Most teachers have not devoted serious thought to the appropriateness of their test-preparation practices. Given the relatively recent arrival of high-stakes testing in education, it is not surprising that scant attention has been given to the appropriateness of various test-preparation practices. Yet, because no decrease in the pressures on educators to promote higher test scores seems likely, it is apparent teachers need to consider seriously what sorts of test-preparation practices are, indeed, appropriate.

■ Assessment Results as Inference Illuminators

Before addressing topics related to test preparation, it is important to remember the function of educational achievement tests. An educational achievement test is employed in order for us to make a reasonable inference about a student's status with respect to the knowledge and/or skills in the curricular aim the test represents. Ideally, of course, an achievement test will sample the curricular aim representatively so the level of a student's performance on the achievement test

figure 1 ■ The Inference-Illuminating Relationship between a Test and the Curricular Aim It Represents

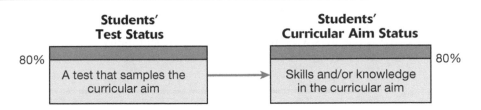

will serve as a reasonably accurate reflection of the student's status with respect to the curricular aim. The nature of this relationship is illustrated in Figure 1 where it is indicated that a student who answered correctly 80 percent of the items in an achievement test would be expected to have mastered about 80 percent of the content in the curricular aim (and its knowledge and/or skills) the test was measuring. The relationship between a student's test performance and the student's mastery of the curricular aim represented by the achievement test, as will be seen later, is a key factor in establishing the appropriateness of test-preparation practices.

Decision Time

Was It Really Wrong?

Judy Jameson is a tenth-grade history teacher in Grant High School. All tenth-graders are given statewide language arts and mathematics tests that must be passed if the students are to receive a state-sanctioned diploma from the district.

The test administration takes place during a two-day period in the school cafetorium and is supervised by Grant High teachers. During those two days, on three occasions Judy overheard Mr. Pelkins respond to students who raised their hands for clarification. Mr. Pelkins did not merely clarify; he told the student what the correct answer was to the test item. After some subtle inquiries, Judy learned that each of the students that Mr. Pelkins had helped was currently in his tenth-grade general mathematics class.

Judy is now trying to decide whether she should do anything about Mr. Pelkins's conduct and, if so, what?

 If you were Judy, what would your decision be?

■ Two Evaluative Guidelines

Two guidelines can be employed by teachers who wish to ascertain the appropriateness of given test-preparation practices. Taken together, the two guidelines provide teachers with advice regarding the suitability of particular test-preparation activities. Here, then, is the first guideline—the *professional ethics guideline*.

Professional Ethics

No test-preparation practice should violate the ethical norms of the education profession.

This first guideline obliges teachers to avoid any unethical test-preparation practice. Ethical behaviors, of course, are rooted not only in fundamental morality but also in the nature of a particular profession. For example, physicians should be governed by general ethical principles dealing with honesty and respect for other people's property as well as by ethical principles that have evolved specifically for the medical profession. Similarly, teachers should not engage in test-preparation practices that involve violations of general ethical canons dealing with theft, cheating, lying, and so on. In addition, however, teachers must take seriously the ethical obligations arising because teachers have agreed to serve *in loco parentis*. Teachers who serve "in place of the parent" take on an ethical responsibility to serve as models of ethical behavior for children.

When teachers engage in test-preparation practices that, if brought to the public's attention, would discredit the education profession, such practices should be considered professionally unethical. This is because, in the long term, such practices erode public confidence in our schools and, as a result, diminish financial support for the schools. Consequently, this erosion of public support renders the education profession less effective and, as a result, leaves children less properly educated.

Thus, according to the guideline of professional ethics, teachers should not engage in test-preparation practices that involve such behaviors as violating state-imposed security procedures regarding high-stakes tests. A growing number of states have enacted serious and widely promulgated regulations so teachers who breach state test-security procedures will have their credentials revoked. Accordingly, teachers should not engage in test-preparation practices that are unethical because there are potential personal repercussions (for example, loss of credentials) or professional repercussions (for example, reduced citizen confidence in public schooling). Most importantly, teachers should avoid unethical test-preparation practices because such practices are *wrong*.

Let's look, then, at the second of our two guidelines—the *educational defensibility guideline*.

Educational Defensibility

No test-preparation practice should increase students' test scores without simultaneously increasing students' mastery of the curricular aim tested.

This second standard emphasizes the importance of engaging in instructional practices that are in the educational best interests of students. Teachers should not, for example, artificially increase students' scores on a test while neglecting to increase students' mastery of the knowledge and/or skills that the test is supposed to reflect.

An appropriate (ethical) test-preparation practice raises not only students' prepreparation-to-postpreparation performance on a test but it also raises students' prepreparation-to-postpreparation mastery of the curricular aim being

figure 2 ■ Appropriate Test Preparation Based on the Guideline of Educational Defensibility

tested. This situation is illustrated in Figure 2 where you can see that a 20-percent prepreparation-to-postpreparation jump in students' mastery was seen both on the test and on the curricular aim it represents.

Conversely, an inappropriate test-preparation practice raises students' pre-preparation-to-postpreparation performance on the test, but not students' mastery of the curricular aim itself. This situation is illustrated in Figure 3 where students' test performances increase, but their curricular aim mastery doesn't.

The result of such inappropriate test-preparation practices is that a deceptive picture of students' achievement is created. The test results no longer serve as an accurate indicator of students' status with respect to a curricular aim. As a consequence, students who in reality have not mastered a curricular aim's content may fail to receive appropriate instruction regarding such content. The students will

figure 3 ■ Inappropriate Test Preparation Based on the Guideline of Educational Defensibility have been instructionally short-changed because inappropriate test-preparation practices led to an inflated estimate of their content mastery. Such test-preparation practices, because they rob students of needed instruction, are educationally indefensible.

■ Five Test-Preparation Practices

We can now turn to a consideration of five common test-preparation practices. These five practices are not exhaustive in the sense that there are no other conceivable test-preparation procedures. The five practices do, however, capture most of the important test-preparation options available to teachers. Some of these involve special instruction rather than regular classroom instruction. *Special instruction* consists of extra preparation sessions, during or outside class, devoted exclusively to the readying of students for tests. In contrast, *regular classroom instruction,* although its focus may be relevant to the content of a test, occurs as part of the teacher's ongoing instructional program. The five test-preparation practices are the following:

1. *Previous-form preparation* provides special instruction and practice based directly on students' use of a previous form of the actual test. For example, if the currently published form of a nationally standardized achievement test is being used on a statewide basis as part of a state's accountability system, the teacher gives students guided or independent practice with earlier, no longer published, versions of the same test.
2. *Current-form preparation* provides special instruction and practice based directly on students' use of the form of the test currently being employed. For example, the teacher gives students guided or independent practice with actual items copied from a currently used state-developed high school graduation test.
3. *Generalized test-taking preparation* provides special instruction covering test-taking skills for dealing with a variety of achievement-test formats. For example, the teacher shows students how to make calculated guesses for certain types of items or how to allocate test-taking time judiciously.
4. *Same-format preparation* provides regular classroom instruction dealing directly with the content covered on the test, but employs only practice items that embody the same format as items actually used on the test. For example, if a mathematics achievement test includes addition problems formatted only in vertical columns, the teacher provides practice with addition problems formatted solely in this manner. Some teachers create "clone" items for same-format preparation activities—such items being almost mirror images of a test's actual items. For many of these "clone" items, the practice items are essentially indistinguishable from the actual items.

5. *Varied-format preparation* provides regular classroom instruction dealing directly with the content covered on the test, but employs practice items representing a variety of test-item formats. For example, if the achievement test uses subtraction problems formatted only in vertical columns, the teacher provides practice with problems formatted in vertical columns, horizontal rows, and in story form.

Applying the Two Guidelines

When these five test-preparation practices are scrutinized according to the guidelines of professional ethics and educational defensibility, only two turn out to be appropriate.

Previous-form preparation violates the educational defensibility guideline because students' test scores are apt to be boosted via such special preparation sessions without concomitant rises in students' mastery of the curricular aim being tested. In addition, because in the public's view this kind of test-preparation practice may be seen as an improper instance of coaching students *merely* for test-score gains, it may be viewed by some as professionally unethical. Previous-form preparation, therefore, is inappropriate. (This same judgment would apply to the use of commercial test-preparation materials based chiefly on specially created "parallel" forms of a currently used test.)

Current-form preparation clearly loses out on both guidelines. Not only is it educationally indefensible but such preparation also constitutes an outright example of cheating. Current forms of the test must be stolen or surreptitiously copied in order to be used in such potentially improper score-boosting special sessions. Teachers who are caught readying their students via current-form preparation should, in fact, be caught.

Generalized test-taking preparation turns out to be an appropriate form of test preparation because such special instruction on how to take tests is, characteristically, rather brief and not seriously deflective of a student's ongoing education. More importantly, because such test-taking preparation readies students to cope with a number of different sorts of tests, students will be less apt to be intimidated by a previously unencountered type of test item. In a very real sense, therefore, generalized test-taking preparation sessions allow students' test performances to be more accurately reflective of their true state of knowledge and/or skill. Such preparation, *if not excessively lengthy,* is clearly appropriate.

Same-format preparation, although it may be ethical, is not educationally defensible. If students in their regular classroom instruction are allowed to deal *only* with the explicit item format used on a test, then those students will be far less likely to generalize what they have learned. Test scores may rise, but comparable content mastery is not apt to rise. Although many administrators may, because of powerful pressures to boost scores, endorse this form of test-preparation practice,

Parent Talk

Mrs. Stern is the mother of Sara, one of your most talented students. Mrs. Stern, it is rumored, will be running for election to your district's school board in the fall. Accordingly, whenever Mrs. Stern raises questions about Sara's education, you always try to be especially responsive. You are no dummy.

When Sara arrived at school this morning, she gave you a brief note from her mother. The note said, "Why is so much time spent in our school, and in your class, 'teaching to the test' this year? Shouldn't our children be learning more than what's on a test?"

 If I were you, here's how I'd respond to Mrs. Stern in person or with a note (if in person, I might reply on bended knee):

"You're right on target to be raising this issue, Mrs. Stern, but I want you to understand an important difference between teaching to the test, in the sense you teach students to do well on particular test items, versus teaching to the test, in the sense you teach the students to master the skills and/or knowledge represented by the test.

"What I do in my class is the latter, and that's also what most of my colleagues do. In other words, we teach directly toward the important skills and knowledge that our tests measure. Those are the key kinds of skills and the significant bodies of knowledge that you and I both want Sara to acquire. But the classroom assessments we use only sample a student's mastery of such knowledge or skills.

"So it would be instructionally unwise for us to teach toward particular test items. We want Sara and her classmates to master skills and knowledge so our students can apply what they've learned in many settings, not merely on a specific test.

"Putting it simply, we do not teach toward a set of test items, but we do teach toward the skills and knowledge our tests represent."

 Now, how would you respond to Mrs. Stern?

it should be resisted because it is educationally unsound. The more "clone" items there are in a set of practice items, the more inappropriate such test-preparation activities are.

Varied-format preparation, in contrast, satisfies both of our two evaluative guidelines. Students during their regular classroom instruction are given practice not only with content as it is conceptualized on the test but also with content conceptualized in other ways. Rises in test scores will, in general, be accompanied by rises in mastery of the curricular aim being tested because students' generalized mastery of the content is being fostered.

table 1 ■ Per-Guideline Indicator of the Appropriateness of Five Test-Preparation Practices

	Guideline Satisfied?	
Test-Preparation Practice	*Professional Ethics*	*Educational Defensibility*
Previous Form	No	No
Current Form	No	No
Generalized Test Taking	Yes	Yes
Same Format	Yes	No
Varied Format	Yes	Yes

Of the five test-preparation variants, then, only varied-format preparation and generalized test-taking preparation satisfy both evaluative guidelines. This can be seen in Table 1.

■ What about "Teaching to the Test"?

If you get into any sort of meaningful discussion of test preparation, it's almost certain that someone will soon use the expression "teaching to the test." This someone should not be you! Here's why.

There are two decisively different meanings people employ when they use the phrase *teaching to the test*. First, they can mean a teacher is directing instruction toward the knowledge, skills, or affective variables represented by the test. Another way to put this same meaning of "teaching to the test" is that teachers are aiming their instruction so students accomplish the curricular aim sampled by the actual test. This is good instruction. A second meaning of "teaching to the test," however, is that it describes teachers who are directing their instruction specifically toward the actual items on the test itself. This is bad instruction.

So, when someone uses the expression "teaching to the test," we can't tell whether they're talking about something swell or something sordid. Conversations that take place about test preparation in which this double-meaning expression is tossed around mindlessly will, almost certainly, end up being mindless conversations.

As a consequence, I implore you *never to use this ambiguous expression* yourself. Rather, say either "teaching to the test's items" or "teaching to the curricular aim represented by the test." To emphasize the importance of this advice, I have summarized it in this box:

NEVER, NEVER SAY:

"Teaching to the test"

SAY:

"Teaching to the test's items"

(or)

SAY:

"Teaching to the curricular aim represented by the test"

If you should momentarily forget my fine advice and find yourself blurting out the foul phrase I've just been castigating, or if you are forced with pepper-spray to say it, be sure to quickly follow up by saying which meaning of the expression you intended. By and large, however, you'll be better off if you expunge the phrase completely from your potential utterances.

If a *friend* uses the phrase, you might gently and supportively seek clarification about which meaning is intended. If an *enemy* uses the phrase, however, I recommend a crisp facial slap on the left or right cheek—depending on either cheek's proximity to you.

One way of thinking about how teachers ought to prepare their students for important assessments is presented in Figure 4. As you can see, a teacher's instruction should be directed toward the body of knowledge and/or skills (it could also

figure 4 ■ Appropriate and Inappropriate Directions for a Teacher's Instruction

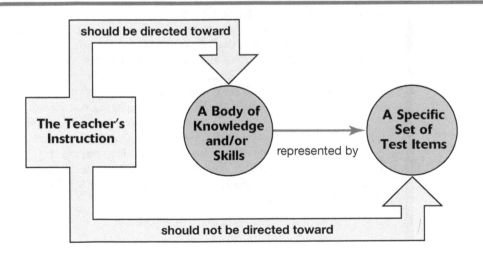

be affect) represented by the test, but not toward the specific set of items doing the representing.

And this way of thinking about test preparation brings us to an important point for teachers to understand. You can only direct your instruction toward the knowledge and/or skills represented by a high-stakes test if there is a suitable description of the assessed curricular aim available. You can't expect a teacher to teach toward a curricular aim if there's no clear description of that aim provided.

Unfortunately, many of the nation's teachers are now experiencing immense pressure to raise their students' scores on high-stakes test that are unaccompanied

but what does this have to do with
Teaching?

Today's teachers find themselves in a terrible bind. Their competence is often being judged on the basis of students' scores on high-stakes tests. And, as a consequence, teachers frequently find themselves pressured by their principals to improve students' scores on the locally anointed high-stakes tests. But many heavily pressured teachers fail to recognize that their principal is often being squeezed just as hard to make sure a school's test scores take a giant jump.

As you'll learn , evaluating a school's staff on the basis of students' scores on certain kinds of standardized tests is fundamentally wrong. Yet that recognition, all by itself, doesn't make the score-boosting pressures on teachers or administrators evaporate.

As a teacher, or a prospective teacher, you really must comprehend the nature of the two test-preparation guidelines offered in the chapter, and you need to understand why it is that some standardized achievement tests measure the socioeconomic makeup of a school's student body—not how well the school's teachers are teaching.

At that point, instead of assuming a school's principal is the "heavy" in this score-boosting frenzy, you need to recognize school principals are, themselves, under substantial pressure to elevate their school's test scores. Accordingly, by the time you wrap up this text, you'll know (1) how to and how not to prepare students for high-stakes tests and (2) what kinds of high-stakes tests give educators—that is, teachers *and* principals—a chance to succeed.

Therefore, why not collaborate *with* your school's principal to explain ways of responding to extant test pressures with test-preparation practices that help, not harm, children. What you need to do is to put the stuff you've learned about formative assessment together with what you learn about test preparation. Then, working collaboratively with your school's principal, figure out a strategy to benefit kids.

by instructionally meaningful descriptions of what those tests measure. And without such descriptions, it is far from surprising many pressured teachers have succumbed to the lure of item-focused teaching.

I've spent a good deal of time reviewing the descriptions of assessed behavior provided by publishers of all the nation's standardized achievement tests, and I can tell you, from a teacher's perspective, the descriptions of these tests' curricular targets fall way short of what teachers need. Oh, of course there are some loose descriptions of objectives or content assessed, but those descriptions just aren't sufficient if a teacher is planning day-to-day instruction.

My point is this: If the high-stakes test on which you're asked to boost students' scores is not accompanied by descriptions of what the test's items *represent,* then you should let the world know you're being put in an untenable instructional position. Teachers should not be forced to play the score-boosting game if obliged to use rules making it certain the teacher will lose. And there's no way to satisfy this chapter's two test-preparation guidelines if a curricular aim's description (suitable for instructional planning) has not been supplied.

■ What Do Classroom Teachers Really Need to Know about Test-Preparation Practices?

As a classroom teacher, you may find your own test-preparation practices may not coincide perfectly with one of the five practices described in this chapter. You'll probably discover, if you are preparing your students specifically for some sort of high-stakes test, however, your approach will be reasonably close to one of the five practices. More important than the five preparation practices, of course, are the two evaluative guidelines. You should review with care your own preparation activities linked to high-stakes tests. The two evaluative guidelines provided here—professional ethics and educational defensibility—will prove useful in such a review.

■ Chapter Summary

This chapter dealt with an important assessment-related issue—namely, how teachers should prepare their students for significant tests. After a recounting of why it is that classroom teachers are under substantial pressure to boost their students' test scores, two evaluative guidelines were supplied by which test-preparation practices can be judged. The two guidelines were (1) *professional ethics,* which indicates that no test-preparation practice should violate the ethical norms of the education profession, and (2) *educational defensibility,* which indicates that no test-preparation practice should increase students' test scores without simultaneously increasing students' mastery of the curricular aim tested. Five test-preparation variants were then described: (1) previous-form preparation, (2) current-form preparation, (3) generalized test-taking preparation, (4) same-format preparation, and (5) varied-format preparation. Having applied the two evaluative guidelines to the five test-preparation practices, it was concluded that the only two practices satisfying both guidelines were generalized test-taking preparation (if brief) and varied-format preparation. Readers were urged to eschew the phrase *teaching to the test*. Readers should also have been urged to eschew the word *eschew*. The chapter was concluded with a discussion of the necessity for the creators of high-stakes tests to supply curricular aim descriptions from which sound instructional decisions can be made.

Self-Check

To see how skillfully you can use the chapter's two guidelines for evaluating teachers' test-preparation practices, you'll now be given five written descriptions of fictitious teachers' test-preparation activities. Your task is to decide, for each description, whether either, neither, or both of the two evaluative guidelines (professional ethics and educational defensibility) have been violated by the preparation activity described. Having done that, decide personally whether you think the preparation activities described were appropriate or inappropriate.

Description One

Mrs. Gordon makes sure she has her sixth-grade students practice in the fall for the nationally standardized achievement tests required in the spring by the district's school board. Fortunately, she has been able to make photocopies of most of the test's pages during the past several years, so she can organize a highly relevant two-week preparation unit wherein students are given actual test items to solve. At the close of the unit, students are supplied with a practice test on which about 60 percent of the test consists of actual items copied from the nationally standardized commercial test. Mrs. Gordon provides students with an answer key after they have taken the practice test so that they can check their answers.

Any violations? _____   If so, which? _____

What's your opinion of this preparation? _____

_____

Description Two

Mrs. Hillard knows the reading test administered to all state eighth-graders contains a set of six fairly lengthy reading selections, each of which is followed by about 10 multiple-choice items dealing with such topics as (1) the main idea of the selection as a whole or the main idea of its constituent paragraphs, (2) the meaning of selection's technical terms that can be arrived at from contextual clues, and (3) the defensibility of inferential statements linked to the selection.

Mrs. Hillard routinely spends time in her eighth-grade language arts class trying to improve her students' reading comprehension capabilities. She has the students read passages similar to those used in the statewide test, then gives her students a variety of practice tests, including written multiple-choice, true-false, and oral short-answer tests in which, for example, individual students must state what they believe to be the main idea of a specific paragraph in the passage.

Any violations? _____ If so, which? _____

What's your opinion of this preparation? _____

Description Three

Because there is a statewide reading comprehension test that must be passed by all high school students before they receive state-sanctioned diplomas, Mr. Gillette, a tenth-grade English teacher, spends about four weeks of his regular class sessions getting students ready to pass standardized tests. He devotes one week to each of the following topics: (1) time management in examinations, (2) dealing with test-induced anxiety, (3) making calculated guesses, and (4) trying to think like the test's item writers. Mr. Gillette's students seem appreciative of his efforts.

Any violations? _____ If so, which? _____

What's your opinion of this preparation? _____

Description Four

Because she is eager for her students to perform well on their twelfth-grade senior mathematics tests (administered by the state department of education), Mrs. Williamson gives students answer keys for all of the test's selected-response items. When her students take the test in the school auditorium, along with all of the school's other twelfth-graders, she urges them to use the answer keys discreetly, and only if necessary.

Any violations? _____ If so, which? _____

What's your opinion of this preparation? _____

Description Five

Mr. Phillips prepares his sixth-grade social studies students to do well on a state-administered social studies examination by having all of his students practice with test items similar to those on the examination. Mr. Phillips tries to replicate the nature of the state examination's items without ever using exactly the same content as it is apt to appear on the examination. He weaves in his test-preparation activities as part of his regular social studies instruction. Most students really don't know they are receiving examination-related preparation.

Any violations? _____ If so, which? _____

What's your opinion of this preparation? _____

_____

Pondertime

1. Can you think of guidelines, other than the two described in the chapter, to be used in evaluating a classroom teacher's test-preparation practices? If so, what are they?

2. How about test-preparation practices? Can you think of any other sorts of test-preparation guidelines that are meaningfully different from the five described in the chapter? If so, using the chapter's two evaluative guidelines or any new ones you might prefer, how appropriate are such test-preparation practices?

3. How do you think classroom teachers can best be prepared to deal with the test-preparation issue in an appropriate fashion?

4. Do you think my rant about the expression, "teaching to the test," was warranted? Why or why not?

Self-Check Key

1. Mrs. Gordon has violated both evaluative guidelines by engaging in what most people regard as downright cheating. Hopefully, you didn't consider this teacher's preparation efforts to be wonderful.

2. Mrs. Hillard is clearly engaged in a version of varied-format preparation. She is violating neither of the two evaluative guidelines. Indeed, because of the likelihood

that she is promoting her students' generalized reading comprehension abilities during her regular language arts evaluation, she is engaging in solidly appropriate test preparation.

3. Mr. Gillette's month-long test-preparation marathon was simply too long. Although both of the two evaluative guidelines appear to have been satisfied, the lengthy test-preparation activities really are costing students a full month of English instruction. To be absurd, let's say Mr. Gillette spent his entire, year-long instructional efforts on generalized test-preparation schemes such as described in this chapter. That kind of approach would clearly be depriving students of an English course. In that sense, particularly if parents discovered Mr. Gillette's students were learning nothing about English, there would surely be some negative repercussion and, as a consequence, an erosion of confidence in the schools. Thus, the professional ethics guideline might have been violated. But even if neither of the two evaluative guidelines had been violated, Mr. Gillette's month-long test-preparation extravaganza was simply too, too long.

4. Mrs. Williamson is engaged in dishonest test preparation that loses out on both evaluative guidelines. Before you think this is a silly and obvious example, you should know many teachers have been fired and had their teaching licenses revoked because of precisely the kind of behavior depicted in this sad scenario.

5. Mr. Phillips satisfied the professional ethics guidelines but lost out on the educational defensibility guideline. Irrespective of whether his students know they were being prepared, and without regard to the inclusion of the test preparation as part of his regular instruction, Mr. Phillips's students aren't likely to be able to generalize the social studies mastery they'll display on the state examination to other settings in which they'll need to possess such mastery.

■ Additional Stuff

Cannell, J. J. (1989). *How public educators cheat on standardized achievement tests*. Albuquerque, NM: Friends for Education.

Hardison, C. M., and Sackett, P. R. (2008). "Use of writing samples on standardized tests: Susceptibility to rule-based coaching and the resulting effects on score improvement," *Applied Measurement in Education, 21,* no. 3 (July–September): 227–252.

Harris, P., Smith, B. M., and Harris, J. (2011). *The myths of standardized tests: Why they don't tell you what you think they do*. Lanham, MD: Rowman & Littlefield.

Lai, E. R., and Waltman, K. (2008). "Test preparation: Examining teacher perceptions and practices," *Educational Measurement: Issues and Practice, 27,* no. 2 (Summer): 28–45.

Mehrens, W. A., and Kaminski, J. (1989). "Methods for improving standardized tests scores: Fruitful, fruitless, or fraudulent." *Educational Measurement: Issues and Practice, 8,* no. 1: 14–22.

Sacks, P. (1999). *Standardized minds: The high price of America's testing culture and what we can do to change it.* Cambridge, MA: Perseus Books.

■ Cyber Stuff

- *Alfie Kohn* is an outspoken critic of the way standardized tests are being currently misused and, as a consequence, how the pressures to raise students' scores on these tests are degrading education. A frequent lecturer on this topic, Kohn has created a website containing a host of references and resources that can be used to oppose the misuse of high-stakes tests. The site is replete with links to the writings of those who share Kohn's views regarding the negative impact of America's preoccupation with test scores. **www.AlfieKohn.org**

- *Caveon Test Security* was established more than a decade ago as an agency "dedicated to detecting, correcting, and preventing test fraud." Caveon offers its clients a range of services such as security audits and data forensics in an effort to minimize cheating—especially on high-stakes exams. A review of this website confirms the lengths to which some will go to improve, even if falsely, their test scores. **www .caveon.com**

- *Education Week on the Web* is the online version of a widely read weekly publication devoted exclusively to educational concerns. Although this online publication deals with a full range of educationally relevant topics, more than a few of its reports focus on assessment, accountability, and evaluation. Because of the perceived "newsworthiness" of stories regarding educators who are coping with assessment-based pressures, frequent visitors to this site are often apt to encounter descriptions of such situations. **www.edweek.org**

■ Extended Applications

It is a truism that the more a person uses something, the more familiar with this something the person becomes. This self-evident notion surely applies to the assessment-related knowledge, skills, and concepts you have been reading about in the foregoing pages. Thus, to provide readers of *Classroom Assessment* with additional opportunities to apply the content contained in this text, this final section contains a variety of exercises intended to give readers an opportunity to use what they've been reading about.

In a sense, of course, the Self-Check exercises found at the close of this chapter provided an opportunity for readers to apply a chapter's content. Nonetheless, the more times you use a concept, skill, or a body of knowledge, the more likely it is that you will master this content so you can employ it in varied situations.

For each of the text, you will find an extended-application exercise calling for you to do some thinking about that chapter's content as it applies to a real-world situation. Each exercise is preceded by a brief introduction setting forth the reason that the upcoming extended-application exercise has been selected.

Because many of these exercises call on you to generate an original response rather than select a response from a set of options, it is difficult to supply an "answer key" for readers' unpredictable responses. So, what you'll find following all the exercises is One Possible Response—an indication of how I would have personally responded to the exercise if I had been asked to do so. Please don't regard my response as the only way to respond to an exercise. After all, by definition, this is only "one possible" response. Instead, please think of my response as a fairly flimsy form of feedback. You can certainly disagree with me, even emphatically, yet still profit from doing the exercise.

Remember, what is being provided in this section. The exercises deliberately intended to extend how you apply the content treated in *Classroom Assessment*. I hope you find these exercises useful in enhancing your understanding of what teachers need to know about classroom assessment.

■ Trolling for Transgressions

Introduction

The most important things in this chapter's consideration of test-preparation practices are the two evaluative guidelines by which teachers can determine if a given test-preparation practice warrants (1) adulation or (2) pelting with rotten eggs. The *professional ethics guideline* and the *educational defensibility guideline* should, therefore, be thoroughly understood by all teachers.

To help you become facile in identifying whether either of these guidelines has been violated, this exercise presents you with 10 brief descriptions of teachers engaged in test preparation, then asks you to indicate whether one or both of the two guidelines has been transgressed. This set of 10 choice-points for you is similar to the 5 self-check exercises in the chapter itself. Clearly, the more adroit you are in spotting guideline violations in colleagues' test-preparation activities, the more likely you'll be able to spot transgressions in any test-preparation activities you whomp up for your own students.

 Exercise Directions: After reviewing each of the following 10 descriptions of a teacher's test-preparation efforts, determine whether either (or both) of this chapter's two test-preparation guidelines has been violated. In essence, you are to decide whether the described teacher activity violates one, both, or neither of the two guidelines.

1. Harriett Harper tries to ready her science students for the state's upcoming annual science tests by giving special attention to each of the state-approved content standards in science that has been identified by the state as "test-eligible." Harriett tries to supply her students with a wide array of practice items focused on those content standards. The practice items include different sorts of

selected-response items as well as constructed-response items, the latter calling for students to both write their responses and present those responses orally. Harriett focuses her instructional attention exclusively on the science content standards that will underlie the impending state science tests.

Any guideline transgression(s)?_____

_____

_____

 One Possible Response: No violation of either test-preparation guideline is present in what Harriett is doing. Although we might regret her decision to focus her instruction *exclusively* on the content standards on which the state science test is to be built, that's often how the rubber hits the asphalt these days in many states. That is, in recent years there has been so much test-eligible content to be assessed that teachers just didn't have time to teach much else. Harriett seems to be promoting her students' generalizable mastery of what's to be learned. There are no guideline transgressions here.

2. Debbie Gia is preparing her third-grade students to take end-of-school-year state accountability tests in reading and mathematics. Because this will be the first time these students have ever taken any sort of standardized test, Debbie believes they will be intimidated by the experience. Accordingly, during the month immediately prior to state testing, Debbie spends about an hour a week, divided into sessions of about 15 minutes each, showing her students samples of the item types they will be encountering. She has downloaded these items from her State Department of Education's website.

   During these "Get-Ready" sessions, Debbie also tells her students how to allocate their test-taking time wisely, and how to make informed guesses when attempting to answer certain kinds of items. Her chief goal in these "Get-Ready" sessions is to reduce students' anxiety about the upcoming tests.

Any guideline transgression(s)? _____

_____

_____

One Possible Response: Debbie seemed to be prepping her third-graders sensibly for their upcoming state "first-time" exams. Her focus on anxiety reduction is commendable. Moreover, her test-prep efforts did not last for an eternity. No guideline violations are seen here.

3. Rod Sherry wants his fifth-graders to perform well on their spring accountability exams. Based on Rod's familiarity with the kinds of items included in his state's Annual Mathematics Appraisals, he makes sure that during the school year, and especially during the three months immediately prior to the state exams, his students receive highly focused pre-exam preparation, but he uses only the specific type of test items used on the upcoming Annual Mathematics Appraisals.

The state's math tests for the fifth-grade consist exclusively of "grid-in" items—that is, items for which students supply their answers by bubbling in certain numbers from a numerical grid supplied along with each item. This "grid-in" approach makes it possible to score students' answers via electronic scanning and thereby permit the state to supply complete reports to each of the state's teachers within one week after the exams are administered. Because "grid-in" items are not used in the state's mathematics tests until the fifth grade, Rod believes his students need all the "gridding-in" practice they can get.

Any guideline transgression(s)? _____

_____

_____

One Possible Response: Rod violated the educational defensibility guideline. By providing his students *only* with practice on "grid-in" items, those students are apt to do all right on the impending statewide exams. But there is life after state accountability exams, and students don't encounter any "grid-in" items in real life. Come to think of it, when was the last time that you personally had to "grid-in" an answer to a math problem? Rod's students' scores on the "grid-in" state tests are likely to be better than those students' actual math mastery if they had been tested in other ways. Rod needs to vary his practice items.

4. In the district where he teaches, John James knows that each spring's accountability exams consist largely of brand-new items. However, it is necessary to make statistical adjustments in order for one year's exams to represent the same challenge to students as all other years' exams. To do so, however, some "anchor" items must be reused on each form so these statistical adjustments are possible. In all, about 15 percent of each form's items are reused. John has a contact in his district's office who has told him which of this year's items will most likely be reused in the next year's exams. Accordingly, John makes copies of those items, then gives his next year's students plenty of practice with the items prior to their taking the spring exams. After all, John concludes, "There will be 85 percent of the items that my students will never have seen!"

Any guideline transgression(s)? _____

_____

_____

One Possible Response: John clearly violates both of the chapter's two test-preparation guidelines. Really, 15 percent cheating is still cheating. If John's conduct were ever divulged to the public, it would reflect negatively on the education profession. In addition to flopping on the professional ethics guideline, John also violated the educational defensibility guideline because, with a 15 percent advantage, his students' spring test scores will surely provide an inflated estimate of students' actual skills and knowledge.

5. Tara Miller teaches Spanish in an urban high school. For several years in a row, students in her school, Kennedy High, have failed to score well enough on the state's annual accountability tests in mathematics. Tara's principal, at a midyear faculty meeting, pointed out if the school's students do not do well enough on the upcoming year's accountability tests, the school is likely to be "restructured."

   In an effort to help her school avoid being restructured, Tara abandons the teaching of Spanish in her five classes altogether for the six weeks leading up to accountability testing. Because she is quite skilled in math, Tara believes she can help her students boost their state math scores sufficiently.

Any guideline transgression(s)? _____

_____

_____

 One Possible Response: This seems to me to be a clear violation of the professional ethics guideline. Tara is selling out. Her intentions may be commendable, but she's supposed to be teaching Spanish to her students. If the public ever learns that Kennedy High's teachers are subverting what they're supposed to be teaching, then it will become apparent the school's teachers are concerned about what will make their school look good, and not about what's educationally good for their students.

6. In her school district, Marian Talbert's annual accountability tests consist of a currently used nationally standardized achievement test that has been "augmented" by about six items per grade level so the test will be better aligned with the district's curricular aims. To help her seventh-grade English students get higher scores on the test, Marian persuades her school's principal to let her buy two sets of commercially published test-prep materials for the test—namely, *Scoring Much Higher* and *Test-Topping*. She devotes at least two class periods a week to these test-preparation materials.

   Only a week before the district's accountability tests are to be administered, a local newspaper publishes an exposé story revealing that almost half of the practice items in the *Test-Topping* booklets were actually taken from the current form of the standardized test being used as an accountability exam. Marian did not know about this, but her school has clearly suffered a public-relations hit because the newspaper story reveals that Marian's school was one of the district's schools using the *Test-Topping* materials.

Any guideline transgression(s)? _____

_____

_____

One Possible Response: This appears to be a violation of both test-preparation guidelines. Marian's students' scores on the accountability test will be higher than they should be—and the public will lose confidence in a profession whose members appear to be relying on inappropriate test-prep materials. If a teacher is going to rely on a set of commercially produced test-prep materials, that teacher needs to make sure the materials are suitable.

7. Marki Fisher tries to get her students to achieve the assessment targets set forth for fifth-graders in her state. Those assessment targets consist of the 13 state-approved reading and math skills the state's board of education has identified as high-priority "power" standards. Marki focuses almost all of her classroom instructional time, as well as every short-duration test she uses, on these 5 reading skills and 8 mathematics skills. Not only does she make these 13 skills the framework for her math and language arts teaching, but she also makes sure to determine her students' evolving skill mastery by measuring their progress using a wide variety of constructed-response and selected-response test items. Marki believes that students' *generalizable* skill mastery is imperative, hence assesses their mastery in myriad ways.

Any guideline transgression(s)? _____

_____

_____

 One Possible Response: This is the way that standards-based instruction makes sense. Marki's aim is to get her students to be able to apply the skills they are learning in a variety of contexts. Her preparation activities are focused on students' attainment of officially approved cognitive skills, but she wants those skills to be so thoroughly mastered that her students can apply the skills in many settings. There are no guideline transgressions here.

8. Billy Joe Merton teaches middle school math classes. His students take the state's spring eighth-grade mathematics accountability test. Because Billy Joe believes the curricula of his classes coincide sufficiently with the state's officially sanctioned mathematical content standards, he never supplies any special test-preparation activities for his students.

Any guideline transgression(s)? _____

_____

_____

One Possible Response: It would be pretty difficult for Billy Joe to violate in this chapter's two test-preparation guidelines because he apparently isn't dishing up any special test prep. The only kind of test preparation that Billy Joe deems necessary is what routinely goes on in his classes. There are, consequently, no guideline transgressions going on here. We hope that Billy Joe is correct about the alignment of his curricula and the state's spring mathematics test. Hopefully, his students call him "Mr. Merton" instead of "Billy Joe."

9. The newly created district reading test in Myra Murray's midwestern school district measures third-graders' ability to comprehend the main ideas of paragraphs. Items in the test call for students to first read a brief paragraph, then select from four multiple-choice alternatives the best statement of that paragraph's main idea. Myra teaches 27 third-graders who will be taking their

first district tests this year (in math and reading), and she thinks her students should have the very best chance to succeed on this important test. Accordingly, all of Myra's in-class reading-comprehension activities dealing with main ideas of paragraphs include only practice items that are essentially identical to the ones that will appear on the end-of-year district reading test.

Myra sets aside no separate "test-prep" sessions for her students. Rather, all of Myra's reading instruction takes place during her regular classroom activities.

Any guideline transgression(s)? _____

_____

_____

 One Possible Response: Although Myra's third-graders will most likely do as well on the district reading test as they can—because Myra's instruction features only the types of main-idea items that will be encountered on the test—her students' test performances are apt to be an overestimate of their ability to comprehend the main ideas in paragraphs. Myra should be more concerned about her students' *generalized* mastery of this skill—no matter how the skill happens to be assessed on the upcoming tests. Myra's preparation activities, although part of her regular instruction, violated the educational defensibility guideline.

10. Stephen Cox believes his fifth-grade students need to become familiar with the sorts of mathematics items they are likely to encounter on the end-of-year state accountability tests. As a consequence, he downloads each year's collection of "released" fifth-grade math items from the State Department of Education's website. He makes sure to work most of these items into his regular instruction and practice exercises, along with other kinds of mathematics test items, but Stephen never indicates that these state-released items are anything "special."

Any guideline transgression(s)? _____

_____

_____

One Possible Response: What Stephen is doing is just fine. He's employing state-released items along with other kinds of items. Stephen is violating neither of the chapter's two guidelines.

■ Glossary

educational defensibility guideline   A guideline for test preparation stipulating that no test-preparation practice should increase a student's test scores without simultaneously increasing his or her mastery of the assessment domain represented by the test.

professional ethics guideline   A guideline for test preparation stipulating that no test-preparation practice should violate the ethical norms of the education profession.

teaching to the test   When a teacher directs instruction toward the assessment domain represented by the test *or* toward the specific items that make up the actual test. Because of this dual meaning, and the confusion apt to result from its use, the expression should be avoided or immediately defined.

The Evaluation of Instruction

M ost teachers, at the conclusion of a set of instructional activities—whether those activities consume an hour, a week, or an entire school year—do not systematically try to determine how successful their instruction actually was. But they should. In this chapter, then, we'll consider ways that teachers can tell whether their just-completed instruction was great or grimy. It's really a rather straightforward task, yet not without some significant sand traps to avoid.

, I want to make sure we are using two sometimes confused labels accurately. In casual conversation, you'll sometimes find educators using the terms *evaluation* and *grading* interchangeably, but these two words really stand for distinctively different education-related activities.

There was a time when educators really didn't distinguish between *evaluation* of students and *grading* of students, but those days have passed. Because program evaluation has now become such a prominent part of educational practice, when most educators encounter the term *evaluation* these days, they think about the evaluation of an educational program such as a school district's newly installed cooperative learning scheme.

When classroom teachers engage in **evaluation**, those teachers are typically arriving at conclusions about the quality of their own instructional efforts. In this sense, therefore, you should think about evaluation as "program evaluation." Because the "program" under consideration in most classrooms is the instructional program provided to students by the teacher, then *evaluation* will be used in this chapter to signify the attempt on the part of teachers to determine how well they're doing instructionally. The evaluation of instruction, then, can be roughly equated with "teacher evaluation" because when teachers evaluate their

From Chapter 15 of *Classroom Assessment: What Teachers Need to Know*, Seventh Edition. W. James Popham.

instructional endeavors, they're really evaluating the quality of the instructional program they put together as well as the way they delivered that program. The focus of *evaluation* in this chapter, therefore, is on teachers' evaluation of their instruction.

In contrast, the focus of **grading** is on *students*. When a teacher grades a student, the teacher is assigning some kind of symbol , such as letter grades of A, B, C, D, or F, that signify "how well the student has done." Although in most classrooms there's surely a relationship between the quality of the teacher's instructional program and the grades students receive, those two notions are really independent. For example, Mrs. Bevins, a third-grade teacher, could evaluate her own language arts program very negatively because her instruction seemed to confuse many students. Nevertheless, Mrs. Bevins would still award grades of A to numerous students who, despite the confusing language arts instruction, effortlessly seemed to grasp the language arts concepts being considered.

Although I've tried to draw a nice, crisp distinction between *evaluation* as the appraisal of an instructional activity and *grading* as the appraisal of a student's performance, don't be surprised if you encounter colleagues who don't slice their appraisal cake in the same way. Some educators (I think mistakenly) refer to the grading of students as the "evaluation" of students. Other educators (also, in my view, mistakenly) talk about "grading" the quality of instruction. So, prepare yourself for some semantic stumbling when you discuss these concepts with others.

There are two types of evaluation bearing on teachers' appraisals of their instructional efforts. *Teachers'* self-evaluation refers to the personal appraisal of the teacher's instructional program for purposes of improving the program. For example, suppose you're teaching a three-week social studies unit on International Cooperation to a class of fifth-graders for the first time. You want to improve the unit so that the next time you offer it, your teaching will be more effective. That's a task for self-evaluation, and students' assessment results will surely help you. *External teacher evaluation,* in contrast, is not improvement focused. This kind of evaluation usually refers to appraisals of teachers' competencies in order to make significant decisions about those teachers such as (1) continuation of employment or (2) awarding of tenure. When teachers are evaluated externally, they're almost always evaluated by an administrator or supervisor.

Classroom teachers usually do their own self-evaluation because they wish to spruce up their instruction. For external teacher evaluation, classroom teachers may be called on to supply evidence (such as students' test results) to supervisors who will then use such evidence evaluatively.

The evaluation of a teacher's instructional effectiveness will also be influenced by the presence of relevant state or federal laws that, for many teachers, may require students' scores on standardized tests to be used for evaluating schools and, by implication, for evaluating the teachers who teach in those schools. If you find yourself teaching a grade level or in a subject field where federal or state accountability tests are given annually, you can bet that your students' scores on those tests will figure into any evaluation of your effectiveness.

■ A Focus on Consequences

You can't tell how well teachers teach by watching them do it. Instead, to determine the effectiveness of a teacher's instruction, we need to focus on the *effects* a teacher's instruction has on students. There are precious few exceptions to this "focus on consequences" strategy for the evaluation of instruction. To illustrate one such exception, on the ineffective end of the quality scale, this would occur if we were to observe a teacher engaging in a series of badly explained, mind-numbing, and off-target activities—all of which were taking place in the midst of loud-talking, misbehaving, and clearly out-of-control students. Anyone walking into such a cacophonous classroom would instantly be able to conclude, with good reason, that some seriously shabby instruction was taking place. At the other end of the quality yardstick—the good end—we might observe a teacher who is carrying out a galaxy of diverse, research-supported instructional practices in a classroom where well-behaved students are clearly engaged in what is taking place and, when asked by the teacher, actively participate in a series of cleverly devised learning activities. This second "does it all perfectly" teacher is likely to be regarded as successful based on just about any evaluative factors we might choose when judging instructional quality. But, with the possible exception of such spectacularly wonderful or spectacularly woeful teachers, we really can't tell by *watching* how successful a teacher is. The vast majority of teachers are neither phenomenally fabulous nor flat-out flops; they're somewhere in the middle. Accordingly, in the vast majority of instances we really need to evaluate a teacher's instruction according to its *consequences*—that is, by determining its effect on students' learning.

To properly evaluate a teacher's instruction, we should employ a rather traditional ends-means model. Using such a time-honored paradigm, the curricular aims sought by a teacher represent the teacher's intended *ends,* whereas what the teacher does in an effort to achieve those ends constitutes the teacher's instructional *means*. When we assess students at the close of an instructional sequence, therefore, we are attempting to determine whether the teacher's instructional means have, indeed, promoted students' attainment of the curricular ends being sought by the teacher.

For years, empirical evidence has shown conclusively that there is no "one best way" to teach something. The instructional procedures used marvelously by a particular teacher in a particular setting with a particular set of students might turn out to be thoroughly ineffectual in the hands of another teacher in a different setting with a dissimilar set of students. Put simply, for almost all teachers, the only way to evaluate instruction accurately is to determine what happens to students as a consequence of the teacher's instruction. And this is where assessment evidence comes bounding onto the scene, *for it is only by using assessment evidence that we can tell what was taught has actually been learned.* Assessment evidence, therefore, helps us arrive at accurate evaluations of a teacher's success, whether this evidence is used as part of a teacher's own self-evaluation or in connection with an externally imposed evaluation of teachers.

If a teacher's instructional success is going to be evaluated on the basis of students' learning, then what evidence of students' learning ought to be employed to arrive at such an evaluation? Well, there are two prominent kinds of assessment evidence that should, if at all possible, be included in any sort of instructional-evaluation sweepstakes. First off, evidence of students' learning that is collected via *classroom assessments* is clearly one source of assessment data to be considered. Second, if a teacher's students are required to complete one or more *external accountability tests*, then students' performances on such tests should definitely be used in the evaluation of instruction.

In a moment, we'll look at ways of collecting both of these kinds of evidence, but please realize that not all results of classroom assessments *or* accountability tests should be treated equally. You tussled with a number of test-development and test-refinement ideas that, clearly, bear on the quality of the data collected by the use of teacher-made classroom assessments. Obviously, there is a profound difference in the persuasiveness of students' test results depending on the caliber of the tests themselves. For instance, let's assume that a teacher's classroom tests assess students' mastery of a set of several genuinely high-level cognitive skills, and those tests do so by using a collection of items that assiduously follow a variety of item guidelines. Students' performances on such a well-built test ought to play a prominent role in evaluation of instructional activities. On the other hand, let's assume that a teacher's classroom test not only measures a collection of trifling curricular aims, but does so with items that reek of wretchedness. In short, this second fictional test measures unimportant stuff and measures it badly. Clearly, students' performances on this second test should be given little if any importance when evaluating a teacher's instruction.

A second source of assessment evidence we should employ to evaluate instructional quality occurs when external achievement tests are used as part of a governmentally required accountability program. Obviously, a teacher has far less influence over the makeup of such tests—in contrast to the teacher's own classroom assessments. But external accountability tests, such as the annual exams administered in accord with a statutorily required accountability program, also vary dramatically in quality. As you will see later in the chapter, many of the accountability tests now being used in the United States are seriously flawed from an evaluative perspective, and thus should really not be employed to evaluate instructional quality. So, just as we saw with the evidence collected by teacher-made tests, the appropriateness of evidence provided by external accountability tests also can vary considerably. It is a mistake to automatically regard external accountability tests as trustworthy merely because they take more time to create and are more expensive to develop than teacher-made tests.

Okay, so when we set out to evaluate instructional quality, two potentially useful kinds of evidence to be considered are students' performances on (1) classroom assessments and (2) external accountability tests. As already noted, because both of these two categories of tests can vary in their quality, caution is clearly warranted when using students' performances on either type of test.

But there's one additional factor to consider when teachers evaluate their instruction, and it's an important one that should be considered every time an instructional evaluation takes place. That additional factor consists of the *unintended side effects of instruction*. With test results, whether from classroom assessments or external accountability exams, teachers have at least a general idea of what's to be assessed, hence they can usually engage in instructional activities aimed at improving students' test performances. But what happens if, although the teacher has not planned on it, some significant side effects on the teacher's students are seen as a consequence of instruction? Shouldn't these side effects be taken into consideration in the evaluation of instruction? Of course they should.

To illustrate, let's say a middle school mathematics teacher has done a simply spectacular job in getting her students to perform well on a series of exams she personally constructed, and she's even seen dramatic increases in her students' performances on the state's annual mathematics assessments. So, clearly, students' scores have soared on both kinds of assessments we have been considering as potential evidence for the evaluation of instruction. Unfortunately, what also happened in this teacher's math classes is that almost all of the students acquired seriously negative attitudes toward math, some of the students claiming privately that they "would never take another math class voluntarily." So, despite the teacher's test-based evidence of success—seen on both classroom tests and statewide accountability tests—a serious side effect seems to have soured this teacher's instructional soufflé. If a math teacher's instruction makes students abhor mathematics, then this constitutes a significant side effect to be taken into consideration when evaluating the teacher. Unanticipated side effects, both negative and positive, should *always* be considered when evaluating instructional quality.

But how, you might be asking, does a teacher identify the side effects of a completed instructional sequence? Well, that task is a truly tough one. As a teacher, what you most need to do is *be on the lookout for any consequences of instruction that you had not foreseen.* You might, as you near the close of an instructional sequence, ask a colleague to help you think about such a question. You might also try to poll your students with anonymous self-. But the chief thing is for you to be *looking for* such unanticipated side effects, and never regard a set of instructional activities as having been properly evaluated without raising the possibility that some unforeseen positive or negative effects might have taken place because of the instruction.

The evidence a teacher uses regarding unforeseen side effects might be collected by fairly traditional data-gathering approaches, or more innovative assessment ploys could be used. And in some cases, side effects will be found without any reliance at all on assessment devices. For example, let's think of a sixth-grade teacher whose hyperdemanding and stressful style, when used with recently arrived immigrant children, apparently leads to massive dropouts on the part of those children. (Fully half of those children have already left school during the current school year.) The evidence of such an adverse side effect might not be collected by using any sort of typical or even innovative assessment tactics. Instead, the school's attendance office might be the source of such information. For identifying side effects, all legitimate sources of information are fair game.

Summarizing, then, to evaluate the quality of your instruction, I encourage you to structure your evaluative strategy around the following three factors:

1. Assessment evidence collected via classroom assessments
2. Assessment evidence collected via accountability tests
3. Evidence pertaining to any positive or negative side effects

As noted before, the quality of the assessment devices used is critical when we set out to appraise instructional quality. Good assessments—ones that measure worthwhile things—typically provide good evaluative evidence. The opposite is also true. We've already taken a look at how teachers can devise appropriate classroom assessments. In the remainder of this chapter, we will be giving serious consideration to external accountability tests because those kinds of tests are currently being used to supply the dominant evidence regarding most teachers' instructional success. But before leaving the evidence available from classroom assessments, let's take a brief look at *how* a teacher can use classroom assessments to collect evaluative evidence regarding the teacher's instructional success.

■ Classroom Assessment Evidence

Most teachers realize that if they collect assessment evidence from their students only *after* instruction is over, they won't be able to determine the effectiveness of the instruction they're trying to evaluate. After all, students might have known already—before any instruction took place—what the teacher was setting out to teach. Thus, whether evidence is being collected for teachers' self-evaluation or for external teacher evaluation, some sort of *pretest versus posttest* data-gathering model is usually employed. Let's consider two such models, both of which can make a contribution to teachers' efforts to evaluate the quality of their instruction.

Pretests versus Posttests

Whether for self-evaluation or external evaluation, the classic pretest-posttest model presented in Figure 1 will prove serviceable for gauging instructional impact. If you assess your students prior to teaching them, then assess your students after you've taught them, any difference between their pretest and posttest performances ought to be chiefly attributable to what went on in between—your teaching.

figure 1 ■ A Classic Pretest versus Posttest Model for Determining Instructional Impact

Certain problems are associated with the classic pretest-posttest scheme for discerning instructional impact, of course, but as a general paradigm for figuring out whether your instruction is making any dents in your students, the approach represented in Figure 1 isn't all that bad. One of the difficulties with the pretest-posttest model you need to watch out for is the possibility the pretest will be *reactive*; that is, it will sensitize your students to "what's important" so they behave atypically when being taught about what was on the pretest. In other words, the effects measured by the posttest will really be a function of your instruction *plus* the pretest. However, if the posttest results for Topic X truly turn out to be what you want when you use a reactive pretest, then you might decide to toss in a pretest every time you teach Topic X.

For purposes of external evaluation, such as when you are being evaluated by school district officials for purposes of continued employment, there's a really difficult problem to consider, and this is the extent to which pretest-to-posttest assessment results for students will be influenced by the caliber of the students you happen to be teaching. If you're teaching a ninth-grade geography class and have been blessed with a group of bright, motivated, and well-informed students, it is certain the pretest-to-posttest gains you obtain will be quite different from the gains you might see if you were teaching a collection of dull, unmotivated students whose conception of geography stops at the boundaries of the schoolyard.

It is imperative, however, that those who use student-assessment data for purposes of external teacher evaluation do so in the context of the situation in which the teacher teaches—the most important feature of which is the specific students being taught. For your own self-evaluation purposes, there's somewhat less need to get caught up with the "dissimilar students" problem. After all, you'll know your own students and will be able to judge whether you have a group of fast-thinking wizards whose pretest-to-posttest gains will be astounding or a group of slow-thinking students whose progress will be substantially less electrifying.

To the extent you're using gain scores (that is, posttest-minus-pretest scores), you should be aware of another technical problem likely to get in your way. If your students do *very* well on the pretest, it's more difficult for them to show gains than if they'd scored lower prior to instruction. When students score very high on tests, they tend to "top out" because of what is called a *ceiling effect*. Sometimes, in fact, if your students score really poorly on a pretest, they'll be likely to score higher on the posttest *by chance alone*. (If you want to intimidate your colleagues during faculty meetings, this is called a *regression effect*, wherein extremely low-scoring (or high-scoring) students tend to regress toward the mean when retested. By casually asserting your "students' progress, of course, might be attributable to a regression effect," you'll surely awe a few of your fellow teachers.)

There's another potential way of dealing with the difficulties of a simple pretest-versus-posttest evaluation design, and that's to use different but *equidifficult* tests. The only problem with this solution is it's almost impossible for busy classroom teachers to create two truly equidifficult forms of a test. So, if the form used as a posttest is easier than its pretest counterpart, the teacher's instruction might look terrific, but students' high posttest performances could be caused chiefly by the softer posttest. Or, worse, if the posttest form is tons tougher than the pretest form, then a pretest-to-posttest comparison might suggest that the impact of the teacher's instruction has been to make students "unlearn" what they knew when they took the pretest. No, two test forms, even if they are intended to be equidifficult, won't save the day.

The Split-and-Switch Design

There is a simple modification of the classic pretest-posttest design that will work for you if you have a reasonably large class of, say, 25 or more students. It's called the *split-and-switch design*, and here's how it works.

First, you need two forms of the test you're going to use as a pretest and as a posttest. The two forms ought to be *somewhat similar* in degree of difficulty, but need not be equidifficult or all that close to it. Let's call the two forms Test 1 and Test 2.

Second, you *split* your class into two roughly equal *half-class* groups, perhaps by counting half-way down your class roster so all students whose last names start with the letters A through L are in Half-Class A, and all students whose last names start with the letters M through Z are in Half-Class B.

Next, you administer one of the two forms to each half-class, but ask students *not* to date their test forms. Ideally, in fact, students should write their names only on the *back* of their completed tests. You should then *code* the two sets of pretests (Test 1 and Test 2) so you can tell they are pretests. You can even use the pretest to help you plan your instruction. But you should not score, or write on, the pretests (on the actual test forms) at this time.

Then you should instruct all your students for as long as you have allowed for the instruction. Suppose, for example, you were trying to teach your students how to write an effective narrative essay. This might take several months or even a full school year. Let's say, however, you devote one full semester to the teaching of this skill.

At the end of instruction, you then *switch* your two half-classes so if Half-Class A took Test 1 as a pretest, it now takes Test 2 as a posttest. Similarly, if Half-Class B received Test 2 as a pretest, at the end of instruction it will receive Test 1 as a posttest.

You then *code* the posttests so *you* can distinguish them, after consulting the codes, from the pretests. You next *mix* together all the copies of Test 1 (both pretests and posttests). You do the same with Test 2.

Next, you, colleagues, or even parents judge the quality of the mixed-together Test 1s. That is, the tests are subjected to **blind-scoring**. The same is then done for the mixed-together Test 2s. *After* all scoring has been done, the codes are consulted so the blind-scored papers are separated into pretests and posttests.

This data-gathering model, one I've called the *split-and-switch design,* provides you with *two* indications of whether your instruction promoted posttest improvement—that is, the pretest-to-posttest changes for Test 1 as well as those for Test 2.

Because the pretest and posttest comparisons are made using the *very same test,* there is clearly no problem caused by differential test difficulty. Moreover, because your students will not have previously seen the posttest they receive, the reactive impact of the pretesting is minimized.

In essence, you have taken two 50-percent samples of your class, at both pretest time and posttest time, to help you determine whether students have made the progress you wish. The split-and-switch design, of course, becomes less accurate as class sizes get smaller, but it does help you dodge some of the more troublesome aspects of the simple pretest-versus-posttest data-gathering model. The evidence this atypical data-gathering design provides can be particularly compelling if you secure *nonpartisans* (such as parents) to supply the blind-scoring.

The split-and-switch design is depicted graphically in Figure 2. If you are not sure yet in how it is supposed to function, please consider the Figure 2 diagram until you see what happens when. Note the appropriate comparisons, and there will be *two,* are signified by the colored arrows.

Teachers can use pretest results to guide their instructional decision-making. And they can use posttest results to assign grades (remembering to make allowances for test forms of differing difficulties). But, of course, no permanent marks should be made on any tests until after they've been mixed together and blind-scored.

The split-and-switch design should be used for determining students' achievement of only a relatively small number of particularly significant cognitive

figure 2 ■ A Split-and-Switch Data-Gathering Design

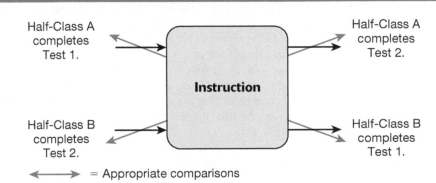

Half-Class A completes Test 1.

Half-Class B completes Test 2.

Instruction

Half-Class A completes Test 2.

Half-Class B completes Test 1.

◄——————► = Appropriate comparisons

outcomes—for instance, a handful of curricular aims calling for students' attainment of truly high-level cognitive skills. If this data-gathering design is overused, students will soon realize that their future "posttest" will be the "pretest" taken by half of their classmates prior to instruction. As a consequence of this realization, some students will start finding out from classmates what they remembered about the "other pretest." However, for measuring students' mastery of a few genuinely significant curricular outcomes, especially when nonpartisan scorers have been employed to judge students' constructed responses, this data-gathering design can provide powerful evaluative data that will be seen as credible even when used as part of an external evaluation of a teacher's effectiveness.

Decision Time

To Buttress or Not to Buttress?

Madeline teaches fifth-graders in an inner-city school. In recent years, her school's students have performed poorly on the state's annual accountability tests. Madeline's principal, Mr. Jenkins, is convinced that the state accountability test is little more than a measure of students' socioeconomic status, and that students' scores on the test definitely do not accurately reflect the instructional success of his school's teachers.

Accordingly, Mr. Jenkins recently issued an invitation to all the school's teachers to evaluate their ability to promote their students' mastery of a high-level cognitive skill in any subject area by collecting pretest-to-posttest evidence regarding whether their instruction was, in fact, successful. The purpose of this activity is to supply evidence to buttress students' scores on the annual accountability test—and to "show the community that our teachers are doing a good job." Mr. Jenkins asks all volunteers to pursue a cognitive skill requiring students to generate their own responses on the pretests and posttests. The instruction should take at least two months to complete, and the collected pretests and posttests would be coded, then mixed together so scorers could not tell whether a student's response was written prior to or following instruction. The test responses would be blind-scored by parent volunteers, then separated into pretest and posttest groups after the blind-scoring had been completed. Mr. Jenkins plans to summarize the results from all participating teachers, prepare a brief report, then send that report to all of the school's parents.

Madeline realizes that if the pretest-to-posttest results are positive, this would surely have a positive impact on parents' perceptions of the faculty's effectiveness. However, if the results are not positive, then this evidence would confirm the view, based on the annual state tests, that the school's staff is not very effective. She must let Mr. Jenkins know by the end of the week whether she will be a volunteer in this proposed activity.

 If you were Madeline, what would your decision be?

What to Assess

Whether you use your students' assessment results yourself for the self-evaluation of your teaching or, in contrast, supply those results to others who will use such evidence for an external evaluation, you still have to decide what to assess. Remember the key factor governing what you should assess in your classroom is always the educational decision(s) you need to make. For purposes of your self-evaluation, you'll have to think through for yourself what kinds of evidence you'll need in order to tinker with or to fundamentally overhaul your instructional activities. Surely you'll want to know how well your students have learned the most important things they were supposed to learn.

You should also seriously consider the assessment of students' *affect*. Affective assessment is of little utility for decisions about individual students because such measurement is too imprecise for defensible inferences about particular students. However, for judging the effectiveness of your instructional efforts, group-based inferences about students' pretest-to-posttest shifts in affect are useful. The split-and-switch design, incidentally, works wonderfully when affective data are being gathered because it minimizes pretest reactivity.

If a classroom teacher is stuck with a small class (tough luck!), so small that a split-and-switch design wouldn't work, then I recommend the straight-out pretest-posttest model with all its problems. You can still use blind-scoring of coded pretests and posttests after having mixed them together. And you can also round up one or more nonpartisan scorers. Such pretest-to-posttest evidence is surely way better than none.

In sum, students' performances on classroom assessments are clearly important when teachers evaluate themselves or when others evaluate teachers. Although there are several important sources of evidence to be used in appraising a teacher's instructional efforts, what happens to students as a consequence of instruction is, unarguably, the most significant source of evidence.

■ Evidence from External Accountability Tests

"If we're going to evaluate teachers, why don't we simply do so by seeing what their students have learned—as shown by those students' scores on significant achievement tests?" This statement, or statements similar to it, can often be heard these days as part of an ever-rising chorus demanding that teachers be evaluated chiefly on the basis of their students' test scores. And the test scores referred to in these entreaties for test-determined teacher evaluation are, almost always, the scores earned by students on externally imposed, standardized accountability tests—not scores on teachers' home-grown classroom tests. This is because most proponents of such an approach to teacher evaluation fear that *teacher-made* classroom tests, if employed to evaluate teachers, will often be softened in a self-slanted manner so that many teachers will appear to be more effective than, in fact, they truly are.

Thus, in the last few years we have seen an enormous increase in the clamor for *test-based teacher evaluation*—that is, teacher appraisals in which the dominant (but not the only) determiner of a teacher's quality is the performance of a particular teacher's students on an externally imposed standardized achievement test. Typically, the tests selected for this purpose are the annual accountability tests that have been administered each year for well over a decade in all of our 50 states. Those state-level accountability tests were required by federal law, especially by recent reauthorizations of the Elementary and Secondary Education Act of 1965. To appraise the teachers in a particular state's schools, these annual accountability tests were often the only available standardized test that appeared to be up to this sort of evaluative task.

In the near future, as mentioned earlier, the anticipated availability of accountability exams generated by two multistate, federally funded consortia is likely to present an attractive alternative for advocates of test-based teacher evaluation. If those two sets of consortium-built assessments become widely available, as planned, during the 2014–15 school year, then the advocates of test-based teacher evaluation can point to a collection of carefully constructed educational assessments that can be used to measure students' achievement status.

It should be noted, however, that the assessments being built by the PARCC and SBAC assessment consortia will be focused on measuring students' mastery of the Common Core State Standards chiefly in mathematics and English/language arts (ELA). Many teachers, of course, are responsible for instruction not addressed by the consortium-built tests (for example, K–2 teachers as well as teachers of the arts, physical education, and various other subjects). Clearly, then, if test-based teacher evaluation is to become widespread in the United States, provisions must be made for supplying suitable measures of students taught by *all* teachers, not only teachers of math and ELA.

The demand for increasingly rigorous teacher evaluation has surely been spurred in part by dissatisfaction on the part of some observers with what they regard as a less than lustrous performance by our nation's public schools. More and more taxpayers are registering dismay with what they regard as the inadequate quality of America's tax-supported schools. This dissatisfaction has often morphed into a straightforward call for teachers to be more stringently appraised, and for the bulk of that appraisal to be determined by the performances of teachers' students on external accountability tests.

Two federal initiatives in 2009 (the Race to the Top Program) and 2011 (the ESEA Flexibility Program) functioned as powerful catalysts for states to overhaul their often dated teacher-evaluation systems. One of those programs, Race to the Top, provided substantial fiscal incentives for those states awarded federal grants from a program funded at $4.35 billion. The other program, the one focused on ESEA flexibility, permitted states to secure a waiver that exempted a state from satisfying certain conditions of NCLB. The Race to the Top Program, therefore, employed a "carrot" while the ESEA Flexibility Program relied on a "stick." To qualify for *either* of these programs, a state's educational officials were required to install a teacher-evaluation system in which teachers must be evaluated using multiple sources of evidence. In that array of evidence, federal officials insisted that student growth must be "a significant factor." These federal initiatives have sparked what most observers regard as an unprecedented re-look at how the nation evaluates its teachers. Clearly, test-based teacher evaluation satisfies the requirement that student growth will be a significant consideration in the appraisal of teachers. I have treated this issue more extensively elsewhere (Popham, 2013).

Following is a four-point logic chain underlying the argument in favor of test-based teacher evaluation.

- *Point 1.* Teachers should be evaluated carefully so that (a) effective teachers can be rewarded and (b) ineffective teachers can either be helped to improve or, if improvement does not transpire, fired.
- *Point 2.* In evaluating a teacher's success, the most important factor must be the depth, breadth, and quality of students' learning that takes place because of instruction provided by the teacher.
- *Point 3.* The depth, breadth, and quality of student learning will best be represented by students' performances on carefully created, externally determined, and properly administered achievement tests.
- *Point 4.* Therefore, the scores of a teacher's students on externally administered exams, such as a state's annual accountability tests, should be the dominant determiner of a particular teacher's evaluated success.

If the foregoing logic chain is to be implemented properly, however, a pivotal requirement is that the tests on which such a teacher-evaluation system is based must be unarguably suitable for this significant evaluative task. In other words, in order for Point 3 to be satisfied, the "carefully created, externally determined, and properly administered" tests must be capable of accurately differentiating between well-taught and badly taught students. When such exams are "carefully created," those who are developing the exams must do their best to make sure the exams can correctly detect the depth, breadth, and quality of student learning. This is easier to say than it is to do. What is imperative, if test-based teacher evaluation is going to work properly, is that the tests being used are sensitive to the *quality of instruction* provided by the particular teacher who is being evaluated.

Instructional Sensitivity

Children learn, thank goodness. But this learning takes place both inside a school and outside of it. Students learn at home from interactions with family members. Students learn at the park or at a shopping mall. Students learn from watching television programs, even reality shows. Students learn darn near everywhere. And

Comparative Estimates of Progress: Student Growth Percentiles

In 2002, when the No Child Left Behind Act (NCLB) first frolicked into American educators' lives, we learned that our schools would soon be seen as unsuccessful unless ever-increasing proportions of students' annual test scores represented "adequate yearly progress" (AYP). The term AYP was defined as the percent of students—overall as well as for students in NCLB-designated subgroups—who were test-classified as "proficient" or "advanced."

But, because NCLB's minimum proportions of AYP proficient-and-above students were federally stipulated, and those proportions became more and more stringent as time went by, many school leaders began to chaff under these required AYP minima. Such educators were dismayed because, although their students may have been displaying substantial improvements in how well they were learning, those increases might not be sufficient to push a school's students over the AYP-required proportions of students who needed to score at proficient or advanced levels on a state's annual accountability tests.

Accordingly, a widespread clamor from the field was heard for schools to be evaluated, at least in part, according to *how much growth* a school's students had displayed—even though this growth might not be enough to reach a given year's AYP targets. For the past several years, therefore, various approaches to the determination of a school's test-based growth have been introduced. Of these, the most widely accepted model has been the system devised by Betebenner (2007). Often referred to as the "Colorado Growth Model" for it was first used on a statewide basis in Colorado, Betebenner's approach has also been adopted by several other states. Because today's teachers are apt to encounter colleagues who approve or disapprove of such growth-focused approaches, a brief description of this increasingly popular model seems in order.

The Colorado Growth Model is predicated on a particular numerical quantity representing an individual student's comparative progress in one school year. This quantity, the heart of Betebenner's approach, is called a *student growth percentile*.

Student growth percentiles are really straightforward to understand, and here's how they work. First off, students who scored at a given point on the *previous* end-of-school-year accountability test (Year 1) are identified. Let's say we're looking at students who earned a scale score of 214 when 300 scale-score points are available. Then, in the next year (Year 2), using those same students (Year 1's 214-scorers), we employ their Year 2 scores to compute how much gain (that is, growth) each student made from the first year to the second year. The amount of gain students make from Year 1 to Year 2, however, is *not* reported according to how many scale-score points those students advanced (or retreated) but, instead, is reported as a *student growth percentile*. On such a percentile scale, students at the 95th percentile have made as much growth as 95 percent of students in the state whose Year 1 scores were 214. Similarly, students at the 40th growth percentile have made as much growth as 40 percent of the state's students with a Year 1 score of 214.

Student growth percentiles, however, are calculated for students with Year 1 scores at *all* points on the score scale. Thus, there is a set of student growth percentiles computed for students with a Year 1 score of 212, another set of student growth percentiles for students with Year 1 scores of 213, and so on—across all Year 1 scores at which students have scored in sufficient numbers to calculate student growth percentiles.

We can calculate a particular teacher's *average* student growth percentile (Betebenner recommends that we use the median, rather than the mean, as this average) based on the performances of that teacher's students on the Year 2 accountability test. But because a given teacher's students will have earned Year 1 scores all over the lot, we base a particular teacher's median student growth percentile on the complete collection of student growth percentiles earned by all the teacher's students. Similarly, such an amalgam median growth percentile could be calculated for all students in an entire school or for the students at a particular grade in that school. The interpretation most often made when a school's (or a teacher's) average student growth percentile is above the 50th percentile is that the school (or the teacher) promoted better than average growth among students. Conversely, an average student growth percentile below the 50th percentile would indicate that whatever growth had been promoted among students, it was below average.

Statistical adjustments can be made in this approach to compensate for the real-world problem that some teachers (and some schools) end up serving very high-achieving students who actually have little room to grow on tests. This is because they are already bumping up against a ceiling effect due to a test's limited difficulty. At the other end of the achievement spectrum, teachers (and schools) dealing with very low-achieving students are working with students who have much more room to grow—because they have scored so dismally on the previous year's tests. Thus, in a sense it may sometimes be "statistically easier" for teachers who instruct particularly low-achieving students to demonstrate that their students have grown during a school year.

If you've never encountered the concept of student growth percentiles, it may take you a bit of time to grasp how they work. Fortunately, these quantities are fairly easy to explain to parents and policymakers. As a way of representing how well a teacher's students perform in a given school year—relative to other students who entered the school year with comparable achievement levels—student growth percentiles, when abetted by an example or two, are intuitively comprehensible to most people.

To the degree that the architects of an accountability program wish to incorporate a legitimate representation of the degree to which students have grown in their mastery of what was to be learned, Betebenner's approach incorporating student growth percentiles is definitely worth considering.

aren't we happy that they do! But when we tie the evaluation of a teacher to students' performances on tests supposedly measuring what students *have learned in school,* we must be reasonably certain that the tests being employed do, in fact, measure what a particular teacher has taught those students. In other words, we need to make certain that any test used to evaluate a teacher's competence can accurately gauge students' mastery of what has been taught. We need, in fact, to ascertain the ***instructional sensitivity*** of a test. Here's what this concept, a remarkably important one when we set out to evaluate teachers or schools, involves:

> *Instructional sensitivity is the degree to which students' performances on a test accurately reflect the quality of instruction specifically provided to promote students' mastery of what is being assessed.*

Notice in the definition of instructional sensitivity that the focus is on *instructional quality*—that is, the caliber of instruction that's directed toward students' achievement of whatever is being measured by a test. An instructionally sensitive test, therefore, would be one that can accurately distinguish between effectively taught and ineffectively taught students. Instructional sensitivity of a test, however, is not an either/or variable. A test need not be *completely* insensitive or *completely* sensitive to instruction. Tests can vary in the degree to which, based on students' performances, they can properly distinguish between students who have been taught splendidly and those who have been taught shabbily.

The push for test-based teacher evaluation comes from a variety of quarters, but sometimes even the most ardent advocates of this evaluative strategy fail to recognize a potential problem with this approach—namely, that if the tests being used for such evaluations do *not* do a good job in distinguishing between successfully and unsuccessfully taught students, then test-based teacher evaluation simply can't work. To illustrate, suppose that a state's education officials have created brand new accountability tests for the specific purpose of evaluating teachers' skills. More specifically, the new tests are to be used so see how well individual teachers have done in promoting their students' mathematics and reading achievements. Further, suppose that the new tests were built by following fairly traditional test-construction practices, and that students' performances on the newly developed accountability tests turn out to be closely linked to the socioeconomic status (SES) of students' families. In other words, when the tests are administered, students from more affluent families almost invariably outperform students from less affluent families—*no matter how effectively those students have been taught.* In other words, SES-status invariably trumps teachers' skills because of the SES-linked nature of the test. Given those circumstances, genuinely skilled teachers in schools serving low-SES kids would often be seen as ineffective (because of their students' weak performances on the new SES-linked accountability tests) while genuinely weak teachers in schools serving high-SES kids would be seen as effective (because of their students' strong performances on the new SES-linked accountability tests).

In such a fictitious scenario, inaccurate decisions would often be made about many teachers' skills, and the ultimate losers in such a situation would be the students themselves. Truly strong teachers might be bounced out of the profession, and truly weak teachers might be retained or even applauded. It is to prevent these sorts of errors, and their subsequent impact on students' educations, that any tests used in test-based teacher evaluation should be accompanied by compelling evidence they are, in truth, instructionally sensitive. (And, by the way, in many states during recent years this "fictitious scenario" is not fictitious at all.)

The Genesis of Instructional Insensitivity

How do educational achievement tests, especially those that are carefully developed by reputable test-development organizations, become instructionally insensitive? Is this some sort of plot, perpetrated by assessment agencies, to subvert the test-based evaluation of the nation's schools and teachers? No, there's no discernible malevolence on the part of those who crank out the standardized achievement tests we have historically used in our schools. Rather, the cause underlying today's instructionally insensitive tests flows from a traditional, long-standing manner in which U.S. psychometricians have viewed the tests they have built and polished. The traditional mission of U.S. educational achievement tests, you see, has been to produce results leading to accurate score-based *comparisons* among test-takers. Indeed, almost a century of large-scale educational testing in the United States has revolved around the creation of comparative score-interpretations. And, giving credit where it is due, educational psychometricians have become darn good at providing such comparative score-interpretations. We can usually do a pretty decent job of determining that Millie's reading scores put her at the 84th percentile whereas Althea's reading scores are only at the 63rd percentile. Conceding that educational tests scores are not as precisely accurate as most people think, it is frequently useful to educators to find out how students compare to one another.

Much of the impetus for the generation of comparative score-interpretations can be traced back to World War I (not World War II) when the United States, having become involved in an unprecedented world conflict, found itself in need of a way to identify young men who would be successful in the Army's officer-training programs. Army officials approached the American Psychological Association (APA) for assistance in developing a suitable screening tool, and soon a committee of APA appointees met at Vineland Training School in Vineland, New Jersey, to develop the *Army Alpha,* a group-administrable intelligence test that presented verbal and quantitative problems to examinees in an effort to get a fix on new Army recruits' intellectual aptitudes. The *Alpha* was administered to about 1,750,000 Army recruits during World War I, and it was regarded as a major success because it allowed test-takers' to be *compared.* The highest-scoring recruits were placed in officer-training programs, and their success in those programs substantially exceeded the success rates of pre-*Alpha* placement efforts. The *Army Alpha* was most certainly an *aptitude test,* for its intent was to locate those Army recruits who had the most cognitive aptitude to succeed in the Army's officer-training programs. Interestingly, however, the comparative assessment strategy employed in the *Alpha*'s aptitude test soon became the prototype for a range of educational assessments—not all of which were focused on the measurement of test-takers' aptitudes.

For example, as soon as World War I was over, several assessment firms in the United States began to create educational *achievement* tests using the psychometric approach embodied in the *Alpha*. To illustrate, the *Stanford Achievement Tests,* a widely used set of nationally standardized achievement tests that have been revised almost a dozen times, were first published in 1923, shortly after the close of World War I. And, although the Stanford Achievement Tests were *achievement* rather than *aptitude* tests, they nevertheless cleaved closely to the comparison-oriented mission of the *Army Alpha*. Indeed, for almost 100 years, the psychometric community in the United States has been committed to the creation of tests intended to yield comparative score-interpretations for test-takers.

One key tenet of assessments intended to yield comparative score-interpretations is that they produce sufficient *score-spread*—that is, differences among test-takers' total scores so that those scores can be meaningfully contrasted with scores earned by other test-takers. For example, other things being equal, for tests intended to provide comparative score-interpretations, it would be better to have a test's items answered correctly by roughly half of the test-takers than for items to be answered correctly by 100 percent of the test-takers or answered incorrectly by 100 percent of the test-takers. Items answered by all or none of those taking a test make no contribution whatsoever to creating the kind of score-spread that contributes to accurate, fine-grained comparisons of test-takers' scores.

Over the years, traditional psychometricans have frequently enhanced an educational test's score-spread by linking its items to socioeconomic status or to students' inherited academic aptitudes. Both SES and inherited academic aptitudes tend to be nicely spread out variables, and they're also variables that are not readily altered. Thus, if an item on an educational test can be linked to either SES or inherited academic aptitude, then this item is likely to produce the kind of score-spread that brings joy to a traditional psychometrician's heart. Let' look briefly at both of these kinds of items.

SES-Linked Items A particularly troubling kind of item on standardized achievement tests chiefly assesses what students have learned outside of school. Unfortunately, you'll find more of these items on standardized achievement tests than you'd expect. If children come from affluent families, then those children are more apt to succeed on certain items contained in standardized achievement tests than will other children whose environments don't mesh as well with what the items measure. Hopefully, the item in Figure 3 will illustrate what's actually being assessed by a number of the items on standardized achievement tests.

This fourth-grade reading item asks students to tell from context what the meaning of a multiple-meaning word is. I have no problem with this as a skill children should acquire. But I have a big problem with the item itself.

figure 3 ■ A Fourth-Grade Reading Item

> My uncle's *field* is computer programming.

■ Look at the sentences below. In which sentence does the word *field* mean the same as it does in the boxed sentence above?

   A. The softball pitcher knew how to *field* her position.

   B. They prepared the *field* by spraying and plowing it.

   C. I know the *field* I plan to enter when I finish college.

   D. The doctor used a wall chart to examine my *field* of vision.

Notice the fourth-grader's task is to figure out how the word *field* is being used in the item's item. And, of course, answer Option C is correct. But please recognize that parents who are physicians, attorneys, or journalists do, indeed, have a *field*. If a child's parents, however, work in a car wash or as a cashier in a convenience store, the child's parents will rarely, if ever, refer to their *field* of employment.

Those parents have *jobs*. Clearly, kids from affluent families in which one or more parents are professionals will be more likely to do well on Figure 3's reading item than will kids whose parents are employed in menial jobs. This item is clearly linked to children's socioeconomic status.

Suppose you're a teacher at a school in which most students come from a genuinely low socioeconomic environment. How are your students likely to perform on a standardized achievement test if a substantial number of the test's items are linked to the affluence of your students' backgrounds? In other words, how will your students do if many of the test's items are SES-influenced? That's right, your students are not apt to earn very high scores. Does this mean your school's teachers are doing a poor instructional job? Of course not.

Conversely, let's imagine you're a teacher in an affluent school whose students tend to be the offspring of upper-class, well-educated parents. Each spring, your students' scores on standardized achievement tests are dazzlingly high. Does this mean your school's teachers are doing a superb instructional job? Of course not.

One of the chief reasons children's SES is so highly correlated with standardized test scores is that there are a number of items on standardized achievement tests really focused on assessing knowledge and skills learned outside of school. Most of such knowledge and skills are more likely to be learned in higher-level SES settings than in lower-level SES settings.

Again, you might ask, Why would developers of nationally standardized achievement tests place such items on their tests? As usual, the answer is consistent with the dominant measurement mission of those tests—namely, to spread out students' test scores so that accurate and fine-grained comparative (norm-referenced) interpretations can be made. Because there is substantial variation in children's socioeconomic strata, and this variation doesn't evaporate overnight, items reflecting such variation are efficient in producing the traditional psychometrician's much-cherished spread in test scores.

Items Linked to Inherited Academic Aptitudes   We turn now to another kind of item favored by traditional psychometricians in their quest for sufficient score-spread in their tests—that is, items linked to the *inherited* academic aptitudes of students. That's right, items hooked up to how lucky a student happened to be from birth.

I wish I believed all children were born with identical intellectual abilities, but I don't. Some kids were luckier at gene-pool time. Some children, from birth, will find it easier to mess around with mathematics than will others. If children came into the world having inherited identical academic aptitudes, teachers' pedagogical problems would be far more simple.

Current thinking among many leading educators suggests there are various forms of intelligence, not just one (Gardner, 1994). A child who is born with less aptitude for dealing with quantitative or verbal tasks, therefore, might possess greater "interpersonal" or "intrapersonal" intelligence, but these two abilities are not tested by conventional achievement tests. For the kinds of items most commonly found on nationally standardized achievement tests, children differ in their innate aptitudes, especially their verbal, quantitative, and spatial aptitudes. And some items on nationally standardized achievement tests are linked directly to such *inherited* academic aptitudes.

Consider, for example, the social studies item in Figure 4. This item attempts to measure a sixth-grader's ability to "figure out" what the right answer is. I don't think the item measures what's taught in school. The item—at least in part—measures what students come to school with, not what they learn there.

In Figure 4's item, look carefully at the four answer options. Read each option and see if it might be correct. A verbally advantaged student, I contend, can figure out that Choices A, B, and D really would not "conserve natural resources"

figure 4 ■ A Sixth-Grade Standardized Achievement Test Item in Social Studies

■ If a person truly wants to conserve natural resources, one good way to do so is to:

A. leave the radio turned on even if no one is listening to it.

B. wash tiny loads instead of large loads in an automatic dishwashing machine.

C. write on both sides of a piece of paper.

D. discard used magazines in the trash.

particularly well; hence, Choice C turns out to be the winning option. Verbally adept kids will have a better time with this item than will their less verbal classmates.

You'll find many such "native smarts" items in any of today's nationally standardized achievement tests. The items I find particularly galling are the ones that measure a child's inborn spatial aptitude. To illustrate, one math item in a current fourth-grade standardized achievement test presents four letters to students (such as "F, L, R, and B"), then asks, Which letter, "when bent in half," will have two equal parts? The answer, in case you weren't born with adequate spatial aptitude, is the B. But what kind of a silly skill is involved in mental letter-bending? Yet, many standardized achievement tests contain items that tap the spatial-visualization aptitudes children have obviously inherited because of the gene-pool lottery.

But why, you might be thinking, do developers of nationally standardized tests include such items on their tests? The answer is really quite simple. Remember, these sorts of items, because they are based on nicely spread out innate academic aptitudes not readily modifiable in school, do a wonderful job in spreading out test takers' scores. The quest for score-spread, coupled with the limitation of having only a few items to use in assessing students, makes such items particularly appealing to those who construct traditional standardized achievement tests.

Yet, items that primarily measure differences in students' inborn academic verbal, quantitative, and spatial aptitudes obviously do not contribute to valid inferences about "how well children have been taught." Would we like all children

Parent Talk

Suppose you're a teacher in a large suburban high school whose students score consistently high on almost any kind of statewide or national test they're obliged to take. Indeed, anyone who knows much about your state's schools would be surprised if your school did not score among the top schools on any standardized achievement test. Nonetheless, at a recent Back-to-School Night, one of your students' parents, Mr. Carney, corners you with a barrage of questions about the meaning of these test results. He prefaces his questions with an indication he is pleased with his daughter's test scores, but then says, "Okay, I know our school serves super-affluent families, and I know students' test scores are always high, but I also know that there is some seriously shabby teaching going on here. When my daughter Wendy has her girlfriends come to our place for sleepovers, they level with Wendy's mom and me. They often tell us about really boring classes they have had to sit through. How can the school's test scores be so darn high, and yet have this sort of poor teaching take place?"

 If I were you, here's how I'd respond to Mr. Collins:

"Well, for openers, Mr. Carney, I'd have to say that I've definitely not heard reports of the sort of weak teaching Wendy's friends have described to you. I'm sure that in a school as large as ours, not all teachers are wonderful, but let's assume—just for the sake of discussion—that some less-than-lustrous teaching is going on in the school. What you want to know is how our school's high test scores can be produced by weak teaching.

"Here's how that sort of thing can happen. First off, you need to know that almost all standardized achievement tests are developed in a very traditional way. That is, those tests are intended to provide *comparative* interpretations of different test-takers' scores—so that the students can be compared with one another. To produce the range of different scores needed for such comparisons, many of the items on these tests are closely linked to students' socioeconomic status—in other words, their SES. As you probably know, SES is a variable that's well spread out, and really doesn't change very rapidly. Kids who come from more affluent families will tend to answer SES-linked items correctly, while kids from less affluent families will tend to miss those same items. This gives a school such as ours a tremendous edge when it comes to such tests. Our school's students are likely to score well on SES-linked items no matter how well or how badly they have been taught. That's just what happens.

"If there are many SES-linked items on a standardized achievement test, you can bet that our school's students will always shine. Personally, what I find myself worrying about is how the teachers who teach low-SES kids feel about this. I might have as easily been teaching students from disadvantaged backgrounds. Remember, Wendy attends a school where, to the outside world, teaching seems to be wonderful. But in a low-SES school, students' scores on SES-linked items are, with few exceptions, destined to be low. It's really not fair."

 Now, how would you respond to Wendy's father?

Determining Students' Progress: With Value-Added Models

As part of attempts to isolate the instructional success of particular teachers, or particular schools, considerable attention has been given to an approach known as a *value-added model*, or VAM. This approach represents a statistical strategy aimed at isolating the cause of students' progress—or lack of such progress. The VAM procedures employ students' prior achievement and/or background characteristics as statistical controls to help isolate the effects on student achievement of specific teachers, schools, or school districts. Relying on often exotic statistical gyrations, VAMs try to contrast the effects on students' test scores of (1) *school-unrelated variables* such as family or friends and (2) the *instructional impact* of a given school or teacher.

The very name given to this statistical strategy usually evokes a positive response from people who are interested in getting a fix on the effectiveness of teachers or schools. After all, when we refer to a "value-added" contribution to students' achievement, we typically think of increases in students' learning attributable to educators *above and beyond what might have taken place simply because students grew older*. Accordingly, the "value-added" label generates a fair amount of support—sometimes unthinking support—from educational policymakers and the public in general. Anything that is "value-added" sounds so darn good. But is this widespread support warranted?

The most widely known VAM is the Tennessee Value-Added Assessment System (TVAAS) devised by William Sanders. However, because the statistical machinery of TVAAS is proprietary, and unavailable to public scrutiny, many proponents of VAMs have sought to employ other VAM approaches. Basically, all of these procedures require data tracking students' academic growth across several years, usually in different subjects, to estimate the contributions that teachers have made to this growth.

Increasing numbers of technical reviewers of value-added procedures, however, have identified several serious methodological problems when such strategies are employed to identify teachers' contributions to students' achievement. To illustrate, a significant shortcoming with these approaches is that VAMs produce a statistically massaged *estimate* of a teacher's relative contribution to a particular student's learning. Making causal attributions for these estimates are most defensible when teachers are randomly assigned to classes and when students are randomly assigned to teachers. As we know, however, randomized assignment of teachers and students is rarely encountered in most school districts. Parents frequently influence the schools their children attend and, beyond that, parents often have a serious say in the teachers to which their children are assigned. The less

(Continued)

random is the undergirding of VAM procedures, the less credible will be the causal inferences about teachers' impact that we can base on these approaches.

Moreover, students' academic progress is influenced by a substantial array of variables beyond a teacher's control—for instance, the physical condition of a school, the instructional resources at hand, the quality of a school's administrators, a district's instructional policies, and the degree of parental encouragement of their children's learning. Because these variables often vary systematically across a district's schools, they can substantially erode the accuracy of VAM conclusions.

Another serious shortcoming of most VAMs is that their use is frequently advocated *irrespective* of the suitability of the achievement tests to be used in the analysis. Elsewhere in this chapter , instructionally *insensitive* achievement tests were described. Such tests often contain numerous items linked closely to students' socioeconomic status (SES). These items tend to be answered correctly more often by students from affluent families than by students from impoverished families. Well, if the results of achievement tests being employed in a VAM are highly correlated with test-takers' SES, all the statistical high-jinks in the world will be unable to transform SES-governed test results into data that accurately gauge teachers' instructional effectiveness. Such tests may permit students' scores to be compared—as is the measurement mission of traditional achievement tests. But such tests—even when all their causality implications have been statistically squeezed out of them—can't tell us which teachers are effective.

A final shortcoming of value-added models is that it is nearly impossible to explain to normal human beings how VAMs work. The statistical operations associated with these value-added strategies are often so esoteric that their opacity defies description.

In a highly readable introduction to the topic of VAMs, Braun (2005, p. 4) concludes that "VAM results should *not* be used as the sole or principal basis for making consequential decisions about teachers." He argues that too many mistakes will be made when VAM approaches use the kinds of data typically available from school districts.

Value-added models, although enticingly labeled and enthusiastically touted by their devoteés, are regarded by most nonpartisans as inappropriate for evaluating the quality of educators' endeavors.

to do well on such "inherited aptitudes" items? Of course we would. But to use such items to arrive at a judgment about a teacher's instructional effectiveness or a school's educational success is absurd.

Avoidance of Instructionally Insensitive Items

It is easy to forget that most educational tests are nothing more than a collectivity of items to which students must respond. If the items are good, the test will be good; but if the items are bad, then the test itself will be similarly bad. So, when we are trying to create an instructionally sensitive accountability test, we must be inordinately attentive to the items themselves. If teachers have effectively taught students to master a curricular aim that's being measured by a collection of, say, 6 to 12 items, will the bulk of those items be answered correctly by the teacher's students? And what about a teacher whose instruction focused on the same curricular aim, but produced a less-than-effective instructional effort? For those same 6 to 12 items, what we need to see is that most of the teachers' students come up with incorrect answers.

One way to discern how many instructionally insensitive items there are on an accountability test is to have a group of properly oriented reviewers—usually experienced teachers—consider each item on the test, one at a time, then respond to a review question such as the following:

> Attention reviewers: Please note the specific curricular aim which, according to the test's developers, this item is assessing, and only then answer this question: *If a teacher has provided reasonably effective instruction to promote students' mastery of the specific curricular aim being assessed, is it likely that the bulk of the teacher's students will answer this item correctly?* (Choose one: YES, NO, NOT SURE).

The nature of the orientation provided for any instructional-sensitivity reviewers should focus on the kinds of factors that might render an item instructionally insensitive. Reviewers must be completely conversant with such factors. For example, consider the following six qualities of an item that might cause the item to be instructionally insensitive:

1. *Alignment leniency.* If an item has been too leniently judged to be in alignment with the curricular aim it ostensibly assesses, that alignment is questionable. Teachers will be trying to get their students to master a specified curricular aim, but the test's items will be measuring something else.
2. *Excessive easiness.* If an item is so very easy that completely untaught students would answer it correctly, then the item is apt to be measuring students' achievement of something other than what the teacher was trying to teach.
3. *Excessive difficulty.* If an item is so very difficult that even marvelously taught students might not answer it correctly, then the item can't distinguish between well-taught and poorly taught students.
4. *Item flaws.* If an item has serious deficits such as ambiguities or garbled syntax, these flaws will prevent well-taught students from answering it correctly, thereby making it impossible for the item to accurately distinguish between well-taught and poorly taught students.
5. *Socioeconomic status links.* If an item gives a meaningful advantage to students from higher SES families, then the item will tend to measure what students bring to school rather than how well they are taught once they get there.

6. *Academic aptitude links.* If an item gives a meaningful advantage to students who possess greater inherited quantitative, verbal, or spatial aptitudes, then the item will tend to measure what students arrive with at school instead of how well they are taught.

By establishing item-review committees to scrutinize all under-development items, much as is currently done by bias-review committees, it would be possible to identify items that might be instructionally insensitive on the basis of one or more of the factors just listed. If, after further analysis, there is a reasonable chance that an item might be insensitive to the accurate detection of instructional quality, then it can be modified or jettisoned from the test before being used. Will we ever completely excise all instructionally insensitive items from our accountability tests? Probably not. However, we need to make sure that the proportion of instructionally insensitive items on any accountability tests—tests presumed to accurately measure the quality of educators' instructional efforts—will be small indeed.

■ What's a Teacher to Do?

Teachers need to make up their own minds about the degree to which students' test performances should figure in the appraisal of a teacher. In my opinion it is foolish for teachers to be evaluated without at least some consideration of the assessed display of students' learning. However, the *degree of emphasis* to be placed on students' test performances should be linked directly to the caliber of the tests being employed to provide such evidence. If an external accountability test, for instance, measures students' mastery of important skills and knowledge that have been approved by relevant policymakers (such as a state board of education), and the test is demonstrably sensitive to instruction, then I'd argue that the results of such a test should play a prominent role in the evaluation of teachers. If no evidence exists that the tests being employed to evaluate teachers are instructionally sensitive, then we should assume the tests are instructionally *insensitive,* and should therefore play a minimal, if any, role in the evaluation of teachers' effectiveness.

This assumption applies not only to the major, externally administered assessments that are used to appraise teachers and schools but also to teacher-made tests that, for teachers whose students are not tested by large-scale assessments, might be created by individual teachers or by groups of teachers. Putting it simply, if policymakers have mandated that students' test performances are to play a key role in the evaluation of teachers, then it may be necessary for teachers to rely on teacher-made tests to supply the needed assessment evidence. Yet, for test-based teacher evaluation to function properly, so evaluation errors are minimized, even teacher-made tests should be fashioned in such a way that they are as instructionally sensitive as possible.

Remember, although the assessments being touted for use in test-based teacher evaluation are almost invariably some form of "achievement test," do not succumb to the widespread misconception that what's measured by such achievement tests represents what's been taught in schools. It is certainly possible that achievement tests do, in fact, assess what students have been taught by their teachers. But it is also possible, especially if the tests have been built by measurement traditionalists, that the tests being employed actually measure what students have brought to school, not what they've learned once they arrive.

Even the staunchest advocates of test-based teacher evaluation typically recommend that factors other than students' test scores play a role in the appraisal of a teacher. For example, evidence based on observations of teachers' classroom activities, students' anonymous appraisals of their teachers, or administrative ratings frequently are mentioned as additional reasons to consider when appraising a teacher. But you're reading a textbook about classroom assessment, and whether the assessments administered in a classroom are teacher-generated instruments or externally created assessments, how much weight to give students' test performances should be heavily dependent on the energy expended in rendering the tests involved as instructionally sensitive as possible.

I recommend you attempt to assess students' mastery of genuinely significant cognitive skills, such as their ability to write effective compositions, their ability to use lessons from history to make cogent analyses of current problems, and their ability to solve high-level mathematical problems. If the skills you choose (1) measure really important cognitive outcomes, (2) are seen by parents and policymakers to be genuinely significant, and (3) can be promoted instructionally by competent teachers, then the assembly of a set of pretest-to-posttest evidence showing substantial student growth in such skills can be truly persuasive. Earlier in this chapter you saw how a split-and-switch design (with blind-scoring of students' responses by nonpartisan raters) can be employed to collect compelling evidence of a teacher's instructional effectiveness. Use of pretest-to-posttest designs to gauge your own instructional success makes much more sense than succumbing to the senselessness of measuring your teaching prowess with the wrong kinds of tests.

Right Task, Wrong Tools

Teachers should definitely be held accountable. The teaching of a nation's children is too important to be left unmonitored. But to evaluate educational quality by using unsound assessment instruments is a subversion of good sense. Although teachers need to produce valid evidence regarding their effectiveness, you've seen that instructionally insensitive accountability tests are the wrong tools for this important task.

If inappropriate standardized tests are chosen by a state's officials to satisfy the provisions of federal accountability laws, you can bet that a good many public schools are going to be labeled as failing when, in fact, they are doing a good instructional job. Equally disturbing, many schools will appear to be doing a stellar job based on their students' test scores, but those high scores are chiefly attributable to the composition of the advantaged students who make up such schools' student bodies. In contrast, instructionally *sensitive* accountability tests are the right kinds of assessments to use when evaluating schools. Teachers should, solo or in collaboration, use whatever influence they can so the proper kinds of accountability tests are used with their students.

What Do Classroom Teachers Really Need to Know about Assessment-Based Evaluation of Teaching?

You must realize that when you use students' test results as indicators of your own instructional prowess, a major determiner of how well your students perform will be the particular students with whom you're working. Even using a straightforward pretest-posttest evaluation approach doesn't circumvent the problem created because of the dissimilarity of different teachers' students. For purposes of teacher's self-evaluation, disparities in students' entry behaviors don't pose all that much of a problem. For purposes of external teacher evaluation, however, disparities in the abilities and motivation levels of different teachers' students should induce caution in the evaluative use of students' test results. Judgments about the caliber of growth attained by a given teacher must be made in the context of the instructional situation in which the teacher is functioning. A useful way of collecting evidence regarding a teacher's instructional effectiveness is the split-and-switch design.

Perhaps one of the most important understandings you should carry from this chapter is the recognition that certain kinds of accountability tests—instructionally insensitive ones—should not be employed to evaluate a teacher's instructional effectiveness. You need to understand *why* such tests are inappropriate for this purpose. And once you recognize why the evidence derived from the wrong kinds of accountability tests is unsuitable for the evaluation of a school staff's quality, then you should see that other evidence, more defensible and more credible, needs to be collected by educators. The public has a right to see how well their tax-supported schools are doing. The public doesn't have the right to do so by using the wrong evidence. It was suggested that *instructionally sensitive accountability tests in concert with teacher-made assessments* could provide accurate evidence of teachers' success.

but what does this have to do with
Teaching?

It is inconceivable to me that an entire profession would allow its members to be judged using the wrong measuring tools. Yet, in education, that is precisely what is going on. And some teachers, largely because they do not understand specifically why certain kinds of accountability tests ought not be used to evaluate schooling, compliantly accept this profound misuse of educational tests. Such teachers may have an intuitive idea that students' scores on some accountability tests don't provide a clear picture of instructional quality, but they can't tell you why.

If, as a teacher, you don't help people understand why it is that particular sorts of accountability tests should not be used to judge instructional effectiveness, then you probably deserve what you'll get—thoroughly inaccurate judgments about your skill. But you're not the only one who gets hurt because of this glaring miscarriage of measurement-based justice. Your students will get hurt too. And *that's* why you need to first understand the ins and outs of this important issue, then you need to let others know about the misuse of certain kinds of tests to judge educational quality.

Who are those "others" you need to acquaint with this issue? Well, start off with your colleagues. Few teachers or administrators really understand, at a meaningful level, why some accountability tests aren't the answer for judging schools. Then there are parents who need to understand. And, of course, there are educational policymakers. They definitely need to learn what constitutes solid evidence of instructional quality and what evidence ought never to be used.

In short, if you don't want your own teaching to be appraised using the wrong microscope, then outfit yourself in evangelical garb and start doing a bit of educative gospel-spreading!

■ Chapter Summary

This chapter argued that the most defensible way to evaluate instruction, whether such evaluations are to be used for a teacher's self-evaluation or for external teacher evaluations, is to focus on the consequence of instruction—that is, the impact of instruction on students. Three sources of evaluative evidence were considered: (1) students' performances on classroom assessments, (2) students' performances on accountability tests, and (3) evidence regarding unanticipated effects of instruction. For the two test-elicited forms of evidence, it was stressed that the caliber of the tests themselves must be considered when deciding how much weight to give certain kinds of assessment evidence.

For the collection of classroom assessment evidence, two forms of a pretest-to-posttest data-gathering design were described: (1) a pretest-posttest design and (2) the split-and-switch design. Instructional sensitivity was described as the degree to which students' performances on a test accurately reflect the quality of instruction specifically provided to promote students' mastery of what is being assessed. When evaluating the quality of instruction, educators were urged to rely exclusively on instructionally sensitive tests. For the identification of unanticipated side effects of instruction, teachers were encouraged to be constantly attentive to the possibility of such unforeseen effects.

Educators were urged to learn more about both the appropriateness and the inappropriateness of certain kinds of evidence regarding instructional quality, then relay their conclusions to concerned constituencies.

Self-Check

For this chapter's self-check exercises, please grapple with a set of binary-choice items. Please judge each of the following ten statements (based on the chapter's contents), as TT (terribly true) or FF (fervently false).

(TT or FF)   1. Because of the nature of their items, some nationally standardized achievement tests assess what students bring to school rather than what those students are taught at school.

(TT or FF)   2. When judging instructional quality, if there is a disagreement between the evaluative evidence supplied by classroom assessments and the evidence yielded by external accountability tests, the evidence from the accountability tests should always trump the evidence from classroom tests.

(TT or FF)   3. One of the most practical ways of reducing the reactive effects of pretesting students is to create two equidifficult forms of a test, then administer one of the forms as a pretest and one of the forms as a posttest.

(TT or FF)   4. Most tests developed by traditional assessment organizations, when considered carefully, turn out instructionally sensitive.

(TT or FF)   5. *Instructional sensitivity* is the degree to which students' performances on a test accurately reflect the quality of instruction specifically provided to promote students' mastery of what is being assessed.

(TT or FF)   6. A test item will be most effective in distinguishing between successful and unsuccessful instruction if responses to the item are highly correlated with students' socioeconomic status.

(TT or FF)   7. Because most items on traditionally constructed standardized achievement tests must contribute to a sufficient spread of scores among examinees, certain items on external achievement tests often end up being closely linked to students' innate academic aptitudes.

(TT or FF)   8. Collection of students' affective predispositions, by using anonymously completed self-report affective inventories—prior to and following instruction—can make a meaningful contribution to the evaluation of a teacher's instruction.

(TT or FF)   9. In general, the bulk of today's teacher-evaluation procedures are both accurate and well understood by most members of the education profession.

(TT or FF)   10. Over the past several decades, American educators have been quite influential in conceptualizing and implementing the evaluation of the nation's teachers.

 # Pondertime

1. If you were devising a plan to promote dramatically improved evaluation of the nation's teachers, how would you go about doing so?

2. Do you think teachers can "blind-score" their own students' tests if those tests are gathered via a split-and-switch design, or should other people do the scoring? Does your answer depend on the kind of test being used?

3. When teachers evaluate themselves (or when supervisors evaluate teachers), various kinds of evidence can be used in order to arrive at an evaluative judgment. If you were a teacher who was trying to decide on the *relative worth* of the following types of evidence, where would you rank the importance of students' test results?
   a. Systematic observations of the teacher's classroom activities
   b. Students' anonymous evaluations of the teacher's ability
   c. Students' pretest-to-posttest gain scores on instructionally sensitive accountability tests
   d. A teacher's self-evaluation
   Would your ranking of the importance of these four types of evidence be the same in all instructional contexts? If not, what factors would make you change your rankings in *some* settings?

4. What kinds of accountability tests are used in your setting to evaluate teachers? How defensible are those tests for such a purpose?

5. Two ways of evaluating students' growth were treated in the chapter: (a) value-added models and (b) progress models based on student growth percentiles. If

you were in charge of a state's teacher evaluation program, and wished to use students' test performances as a key factor in appraising your state's teachers, which *one* of these two approaches would you choose. And, of course, why?

Self-Check Key

1. TT	3. FF	5. TT	7. TT	9. FF
2. FF	4. FF	6. FF	8. TT	10. FF

■ Additional Stuff

American Educational Research Association. (1999). *Standards for educational and psychological testing.* Washington, DC: Author.

Barton, P. E. (2007/2008). "The right way to measure growth," *Educational Leadership, 65,* no. 4 (December/January): 70–73.

Betebenner, D. W. (2007). *A primer on student growth percentiles.* Dover, NH: National Center for the Improvement of Educational Assessment.

Braun, H. I. (2005). *Using student progress to evaluate teachers: A primer on value-added models.* Princeton, NJ: Educational Testing Service.

D'Agostino, J. V., Welsh, M. E., and Corson, N. M. (2007). "Instructional sensitivity of a state's standards-based assessment." *Educational Assessment, 12,* no. 1: 1–22.

Gardner, H. (1994). "Multiple intelligences: The theory in practice." *Teacher's College Record, 95,* no. 4: 576–583.

Nichols, S. L., and Berliner, D. C. (2008). "Why has high-stakes testing so easily slipped into contemporary American life?" *Phi Delta Kappan, 89,* no. 9 (May): 672–676.

Popham, W. J. (2009). *Unlearned lessons: Six stumbling blocks to our schools' success.* Cambridge, MA: Harvard Education Press.

Popham, W. J. (2010). *Everything school leaders need to know about assessment.* Thousand Oaks, CA: Corwin.

Popham, W. J. (2013). *Evaluating America's Teachers: Mission Possible?* Thousand Oaks, CA: Corwin.

Stronge, J. H. (Ed.). (2006). *Evaluating teaching: A guide to current thinking and best practice* (2nd ed.). Thousand Oaks, CA: Corwin Press.

■ Cyber Stuff

- *AdvancED* accredits schools and districts not only in the United States, but worldwide—currently supplying accreditation services in about 70 nations. In all, AdvancED serves more than 27,000 public and private schools and districts. Formed in 2006 through the amalgamation of several major educational accreditation associations, AdvancED provides a website illustrative of an accreditation approach to school evaluation. This website not only lists the organization's products and services but it also describes key aspects of how AdvancED believes accreditations of schools and districts should be carried out. **www.advanc-ed.org**

- *ASCD, Formerly the Association for Supervision and Curriculum Development,* established in 1943, is an international organization representing 160,000 educators from more than 100 nations. Its website contains an excellent search-capability focusing on ASCD-distributed products and services. For example, a recent search for "assessment" produced more than 5,000 entries. ASCD's considerable array of conferences and training sessions is described on this comprehensive website. **www.ascd.org**

- *The National School Boards Association (NSBA),* founded in 1940, is a not-for-profit federation of school boards across the United States. It represents 90,000 school-board members who govern nearly 14,000 local school districts serving almost 50 million public school students. Intended to assist those who deal with public school issues, this website contains a search-capability that can isolate substantial numbers of resources related to such topics as assessment. **www.nsba.org**

■ Extended Applications

It is a truism that the more a person uses something, the more familiar with this something the person becomes. This self-evident notion surely applies to the assessment-related knowledge, skills, and concepts you have been reading about in the foregoing pages. Thus, to provide readers of *Classroom Assessment* with additional opportunities to apply the content contained in this text, this final section contains a variety of exercises intended to give readers an opportunity to use what they've been reading about.

In a sense, of course, the Self-Check exercises found at the close of this chapter provided an opportunity for readers to apply a chapter's content. Nonetheless, the more times you use a concept, skill, or a body of knowledge, the more likely it is that you will master this content so you can employ it in varied situations.

For each of the text, you will find an extended-application exercise calling for you to do some thinking about that chapter's content as it applies to a real-world situation. Each exercise is preceded by a brief introduction setting forth the reason that the upcoming extended-application exercise has been selected.

Because many of these exercises call on you to generate an original response rather than select a response from a set of options, it is difficult to supply an "answer key" for readers' unpredictable responses. So, what you'll find following all the exercises is One Possible Response—an indication of how I would have personally responded to the exercise if I had been asked to do so. Please don't regard my response as the only way to respond to an exercise. After all, by definition, this is only "one possible" response. Instead, please think of my response as a fairly flimsy form of feedback. You can certainly disagree with me, even emphatically, yet still profit from doing the exercise.

Remember, what is being provided in this section. The exercises deliberately intended to extend how you apply the content treated in *Classroom Assessment*. I hope you find these exercises useful in enhancing your understanding of what teachers need to know about classroom assessment.

Jordan Shows Her or She Knows

Introduction

In the musical comedy *The Unsinkable Molly Brown* there's a song Molly sings in an effort to convince the "beautiful" (uppity) people of Denver, Colorado, that—despite her low beginnings—she's a worthwhile person. During that song, Molly belts out the following line: "To show you know, you've got to show you know you know!"

Well, this Extended Applications exercise is based on the idea that today's teachers really need to understand what's going on with respect to teacher evaluation—and they need to show the world that they do, indeed, understand it. Moreover, because many teachers know little about the way their co-workers should or shouldn't be evaluated, any teacher who truly understands what's up regarding teacher evaluation really needs to spread the word.

In this exercise, to give you some practice in dealing with key issues related to teacher evaluation, you are to do a spot of make-believing. More specifically, you are to pretend you've just finished reading an extensive article about the evaluation of teachers. Now, and here you'll need to ratchet up your pretending prowess, please pretend you're sitting in a school's staff lounge and a half dozen of your colleagues, having learned that you've read about this topic, are peppering you with questions about the evaluation of teachers. This exercise calls for you to answer those questions and, in the process, better formulate your own thinking about the issues under consideration.

For this exercise, you've been assigned the imaginary name of Jordan, one of those unisex names permitting you to play the Jordan part as a boy-Jordan or a girl-Jordan without any threat to your gender image. Try to come up with your own responses *before* taking a gander at the One Possible Response answers to your colleagues' questions.

 Exercise Directions: For this exercise, please assume your name is Jordan and you've agreed to answer questions from some colleagues regarding the ways teachers should/shouldn't be evaluated.

1. *Betty's question:* "Jordan, remember at our first faculty meeting of the year, when Principal O'Malley urged us to always use pretests if we were going to employ posttests to gauge our own success? Because our students *rarely* know what we're trying to teach them, at least initially, why is pretesting actually necessary?"

Your answer: _____

_____

_____

The Evaluation of Instruction

 One Possible Response: "First off, you need to remember these days we're smack in the middle of an accountability fishbowl, and the reason underlying all these externally imposed accountability requirements is *incredulity*. That's right, the world doubts whether today's teachers are doing a satisfactory instructional job. So, to demonstrate to an incredulous world that we really are able to promote worthwhile improvements in our students' achievement, we must demonstrate, *prior* to instruction, our kids were unable to do the things that, *after* instruction, they are able to do. Not only will pretests and posttests supply 'proof to the world,' Betty, but good pretesting—because it can be diagnostic—can help us all do a better job of teaching."

> 2. *Samantha's question:* "You've surely heard, Jordan, that a group of citizens has been aggressively lobbying our district school board to evaluate the district's teachers primarily on the basis of our students' scores on a spring-administered nationally standardized achievement test. Would that be a sensible thing to do?"

Your answer: _____

_____

_____

 One Possible Response: "No, Samantha, this would be a truly dumb thing to do. You see, nationally standardized achievement tests are intended to permit comparisons between a test taker's performance and the performances of previous test takers in the test's 'norm group.' But, in order to create sufficient score-spread so these comparative interpretations are possible, the developers of nationally standardized achievement tests include items that tend to be remarkably impervious to in-school instruction. Accordingly, current nationally standardized achievement tests are *instructionally insensitive* and, as such, would be ghastly tests to rely on when evaluating teachers. These tests tend to measure the socioeconomic composition of a school's student body, not the effectiveness with which those students have been taught."

> 3. *Greg's question:* "After what you just told Samantha, can we then put our money on standards-based tests? Are those sorts of accountability tests the kind we should be urging our state's officials to use when appraising the state's teachers?"

Your answer: _____

_____

_____

One Possible Response: "I wish it were that simple, Greg, but there are only *particular* standards-based accountability tests that can do the teacher-evaluation job properly. Most standards-based tests, unfortunately, are every bit as instructionally insensitive as are nationally standardized achievement tests. If a standards-based test tries to measure students' achievement of too many curricular aims, and fails to provide instructionally useful results for teachers, it is almost certain to be instructionally insensitive. To evaluate teachers properly, a standards-based test must be *demonstrably* sensitive to the detection of effective and ineffective teaching."

4. *Lamar's question:* "What, then, is an instructionally sensitive standards-based accountability test?"

Your answer: _____

_____

_____

➤ **One Possible Response:** "Lamar, a standards-based test that's instructionally *sensitive* must possess four attributes. First, it should measure only a modest number of curricular goals, more like 5 to 10 than 30 to 60. But, because those goals are fewer in number, they must be incontestably significant—typically representing very high-level cognitive skills. Second, the test should be accompanied by clear, teacher-palatable descriptions of every skill or body of knowledge being assessed. This allows teachers to direct their instruction toward well-understood, important curricular targets instead of toward specific test items. In addition, Lamar, an instructionally sensitive standards-based test must supply reports of each student's status with respect to every curricular aim measured by the test. Thus, per-aim reporting plays a major role instructionally for each student and, over time, in helping teachers improve their instructional activities. And, finally, a serious effort must have been made to eliminate from such a test any items apt to be instructionally insensitive."

5. *Felipe's question:* "Jordan, how many content standards can a well-conceived standards-based test effectively measure?"

Your answer: _____

_____

_____

➤ **One Possible Response:** "In truth, Felipe, that's a judgment call, but it is governed to a large degree by the need to report a student's status with respect to each curricular aim that's been assessed. So, for instance, if it were estimated that it took about 8 to 10 items to measure each of the curricular targets—that is, skills or bodies of knowledge to be assessed—and you had only an hour or so for kids to be tested, you'd probably not want more than 6 or 7 content standards to be measured. But remember, Felipe, those content standards must be formulated at a "grain-size" that makes instructional sense to teachers. If the grain-size is too broad, then neither teachers nor students end up knowing what it is a student can or can't do."

6. *Collette's question:* "Why do some people recommend that we get our pretest-posttest results blind-scored?"

Your answer: _____

_____

_____

The Evaluation of Instruction

 One Possible Response: "That's an interesting question, Collette, and once more it stems from the public's incredulity about the quality of today's schooling. If you contrast your students' posttest performances with your students' pretest performances, and there are many constructed-response items involved, you really do need to have them blind-scored (with precoded pretests and posttests mixed together). Ideally, this blind-scoring would be carried out by nonpartisan folks such as parents or members of the business community. The more patently objective the test-scorers are, and the less they know about when a test was completed (in relation to your instructional activities), the more accurate will be the scoring and the more credible will be the results."

7. *Sara's question:* "I've heard you mention the split-and-switch model as one way of collecting pretest-to-posttest data about the impact of your teaching. But, Jordan, why is it better than just a simple no-split and no-switch pretest-posttest approach?"

Your answer: _____

_____

_____

 One Possible Response: "The split-and-switch approach allows you to effectively get around the 'reactive effects' of pretesting—effects that can distort your conclusions about the impact of your teaching. It also gives you *two* 50-percent samples of the degree to which your students' performances changed from before instruction to following instruction."

8. *Clyde's question:* "Jordan, my classes are usually quite small, sometimes not even reaching 20 students. Can I still use the split-and-switch model?"

Your answer: _____

_____

_____

 One Possible Response: "With small classes, Clyde, it makes more sense to simply use a pretest-to-posttest one-group model—but still employing blind-scoring with nonpartisan scorers. Because the split-and-switch approach requires a teacher to chop a class in half, two half-classes of too few students are apt to provide only shaky estimates of your instructional impact."

9. *Melinda's question:* "Jordan, do experts in teacher evaluation think it is okay to use multiple data sources to evaluate teachers, or should the only legitimate data sources for judging teachers be their students' scores on state-level accountability tests?"

Your answer: _____

_____

_____

One Possible Response: "I don't pretend I'm an expert in teacher evaluation—at least not too often—but I believe any thoughtful person wants to see *more*, not *less* evidence of a teacher's impact on kids. But what's important, Melinda, is the *quality* of the various kinds of evaluative evidence being gathered. I can think of a scad of self-serving evidence regarding a teacher's skill—evidence that any right-thinking person would instantly reject. Not all indicators of a teacher's competence are created equal. As much accurate and credible evidence of a teacher's skill as we can sensibly come up with should be incorporated into any judgment about a teacher's instructional prowess. *If* a state-level accountability test is an appropriate one for such evaluations—*and most, at least in the past, have not been*—then such a test might play a major, but not exclusive, role in evaluating the teacher's success."

10. *Randall's question:* "What about these new consortium-built tests, Jordan? They've been built with considerable financial support from the federal government, about 175 million each for the Smarter Balanced Assessment Consortium and the Partnership for the Assessment of Readiness for College and Careers. When those well-funded tests trot out of their test-building factories, many people will surely want to see these tests used in the evaluation of teachers. Will the quality of these new tests be up to that task?"

Your answer: _____

_____

_____

 One Possible Response: "That's a terrific question, Randall, and it has been troubling more than a few educators ever since the building of the SBAC and PARCC tests got under way. Because we will have a pair of almost "national" tests at hand, many proponents of test-based teacher evaluation will want to see the consortium-built tests heavily featured in any sorts of serious teacher-evaluation undertakings. Yet, even though the pressure will be on to use these new tests in teacher-evaluation programs, we must still be sure the tests are able to accurately distinguish between well-taught and poorly taught students. We need to see what sorts of evidence the tests have attesting to their instructional sensitivity of the new consortium-built assessments. In my view, Randall, if these new consortium-built tests are not *demonstrably* sensitive to instruction—and accompanied by a raft of evidence to that effect—then we should not be using them to evaluate teachers!"

■ Glossary

blind-scoring When a student's tests are judged without the judges' knowing whether a test was completed as a pretest or as a posttest.

evaluation An appraisal of the worth of an educational program or, in the case of classroom teachers, either the effectiveness of an instructional activity or the competence of the teacher.

grading An assignment of a quality-designating label (numerical or verbal) to describe the caliber of a student's work.

instructional sensitivity The degree to which students' performances on a test accurately reflect the quality of instruction specifically provided to promote students' mastery of what is being assessed.

reactive The often confounding effect of early assessment on a student's subsequent learning, most vividly seen in the impact caused by preassessment of an affective variable, wherein the student is unduly sensitized to the affective variable with which a teacher is concerned.

regression effect A well-known statistical phenomenon in which extremely high scorers or extremely low scorers will, when retested, tend to earn scores closer to the mean of the score distribution.

score-spread The degree to which a set of test scores is dispersed, or spread out.

split-and-switch design A data-gathering design in which a class is split into two halves, each half taking a different pretest. Then, after instruction, the tests are switched so that students take the other test form. Two comparisons are then made between students' pretest-versus-posttest performances on the same test form.

student growth percentile A norm-referenced representation of students' relative changes in test performances during a single school year—such changes being represented on the current test by percentile comparisons of all students who had scored identically on the prior year's test. The growth of a given teacher's students would therefore be determined by an average of those growth percentiles based on different starting points.

test-based teacher evaluation Teacher appraisals in which the dominant determiner of a teacher's quality is the performance of a particular teacher's students on an externally imposed standardized achievement test.

value-added model (VAM) A statistical procedure intended to employ students' prior achievement and/or background characteristics as statistical controls to estimate the effects on student achievement of specific teachers, schools, or school districts.

Assessment-Based Grading

Teachers give grades. One supposes when the original blueprints for "teacher" were drawn, there must have been a mandatory grade-giving component included somewhere. Other than tradition, however, why is it that teachers dispense grades to students so regularly?

The answer's fairly simple. A teacher needs to let students know (1) how well they're doing, as when a teacher assigns interim grades on various assignments during the course of the school year; and (2) how well they've done, as when a teacher dishes out end-of-year grades. For teachers to find out how well they've *taught*, the level of students' achievement must be determined. For students to find out how well they've *learned*, the extent of their achievement must also be determined.

Although, as you'll soon see, there are a number of factors teachers sometimes consider when grading students—other than simply how well those students performed on classroom assessments—there's little argument that a *major* consideration in the grade a student receives should be the quality of the student's assessment performances. In this chapter, we'll be looking at different ways those assessment results can be incorporated into students' grades.

■ The Purpose of Grading

How teachers grade their students stems chiefly from what those teachers believe the purpose (or purposes) of grading should be. I know, as a beginning high school teacher, my understanding of the potential purposes of grading was almost nonexistent. Oh, sure, I knew that good grades should be given to students who

From Chapter 16 of *Classroom Assessment: What Teachers Need to Know*, Seventh Edition. W. James Popham. Copyright © 2014 by Pearson Education, Inc. All rights reserved.

performed well on my tests, and that students who performed poorly on those tests should end up with low grades. After all, teachers who—as students themselves— have gone through years of schooling surely recognize that students' test performances and students' grades are closely linked. But is that all there is to it? In truth, when I began teaching, I simply had not devoted any thought, *any at all,* to how I was going to grade my students. In retrospect, I'm certain I made a number of bone-headed grading mistakes as a tyro teacher.

The mission of this chapter in *Classroom Assessment* is to encourage you to give some serious think-time to the topic of grading. In almost every school setting, teachers will need to grade their students. And although teachers will probably never acquire a precise, zero-errors grading strategy, teachers can at least come up with a defensible way of thinking about this important task. Such defensibility begins by a teacher's understanding the purpose of grading.

Susan Brookhart (2009), who writes often and well about grading, contends that the primary purpose for grading, whether for individual assignments or report cards, should be to communicate with students and parents about students' achievement of curricular aims. At first glance, this sensible statement might appear to be little more than the sort of educational platitude teachers routinely encounter. It isn't. Indeed, if you agree with what Brookhart thinks the purpose of grading should be—namely, *communicating information to both students and their parents about students' goal attainment*—then this stance will profoundly influence how you grade your own students.

Brookhart's conception of grading identifies not only *who* are the targets of the information that's being communicated (in this instance, students and parents) but also *what* is being communicated (in this instance, students' goal-attainment status). You'll find most educators agree that the target audiences of grading should be students and their parents. Where more disagreement bubbles up, however, is with what's being communicated to those audiences. Brookhart's exclusive focus is on *goal attainment.* But some educators want grades to communicate not only students' goal attainment but also to incorporate evaluations of students' effort, attendance, attitudes, classroom behavior, and so on. Clearly, if teachers are grading students only on the basis of students' goal attainment, those teachers will arrive at substantially different grades than will teachers who try to incorporate such factors in their grading as students' attitudes and effort.

As Brookhart (2009, p. 4) points out, "In a perfect world, there would be no need for the kinds of grades we use in school today." She would prefer replacing grades on individual assignments with discussions about strengths and weaknesses—based on a student's progress toward goal attainment—and these discussions would take place among students themselves as well as between the student and the teacher. The focus would be on how to improve. There would be no "failures" because students would continue with additional tasks and assignments until a curricular aim had been achieved. All performances would be seen as capable of being improved. As she points out, however, "The demands of schooling as we know it have kept us from reaching that utopia" (p. 4). Yet, even in such a utopian educational world, the focus of all these improvement-oriented evaluative discussions among teachers and students would revolve around the level of students' goal attainment. Thus, whether you are a seasoned teacher or a teacher-in-training, an early decision you must make is precisely *what it is* that you want to be communicating to your students and to their parents.

Okay, what about teachers giving grades—at least in part—on the basis of their students' effort, attitudes, levels of class participation, behavior, attendance, tardiness, and punctuality in assignment submission? Should factors such as these have *any* role in the awarding of grades? Well, Ken O'Connor thinks not.

O'Connor is another colleague who has devoted much of his career to helping teachers decide how best to award grades to their students. "For grades to have real meaning," wrote O'Connor, "they must be relatively pure measures of each student's achievement of the learning goals" (2009, p. 90). He, too, advocates that teachers relate their grading procedures to learning goals. In fact, he recommends that when officially sanctioned content standards exist, as is true now in almost all jurisdictions, students' achievement of those standards should be the *only* determiner of students' grades. O'Connor would definitely supply students and their parents with information about such factors as class participation or punctuality in assignment submission, but this would be done separately. (We'll look at techniques for doing so later in the chapter.)

I must confess that the laser-like focus on using students' attainment of curricular aims as an exclusive grading criterion, the stance taken by both O'Connor and Brookhart, was surely not the way I approached grading when I was a neophyte teacher. I sometimes gave higher than deserved grades to certain underachieving students as a way I thought might jolt them into an "I can do it" mood. I also graded some students according to what I believed were the levels of effort they were giving to their studies. I graded hard-working, albeit low-performing, students generously, while also grading lazy, yet high-performing, students harshly. I also used the lure of high grades as a motivation ploy—that is, as a way of getting students to study harder. In hindsight, my grading practices would have earned condemnation from my friends Sue Brookhart and Ken O'Connor. They would have been right. My grading practices were an ill-conceived mess.

When I became a college professor, merely because students' achievement seemed to be the only thing my fellow professors deemed worth grading, I nestled into a comfortable, achievement-dominated approach to grading. But this professorial grading stance was not dictated by careful thought on my part. Rather, it was a knee-jerk acceptance of my peers' expectations.

So, with the hope that my now-confessed grading sins will ultimately be forgiven, I want to go on record as saying the central grading position taken by O'Connor, Brookhart, and those who share their views, is one I recommend to you with enthusiasm. I now believe that truly defensible grading requires the teacher to make students' achievement of clearly understood curricular aims the solitary consideration in determining the grades to be communicated to students and parents. For report-card grading, this typically means the teacher will be relying on assessment-based evidence concerning students' status regarding the curricular aims themselves. For assignment grading, or for grading en route assessments, the teacher must decide on the contribution those assignments and en route assessments will make to students' mastery of the target curricular aims. Certain en route tests, for example, may deal with knowledge or subskills deemed more significant to students' mastering the target curricular aims than will other en route tests. The more significant tests (or assignments) would obviously carry more grading weight than would the less significant ones.

I realize that all curricular aims are not created equal. Many teachers simultaneously promote their students' attainment of several curricular aims, and some curricular aims are more important than others. It is perfectly acceptable, therefore, for a teacher to assign more significance to some curricular aims than to others. If teachers try to make their grading decisions transparent rather than cloud-cloaked, a teacher can announce in advance which curricular aims, if any, are regarded as more significant than others. The same sort of thinking would apply to the assignment of grades for en route tests or for grades given to students' assignments. Those aimed at more important curricular aims would be assigned more grade-determining import than would those aimed at less significant curricular aims.

To review, then, when arriving at a sensible stance regarding grading, teachers must first make up their minds about what the fundamental purpose of grading is. I have suggested teachers adopt a position that grading should be regarded as a communication activity aimed at students and their parents, and that this activity should be based exclusively on a student's status with respect to the mastery of curricular aims. I understand that, in many settings, a teacher has little choice about which curricular aims should be regarded as important—because governmental agencies will have already made those curricular decisions. Thus, in those settings, teachers will characteristically endorse students' attainment of officially sanctioned curricular aims. Accordingly, what's communicated to students and parents will be a student's status regarding each of these official curricular aims. In sum, I recommend without reservation that you adopt a grading strategy based only on students' goal attainment.

How Does Goal-Attainment Grading Take Place?

Let's assume that you see a mite of merit in the idea of linking students' grades to their progress in mastering curricular aims. How, precisely, would a teacher go about using this approach? Let's take a look at a few nuts-and-bolts of such a goal-attainment grading strategy.

I am presuming that teachers will want their grading approaches to be as transparent as is practical. I know that some teachers might prefer to keep grading a mysterious enterprise. Most such teachers, of course, are reluctant to bring their grading practices into the sunlight chiefly out of fears that those practices would be found wanting. This is all too understandable. My early grading practices were so deplorable that the only way I could have defended them was by hiring well-armed mercenaries. But if teachers accept the view that the grading of students is a less than completely scientific enterprise, and mistakes will inevitably be made, then letting the world know what went into the teacher's grading decisions seems so much more responsible than trying to camouflage what transpired while grades were being determined.

- ■ *Step 1: Clarifying curricular aims.* The first step in any grade-giving approach that's wedded to students' attainment of curricular aims is to make certain all participants in the grading game understand the nature of the curricular aims involved. What this means, in practice, is that teachers must provide *understandable* renditions of all curricular aims to those involved—specifically, to students and parents. Sometimes those understandable versions of curricular aims will employ identical language for both students and parents. In most instances, after students have entered middle school, any statements of curricular aims thought suitable for students will probably also be suitable for their parents. But for younger children, especially those in primary grades, separate "kid-friendly" versions of curricular aims are usually needed in addition to the descriptions of curricular aims provided for parents.

  These statements of curricular aims are often more readily understood when accompanied by illustrative test items. It helps both students and parents to see sample items that might be used to assess a student's mastery of a particular curricular aim. Care must be taken, however, to indicate that these sample items do not exhaust the assessment techniques that might be employed to measure students' mastery. The accompanying items should be identified as "illustrative, but not exhaustive" examples of how students might be asked to display mastery of a particular curricular aim. We want our students to master a curricular aim so they possess a truly generalizable mastery of this aim, not merely one way of displaying such mastery. Genuine mastery of a curricular aim signifies that a student can display this mastery in a variety of ways, not only one or two.

  To truly understand the nature of a curricular aim, it is often necessary for us to know the nature of the criteria by which a student's mastery of the aim will be determined. Such criteria are the factors to be used in determining the student's level of aim mastery. For instance, when judging the quality of a student's ability to write expository essays, the scoring guide/rubric that's employed for this purpose might isolate judgmental criteria such as the quality of an essay's (1) organization, (2) content, and (3) avoidance of mistakes involving the mechanics of writing. When the absence of such criteria would appreciably reduce someone's understanding of what mastery of a curricular aim really means, then the teacher must identify and, if necessary, explain what those criteria are.

  For both the improvement of instruction as well as for the clarification of a grading process, it is almost always helpful to supply students with

Assessment-Based Grading

examples of acceptable and unacceptable responses to assessments or to assignments. When students are just starting to learn about something, for example, when they're just beginning to acquire mastery of a sophisticated new skill, it typically makes sense to provide exemplars at the extreme ends of the quality continuum. For example, once more using our expository-essay example, a teacher could pass out a truly terrific expository essay as well as one that was sublimely shabby. Ideally, both examples would be actual responses made by previous students. Later, when students become more conversant with the nature of the curricular aim being sought, exemplars exhibiting more fine-grained differences in quality could be distributed. The idea here, of course, is to help students understand what is being sought and how students' mastery of it will be appraised.

- *Step 2: Choosing goal-attainment evidence.* After identifying and describing the curricular aims (goals) on which grades are to be based, the teacher then decides on the *evidence* that will be used to help arrive at a determination of the student's progress toward mastery of each curricular aim being sought. It is altogether appropriate to let parents, as well as students, know what's coming in the way of evidence-eliciting assessment approaches. Well-described goals communicate effectively to students and parents. Well-described goals along with well-described assessments communicate *really* effectively to students and parents.

  Most of today's teachers, when they were students themselves, saw their teachers typically rely on important exams to assign grades. To illustrate, a final-exam grade counted more toward an end-of-course grade than did a midterm exam or weekly quizzes. The final exam was, in other words, the test that made the most difference in the grade a student received. It is the assumption in such instances, and this is often a warranted assumption, that the more significant the exam, the more influential should be its contribution to a teacher's judgment about a student's mastery of curricular aims. In many instances, this may be true. But sometimes it isn't.

- *Step 3: Weighting goal-attainment evidence.* The third step in goal-attainment grading calls for the teacher to judge whatever assessment evidence is available regarding students' goal-attainment status. Here's what's typically going on when a teacher arrives at a judgment about a student's mastery of a specific curricular aim. First off, the teacher decides what evidence might be germane to a "goal-mastery" decision. Perhaps there are two homework assignments the teacher's students were obliged to complete, as well as one classroom quiz, and also about 40 percent of the items on the midterm exam. Well, when the teacher looks at those four chunks of evidence, it is up to the teacher to decide which evidence will best support an interpretation about a student's mastery of this particular aim. It may well be that the two homework assignments actually give the teacher a better idea about the student's mastery-status than the evidence provided by either the classroom quiz or the items on the midterm exam. What the teacher must do, then, is decide how much weight to

412

give each source of evidence, and be prepared to let any concerned individuals know about the nature of those weighting decisions. Again, transparency is the motive here. If grades are to be awarded on the basis of the degree to which a student has mastered a curricular aim, then a teacher should make clear (1) the evidence being relied on when the teacher makes those mastery-inferences and (2) the teacher's judged importance of this evidence.

Over the yearsI advocated assigning more grading weight on the basis of the type of assessment involved, with final exams and midterm exams trumping en route quizzes and homework assignments. I hope I was assuming that those exams would supply the most useful evidence in helping teachers arrive at inferences about students' goal attainment. But, for the record, if you have adopted the grading posture recommended so far in this chapter, it may well be that your most significant evidence in support of an inference about students' goal attainment might come from "lesser" exams. All you need to do is decide how much significance to assign to different sources of evidence, and then let the world know—preferably in advance—what your weighting decisions were.

- *Step 4: Arriving at a final goal-attainment grade.* Let's assume there are several curricular aims being pursued, and there are several sources of assessment-evidence at hand related to each of those aims. This is when the teacher focuses on the overall status of a student with regard to the attainment of the complete array of goals. More-important goals will count more than less-important goals. More-significant assessment evidence of goal attainment will be counted more heavily than will less-significant assessment evidence of goal attainment. Clearly, arriving at a reasonably coalesced conclusion with so many things to keep track of is not a task for the dull-witted. But, in the final analysis, that's what grading boils down to. And, at least with the overriding grading consideration being a student's attainment of goals, a teacher is at least playing an understandable grade-giving game.

Elementary school teachers, of course, often are concerned about grading considerations of less interest to teachers in middle schools or high schools. For instance, first-grade teachers may think a significant *educational* aim in their classrooms is to have children develop self-control in a social setting. For example, a 7-year-old boy who pounds on male or female classmates during recess would not be behaving in an appropriate manner, nor would a 7-year-old girl who pounds on male or female classmates during recess. (A teacher afflicted with many such students might consider establishing a "cooperative pounding group.")

As students become older, a teacher's grading scheme might be based on typical academic criteria. Teachers who work with younger children will often need to describe—and weigh—a much more developmentally appropriate set of factors. The essentials of such teachers' grading practices are identical to the approach used in later grades. But elementary teachers need to think through what they regard as relevant curricular aims, describe them, then weigh their contribution to a child's grade.

■ Grade-Giving Specifics

When teachers award grades, there are several options available to them. For final, end-of-term or end-of-year grades, it is necessary to adhere to whatever grade-descriptor system has been adopted by the district. Thus, if the district's policy is to use grades of A, B, C, D, or F, then the district's teachers must use those grades even if, during the course of the year, the teachers employed a different grade-descriptor scheme in class. Although many school districts, or schools within those districts, have grading policies that are quite general, some grading policies are particularly restrictive—setting forth specific limits on the percentages of particular grades that can be awarded by teachers.

Generally speaking, there are three major options available to teachers when they describe how well a student has performed. Teachers can use (1) letter grades, (2) numerical grades, or (3) verbal descriptors. Most of us are familiar with *letter grades* because such grades have been widely used for a long, long time. A grade of A is yummy and a grade of F is crummy. In some districts, teachers are also allowed to add pluses or minuses to letter grades, thus transforming a grading scale that has 5 points (A, B, C, D, or F) to one with 15 points. We can assume that a grade of F– reflects genuinely abysmal rock-bottom performance. A *numerical grading system* is usually organized around some chosen number of points such as 100, 50, or 10. Students are then given a number of points on each classroom assessment so that when students see their grade for the assessment, they realize they have earned, for example, "7 points out of a possible 10." *Verbal descriptors* are used instead of numerical or letter grades when teachers rely exclusively on phrases such as "excellent," "satisfactory," and "needs improvement." The number of such phrases used—that is, the number of possible verbal-descriptor grades that might be employed—is up to the teacher. If verbal-descriptor grades are used throughout an entire district, the choice of verbal descriptors is typically determined by district officials.

One increasingly common form of a verbal-descriptor grade is the *achievement-level* classification system used to describe performance on the National Assessment of Educational Progress (NAEP). When NAEP tests are administered, students' performances are classified as Advanced, Proficient, Basic, or Below Basic. (Although "Below Basic" is not an official NAEP-designated reporting category, it is typically employed so that students' totals add up to 100 percent!) This four-category achievement-level classification model has become widely used across the United States. Because the NCLB Act called for states to use at least three of these descriptive labels (that is, *Basic, Proficient,* and *Advanced*), many states simply adopted the NAEP four-category model. Thus, the use of the NAEP achievement-level labels is clearly a prominent variation of verbal-descriptor grades used in the United States. A number of districts have tried to devise *standards-based report cards* wherein the quality of each student's mastery of each content standard (curricular aim) is described. In many instances, the level of detail being used in such reporting systems has proven overwhelming to students, their parents, and more than a few teachers.

These standards-based report cards, a fundamentally sensible approach—especially given the increasingly widespread advocacy of basing grades dominantly on the basis of students' attainment of curricular aims (content standards)—is dependent on the *artistry* of those who crafted the content standards in the first place. If the grain-size (breadth) of the content standards is too small, then teachers end up being obliged to evaluate students' status with respect to an often overwhelming litany of such standards. The teachers might know what each content standard means, but there are simply too darn many of them! As a result, teachers tend to give less than careful attention to the whole array of standards, and both students and their parents become overwhelmed. In contrast, if the grain-size of the standards is too large, then what the content standards truly mean sometimes vanishes into too-general verbiage. That's why it truly takes verbal artistry for those who craft standards-based report cards to arrive at versions that make those report cards educationally useful. I have seen many examples of standards-based report cards, all of them well-intentioned. I have seen few examples of standards-based report cards I regarded as educationally useful.

The only sensible way to wrestle with the grain-size dilemma when relying on standards-based report cards is to *prioritize, prioritize,* and, for good measure, *prioritize.* If standards-based report cards can be structured around a manageable number of understandable curricular aims, then the standards set forth in such report cards can be crafted at a suitable grain-size so this grading strategy pays off for both teachers and students. If grading is seen as a way of communicating about a student's level of goal attainment, then it is difficult to conceive of an approach to report-card grading that is not chiefly dependent on the quality of the content standards involved.

In contrast to more traditional letter grades, or even some of the alternative grading descriptors considered earlier, teachers should recall the dividends of *descriptive feedback* . Descriptive feedback is rooted in a three-step operation in which the teacher lets the student know (1) what the curricular aim is—or what the building blocks are leading to master of the aim, (2) where the student is in relation to that aim's attainment, and (3) what the student should do to reduce the gap between the student's current status and desired status. Insofar as possible, teachers should try not to dispense grades that have few implications for students' learning. Instead, teachers should replace those grades with descriptive feedback whose function is to guide students toward the achievement of the curricular aims which, if the teacher adopts a goal-attainment approach to grading, will ultimately determine the student's grade.

Evaluative Options

Let's look at three common grade-giving approaches. Each of these approaches can be used not only for end-of-term or end-of-year grades but also for grading the classroom assessment performances and assignments of students during the school year. In other words, these grading approaches can be applied whether you are assigning Johnny an end-of-term grade in your science class or grading his two-week experiment dealing with "Psychological Depression in Earthworms."

You're probably already familiar with the three grading approaches to be described because, when you were a student, you most likely encountered them all:

- *Absolute grading.* When grading *absolutely,* a grade is given based on a teacher's idea of what level of student performances is truly necessary to earn, for instance, an A. Thus, if an English teacher has established an absolute level of proficiency needed for an A grade, and in a given class no student performs at the A-level of proficiency, then no student will get an A. Conversely, if the teacher's absolute grading standards were such that all students had performed beyond the A-level requirements, then the teacher would shower these students with A grades. An absolute system of grading has much in common with a criterion-referenced approach to assessment. If the teacher has adopted a goals-attainment approach to grading, then an absolute implementation of this strategy would revolve around a teacher's judgment about the levels of goal attainment needed for all to-be-awarded grades.

  The major argument in favor of an absolute approach to grading is that there are, indeed, legitimate levels of expectation for students that, although judgmentally devised by teachers, must be satisfied in order for specific grades to be awarded. And, of course, it is always the case that people form their absolute expectations based on seeing how folks usually perform. Thus, there's a sense in which *absolutes flow from relatives*.

- *Relative grading.* When teachers grade *relatively,* a grade is given based on how students perform in relation to one another. Thus, for any group of students, there will always be the *best* and the *worst* performances. Those students who outperform their classmates will get high grades irrespective of the absolute caliber of the students' performances. Conversely, because some students will always score relatively worse than their classmates, such low scorers will receive low grades no matter what. This system of grading is somewhat analogous to a norm-referenced approach to assessment.

  As noted earlier, there is a sense in which even a teacher's *absolute* expectations regarding the level of performance needed to achieve an A, B, C, D, or F are derived from years of working with students and discerning how well similar students are usually capable of performing. But a relative grading system uses the students *in a given class* as the normative group, and does not take into consideration all the students whom the teacher has taught in the past.

  The chief argument in favor of a relative system of grading is that because the quality of the teacher's instructional efforts may vary, and the composition of a given group of students may vary, some type of class-specific grading is warranted. Teachers who use a relative-grading approach tend to appreciate its flexibility because their grading expectations change from class to class.

- *Aptitude-based grading.* When grading on *aptitude,* a grade is given to each student based on how well the student performs in relation to that student's academic potential. To illustrate, if a particularly bright student outperformed all other students in the class, but still performed well below what the teacher believed the student was capable of, the student might be given a B, not an A. In order to grade on aptitude, of course, the teacher needs to have an idea of what students' academic potentials really are. To estimate each student's academic aptitude, teachers either need to rely on the student's prior performance on some sort of academic aptitude test or, instead, must form their own judgments about the student's academic potential. Because academic aptitude tests are being administered less frequently these days, in order to use an aptitude-based grading approach, teachers will generally need to arrive at their own estimate of a student's potential.

  The main argument in favor of aptitude-based grading is it tends to "level the playing field" by grading students according to their innate gifts and, thereby, encourages students to fulfill their potential. A problem with this grading approach, as you might guess, is the difficulty of deciding on just what each student's academic potential really is.

As indicated earlier, any of these three grading approaches can be used to assign grades for individual efforts of students, such as their performances on a short essay examination, or for arriving at a student's total-year grade. For instance, it would be possible to use any of the three grading approaches in order to arrive at students' portfolio grades—grades dispensed in letter, numerical, or verbal form.

What about Effort?

Students' effort is, educationally, so profoundly important. If a teacher can engender in students the inclination to expend effort in their school and nonschool endeavors, those students will be well served in the future. Students who believe the level of their effort will make the most difference in their success will be students who are more likely to succeed than will their classmates who rely on luck or on inherited smarts to carry them through life.

Okay, if students' effort is so significant, why shouldn't we take it into consideration when we grade students? In other words, why shouldn't we give higher grades to kids who put out the effort—regardless of their assessed levels of achievement? Regrettably, as Wormeli (2006) points out, "We don't have a commonly accepted, legally justifiable, non-subjective method for measuring how hard or sincerely someone is working" (p. 108). This single sentence, sadly, torpedoes any hope of a worthwhile "effort-grading" approach. Even if, as a teacher,

Decision Time

Should Level-of-Effort Be Rewarded?

Karl Kramer teaches second-graders at Twelfth Street Elementary School. He's been doing so for six years. During the past year, however, Karl has seriously been reconsidering his whole approach to grading. This reconsideration was stimulated by three students who in the past would have been placed in some form of special needs program, but now have been included in Karl's second-grade class.

Although the three students, Marie, Floyd, and James, are having difficulty with much of the content treated in class, all three are obviously trying hard to succeed. In fact, if Karl were to grade on effort alone, the three students would probably get the highest grades in class.

In the past, Karl has given no credit for student effort when grades were awarded. Now, however, he finds that he's rethinking that decision.

 If you were Karl, what would you do?

you would desperately like to incorporate effort into your grading approach, *you can't get an accurate fix on your students' effort levels*. Although you might identify anecdotal evidence that seemingly tells you how hard a student is trying, such evidence can be misinterpreted. And such evidence *is* misinterpreted—way too often. We simply don't have an effort-determining measuring stick on which we can rely.

Let's suppose a teacher (we'll call him Elmer) cares so much about incorporating effort into students' grades, he goes totally overboard to try to accurately identify a student's level of effort. Indeed, in this fictional fantasy, Elmer even rents a set of pricey lie-detection equipment, and also hires an expensive lie-detector technician to operate it. Okay, there is Elmer and the technician (in the teachers' lounge), interviewing students one at a time to reach a conclusion about each student's level of effort. What scale will Elmer employ to represent students' effort levels? Will the scale range from 10 for "Loads of Effort" to a 1 for "Little Effort"? And what about the personal judgments of our truth-telling students when they try to identify their own levels of effort? Is a self-identified effort level of 9 by Sally Lou the same as a self-identified effort level of 9 by Billy Bob? When we are dealing with such a covert, person-specific variable, even completely honest respondents can't help us arrive at an unerring fix on students' levels of effort. Effort levels are decidedly squishy. Effort is almost as elusive as it is important.

Accordingly, teachers who try to incorporate effort into their students' grades are usually fooling themselves. They simply can't arrive at an accurate identification regarding a student's effort associated with a given assignment or a particular assessment.

What about Those Important Intangibles?

Suppose that a teacher accepts the central grading guideline that's been endorsed in this chapter—namely, that students' grades should be based only on the degree to which a student has achieved the curricular aims set forth for the student. What about the many variables other than goal attainment that most teachers regard as important? If those are significant education-related variables, shouldn't teachers find a way to let students and their parents know how a student is doing with respect to, for instance, *social skills* (such as showing respect for classmates and adults) and *study skills* (such as working independently)? The answer is definitely *yes*. But the way to communicate such information is not by trying to piggy-back it onto a goal-attainment grade. Rather, the solution is to employ report cards embodying what O'Connor (2009, p. 238) calls "expanded format reporting" in which teachers render judgments about what I'll call *evaluative factors*.

These evaluative factors are the educationally relevant variables that educators believe students and those students' parents should know about. For instance, we know that "effort" is a potent consideration in the way a student prospers—not only in school but also after schooling is over. Yet, there's no way of accurately measuring an individual student's effort level. Nonetheless, if a report card clearly indicates that a teacher's estimate of a student's level of effort is just that, *a judgment-based estimate,* then both students and parents may benefit from those estimates.

As a practical matter, of course, individual teachers cannot craft their own report cards, so what's on a report card is typically decided at a district, state, or provincial level. Typically, an expanded format report card lists a series of evaluative factors, then provides an interpretation key so that a teacher can indicate whether—for each listed evaluative factor—a student is, for example, "Excellent, Good, Satisfactory, or Needs Improvement."

Ideally, the report card itself, or an accompanying letter, will provide an explanation regarding the judgmental nature of the teacher's estimates regarding each evaluative factor that's included in an expanded format report card. Such "disclaimer" explanations can play a powerful role in educating both parents and students about the difference between "teacher's *evidence-based* grades about a student's goal attainment" and "teacher's *judgmental estimates* regarding a student's status on key evaluative factors."

In Figure 1 you will find an example of an expanded format report card in which, at the right, you see a listing of the five curricular aims (called goals in this instance) and a place where at the close of every quarter, a student's status with respect to each goal is to be given a "mastery-status grade" by the teacher—namely, *Complete Goal Mastery (CGM), Developing Goal Mastery (DGM),* and *Inadequate Goal Mastery (IGM).* A total-course grade is supplied at the bottom of each quarter. (In this example, the total-course grade would be based on a teacher's judgment about the student's composite goal mastery.) On the right of Figure 1's report card, you will see two sets of evaluative factors (Social Skills and Study Skills), each of which is given a mark by the teacher on the basis of the teacher's judgmental estimate of whether the student's effort to improve has been *Consistent* (3 points), *Inconsistent* (2 points), or *Minimal* (1 point).

As you consider the report card presented in Figure 1, I'm sure you will realize that the mastery-status grades or, indeed, the overall course grade itself, is going to make no sense if the persons on the receiving end of such a report card do not understand the nature of the five goals on which the course grades will depend. This information (distributed at the beginning of the school year in this illustration) needs to be written in language readily understandable both to students and parents. Providing an additional description of those goals whenever report cards are issued is usually a smart move.

Again, recognizing that not all of a district's teachers are apt to have a hand in carving out the specifics of how a district's report cards are constructed, there may be some occasions when you might actually have an opportunity to register your personal preferences regarding the structure of district report cards. If you do have a chance to toss your ideas into such mix, please remember that in the reporting of students' grades, a profound truth is that "less is more." Too many grading dimensions incline both students and parents to become so swamped with information that they end up paying only superficial attention to any of those dimensions. And,

figure 1 ■ An Illustrative Expanded Format Report Card

Student's Name: _____

Goal Mastery

Interpretation Key: The letters below indicate a student's assessment-based mastery of each goal. Goal descriptions were distributed at the beginning of school. The *overall grade* (A, B, C, D, F) represents a student's overall goal mastery.

Mastery Status Grade:

CGM = *Complete Goal Mastery*

DGM = *Developing Goal Mastery*

IGM = *Inadequate Goal Mastery*

Curriculum Goals

Goal 1				
Goal 2				
Goal 3				
Goal 4				
Goal 5				
verall Grade				

Social Skills Factors

Respects classmates				
Follows rules				
Is self-disciplined				

Evaluative Factors

Interpretation Key: For the factors listed to the right, you will find a teacher's *judgmental estimate* of the student's effort to improve.

3 = *Consistent*

2 = *Inconsistent*

1 = *Minimal*

Study Skills Factors

Stays on task				
Organizes work				
Uses time well				
Employs technology				

of course, if there are too many grading tasks for teachers to undertake, they will typically end up racing through the "grading agony" as quickly as they can—often thoughtlessly. Really influential report cards will be crafted so that the number of judgments a teacher must make are intellectually manageable. This will lead to a modest, understandable interpretation task for both students and their parents. This will also lead to teachers' more thoughtful decisions regarding students' grades.

Electronic Record Keeping

Although many seasoned teachers have traditionally kept records of their students' accomplishments by making handwritten entries in a gradebook, the dramatic increase in the use of teacher-friendly computers promises to alter that practice. As more and more youthful, computer-canny teachers enter the field of education, we will surely see marked expansions in the use of computer-based records regarding students' performances.

Parent Talk

Imagine that one of your students' parents, Mrs. Aquino, wants to discuss her daughter's grade in your class. Specifically, she wants to know, "What goes into Mary's grade?"

 If I were you, here's how I'd respond to Mrs. Aquino:

"I'm delighted you want to look into how Mary is graded in my class. What I'd like you to do is look over my classroom information system I've been able to get up and running this year on my lap-top computer. Why don't you come to my class before or after school and I'll show you how I arrive at each of the components contributing to Mary's grade. I'll also show you how I've tried to weight the grade-determination importance of certain tests and other assignments Mary and her classmates complete. I am especially concerned about the progress Mary is making toward the nine state-set curricular aims that are to be achieved by students this year.

"What you need to understand, Mrs. Aquino, is that any grade given to any student is almost always a teacher judgment based on an amalgam of different sorts of evidence. And, to be honest, because teachers' judgments are involved, and teachers are altogether human, there will invariably be some teachers' errors in grading.

"But I assure you, the other teachers in our school and I are trying to do the fairest and most accurate job we can when we grade our students. Why don't you visit and we can review what goes into Mary's grade?"

 Now, how would you respond to Mrs. Aquino's concerns?

A number of readily usable programs to help teachers keep track of their students' performances now exist, and more will surely be available in years to come. The mission of these electronic grading programs is to simplify the teacher's tasks, so even a rudimentary notion of how to use a computer will allow teachers to save tons of record-keeping time. Some observers of America's classrooms predict, within a decade or so, teachers' entering grades by hand in a traditional gradebook will be quite rare.

Student-Involved Grading Conferences

One useful supplementation to the exclusive reliance on traditional report cards is the use of grading conferences. Grading conferences, when first introduced, usually involved only teachers and students' parents. Increasingly, however, these conferences are taking place in which students themselves play a role. There is, of course, a considerable range of involvements for students in such grading conferences. This range starts off with the student being present but not taking any part—other than being a listener—in the conference. At a greater level of involvement, the student participates actively in the conference. At the most substantial level of involvement, the student actually *leads* the grading conference. Clearly, for most variations of student-involved grading conferences, students will need to be carefully prepared by their teachers so that the resulting conferences will be maximally productive. (The vast majority of students possess no experience in grading themselves, and definitely no experience in supplying *goal-attainment* grades for themselves.) Remember, if the grading conference is based on a goal-attainment conception of grading, then all three parties in the conference (student, teacher, and one or both parents) will need to consider the *evidence* regarding a student's level of goal mastery. And that, of course, is where assessment provides the key information around which the grading conference is structured.

Let's recall that the basic purpose of grading is for teachers to communicate to students and parents the degree to which a student is making progress toward the goals this student is supposed to master. To the degree a teacher accepts this conception of grading, then when students understand the chief thrust of the grading process—by being actively involved in that process—this provides those students with information they need not only to evaluate their own achievements but, just as importantly, to monitor their ongoing progress toward goal attainment. Student-involved grading conferences can be a powerful *instructionally* relevant way of grading students so that they and their parents comprehend, if they are the recipients of descriptive feedback, where students currently are and what students need to do in order to achieve complete goal mastery.

Grading's Inherent Imprecision

Wouldn't it be nice if teachers never made mistakes when they grade students? But, as you probably know all too well from having been the recipient of too-low or too-high grades during your own years as a student, teachers do make grading errors. Certainly, teachers don't want to make mistakes in the grades they give to their students. However, grading is a judgment-based enterprise in which flawed decisions will surely be made.

Fortunately, in the long haul, such errors tend to balance one another out. There are three kinds of rater bias—namely, generosity bias, severity bias, and central-tendency bias. It is true that many teachers are biased in one of these three ways when they grade their students. Thus, over the years, a given student will probably be on the receiving end of some undeserved high grades and some unwarranted low grades. What you need to remember is that if you do the best job you can in dispensing grades to your students—that is, if you assign grades carefully and with the kind of deliberateness suggested in this chapter—you'll have done your grading as well as you can. Human judgment, as potent as it is, is not flawless. And it certainly isn't flawless when it comes to grading students.

What Do Classroom Teachers Really Need to Know about Assessment-Based Grading of Students?

It is now apparent to me that adoption of a goal-attainment approach to grading makes solid educational sense, and that separating grading from a teacher's judgments about other evaluative factors is the way to proceed. First off, there will be greater clarity about grades on the part of teachers who base their grades on students' goal attainment of well-described goals. Students and parents will better understand the resultant grades than they would understand such traditional grading approaches as simply comparing the relative achievement levels of the students in a particular classroom.

But equally important as the communication dividends derived from goal-attainment grading is the manner in which such an approach will mesh with the way teachers should approach their *instructional* tasks. Let's face it, the chief reason teachers teach kids is to help those kids acquire skills and knowledge. The skills and knowledge to be promoted by teachers are called *goals, curricular aims,* or some synonymous label. Those are the *ends* of a teacher's instruction, and *teaching* is what the teacher does to promote students' mastery of those curricular ends. Indeed the quality of a teacher's instructional efforts should be dominantly evaluated on the basis of whether the teacher has promoted students' attainment of curricular goals. So, from an instructional perspective focused on students' goal attainment, why not devise a student appraisal system that meshes perfectly with the fundamental reason teachers teach?

but what does this have to do with
Teaching?

The purpose of teaching is to bring about worthwhile changes in boys and girls. Most of these changes focus on students' acquisition of knowledge and skills. In truth, the very act of teaching can be seen as the use of the instructional means a teacher used in order to promote students' attainment of worthwhile ends—that is, curricular goals. If this is to be the teacher's chief aspiration—to have students master the curricular aims set forth for those students—why not evaluate students according to precisely the same framework? To the degree that both the teacher and the teacher's students are using the same targets to orient their activities, and to judge the success of those activities, then the resulting synergy from having both teacher and students pursuing identical aspirations will surely prove educationally beneficial. Goal-attainment grading pushes students to attain the very same goals the teacher wants those students to attain. Instruction will follow aspiration. Learning, too, will follow aspiration. Evaluative structures alter conduct. Why not alter students' conduct in a manner that leads to a greater likelihood of goal attainment?

Grading based on students' goal attainment, therefore, is an approach that makes sense from both an evaluative perspective and an instructional perspective. Regarding those other important factors that teachers would like to communicate, adoption of an expanded reporting format seems to be the way to go, as long as the evaluative factors don't overwhelm. Remember, the converse of "less is more" embodies every bit as much truth—namely, "more is less." An expanded format report card whose grade emphasis is students' goal attainment, yet that deals with a modest number of evaluative factors other than goal attainment, seems to represent the most sensible way to proceed.

■ Chapter Summary

Conceding that the grading of students is a process fraught with imprecision, the chapter argued that the most defensible system of grading should be rooted in teachers' judgments about the degree to which students have mastered the curricular aims a teacher is promoting for those students. The guiding premise of the chapter was that the purpose of grading is for teachers to communicate with students and their parents about the degree to which students have attained the goals they are supposed to achieve. Thus, a goal-attainment approach to grading was advocated.

Four steps for teachers when implementing a goal-attainment approach to grading were presented: (1) clarifying curricular aims, (2) choosing goal-attainment evidence, (3) weighting goal-attainment evidence, and (4) arriving at a final goal-attainment grade.

Regarding the incorporation of factors other than assessment-based evidence of a student's goal attainment, it was suggested that an expanded format type of report card be employed to allow the teacher to provide judgmental estimates regarding the student's status with respect to these educationally relevant variables. However, it was stressed that the *grades* awarded by teachers should be based exclusively on assessment-obtained evidence of goal attainment rather than attempt to incorporate any of these other factors.

Self-Check

We'll close out this chapter with a short set of self-check exercises. In truth, teachers' grading of their students is an endeavor for which one can proffer preferences about how it should be done, but there are simply no "right" or "wrong" answers to most questions one could pose about grading. Suppose, for example, a teacher adopts a totally norm-referenced approach to grading in which the teacher strives, assessment evidence notwithstanding, to make certain that students' grades end up resembling a bell-shaped curve (with only a few A-level grades and a few F-level grades). This teacher would not be guilty of a felony, or even a misdemeanor. A number of different approaches to grading have been adopted by teachers, and many of them have merit. There are few unequivocally correct or incorrect answers when it comes to grading.

So, for this final exercise, I want you to suspend your personal judgment about how *you* would prefer to approach grading yourself and, instead, just for purposes of this exercise, try to get your head inside a goal-attainment approach to grading. What I want you to do is consider each of the following five vignettes, then decide whether the teacher described was a GGAG or not. GGAG, in the case of a female teacher, stands for a Good Goal-Attainment Gal. And, as you might have already guessed, in a vignette describing a male teacher, GGAG stands for a Good Goal-Attainment Guy. Your task is to decide, for each vignette, whether the teacher described is a GGAG—or not. You will find this Self-Check most useful if you refer to the Self-Check Key immediately after making your GGAG-decision for *each* vignette.

Vignette 1: George's Geography Grades

George has recently been asked by his principal to teach a geography course in the high school where he has taught for the past four years. Although George has never taken a college-level course in geography, his principal assures him that he can "pull this off with ease." The emergency situation was caused by the sudden illness of the school's regular geography teacher, Mr. Hibbard, just before the start of the school year.

As he surveys the materials that Mr. Hibbard has left him, George sees there are five major curricular outcomes students are supposed to achieve during the one-semester course. However, as far as George can see, Mr. Hibbard's exams seem to be based more on the content covered in the course's geography textbook than those exams dealing specifically with the five curricular outcomes. Nonetheless, after reviewing the five curricular goals Mr. Hibbard has described to him in an e-mail, and prominently posted on the classroom bulletin board, George is increasingly convinced that much of the content in the textbook (and on Mr. Hibbard's midterm and final exams) is not very relevant to the five "Geography Goals" emphasized by Mr. Hibbard. Given his modest familiarity with geography, however, George is delighted that Mr. Hibbard has left his exams to be used if George chooses to employ them. George definitely plans to do so.

George urges his students to pay careful attention to the five goals as they study their geography material throughout the semester. He then determines each student's grade primarily on the basis of the two major exams in the course—that is, 50 percent for the final exam; 35 percent for the midterm exam; 10 percent for short, in-class quizzes; and 5 percent for class participation.

Is George a GGAG? (YES or NO)

Vignette 2: Belinda's Building Blocks

In her fourth-grade class, Belinda has recently tried to rely heavily on the formative-assessment process in pursuing the language arts curricular aims identified by her state's department of education as "Mandatory Language Arts Expectancies." In all, there are 13 such expectancies her students are supposed to master, 8 in reading and 5 in writing. For each of these 13 expectancies, Belinda has identified either 1 or 2 "building blocks"— that is, subskills or bodies of enabling knowledge she believes students must master en route to their achievement of the specific expectancy involved. Belinda weights the importance of each of the building blocks as a contributor to students' mastery of the expectancy, then bases her during-the-year grades on students' mastery of the most heavily weighted building blocks.

When the school year is nearing its conclusion, Belinda plans to measure her students' mastery of each of the 13 expectancies directly, and to grade students on their expectancy attainment. But during the bulk of the school year, she is only assessing students' building-block learning.

Is Belinda a GGAG? (YES or NO)

Vignette 3: Grading What's Most Important

Leonard teaches four general science courses in an urban middle school. He is familiar with the substantial body of research evidence indicating that students' level of effort is a powerful predictor of their subsequent success in school and, perhaps more importantly, later in life when school years are only a memory. Accordingly, when Leonard grades his 114 students each term, he never grades them simply on the basis of how well they have achieved the six curricular aims around which his science course is organized. Rather, for each student he tries to reach an informed judgment about that particular student's level of effort in the science course. He tries to observe students closely during the course, and often makes judgments about each student's effort level on a one- to five-point scale. Leonard always makes this mix of effort and goal achievement well known to his students in advance, feeling it only fair, as he says, to "lay his grading cards on the table." Moreover, he believes that his effort-oriented grading system will spur his students to work harder in the course.

Is Leonard a GGAG? (YES or NO)

Vignette 4: Sarah Scales Back

In the midwest state where Sarah teaches third-graders, the state's school board has officially endorsed an exceedingly large number of "learning objectives." Because Sarah wants to organize her instruction, as well as her grading practices, around a set of intended curricular outcomes, and because she believes the state's learning objectives are too numerous, she decides to prioritize those objectives by focusing only on a half-dozen of the most important ones.

Her school district's report cards call only for an "overall achievement" grade (not broken down by particular objectives), so Sarah lets all her students—and their parents—know *which* objectives she will be using as the chief foci for her instruction and for her grading. A description of each of those six objectives, along with two sample items that might be used on a test assessing student's achievement of that objective, is sent home with each student at the start of the school year. Sarah then grades her students, using evidence from formal and informal assessments, according to how well she believes a student has mastered the six objectives. Although the students and parents seem to appreciate the way Sarah is grading her students, several teachers in her school chide her for dealing with only 6 objectives out of a state-approved set of 34 third-grade objectives.

Is Sarah a GGAG? (YES or NO)

Vignette 5: Harry Handles Heterogeneity

In the school district where Harry teaches fifth-graders, a number of recent demographic changes have occurred so that most schools now serve very divergent groups of students. In his own fifth-grade class, Harry finds that roughly half of his students have come from schools with excellent instructional programs, and half have come from schools where instruction has been less than stellar. His students' entry-level achievement, therefore, varies enormously. When Harry communicates about grades to parents and students during midyear and end-of-year grading conferences in which students take part, he makes no grading allowances for differences in students' prior instruction. The only factor Harry uses, as he presents his midyear and end-of-year grades during these conferences, is the degree to which each student has accomplished the curricular goals identified by Harry's district for fifth-graders.

Is Harry a GGAG? (YES or NO)

 # Pondertime

1. If you were asked to make a presentation to a district school board in which you both defend and criticize a goal-attainment approach to grading students, what would your chief arguments be on both sides of this issue?

2. How do you think a teacher who is a "goal-attainment grader" should best cope with a situation in which teachers are asked by their district's administrators to promote students' attainment of a patently excessive number of curricular expectations?

3. If you were trying to help a new teacher adopt a defensible grading strategy, what advice would you give that teacher about the importance of descriptive feedback and how to communicate it to students and parents?

4. Assume that you are a member of a school-district design team whose responsibility is to devise a brand-new expanded format report card for the district. The main focus of the report card, according to the district's school board, is definitely to be on students' mastery of the district's curriculum objectives, but there is also to be a section for teachers to supply estimates of students' standing on such significant variables as "level of effort expended on school tasks." If you wanted to make sure there were not too many of these other variables to be unwieldy, which variables would you recommend be included on the report card? To keep district teachers' evaluation tasks manageable, be sure to include no more than a half-dozen such variables in your recommendations.

Self-Check Key

Vignette 1

Regrettably, George is not a good goal-attainment guy; he's definitely not a GGAG. Although he tosses some lip service in the direction of the five curricular goals identified by Mr. Hibbard, George still uses Mr. Hibbard's exams even though he has concluded that what is on those exams does not mesh well with the five goals. George's approach to grading is similar to that of many teachers who may have identified a set of curricular goals, but whose assessments do not deal dominantly with measuring students' mastery of those goals.

Vignette 2

Although most of Belinda's school year grading centers on the building blocks she regards as requisite precursors to her students' mastery of the 13 expectancies, it appears that she will—near the close of the school year—directly assess students' expectancy attainment. This approach undoubtedly qualifies Belinda as a good goal-attainment gal (GGAG). Because the building blocks are seen by Belinda as contributory to students' mastery of the 13 language arts goals (expectancies), it is perfectly reasonable to base her along-the-way grades on students' attainment of such building-block mastery. At the end of the school year, hopefully when the formative-assessment process has helped students learn what they are supposed to learn, then Belinda will switch to a procedure in which she will grade on the basis of students' achievement of the 13 expectancies. Belinda is, clearly, a GGAG.

Vignette 3

Even though we can sympathize with Leonard's attempt to get his students to expend more effort in their science studies, and to use his estimates of their effort levels when he grades them, this does not make him a GGAG. He may, indeed, be a good guy. And he may be happy with his approach to grading. But because goal-attainment grading relies *exclusively* on students' degree of goal mastery, Leonard's melding of students' effort and their achievement removes him from the GGAG gang. This would be true even if he could come up with *accurate* estimates of students' levels of effort. And the probability of those effort estimates being accurate, especially when Leonard teaches so many students, is truly teensy.

Vignette 4

Teachers in all sorts of settings these days are encountering the sort of too-many-targets curricular demands faced by Sarah. Her decision to engage in some curricular prioritizing, then focus her instruction and grading on a limited number of the highest priority objectives represents a reasonable response to an unreasonable set of curricular expectations. Because Sarah is up-front in communicating her plans to both parents and students, in my view she should go into the goal-attainment grading hall of fame. She is, most definitely, a GGAG!

Vignette 5

Harry gets full marks for his goal-attainment exclusivity when it comes to grading. We can hope that, during the twice-a-year grading conferences—happily involving students—Harry provides plenty of descriptive feedback so that both parents and students know how students can improve in their mastery of the district's curricular goals. But background heterogeneity aside, Harry is clearly opting for goal attainment when he grades. He is definitely a GGAG.

■ Additional Stuff

Brookhart, S. M. (2009). *Grading* (2nd ed.). New York: Merrill.

Brookhart, S. M. (2011). *Grading and learning: Practices that support student achievement.* Bloomington, IN: Solution Tree.

Guskey, T. R. (Ed.). (2008). *Practical solutions for serious problems in standards-based grading.* Thousand Oaks, CA: Corwin Press.

O'Connor, K. (2009). *How to grade for learning: Linking grades to standards* (3rd ed.). Thousand Oaks, CA: Corwin Press.

O'Connor, K. (2011). *A repair kit for grading: 15 fixes for broken grades* (2nd ed.). Boston: Pearson.

Sadler, P. M., and Good, E. (2006). "The impact of self- and peer-grading on student learning," *Educational Assessment, 11,* no. 1: 1–32.

Wormeli, R. (2006). *Fair isn't always equal: Assessment and grading in the differentiated classroom.* Portland, ME: Stenhouse Publishers.

Wormeli, R. (2011). "Effective grading in standards-based schools," *Educational Leadership,* 69: no. 3, November: 40–44.

■ Cyber Stuff

- *Alberta Assessment Consortium* is a not-for-profit partnership of educational organizations in Alberta, Canada, focused on the use of educational assessment to improve the caliber of students' learning. The sophisticated website offered by this consortium offers a wide range of assessment-relevant resources. Most of the resources available on this website, however, are restricted to individuals working in educational organizations that are consortium members. **www.aac.ab.ca**

- *Grading: Selected Resources for the Middle School Teacher* deals with grading-related topics that have relevance for middle school teachers, but also teachers at other grade levels. This website is chiefly a collection of links to other grading-related sources, many of which deal head-on with issues of concern to those teachers trying to rethink their own grading strategies. **www.middleweb.com/Grading.html**

- *The Learning Community,* established in 1993, is a nonprofit organization focused on parent education. Its website provides thousands of articles, tips, videos, and links to resources suitable for helping parents be successful in dealing with their children, both at school and at home. A number of this website's materials are related to parental expectations regarding how their children should be graded at school. **www.thelearningcommunity.us**

- *Vanderbilt University Center for Teaching* was founded in 1986 to advance teaching excellence in the College of Arts and Science, and expanded in 1997 to serve the entire university. Its website is aimed at those involved in postsecondary education. Nonetheless, a useful section of the site is devoted to issues associated with grading. A number of site resources on this topic can be found by directing the site's search process to focus on grading. **www.vanderbilt.edu/cft/**

Extended Applications

It is a truism that the more a person uses something, the more familiar with this something the person becomes. This self-evident notion surely applies to the assessment-related knowledge, skills, and concepts you have been reading about in the foregoing pages. Thus, to provide readers of *Classroom Assessment* with additional opportunities to apply the content contained in this text, this final section contains a variety of exercises intended to give readers an opportunity to use what they've been reading about.

In a sense, of course, the Self-Check exercises found at the close of this chapter provided an opportunity for readers to apply a chapter's content. Nonetheless, the more times you use a concept, skill, or a body of knowledge, the more likely it is that you will master this content so you can employ it in varied situations.

For each of the text, you will find an extended-application exercise calling for you to do some thinking about that chapter's content as it applies to a real-world situation. Each exercise is preceded by a brief introduction setting forth the reason that the upcoming extended-application exercise has been selected.

Because many of these exercises call on you to generate an original response rather than select a response from a set of options, it is difficult to supply an "answer key" for readers' unpredictable responses. So, what you'll find following all the exercises is One Possible Response—an indication of how I would have personally responded to the exercise if I had been asked to do so. Please don't regard my response as the only way to respond to an exercise. After all, by definition, this is only "one possible" response. Instead, please think of my response as a fairly flimsy form of feedback. You can certainly disagree with me, even emphatically, yet still profit from doing the exercise.

Remember, what is being provided in this section. The exercises deliberately intended to extend how you apply the content treated in *Classroom Assessment*. I hope you find these exercises useful in enhancing your understanding of what teachers need to know about classroom assessment.

Critiquing Teachers' Grading Practices

Introduction

For this final Extended Applications exercise, your task will be to appraise the grading practices of five fictional teachers. Given what you have already read in this chapter, it should be clear that there is no definitive "one and only one way for teachers to grade their students." Nonetheless, a position taken in this chapter was that one defensible way to grade students was to focus on their achievement of the sorts of curricular aims so widely formulated these days as a state's or province's official content standards—in other words, its goals. Thus, for purposes of this exercise, please critique the following teachers' grading-related actions according to the view of *goal-attainment grading* advocated in the book's final chapter.

Simply read the brief account of each teacher's actions, then assume that you had been asked by the teacher, in the spirit of constructive collegial criticism, to put forward your analysis of the teacher's grading-related actions. After having registered your own critique of the teacher's decisions, then consider the reaction embodied in the One Possible Response.

 Exercise Directions: Please read each of the five grading-relevant descriptions that follow, then provide a brief critique—negative, positive, or mixed—of the teacher's actions. Frame your critique according to a goal-attainment conception of grading.

1. *Clarice cleaves to clarity.* Clarice Johnson teaches primary children, typically first-graders or second-graders. Her approach to grading these young children is rooted in what she believes is her most important job: getting her students to master the high-priority "power" curricular aims identified by her district's administrators and thereafter approved by the district's school board. Fortunately, in each subject area she teaches, there are only a few Power Goals to be promoted. Her initial task each year is to provide her students and those students' parents with as clear a description of the district's Power Goals as she possibly can. She has spent a substantial amount of time devising clear statements of each goal, along with examples of test approaches that might be employed to verify students' status regarding each goal. To conserve both time and paper, her descriptions of the Power Goals are written only for her students' parents. She believes that those parents can then help their children understand what the Power Goals in each subject actually are.

What is your appraisal of Clarice's actions? _____

_____

_____

 One Possible Response: Clarice certainly seems to sense the importance of clarifying the goals she hopes her students will achieve, but she missed 50 percent of the intended audience. By communicating information about the nature of the goals only to her students' parents, she fails to let the students in on the grading game. It will most likely be necessary for her to develop different materials for these primary-grade children than the goal-descriptive materials she devised for parents. But students, as well as their parents, are integral participants in goal-attainment grading. Students who are kept out of the curricular-intention clarification loop are students who can't profit optimally from goal-attainment grading. And the idea Clarice has of counting on parents to describe the district's Power Goals to their children represents woefully wishful thinking.

2. *Gordon dots every* i *and crosses every* t. Gordon Grover teaches high school English classes and, after almost a decade of what he now regards as "sloppy grade-giving," has decided to fully embrace goal-attainment grading. Each year, for every one of his classes, Gordon spends considerable time clarifying the

nature of his course curricular goals—and he does this not only for his students but also for their parents. After the excursion in goal clarification, he chooses the kind of assessment evidence he will use to arrive at an end-of-course estimate of each student's goal-attainment status. He also decides how much weight to give different sources of evidence when more than one kind of assessment result will be at hand. Gordon communicates these decisions to his students and their parents. Finally, he arrives at an overall grade in English for each student based on an amalgam of all the goal-attainment evidence he has assembled. As with the other aspects of his grading approach, Gordon communicates with parents and students the steps he used to arrive at students' grades based on the course goals and different students' mastery of those goals.

What is your appraisal of Gordon's actions? _____

_____

_____

One Possible Response: Gordon appears to be making a sincere effort to carry out the four major operations called for when teachers use a goal-attainment approach to grading: (1) clarifying curricular aims, (2) choosing goal-attainment evidence, (3) weighting the goal-attainment evidence, and then (4) arriving at a final goal-attainment grade for each student. Gordon appears to be bent on keeping parents actively informed about their students' grades. From a goal-attainment grading perspective, Gordon gets piles of plaudits.

3. *Flora flaunts formative grades.* Flora Gallimore, a high school science teacher, has become a strong proponent of formative assessment in her classes during the past two years. Although she professes a commitment to goal-attainment grading, she invokes this approach only on a small number of grade-determining exams she uses at the conclusion of any extended-duration instructional units (usually lasting at least a month or more). Having already communicated with parents and students about how she will be calculating goal-attainment grades, she then tries to grade each child according to how well that child has mastered the science goals set forth in her classes. However, all of the classroom assessments—both formal and informal—she uses during her regular instruction are never graded. The purpose of these assessments, says Flora, is "exclusively to help students figure out how to learn what they need to learn."

What is your appraisal of Flora's actions? _____

_____

_____

One Possible Response: Flora's decision not to grade any of her students' assessments used as part of the formative-assessment process is completely consonant with a goal-attainment conception of grading. If she wishes to use her ongoing assessments to help students master her curricular goals, then later use other exams to verify students' final levels of goal-attainment, this makes instructional sense. Why base students' grades on the early stages of learning when those students have yet to really master what is being taught? If the function of tests during the formative-assessment process is patently designed to help students learn, not to grade them, then most students will become more willing to "try-and-fail," because "failing" does not count against them.

4. *Edgar lauds effort.* Edgar Elmore teaches social studies classes in a suburban, high-achieving school. Most of the students in the school come from fairly affluent families, but Edgar is continually disappointed in the levels of effort his students seem to be putting into their studies. What he finds particularly vexing is that most of his students, even without expending much visible effort, score really well on Edgar's exams as well as on the state accountability tests that the school's students are obliged to take each spring. Accordingly, Edgar not only encourages his students to try much harder in their studies but he also devises a "score-plus-effort" grading system. He computes a student's grade on major exams covering the chief segments of his courses *as well as* a level-of-effort judgment made by Edgar about each student. Because his students recognize the importance of effort expenditure, there are few complaints from students about this new grading approach.

What is your appraisal of Edgar's actions? _____

_____

_____

 One Possible Response: Although we can appreciate why Edgar has become enamored of effort, particularly working with a collection of students who do not seem to be displaying much of it, his approach represents a serious departure from goal-attainment grading. The most serious drawback with Edgar's well-intentioned plan is that *he cannot accurately estimate each of his students' individual level of effort.* Without being able to do so, his fine-sounding grading approach collapses.

5. *Sandra prioritizes the grading game.* Sandra's school district has determined that the district's students are to be graded according to the degree to which they have mastered the district-specified content standards in each subject. There are many of these content standards, and because Sandra teaches fourth-graders in multiple subjects, if she based a grade on all of the district's content standards, she would be basing a grade on well over 100 goals—clearly, as she says, "Way too many!" As a result of this analysis, Sandra has decided on the most significant curricular aims (content standards) in each of the subjects she teaches, but never more than six per subject. She sends a note home to parents, and she also informs her students, that even though she will attempt to provide instruction for the full set of more than 100 goals, she will grade students only on their accomplishment of the high-priority goals that she has identified. Given the reduced number of goals, Sandra is able to develop clear descriptions of those goals for her students' parents, and has also created simplified versions of those descriptions for her students. Finally, she supplies students with examples of high-quality and

low-quality student responses to illustrate the nature of the goals being sought. These examples are also supplied to any parent who requests them.

What is your appraisal of Sandra's actions? _____

_____

_____

 One Possible Response: Sandra made a sensible decision, one consonant with the overall intention of a goal-attainment grading strategy. In particular, by assuring her students' parents that she will try to give instructional attention to the full array of district-sanctioned curricular goals, she makes clear that she will attempt to *teach* as much of the state-approved curriculum as she can, but she will *grade* her students on the basis of only the highest priority curricular goals.

Index

440

441

445